CONSPIRACY *of* INTERESTS

Iroquois Dispossession and the Rise of New York State

Laurence M. Hauptman

Syracuse University Press

Copyright © 1999 by Syracuse University Press
Syracuse, New York 13244-5160
All Rights Reserved
First Edition 1999
99 00 01 02 03 04   6 5 4 3 2 1

The paper used in this publication meets the minimum
requirements of American National Standard for Information
Sciences—Permanence of Paper for Printed Library Materials,
ANSI Z39.48-1984.∞

This book was published with the assistance of the John Ben Snow Foundation.

LIBRARY OF CONGRESS CATALOGING-IN-PUBLICATION DATA

Hauptman, Laurence M.
    Conspiracy of interests : Iroquois dispossession and the rise of New York State /
Laurence M. Hauptman.
        p. cm. — (The Iroquois and their neighbors)
    Includes bibliographical references and index.
        1. Iroquois Indians—New York (State)—Government relations.   2. Iroquois
Indians—Land tenure—New York (State).   3. New York (State)—History—1775–1865.
    I. Title.   II. Series.
    E99.I7H28 1998
    974.´03—dc21
    ISBN 0-8156-0547-1 (cloth : alk. paper)

Manufactured in the United States of America

For Ruth, Beth, and Eric

The increase of the population of this state [New York], especially of the western portion, has been so rapid as to attract the attention of intelligent men throughout Christendom. Sixty years ago, the whole section of the state from Utica to Buffalo was all a wilderness, occupied only by tribes of roving Indians. It now embraces twenty-eight counties and more than a million of inhabitants, enjoying all the comforts and many of the elegancies of civilized life, distinguished for general intelligence and enterprise, and rapidly advancing in numbers, and all the elements of social prosperity and power.

—John Disturnell, *A Gazetteer of the State of New-York* (1842)

Laurence M. Hauptman is professor of history at the State University of New York at New Paltz and is author of many books and articles in Native American studies, including *The Iroquois in the Civil War: From Battlefield to Reservation*, *The Iroquois and the New Deal*, and *The Iroquois Struggle for Survival: World War II to Red Power*, each published by Syracuse University Press. He has worked for the Wisconsin Oneidas, the Mashantucket Pequots, and the Seneca Nation of Indians as a historical consultant, and in 1997 he received an award of commendation from the Seneca Nation for his expert testimony that contributed to congressional legislation in the Seneca-Salamanca lease controversy. In 1987 and again in 1998, Hauptman received the Peter Doctor Memorial Indian Scholarship Foundation Award for distinguished service in his research and writings on American Indians.

CONTENTS

ILLUSTRATIONS

FIGURES

PREFACE

Historians writing about the Iroquois Indians in the period between the end of the American Revolution and the Civil War have largely focused on such topics as the federal treaties of the era; the activities of speculators in Indian lands such as the Phelps-Gorham, Holland, and Ogden Land Companies; on Iroquois political factionalism that weakened the Indian polity; on the War of 1812 in Iroquoia; and on the religious history of the Six Nations, whether the origins and establishment of the *Gaiiwio*, the Code of Handsome Lake, or the proselytizing of Christian missionaries. Indeed, as I show in this book, transportation interests, combined with land speculation and national security forces, permanently transformed Iroquoia between the end of the American Revolution and the Civil War. Even before the completion of the New York and Erie Railroad in 1851, the improvement of harbors and navigable rivers, the firm establishment of a New York State boundary as a result of a United States–British Canada commission, and the building of numerous canals and roads had completely changed the Indian world from the Oneida country in the east to the Seneca country in the west.

Three interlocking forces—transportation, land, and national defense—helped create an urban industrial corridor in the heart of Iroquoia. The rise of metropolises such as Utica, Syracuse, Rochester, and especially Buffalo in this period was phenomenal, making it one of the fastest growing regions of the United States. At the turn of the nineteenth century Indian isolation, especially in western New York, gave way to a flood of emigrants who either passed through the region on their way to the Midwest or settled within the corridor. This massive settlement—the sudden appearance of hundreds of thousands of non-Indian taxpaying citizens in their midst—added fuel to attempts to Christianize, educate, concentrate, or remove the Indians from the state. Albany politicos also pushed for state jurisdiction over the Indians: the creation of a statewide system of schools, attempts to tax the Indians for the building of highways, incorporating and charting the new republican form of government for the Seneca Nation under state law, and unilaterally taking Indian lands without federal supervision or United States Senate approval. Thus, this period is an important epoch in Iroquois–New York State relations, one that has contemporary implications on Indian land claims, on the state's power to tax Indian nations, and in many other areas of that present relationship.

Conspiracy of Interests: Iroquois Dispossession and the Rise of New York State goes beyond simply recounting the tragedy that befell the Indians in New York. The memoirs and letters of individuals involved in creating the transportation network, gazetteers, travelers' accounts of the times, tribal memorials to Albany and Washington, and individual Indian correspondence do describe the world of the Iroquois in a time of crisis; however, this story does not merely show how white politicos and land speculators tricked the Indians but also clearly demonstrates how the Iroquois themselves developed strategies to meet these challenges. The Iroquois in this period delayed their loss of Buffalo, saved Oil Spring Reservation, regained part of the Tonawanda Indian Reservation, established and institutionalized their native religion, held onto their cultural traditions, and stymied annual Albany efforts to concentrate or remove all Iroquois nations from east of the Mississippi. Even though the Iroquois lost more than 99 percent of their lands, their presence today remains in central and western New York, whereas the great cities created during the transportation revolution—Utica, Syracuse, Rochester, and Buffalo—have rapidly declined in the last half-century. Thus, ironically, the so-called vanishing race, the American Indians, in some ways have outlasted the forces that were unleashed in the promotion of frontier settlement.

The book's beginning point is the end of the American Revolution at a time when the Iroquois were weakened and split. In 1784 few white men were west of the Mohawk River. New York State was an undefined universe and the Articles of Confederation government in Philadelphia was bankrupt. In the need to develop a postwar economy and to establish its foundations, state and federal governmental officials and land companies and individual speculators began treating with the Oneidas, mostly American allies in the war, who sat athwart the major trade routes of central New York. Later, when the land and transportation thrust shifted westward, these same interests largely treated with the Senecas, most of whom had sided with the British during the war. Hence, the book focuses on these two key Iroquois nations because their role in the making of the Empire State was pivotal, much more significant than that of their relatives among the

Cayuga, Mohawk, Onondaga, and Tuscarora. Although these other four communities are mentioned, the primary focus in the book is on the Oneida and Seneca role in the shaping of the Empire State. It also should be noted that although the Iroquois in Canada, especially along the Grand River, were also affected by the transportation revolution, especially canals, the exclusive focus of this study is on New York State.

The end date of this study is 1860. Although canals were in decline long before this time, railroads, a force I wrote about previously in *The Iroquois in the Civil War* (1993), by then had an impact on Iroquoia. By 1860 the Genesee Valley Canal had been completed, an event that reduced the size of the Oil Spring Reservation by creating the Oil Spring Reservoir, now better known as Cuba Lake. This canal, built at the very end of the canal era, was the last one that had any impact on the Iroquois. Moreover, in the late 1850s, the last federal accord with the Iroquois in New York was made with the Tonawanda Senecas. In that treaty the Tonawanda Senecas were "allowed" to repurchase their lands, stolen in 1826 and 1838 to 1842. In return they agreed to allow New York State to hold these lands in trust, a further erosion of their sovereignty and indicative of a world that was no longer separate from Albany.

Hence, by the Civil War, despite being federally recognized Indians, the Iroquois world was slowly incorporated into a new reality, the Empire State. The Indians could no longer dismiss Albany as irrelevant to their existence. With state roads, state canals, state laws, and state educational institutions, the Iroquois were affected at nearly every turn by a growing state presence. By 1861 the New York Central Railroad network was completed, an event that marked the rapid decline of canals in the late nineteenth century, but an event, albeit beyond this present study, that had further effects on Iroquois life in New York State. In sum, Indian dispossession was not merely an unfortunate consequence or unexpected result of state transportation, land settlement, or defense policies, but an integral part of those policies.

Conspiracy of Interests: Iroquois Dispossession and the Rise of New York State emanates out of twenty-five years of research. When I first set foot in Salamanca, New York, an old railroad company town, in 1972, I became aware of how transportation shaped the Seneca world. In 1976 while standing at the observatory of the Eisenhower Locks at Massena, New York, I witnessed the Herculean power of midtwentieth-century technology, namely the creation of the St. Lawrence Seaway, which I wrote about a decade later in *The Iroquois Struggle for Survival: World War II to Red Power* (1986).

Indeed, the seaway along with the Kinzua Dam and the Niagara Reservoir had a devastating impact on Iroquoia and shaped the present-day Iroquoian world in New York. From 1986 to 1988, in preparing a Rockefeller Public Policy Institute report on the nature of contemporary New York State–Iroquois relations, I focused much attention on the histories of Routes 17 and 81 and New York State transportation policies since the 1950s. While a visiting scholar at Saint Bonaventure University, I became caught in the middle of the "Seneca Tax War of 1992," unable to travel on two of the main highways through Seneca country in western New York—Route 17 and the New York State Thruway—which were temporarily shut down in an Indian protest. A similar protest occurred in the spring of 1997.

My interest in transportation policies was also shaped by my three-year stint as trustee of the Delaware and Hudson Canal Society Museum in High Falls, New York. I acknowledge with appreciation the museum's past and present directors, Susan Lewis and Vicki Doyle, and trustee Donald Martin for making me a "canawler." They, and especially Craig Williams of the New York State Museum, helped educate me about the canal era. Because of Williams's unique expertise in the canal records of New York State, I was able to piece together this story. Williams also assisted me in reproducing some of the illustrative materials that I have included in this book. Philip Lord, Jr., chief of the Historical Survey of the New York State Museum, shared his expertise with me on the Western Inland Lock Navigation Company and early transportation development in central New York. I also thank James Folts and William Evans of the New York State Archives and James Corsaro, director of the New York State Library's Manuscript Division, for their assistance in guiding me through the rich collections in the Cultural Education Center in Albany. Mary Bell of the Buffalo and Erie County Historical Society, Frank Lorenz and Waltraut Wuensch of the Hamilton College Library, and Karl Kabelac and Mary Huth of the Special Collections and Rare Book Room of the Rush Rhees Library at the University of Rochester also provided valuable assistance in the preparation of this book. I also thank Richard Wiles, editor of the *Hudson Valley Regional Review,* and Wendell Tripp, editor of *New York History,* for allowing me to reprint chapters 1, 11 and 12 of this book; earlier versions of this material appeared in their fine journals in 1996, 1997, and 1998.

I also acknowledge the assistance of several colleagues at the State University of New York, New Paltz. Most importantly, Jo Margaret Mano, associate professor of Geography, a true expert on early New York State cartographic records and on the life and public career of Simeon De Witt, the first surveyor-general of the State of New York, deserves special recognition. She graciously shared her expertise and introduced me to important studies in the geographic literature. Ben Simpson, one of Dr. Mano's former students, contributed his cartographic skills to produce four original maps for the book. Donald Roper, associate professor of History emeritus at the college, a scholar of New York State history, discussed with me the early political and legal history of the Empire State and provided me with valuable leads and bibliographic references. Joan Walker, the secretary of the History Department, typed all the numerous letters of inquiry required in my research. Librarians Barbara Petruzzelli and Wilma Schmidt of the Sojourner Truth Library at the college provided valuable assistance in securing my interlibrary loan requests. The college administration at SUNY, New Paltz, provided initial seed money, an internal grant in 1987 for the project, a small travel award for research in 1996, and release time from one course in the spring of 1997, which facilitated the completion of the project.

Over the past decades I have had the opportunity to refine this project by discussions with others. Attorneys George Shattuck, Arlinda Locklear, and Derril Jordan have been quite helpful. Nearly fifteen years ago, Shattuck first suggested to me that Oneida Indian history after the American Revolution was directly affected by waterway routes westward. Three Allegany Senecas deserve special mention for their help: Calvin John, former president of the Seneca Nation, and Duwayne "Duce" Bowen, former assistant to the director of the Seneca Nation's Maps and Boundaries Division, both of whom have the expertise on the history of the Oil Spring Reservation; and Judy Greene, former director of the Seneca-Iroquois National Museum in Salamanca. Gordy McLester, former tribal secretary of the Oneida Nation of Indians of Wisconsin, helped me understand the complexities of the Oneida Indian world from the American Revolution through the 1840s. My friend David Jaman provided me with frank and helpful comments about this manuscript.

I dedicate this book to my wife and two children who tolerated my frequent ramblings and my compulsive work habits. I could not have completed this project without their support.

New Paltz, New York
December 1997

CONSPIRACY OF INTERESTS

CHAPTER I

_____

Introduction: Ditches, Defense, and Dispossession

On October 26, 1825, the *Seneca Chief* out of Buffalo became the first boat to enter the newly opened Erie Canal. On board this vessel were leading New Yorkers associated with the state's canal development. Besides its honored guest Governor De Witt Clinton, the assemblage included Stephen Van Rensselaer, Robert Livingston, and Thurlow Weed, prominent men who were to play a major part in the rise of the Empire State. The *Seneca Chief,* part of a four-boat flotilla at the start, was elegantly decorated for the festive occasion. Its one cabin was adorned with two George Catlin paintings. The first was a scene of Buffalo harbor, a section of Lake Erie, Buffalo Creek, and its junction with the Erie Canal. The second portrayed, on its left, a figure of Hercules in a seated position, resting after arduous labor, with the center of the painting showing a section of the Erie Canal with Governor De Witt Clinton, in a Roman toga, symbolically flinging open the canal lock gate; the right side of this second painting was occupied by Neptune holding his trident erect in his chariot of shell drawn by sea horses.[1]

The four-boat flotilla also included the *Noah's Ark,* outfitted at Grand Island, then called Ararat, on the Niagara River strait, with a cargo of "specimens": birds, fish, insects, two bear cubs, and two Seneca boys. A third boat, the *Young Lion of the West,* was filled with produce—flour, butter, apples—cedar tubs, wooden pails, brooms, and representative samplings of upstate wildlife, including wolves, foxes, and raccoons. This grand voyage of American progress was joined by another boat, which actually became the second in the flotilla, the *Niagara of Black Rock,* with General Peter Buell Porter, a major actor in Iroquois history, in an honored place on board.

Although there were some protests against the canal at Rome and

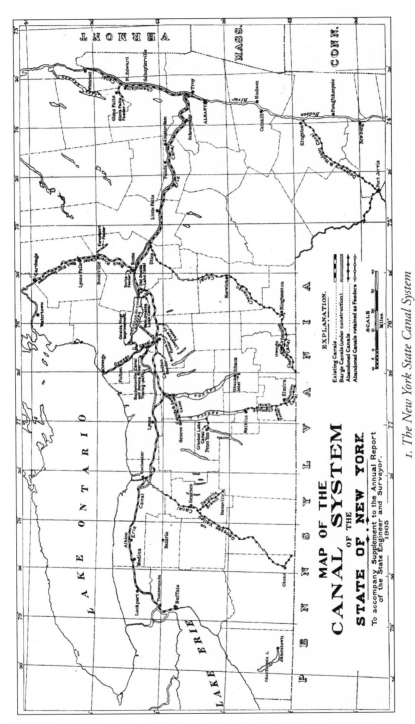

1. *The New York State Canal System*

Reprinted from Noble E. Whitford, History of the Canal System of the State of New York (1905)

Schenectady and later in the Hudson Valley as well, the flotilla made its way largely triumphantly down the artificial river, stopping at Lockport, Rochester, and Syracuse where celebrations took place. When the boats reached Albany, the noted politicos Ambrose Spencer, John Tayler, and Martin Van Buren, all associated with the Iroquois, met the flotilla and held a banquet in honor of this resounding technological civil engineering project. After the flotilla left the canal at Albany, two powerful steamboats towed the entire fleet down the Hudson River where the boats arrived in New York harbor on November 4, completing the 425-mile voyage.[2]

After pouring a keg of Lake Erie water into the Atlantic, Governor De Witt Clinton, Magnus Apollo, dedicated the canal, commemorating "navigable communication, which has been accomplished between our Mediterranean seas and the Atlantic Ocean" as a result of eight arduous years of work, "by the wisdom, public spirit, and energy of the people of the state of New York; and may the God of Heavens and the Earth smile most propitiously on this work and render it subservient to the best interests of the human race."[3] The Erie Canal in many ways made New York the Empire State. Yet, this and other elements of what George Rogers Taylor dubbed "the transportation revolution," originally conceived in New York in the 1780s and continuing to the Civil War, also led to the undoing of the Iroquois.[4]

This great transformation fits the pattern described by geographer John R. Borchert in a seminal article written more than thirty years ago. To Borchert, the evolution of American metropolitan areas required two essential ingredients: great migrations and major changes in technology. "Both factors have repeatedly been given specific geographical expression through their relationship to resource patterns." Borchert added, "Great migrations have sought to exploit resources—ranging from climate or coal to water or zinc—that were either newly appreciated or newly accessible within the national market." The noted geographer concluded, "Usually, of course, the new appreciation, or accessibility had come about, in turn through some major technological innovation." In terms of the Empire State, as the cargo of the *Seneca Chief* in 1825 demonstrates, the new technology of canal building combined not only to bring massive population west but to make Syracuse the primary salt city of the United States; Rochester, the primary flour and flower city of the United States; and Buffalo, the primary granary depot of the United States in the decades before the Civil War.[5]

De Witt Clinton

Courtesy of the New York State Library, New York State Museum and Craig Williams

A central focus of Albany policymakers throughout much of the early history of the state was to gain control of access routes to transportation. The first part of the transportation puzzle was Whitestown, the area in and around today's Utica, the so-called Gateway to the West, which had a waterway passage to Oneida Lake and Lake Ontario, except for a short portage, the "Oneida Carrying Place," between the Mohawk River and Wood Creek. In the initial years Oswego was the primary terminus for the inland waterway system. Although river boat traffic increased steadily after the American Revolution, New York, a third-rate state in the 1780s, could not have secured its present borders and become a populated universe without a greater commitment to transportation. Individual, state, and national officials came together in making New York the Empire State, promoting the migration of taxpaying citizens to settle on lands in central and western New York. Subsequently, after the War of 1812, Buffalo and its environs (Black Rock) became the Holy Grail, the ultimate prize sought by master planners, private interests, and public officers.

Demographic changes spurred by the new transportation network prove this point. The population along the western section of the Erie Canal increased five times as rapidly as in areas farther away from the artificial river.[6] Madison County in central New York had fewer than 1,000 non-Indian settlers in 1800 but grew to 39,000 by 1830.[7] In 1790 approximately 1,000 non-Indians lived west of Seneca Lake; sixty years later, more than 660,000 non-Indians lived in western New York.[8] As a result of the transportation revolution, Rochester grew from nothing in 1814 to a thriving city of more than 36,403 people by 1850. A similar increase occurred in Utica and Syracuse (see tables 1 and 2).[9] The most outstanding change, however, came in Buffalo, a city incorporated in 1831. The Queen City of New York grew to 81,129 people by 1860, making it the ninth largest city in the United States by the time of the Civil War.[10]

In the 1790s the Holland Land Company's vast empire was largely isolated from the rest of New York State because of nonexistent transportation networks, was unattractive because of its frontier character, and was under threats of invasion by British and British-allied Indians from across the Canadian border. It is little wonder that, in each of his annual reports, Joseph Ellicott, the chief agent of the Holland Land Company, argued for private or public subsidies to build roads, which he envisioned would foster rapid settlement. Nearly every report Ellicott made to Paul Busti, the com-

TABLE I

Population Increases in Madison and Oneida Counties, New York, 1790–1855

County				year		
	1790	1800	1814	1825	1840	1855
Madison	—	8,036	26,276	35,646	40,008	43,687
Oneida	1,891	20,839	45,627	57,847	85,310	107,749

TABLE 2

Population Increases in Ten Western New York State Counties, 1790–1855

County				year		
	1790	1800	1814	1825	1840	1855
Allegany	—	—	2,207	13,184	30,254	42,910
Cattaraugus	—	—	537	6,643	28,872	39,530
Chautauqua	—	—	4,259	20,689	47,976	53,380
Erie	—	—	6,201	24,316	62,465	132,331
Genesee	—	—	9,435	20,708	28,705	31,532
Livingston	—	2,448	13,181	26,731	42,498	37,943
Monroe	—	1,192	11,178	39,108	64,902	96,324
Niagara	—	—	1,276	14,069	31,132	48,282
Orleans	—	—	1,524	14,460	25,127	28,435
Wyoming	—	—	5,411	22,307	34,245	32,143

pany's director, or to the Dutch investors mentioned roads and their importance or expressed frustrations about the lack of roads or their disrepair, which retarded non-Indian settlement.[11] He even rationalized spending company moneys on these projects because "it has been the means of bringing the Land in Demand and enhancing its Value by promoting Intercourse with the various Parts of the Territory."[12]

During the first decades of the nineteenth century, western land traffic through New York by oxcart, horseback, or on foot was followed in rapid succession by stagecoach, river and canal boats, and railway. In the first years of the nineteenth century, the road system in New York State was either nonexistent or abysmal. At the turn of the century, the famous Buffalo Road (the Buffalo-to-Batavia road), which subsequently became part of the Genesee Turnpike, was perhaps the best road in the state, even though it was little more than an improved Indian trail incapable of carrying large freight by teamsters. The Ridge Road, described by De Witt Clinton as a "great natural turnpike," ran seventy-eight miles east-west from the Genesee

River to Lewiston. This Indian path was improved and formally laid out as a major turnpike by the Holland Land Company in 1807–8. By that time, incorporated turnpike road and bridge companies operated in New York although they were often useless—limited in distance of operation, affected by weather conditions, and often in a state of poor maintenance and disrepair.

The first great main artery, today's State Road 5 from Albany to Buffalo—known at times as the Seneca Trail, the Genesee Turnpike, the Seneca Turnpike, or the Great Western Turnpike—brought emigrants through Utica, Auburn, and Geneva. Built in separate sections at different times, this road, which was established by the first state grant of land for a right-of-way, was begun in the 1790s and completed only during the War of 1812. After carrying troops west in that conflict, the great road, which went directly through Oneida lands in central New York, provided access to stagecoaches carrying passengers and the United States mail until its decline three decades later with the advent of railroad competition. It is important to note that Indian leaders, Red Jacket and others, petitioned from 1802 onward for free and unlimited passage on turnpikes, bridges, and ferry service.[13]

The connections between Iroquois land dispossession and the transportation revolution can be seen in several distinct ways. State transportation concerns seriously affected the Oneidas in the period from 1785 to 1815 and led to periodic extinguishment of Indian land rights along the Genesee Turnpike, which passed through the Oneida "Castle." The direct relationship between canal building and Indian dispossession is clearly evident in the journals of Benjamin Wright, the chief engineer of the Erie Canal. In 1816 Wright wrote about the advantages of a branch canal to connect Oneida Creek to the Erie Canal. He insisted that by uniting the two, "the State property now owned and that owned by the Indians *which will soon become State property*" (emphasis mine) "will be trebled in value."[14] Even as late as 1829 the state, under the governorship of Martin Van Buren, "acquired" Oneida lands for this purpose through an illegal agreement with the Oneida's First Christian Party in clear violation of the Trade and Intercourse Acts that required federal approval and/or the presence of a federal commissioner to supervise the proceedings.[15]

The Grand Canal, the Erie, completed in 1825, is largely the focus of part 2 of this book and was significant to the Senecas' loss of Buffalo and their Genesee lands by 1838. Much later, in 1858, the Genesee Valley Canal, one which connected the Erie Canal south of Rochester to the New York and Erie Railroad and the Allegheny River valley just east of Olean, was completed. This Albany-sponsored boondoggle initiated by the New York State Board of Canal Commissioners required a feeder to supply the water needs of the canal. By damming the Genesee River at the Oil Spring Indian Reservation, a 1,600-acre reservoir, the largest artificial body of water in the state at that time, was created by state engineers in a series of "takes" between 1858 and 1871. A portion of Seneca lands was illegally condemned to form Oil Spring Reservoir, now known as Cuba Lake. When the canal was abandoned in 1878, after only two decades of use, the lake became one of the major tourist areas of southwestern New York State.[16]

The connection between Iroquois land dispossession and the transportation revolution can also be seen by examining the makeup of the New York State Board of Canal Commissioners, founded as a state agency in 1810 at the behest of De Witt Clinton, who at that time was a respected scholar of "Iroquois antiquities."[17] In the first decade of its operation sixteen men served on this powerful state board. Besides representatives from prominent old New York families such as the Livingstons and Van Rensselaers and heroes of the early republic such as Robert Fulton and Gouverneur Morris, the board also included the powerful governor De Witt Clinton; Clinton's cousin, Simeon De Witt, the state's surveyor-general; Joseph Ellicott, the chief land surveyor and agent of the Holland Land Company; Peter B. Porter, also connected to the Holland and later Ogden land companies and the founder of Black Rock, western New York land speculator, military hero of the War of 1812, state Indian negotiator in 1815, federal boundary commissioner under the Treaty of Ghent and later secretary of war; and Henry Seymour, a representative from central New York, father of Governor Horatio Seymour who, next to De Witt Clinton, was the state's greatest promoter of canals and was the grandfather of Horatio Seymour, Jr., later chief engineer of the Erie Canal.[18] Hence, politics, land speculation, and transportation were wedded in an effort to build New York, making a third-rated northern state behind Pennsylvania and Massachusetts into the "major player," the Empire State.[19]

The New York State Board of Canal Commissioners, the New York State Surveyor-General's Office, headed by Simeon De Witt from 1784 to the 1830s, and the land companies such as the Holland Land Company, had an incestuous relationship, working against Indian interests. For example,

Simeon De Witt

Courtesy of the New York State Library and James Corsaro

Moses De Witt, Simeon's cousin, was a leading speculator in military tract lands after Simeon's survey laid it out. Peter B. Porter's brother, Augustus, worked as the surveyor for the Holland Land Company after the Treaty of Big Tree of 1797, and he and Peter also both made financial killings by the extinguishment of the so-called New York Reservation strip lands north of the Buffalo Creek Reservation in the federal treaty with the Seneca in 1802. As early as 1798 Joseph Ellicott, the Holland Land Company agent, served as a deputy surveyor under the auspices of Simeon De Witt, which authorized Ellicott to fix legally the boundaries of the Mile Strip along the Niagara River.[20]

Well before the creation of the New York State Board of Canal Commissioners, New Yorkers were predicting the rise of the Empire State. One of the earliest architects of this dream was Christopher Colles, the first

Christopher Colles

Courtesy of the New York State Library, New York State Museum, and Craig Williams

great civil engineer in the history of the Empire State. Born in Ireland around 1738, where he studied science, he emigrated to America where by the early 1770s he was lecturing on civil engineering, focusing on creating New York City's water system and improving inland navigation. During the American Revolution he was an instructor in artillery under Baron von Steuben, teaching the principles of projectiles. He, along with Simeon De Witt, was also involved in survey and mapping experiences during the war years that took him throughout the Middle Atlantic states. After the American Revolution, Colles was the first to propose the linking of the Hudson River with the Great Lakes by means of natural and artificial waterways (canals).[21]

Colles's idea was published in pamphlet form in 1785 as *Proposals for the*

Speedy Settlement of the Waste and Unappropriated Lands on the Western Frontiers of the State of New York, and for the Improvement of the Inland Navigation Between Albany and Oswego. Hence, by very definition, Colles interpreted Iroquoia as "waste and unappropriated lands" in need of state development, arguing on political, economic, and national security grounds.[22]

The proposal led to the introduction of a bill "for improving the navigation of the Mohawk River, Wood Creek and Onondaga River, with a view to opening an inland navigation to Oswego and for extending the same if practicable to Lake Erie."[23] Later, in 1789, Colles distributed the first American tour guide or road book, *Proposals for Publishing a Survey of the Roads of the United States,* which included an elaborate broadside-styled title page and eighty-three small road maps.[24] In 1808, still interested in canal development, Colles published his *Proposal of a Design for the Promotion of the Interests of the United States of America, Extending Its Advantages to All Ranks and Conditions of Men by Means of Inland Navigable Communication of a New Construction and Mode* in which he advocated the revolutionary idea that a canal should be constructed out of timber and above ground with perpendicular sides so that goods could be loaded and unloaded along the entire route.[25]

Elkanah Watson, Colles's contemporary and major land speculator in military tract lands, was the great propagandist for canals in the early republic. Although there were other self-styled promoters of canals, such as Jesse Hawley, Watson, because of his early business, banking, and land-speculating successes, was much more influential. Born in Plymouth, Massachusetts, in 1758 of Pilgrim stock, he was trained as a businessman, having served a valuable apprenticeship with the Brown family, the merchant barons of Providence, which led him to travel throughout the American colonies on their behalf. During the American Revolution he carried dispatches and money to Benjamin Franklin in Paris, then American rebel representative at the French court. In France he attended the clerical college of Ancenis. As a result of these experiences, after the war, on his own he established himself in banking and various mercantile enterprises. Because of his extensive European travels in the decade before his move to Albany in 1789, he had become impressed with canals, especially those of Holland, and corresponded throughout the 1780s with Washington and other prominent Americans

Elkanah Watson

Courtesy of the New York State Library, New York State Museum, and Craig Williams

about the feasibility of developing a system of American canals; however, Watson's final conversion to Erie Canal development came between 1788 and 1791.[26]

In 1788 this peripatetic businessman attended an Indian treaty negotiation at Fort Stanwix. In his extensive memoirs Watson recorded his journey through the Mohawk country to Fort Stanwix, now Rome, New York. After describing the Indians on route, Watson then envisioned the future of the area, predicting accurately the rise of central New York:[27]

> In contemplating the situation of Fort Stanwix, at the head of batteaux navigation on the Mohawk river, within one mile of Wood creek, running west, I am led to think this situation will, in time, become the emporium of commerce between Albany and the vast western world above.
> Wood creek is, indeed, small, but it is the only water communication with the great lakes. It empties into Oneida lake; thence down the Onondaga and Oswego rivers to Lake Ontario, at Fort Oswego, where the British have a garrison.
> Should the Little Falls be ever locked,—the obstructions in the Mohawk river removed,—and a canal between said river and Wood creek, at this place, formed, so as to unite the waters running east, with those running west;—and other canals made, and obstructions removed to fort Oswego,—who can reasonably doubt but that by such bold operations, the state of New-York have it within their power, by a grand stroke of policy, to divert the future trade of Lake Ontario, and the great lakes above, from Alexandria and Quebec, to Albany and New-York.

Leaving Fort Stanwix, Watson concluded "that a canal communication will be opened, sooner or later, from the great [*sic*] lakes to the Hudson."[28] Three years later, at the insistence of Watson, three prominent New Yorkers— Jeremiah Van Rensselaer, Stephen N. Bayard, and Philip Van Cortlandt—all major investors in the military tract, toured New York with the aim of canal development, which passed through Oneida, Onondaga, Cayuga, and Seneca Indian lands. After traversing north of the Oneida Indian Reservation and leaving Oneida Lake, Watson wrote:[29]

> This lake is thirty miles long, and from five to eight broad. We are now sailing parallel with the Ontario ocean, which I hope to see, and at least enjoy in delightful anticipation the prospect of a free and open water communication from thence to the Atlantic, via Albany and New-York.
> In giving a stretch to the mind into futurity, I saw those fertile regions, bounded west by the Mississippi, north by the great lakes, east by the Allegany mountains, and south by the placid Ohio, overspread with millions of freemen; blessed with various climates, enjoying every variety of soil, and commanding the boldest inland navigation on this globe; clouded with sails, directing their course towards canals, alive with boats passing and repassing, giving and receiving reciprocal benefits from this wonderful country prolific in such great resources.

The expedition then went north toward Oswego, visiting the camp of Moses De Witt. Twenty-five miles south of Oswego, the party was visited by "several troublesome Indians of the Onondaga tribe," some of whom were intoxicated. Despite Watson's frequent outrage in his journals about drunken Indians, he then traded alcohol and biscuits for salmon and eels with the "old Kiadote King of the Onondaga Indians," his "queen" "Kanastoretar," and several other Onondaga "warriors."[30] Throughout his memoirs he frequently alluded to the potential of a future canal between Onondaga country and Oswego and to the emergence of a great city, predicting the future rise of Syracuse, emerging within the environs of central New York because of its geographic position and its access to salt:[31]

Providence has happily placed this great source of comfort and wealth, precisely in a position accessible by water in every direction. When the mighty canals shall be formed and locks erected, it will add vastly to the facility of an extended diffusion, and the increase of its intrinsic worth. . . . Whenever works are properly constructed on a large scale, the salt may be delivered for twenty-five cents a bushel, probably less; but the expense of transportation under present obstruction, will limit its consumption to the western country.

By the end of the 1790s Watson had become a leading banker in Albany, promoted the interests of two canal companies as well as a stage line from Albany to Schenectady, and secured a future charter for a canal in western New York. Because of his Federalist/anti-Clintonian politics, his political influence waned in New York in the first decades of the nineteenth century, leading him into retirement in the Berkshires of Massachusetts. Later, his book, *History of the Rise and Progress and Existing Condition of the Western Canals in the State of New York,* published in 1820, became the bible for promoting canals. Indeed, it reads as a great commercial prospectus for central and western New York, much like a modern state, federal, or foreign investment brochure.[32] A quarter-century after his famous 1791 tour, Watson returned to central New York. His comments are revealing:[33]

At Syracuse I resumed my carriage. It was impossible for me to contemplate Syracuse, Salina and Liverpool, all thriving villages situated in the vicinity of Onondaga Lake, and devoted to the manufacture of salt, of which they produce nearly a million of bushels annually, and not recur to my expedition by water, thirty-seven years ago, to this same lake. What a transition! The country was then in its primeval condition, roamed over by savage tribes, and only occupied here and there by scattered white inhabitants. No roads existed, and not even a gristmill west of the German Flats. Behold now, as it were, an old country, possessed by a vigorous and intelligent population, fine turnpike roads, prosperous villages and large and beautiful towns, numerous stage-coaches all plying in every direction in the midst of elegant and commodious farm-houses, excellent and highly cultivated farms, matured orchards, and above all, the Erie canal in active progression, with fifteen hundred men at work in its construction within sixty miles of this place, and splendid packet-boats already building for the transportation of passengers from Lake Erie to the Hudson. Inexhaustible beds of gypsum are revealed here, which will tend to stimulate the advancing improvements in agriculture.

Colles the engineer and Watson the promoter were part of larger forces at work in the early republic, namely, national political leaders such as John C. Calhoun, De Witt Clinton, Albert Gallatin, Gouverneur Morris, and Philip Schuyler, each of whom was responsible for adding elements to the formula for making New York the Empire State. Morris, later a New York State canal commissioner, had seen the emerging canal system in Great Britain on a visit in 1761 and had become the "chief patron of internal improvement" in New York State from the American Revolution onward. It is important to note that Morris held title to thousands of acres of land along the St. Lawrence River and stood to benefit by improving transportation networks in the state.[34]

Connected to Watson was Philip Schuyler, the Federalist scion in New York. Schuyler was without doubt *the* major player in securing Oneida lands for the evolving transportation network. The omnipotent Schuyler, using his past connections to these Indians and drawing on his powerful family and political alliances, can be considered the founding father of New York State's transportation revolution. This prominent Albanian, the former general and United States senator from New York, was the founder and president of the Western Inland Lock Navigation Company, the precursor to the Erie Canal which was incorporated in 1792 and was designed to open a navigable channel from Albany to Seneca Lake and Lake Ontario to market potash, wheat, lumber, and salt. Schuyler's and Watson's goal, which they successfully accomplished, was to open a linked channel that combined natural waterways, improved natural waterways, and short canals.

Schuyler's early efforts led to the passage by the New York State Legislature of "an act for establishing and opening lock navigations within the State." As early as 1793, "Wood creek, the stream which flows into Oneida Lake, was cleared of fallen timber and straightened to the extent of shortening its length more than seven miles." By the following year thirteen minicanal channels had already been illegally cut through Oneida territory. Thus, by the mid-1790s the transportation revolution had come to Oneida

Philip Schuyler

Courtesy of the New York State Library, New York State Museum, and Craig Williams

Indian territory and had been initiated by the New York politician most closely associated with the Oneidas during the American Revolution. Although Schuyler's landed investments were in Albany and Saratoga Counties, he also had leased lands in the environs of present-day Utica, right in the path of future canal development.[35]

In 1808, at the time of Jefferson's embargo crisis with Great Britain, Secretary of the Treasury Albert Gallatin made his famous report on internal improvement. While New York State's preliminary canal surveys were being undertaken by James Geddes and Simeon De Witt, the Gallatin report called for the expenditure of federal moneys of two million dollars annually on canals and roads. Gallatin proposed making a series of canals between the Hudson and Lake Erie part of a system of economic planning and security to strengthen the nation as a whole.[36] Hence, Gallatin, as a result of the looming war clouds on the horizon, added another dimension to the equation, namely national security concerns.

De Witt Clinton's private canal journal, written in the summer of 1810 while touring in his capacity as a founding member of the New York State Board of Canal Commissioners, is one of the essential clues to understanding the rise of the Empire State. Although intended only as a record of his own thoughts, the journal illustrates Clinton's mind-set and indicates how he formulated policies both as governor of New York State and as canal commissioner. Indeed, the journal, much like Watson's writings, reads as if it were a modern prospectus put out by the United States Department of Commerce promoting investment in foreign lands. Throughout, Clinton commented about the vast potential of central and western New York.

Clinton observed that New York State offered rich opportunities to take advantage of its natural bounties. Chief to it, according to Clinton, was its large availability of salt. Frequently describing salt boats and salt production in central New York, he emphasized the central importance of this trade in the early years of the nineteenth century, especially the state's export trade of the commodity to both Pennsylvania and British Canada. It is important to note that Clinton mentioned one Peter B. Porter, who had leased the state lands around Niagara Falls to carry out his salt trade enterprise.[37] Although salt was thoroughly emphasized in Clinton's journal, the governor also described other current money-making activities or those with substantial economic potential. These varied from wheat farming, apple harvesting, and growing ginseng for materia medica to fishing, cattle raising, and gypsum mining. Clinton even mentioned the future of hydraulic energy development near Niagara Falls.[38]

Clinton's journal reveals the hypocritical thinking of men in power in that age. Clinton lauded his political allies when they dabbled in Indian real estate but had no praise for his political enemies or those of the Catholic persuasion. To him, Joseph Ellicott and the operations of the Holland Land Company were "admirable" in both "management and method." Nor was Magnus Apollo critical of the unquenchable appetite of Peter B. Porter, pointing out his business acumen in buying one thousand acres along the Ridge Road in Seneca country at the ridiculous price of twelve shillings per acre! In contrast, Clinton attacked his Federalist enemy, Assemblyman James Dean, the trader-interpreter-cultural broker to the Oneida and Stockbridge, for his duping the Indians out of their lands; and Angel De Ferriere, a French trader intermarried with the Oneida, the family of Lewis Denny, who emerged as a leader within the First Christian Party, and who, according to Clinton, "forced land sales to the State of New York"!39

Taking advantage of the crisis of the War of 1812, New York politicians led by De Witt Clinton, after his official tour as a canal commissioner in 1810 and long enamored with canals, proposed a radical idea—state funding for public works. Despite the success of inland navigation by Durham boats throughout this period, promoters of the scheme used the rationale that the crude and inadequate turnpike toll roads, always in a state of disrepair, retarded the war effort. Hence, transportation and defense needs to counter the British lion—much like the cold war arguments of the 1950s made by Robert Moses in the advocacy of the Tuscarora Reservoir and the St. Lawrence Seaway projects—"required" the Iroquois to lose their lands as "sacrifice areas" for the state's and nation's progress.40 It is important that no party had a monopoly on virtue relative to Indians from 1784 onward. Whatever the party between 1784 and 1860—Federalist, Jeffersonian, Clintonian, Democrat, or Whig—America's idea of progress was scarcely inclusive of Indians remaining on *all* their lands or, for that matter, remaining culturally and politically separate.

Clinton's attitudes toward the Iroquois explain much. Seeing himself as an "authority" on the Six Nations, he regarded Indian religion as superstition and was "dubious of efforts to christianize the Indians." To the future governor the Indians were much like wild beasts that had to give way to progress. Clinton predicted, in an address before the New-York Historical Society in 1811, that the "minister of destruction is hovering over them [the Iroquois], and before the passing away of the present generation, not a single Iroquois will be seen in this state [New York]."41 His promotion of canals was to contribute directly to undermining the Iroquois, removing many of them west and north, and dispossessing them from Buffalo Creek, the focal point of his grand design in making New York the Empire State.

Although the federal government did not fund the Erie Canal, the secretary of war from 1817 to 1825, John C. Calhoun, saw canals as strategic in helping to populate and to develop rapidly the northern reaches of the United States from central New York to Michigan. Although Anglo-American rapprochement was President Monroe's and Secretary of State John Quincy Adams's strategy, American policymakers and the American public at large were seriously affected in their thinking by forty years of tension and wars with Great Britain. American claims of depredations committed by the British and their Indian allies on the Niagara frontier were extensive after the War of 1812. Because of the difficulties in transporting goods, ordinance, and men by turnpike toll roads during 1812–15, transportation issues came to the fore. Gallatin's plan was revived because of the "imperative need for military roads to critical frontiers" as part of a national plan of defense, most emphatically championed by Secretary of War John C. Calhoun.[42]

Calhoun as secretary of war was the major formulator of both defense and Indian policies and proposed a change in the direction of both areas. Calhoun's grand design was to strengthen United States defenses by settling the disputed northern boundary with British Canada, urging the Indians in the strongest language, but without formal military coercion, to see the value of leaving their New York homeland for lands in the west. Calhoun also advocated the encouragement of local state-funded internal improvements such as roads and canals, which he deemed necessary for the quick settlement of the northern reaches of the nation and which he believed would guarantee national security.[43] The brilliant South Carolinian discussed the possibilities of Indian removal from New York State with the motley likes of Henry Clay, Reverend Jedidiah Morse, Indian subagent Jasper Parrish, territorial governor of Michigan Lewis Cass, and with the prominent land jobber, David A. Ogden.[44]

Ogden, the former congressman, Holland Land Company attorney based in New York City, and founder of the Ogden Land Company in 1810, had long advocated the goal of concentrating Indian populations in the state or tribal removal from New York and had long expounded the centrality of acquiring Buffalo. He argued that little more than two thousand Indians at Buffalo Creek retarded the growth of this important place, that the Indians were depraved—mostly "alcoholics," "liars," and "prostitutes"—and that they paid no taxes and did not contribute to local improvements such as roads.[45]

Although Calhoun apparently did not trust Ogden and was suspicious of his motives, the secretary of war did insist in a letter to the Speaker of the House Henry Clay in December 1818 that the Indians should no longer "be considered as independent nations. Our views of their interests, and not their own, ought to govern them." He added that by "a proper combination of force and persuasion of punishments and rewards, they ought to be brought within the pales of law and civilization." To him, "savage customs" "cannot, and ought not, be permitted to exist in an independent condition in the midst of civilized society." Calhoun viewed the Indians as capable of transformation, civilization, and citizenship if led to accept individual ownership, more concentrated landholdings "within reasonable bounds," and American law and jurisdiction.[46]

Hence, because of his vision of transforming the Iroquois, Calhoun was not satisfied with simply seeking easements through Indian lands. Indeed, Calhoun considered concentrating the Iroquois away from the northern border at the Allegany Indian Reservation and saw the value of relocating the Iroquois to the west, first considering Arkansas, then Illinois, and finally the Michigan Territory which included present-day Wisconsin. For "their own good" they had to be isolated from the evil temptations of the rampaging frontier such as alcohol or continued British machinations. Military force was not necessary to remove them because the Indians would eventually see for themselves, Calhoun thought, that their ultimate fate required them to live like white Americans or move beyond American settlement. In an age of transportation revolution, this was the accepted American shibboleth, namely, the inevitability of progress and the decline of the "vanishing race."[47] Thus, to "save" the Indian the Iroquois had to be convinced that removal was in their "best interests."

Calhoun believed that commerce, military defense, and inland transportation "were closely allied, especially at the great estuaries and harbors where land and water communications met."[48] In this vein he issued his "Report on Roads and Canals" in 1819. Based on Gallatin's earlier report and New York State's building of its grand canal, Calhoun was well aware of the strategic importance of Buffalo, receiving frequent news from Morse, Ogden, Parrish, and Eleazer Williams about the Indians in that region.[49]

More cautious in his approach than most of the secretary of war's correspondents, Jedidiah Morse, who served as Calhoun's special emissary, made a national report in 1820 after his extensive visits through Indian country. It is important that, on his visit through the Indian communities in New

York, he was accompanied "for three or four days" by "Governor Clinton, General S. Van Rensselaer and other gentlemen, Commissioners" who were going to visit the "Grand Erie Canal" construction. Not surprisingly, Morse, the prominent missionary who had first visited in Iroquoia in 1796, extensively described the canal, especially its ninety-six-mile completed portion from Utica to Montezuma and the flourishing salt manufacture along a 1.5-mile branch at Salina in the vicinity of the city of Syracuse.[50] Although an advocate of Indian removal to the Fox River of Wisconsin, which he saw as a way to isolate and save the Indians from the rapid push of white settlement, Morse was quite deliberate in pushing removal before Indian councils at Buffalo Creek. Morse warned Clinton about approaching the Indians on the subject: "I did not touch [at Buffalo Creek] on the delicate subject of their *removal and colonization* [Morse's emphasis]. Things are not yet ripe for a discussion of a subject on wh[ic]h there is a diversity of opinions warmly supported on both sides among the Whites and Indians."[51]

Right to the end of his tenure as secretary of war, Calhoun looked at Iroquoia as central to the defense needs of the nation. To him the changes underway required and set in motion by canal building were essential to his overall national security planning. In December 1824, just before his ascendancy to vice-president, Calhoun wrote President Monroe, insisting the near-completed Erie Canal and other planned canal ventures were "of the highest *national* [Calhoun's emphasis] importance in a commercial, military and political point of view."[52]

Thus, ditches—improved navigable rivers and later canals—were to affect Iroquoia permanently. Besides tourists, they brought tremendous population and expanded agriculture, industry, and mining. In addition to creating a metropolitan corridor, canals affected the Iroquois, as did railroads later, in other ways. New York State canal records have occasional references to land takes and physical damage to both individual Indian and tribal property caused by the expansion of various canal projects.[53] Indians were also employed in building and repairing canals, roads, and tracks, thus ironically serving as foot soldiers in the transportation revolution that was seriously undermining their way of life. One such individual was Ely S. Parker, the Tonawanda Seneca sachem, who later served on General Grant's staff during the Civil War and who became commissioner of Indian Affairs in 1869. Parker worked as an axeman on the Genesee Valley Canal project in 1849

Ely S. Parker
Courtesy of the National Archives

and later served as a deputy engineer for the New York State Board of Canal Commissioners in its Rochester office until 1855.[54]

Although it was a short-lived phenomenon nationally, the canal era made central and western New York unrecognizable. The changes wrought were dramatic, permanently affecting the Indians. Forcing the Iroquois out of Buffalo not only resulted in removing the Indians but also led to the reestablishment of the League's ritual center at Onondaga. Besides the intrusion of the outside world and the loss of significant acreage in this period, land dispossession spurred major litigation, including the so-called Kansas claim, settled a half-century later. Other claims remain unsettled today, including the Oneida land claim and the Grand Island, Genesee Valley, and the Cuba Lake claim (Oil Spring) of the Seneca. In this important period other communities such as the Oneidas became a widely separated people with many tribal members dispersed to Wisconsin and southern Ontario. Perhaps as important was the increased role of New York State in Iroquois affairs, starting with state legislative enactments in 1813 and increasingly substantially by the 1840s and 1850s. The Albany presence in Iroquoian life, one resented by the majority of the Indians, included issues that still remain a source of New York State–Indian tensions, including the right of the state to tax Indians on reservations.

The relationship between settlement patterns and transportation was a reciprocal one. Euroamerican settlers who came into central New York, as geographer Richard H. Schein has carefully noted, were no seekers of "self-imposed isolation" attempting to merely escape the more heavily settled east. To them the "sooner the frontier could be physically connected to the east the better." Thus, roads—local and interregional—and canals were advocated and promoted, which also meant land values would rise and land speculation would also increase, especially at key junctions of rivers or along the routes of roads and canals. Thus, as Schein has noted, the establishment of an adequate transportation network was crucial to the colonization process.[55] The first of these pressure points was central New York, especially the land of the Oneidas.

PART ONE

The Oneida Country: Gateway to the West

Utica in 1819

Courtesy of the New York State Library, New York State Museum, and Craig Williams

CHAPTER 2

The Oneida Carrying Place

No other Indian community in New York State was affected more by the transportation revolution than the Oneidas. The Oneida lands, totaling more than five million acres in 1784, were the necessary ingredient for the rise of the Empire State. With its center in Oneida and Madison Counties, these lands were situated at a vital transportation crossroads that was essential for New York's economic growth after the Revolution. To private and state interests, the relatively small number of Oneidas—780 in the Oneida homeland and 30 in the Genesee valley in 1792—stood in the way of "progress."[1] What happened to the Oneidas set the pattern of state-Indian relations right through the Jacksonian era. For New York State to expand east-west and north-south, private entrepreneurial interests in conjunction with Albany officials, whether Federalists, Jeffersonians, Clintonians, Democrats, or Whigs, and subsidized by public funds, constantly picked away at Oneida lands from 1785 onward until the early 1840s.

The Oneidas, already severely fractionated in their polity and religion, largely found it impossible to resist these pressures, leading a majority of the community eventually to migrate for its protection and survival west to Wisconsin in the period 1822 to 1838 or to Ontario from 1839 onward. The incredible pressures placed upon the community as a result of this transportation revolution explain in part why the bulk of the community followed the controversial Indian missionary, Eleazer Williams, a charismatic but unbalanced ecclesiastical leader of Mohawk ancestry, into the wilderness of eastern Wisconsin, where the largest contemporary Oneida community still resides.[2]

The boundaries of the Oneida territory had been formally recognized in the federal Treaty of Fort Stanwix in 1784 (see map 2). From Wood Creek, it ran southeast along the Unadilla River to the Susquehanna and then to the Delaware. On the north, it went from East Canada Creek to West Canada Creek, near today's Poland, New York, and then west across the headwaters of the Black and Oswegatchie Rivers and northwest to the St. Lawrence River, following the shoreline of Lake Ontario southward to nearly the rift of the Onondaga River valley. It then ran due south to a point five miles west of the outlet of Oneida Lake and then southeast to Chittenango Falls on Chittenango Creek and Cazenovia Lake. The boundary line then returned to its starting point via the headwaters of the Oswego River and the course of the Susquehanna. The Oneidas' twenty-seven known villages were within this vast territory, mostly in present-day Madison County, but they controlled an extensive hunting territory that stretched from the St. Lawrence River valley to what is today's Pennsylvania line. Despite one of the smaller populations within the historic Five Nations in the seventeenth and eighteenth centuries and bounded by more vociferous Iroquoian neighbors the Mohawks and Onondagas, the Oneidas, largely because of their favorable geographic position at the crossroads of water transportation to great rivers—Delaware, Mohawk, St. Lawrence, and Susquehanna—and to one of the Great Lakes, Lake Ontario, were without doubt more significant in the colonial period than most scholars have acknowledged.[3]

Ancient trade routes coming from the east into Oneida country started up the Mohawk River, dividing into two at the river's headwater. One navigable branch went as far as today's Rome, where canoes were picked up at this strategic "carrying place" and transported two miles overland and then relaunched into Wood Creek, following a winding course to Oneida Lake. Then the canoes were paddled down the Oswego River on Lake Ontario to Fort Oswego or up the Seneca River. The second route began at the ford at today's Utica (Unundadages) and followed the overland Seneca Trail westward by way of Oneida Castle—today's Vernon, New York—to Onondaga, Cayuga, and Seneca country.[4]

This region, whose center was the short portage between the Mohawk River and Wood Creek, the so-called Oneida Carrying Place, was strategic for both the Iroquois Indians and the later Euroamericans (see map 2).[5] To the southeast are the headwaters of the Mohawk, which flows eastward until it joins the Hudson, which connects to the Atlantic Ocean at New York City. On the north is Wood Creek which, along with Fish Creek, Oneida Lake, and the Oswego River, was a major passageway to Lake Ontario and the rest of the Great Lakes. Control of these water routes was essential for colonial commerce in furs and for military defense of the colonies, leading to the building of the British bastion of Fort Stanwix, constructed in 1758, at the Oneida Carrying Place, one of the strongest fortifications in North America. During the American Revolution, General Philip Schuyler rebuilt Fort Stanwix, which was renamed in his honor and which became central to American and Oneida military operations in central New York against the British and their allied Indians.[6] The Oneida Carrying Place's importance cannot be fully understood in today's space age. Two National Park Service archaeologists observed its strategic value:[7]

During the spring thaws, when both watersheds were full, the distance across the portage was only one mile, while in the fall, after a drought, a man might have to walk five miles to find water deep enough to launch a bateau. . . . The importance of this portage can only be realized when one understands how poor the roads and trails were in colonial days. Most were mere ruts worn in the soil by travelers and were extremely difficult to negotiate on horseback, let alone by wagon. Rivers were the principal arteries of transportation and bateaus were developed to hold several tons of cargo. They could be propelled by three men paddling or, if the wind was right, with a sail. The Oneida Carry offered the second shortest route from the Atlantic to the Great Lakes. The St. Lawrence River, under French control until 1760, was the shortest.

The Oneidas had long been aware of the natural advantages of their homeland. The rolling hills around Oneida Castle had provided the Indians with fine hunting grounds. Oneida Lake and the numerous river systems and waterways of the region teemed with fish, including bass, eel, pickerel, salmon, and whitefish. The Dutch-American intellectual Francis Van der Kemp, who in 1794 settled on lands obtained from the Oneidas by George Scriba, a major land speculator, described the richness of this fishery:[8]

Both Salmon rivers emptying in Lake Ontario, to the north of this tract of land and the Fish creek in Oneida Lake, are in the spring and fall, full of salmon. One Oneida Indian took with his spear, forty-five salmon in one hour. They are equal to the best which are caught in the rivers of the Rhine and Meuse. The eel of the Oneida Lake is equal to the best of the Holland market, and far surpasses every kind which I have ever tasted here, in size, in fatness, in tenderness of the fish.

Yet fishing was not the primary way the Oneidas maintained themselves, and at times they appeared to outside observers as "disinterested" about their great fishing resources at Oneida Lake.[9] The importance of fishing to the Oneidas was clearly manifested, however, in their transactions about the lands of the lake. According to Friedrich Rohde, a German geologist travel-

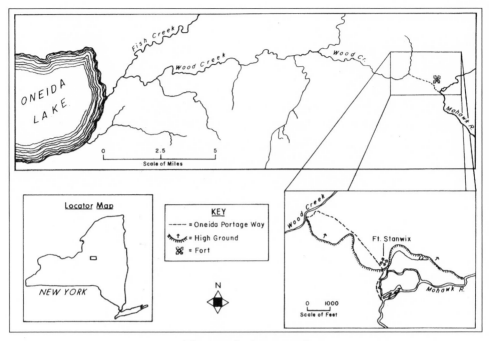

2. The Oneida Carrying Place

Original map by Ben Simpson

ing through the region in 1802, the "Indians stipulated upon selling this district that the woods for 1/2 mile wide on either side should not be cut down, because they believe that by denuding the creek of woods would harm the fishing."[10] The extremely copious fishing resources and the territory's timber value and salt-mining potential were mentioned by nearly every major non-Indian observer from Elkanah Watson to Jeremy Belknap to De Witt Clinton.[11] Van der Kemp added:[12]

Everywhere are salt springs, and but few miles from Oneida Lake in Onondago is a copious salt lake, encircled with salt springs, the domain of the people of the State of New York. A considerable quantity is already transported to Canada, and [a] thousand American families make never use of any other. How the copiousness must be increased when rock salt too is manufactured and carried to the South and West of our immense continent.

This country, so abundant in water and fish, is, if possible, yet more profusely endowed by our bountiful maker with wood. Every kind of timber of the northern and eastern States, is here in the greatest plenty and perfection: butternut, walnut, white oak, sugar maple, chestnut, beech, black ash, pine, hemlock, the lime tree, white wood or canoes wood, and several other species.

To Van der Kemp even the lonely individual pioneer without the immediate wherewithal to survive off farming could maintain himself and his family in this region: "Providence has in this district graciously provided even to satiety. Never did I see a country where all kind of fish was so abundant and good."[13]

Two years later, Belknap as Watson earlier, recognized that these waterways also offered other advantages, long known and used by the Indians: communication and trade. The Indians had used these waterways for trade, diplomacy, and warfare, stretching south into Pennsylvania and north into southern Ontario. Belknap in 1796 commented specifically about the strategic value of Oriskany Creek and the surrounding new white settlements of Clinton, Paris, and Whitestown: "It is a central situation and a good place for trade."[14] The area at Steuben, between New Hartford and Clinton, in the heart of Oneida country, was one of the key strategic positions of the state. One missionary in 1802 observed that at the high ground there, a person on a clear day could see thirty-five miles to the northwest, specifically Oneida Lake; the Catskill Mountains to the southeast and southwest; and, by climbing to the tops of the trees, as far north as Ontario.[15]

South of Oneida Castle was one of the richer areas of agriculture in New York State, the Chenango valley, used by the Indians for centuries in their slash-and-burn methods of farming maize, beans, and squash. The summit of the area, nearly two thousand feet above sea level, helped the Indians defend and safeguard their villages. Moreover, the forests of the region were filled with beech, chestnut, elm, hemlock, maple, oak, and pine, and with basswood, most serviceable as it could be split easily into rough slabs or could be carved in the early spring, serving the Oneidas as masks for the False Face Society. Thus, the location of the Oneida's principal village, Oneida Castle, Canowaroghere, or *Ganowarohere*—in Oneida meaning "where there is a skull impaled," according to Lewis Henry Morgan— allowed these Indians access to "not only some of the finest agricultural districts of the state, but the most attractive localities in its central part."[16]

Because of these natural advantages, the fate of these Indians was set long before their eventual removal from the state. Indeed the thirty-year period, 1785 to 1815, was the decisive era. The eminent geographer D. W. Meinig has labeled the process of non-Indian settlement in central New York as "geographic prediction." White entrepreneurs sought strategic sites that by the "qualities of their position would become important settlements." Meinig observed that the process involved the "attempt to foresee which would be the critical points of 'spatial interaction' (junctions, ports, manufacturing nodes, regional supply centers, etc.) once the whole state developed beyond the pioneer stage."[17]

Entrepreneurs seeing the natural advantages of the central New York landscape promoted the founding and rise of the region's major cities—Utica, Syracuse, and Rome—and the development of integrated navigation systems such as the Western Inland Lock Navigation Company. They also advanced the construction of four canals—the Black River, Chenango, Erie, and Oneida Lake Canals—and the building of the first state road, the Genesee Turnpike, sometimes called the Seneca Turnpike (Route 5). This turnpike in the beginning extended from New Hartford (originally the Oneida village of Chicugughquate or Kidneys) to Canandaigua and ran through the southern end of the principal Indian settlement of Oneida Castle. Consequently, Oneida County was established in 1798 and Madison County became a separate administrative unit by 1806 (see map 4). Importantly, west of Oneida was the rising city of Syracuse, with its nearby salt mines at Salina and the vast lands of the New Military Tract, the former estate of Indians allied to the British in the American Revolution. This great salt deposit around Onondaga Lake was frequently mentioned by entrepreneurs, missionaries, and politicians in this period and salt mining was seen as the great industry for the emerging center of the state.[18] Thus, for Utica to emerge economically and for the military tract to be populated, a new, viable transportation network had to be established. Moreover, the city fathers of Rome (which is largely northwest of Oneida territory), although slower to develop a growth strategy, saw themselves in competition with the better-located Utica. Rome city fathers saw the survival and future of their city as contingent upon promoting and extending economic tentacles east to Oneida Lake and north into the Adirondacks. The rivalry of these two cities and their battle for dominance spilled over and affected the Oneidas.

Any and all east-west and north-south development required the extinguishment of Oneida title to these lands or, at least, the separation of these Indians from their homeland. Road building and canal building, the creation of inland navigation centered in and around Oneida Lake, became central to the process of Indian dispossession from the late 1780s onward and continued unabated until the majority of Oneidas had been removed from New York State by the 1840s.

New York State's extinguishment of Oneida title in this period has been deemed by the United States Supreme Court as a clear violation of the federal Trade and Intercourse Acts because a federal commissioner was never present nor was United States Senate approval secured.[19] William Bradford, the attorney general of the United States, as well as Timothy Pickering, the United States commissioner assigned to negotiate with the Oneidas and other members of the Six Nations (who was later secretary of war), saw these state "accords" with certain Indian "leaders" as clear violations of federal law and warned Washington officials and tribal leaders about these violations.[20] To be sure, the taking of Oneida lands in the period was actually accomplished by a vast conspiracy of interlocking forces—land and transportation interests—that took advantage of the real fears caused by New York State's proximity to the enemy, British Canada, to generate calls for Indian removal. It should be pointed out, however, that despite Pickering's warnings, the federal government did little to carry out its fiduciary responsibility to the Indians as set forth in treaties to protect them against state actions and, therefore, it cannot be exempted from blame for what befell the Indians.[21]

These actions occurred before conflict-of-interest laws in an age when regulations on insider trading did not exist. In many ways the strategy used was what George Washington Plunkitt, that extraordinary late-nineteenth-century Tammany Hall politician, later labeled "honest graft."[22] Well-positioned players, often presenting themselves as protector friends of the Indian, saw their opportunities and took advantage of their inside track with the Oneidas. Although the Indians had little power to resist the non-Indian world, the nature of Oneida society after the American Revolution in part allowed them to be manipulated and to succumb to the intense pressures that sought their quick exit from the Carrying Place and from almost all of their lands in central New York.

CHAPTER 3

The Good Indians at the Crossroads

While transportation, land, and national defense interests were coming to the fore in Albany and Washington, the Oneida Indian world was increasingly beset with internal problems. Despite the ideal of working through consensus, the Oneidas had actually become increasingly divided throughout the colonial era, with major splits between the sachems and the warriors. From the beginnings of the American Revolution onward the Oneida Indians rarely spoke with one voice. "Representatives" of all factions within the Oneida polity, never a cohesive whole, ceded land to New York State in numerous illegal transactions from 1785 well into the 1840s. In the process of facing unrelenting white pressures to secure and to settle upon their land base, the Oneida community in New York further fractionated, splintering into three communities that exist to the present day.

Religious and political factionalism and social disintegration, manifest in increasing alcohol abuse and internecine violence in addition to economic dependence and class distinctions, were all apparent in the Oneida community in this post–Revolutionary War period.[1] While becoming increasingly divided, however, the Oneidas, it is clear, cultivated their role as "good Indians," attempting to stymie pressures for removal. They tried to stem the tide by leasing or ceding lands to individuals whom they deemed friends and whom they believed could prevent the flood of settlement into their central New York State homeland. Although this strategy proved faulty in retrospect, it was one of conscious design, one long used by the Oneidas as a survival strategy.

Although some Oneidas had splintered off and joined the sizable contingent of the Six Nations on the British side during the American Revolution, the vast majority of Oneidas, encouraged by their pro-American missionary

Samuel Kirkland, faithfully served George Washington's rebel army (as did the Oneida's allies the Tuscaroras). Eleven Oneidas served as officers in the American army, and, to this day, Oneida folklore is filled with references to their service in the patriots' quest for independence. Among the Oneida heroes of the Revolution are Peter Bread, Blatcop, Henry Cornelius (later the founder of the Handsome Lake religion among the Oneidas), Hanyost, Paul Powless, and Thawengarakwen (Honyery Doxtator). These men were hailed for their service to the American cause, especially for their heroism at the Battle of Oriskany in 1777. Blatcop, one of the Oneida warriors there, under intense British fire heroically charged the enemy three times during this major battle of the Saratoga campaign while Dolly Cobus, Honyery Doxtator's wife, took her husband's place in the battle after he had been wounded in the right wrist. Hanyost distinguished himself at the siege of Fort Stanwix as a lieutenant under General Peter Gansevoort's overall command. Moreover, Skenandoah and Good Peter, despite their advanced ages at the time, faithfully served the Americans as messengers from General Philip Schuyler, only to be arrested and harshly confined as prisoners of war by the British in 1780.[2]

In the postwar crisis period affecting the Oneidas, these warriors frequently referred to their faithful service, appealed for compensation in the form of military pensions, or attempted to play on their past service to Washington to secure federal protection from New York State's aggressive actions. The Oneidas also tried to make themselves indispensable to the white settlers in other ways. The Oneidas even allowed the Stockbridge Indians to formally resettle in their central New York territory. Brothertown Indians, several distinct communities from Long Island, Massachusetts, Connecticut, and Rhode Island, were also allowed to enter the Oneidas' homeland and to seek protection among these Iroquois people. Both moves were encouraged by their missionary Samuel Kirkland and by American officials who saw the advantage of concentrating friendly Indian populations.[3] Besides, these new adoptees fit into the Oneida cultural and historic role within the Iroquois polity because for the previous century they had resettled refugee Indians such as the Conoy, Munsee, Nanticoke, Susquehannah, Tuscarora, and Tutelo Indians within their territory.[4]

In the early fall of 1784 François Marbois (later the Marquis de Barbe-Marbois), at the time, the secretary to the French legation in the newly established United States, visited Oneida country. The visit of Marbois, an

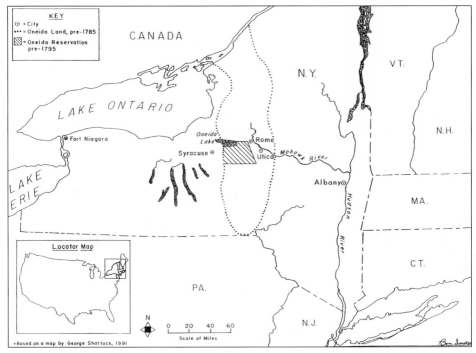

KEY
⊙ = City
••• = Oneida Land, pre-1785
▨ = Oneida Reservation pre-1795

CANADA

LAKE ONTARIO

N.Y.

VT.

N.H.

Fort Niagara

Oneida Lake

Rome

Syracuse ⊙

Utica ⊙

Mohawk River

Albany ⊙

LAKE ERIE

Hudson River

MA.

Locator Map

C.T.

PA.

N

0 20 40 60
Scale of Miles

N.J.

•Based on a map by George Shattuck, 1991

Ben Simpson

3. The Oneida Country after the American Revolution

Original map by Ben Simpson

old acquaintance of Lieutenant Colonel Hongarry [Honyery] (also called Thehoghwennagaloghwen or "Grasshopper"), the Oneida Indian head warrior of the Wolf Clan and a hero of the American Revolution, occurred at a pivotal time in Iroquois history. Marbois remarked at the large number of Indian refugees—Stockbridge, Narragansetts, Mohicans, and Niantics— who had been recently allowed to settle on "a piece of land six miles square" within the Oneida territory. The French diplomat then carefully noted that the Oneidas possessed "sixty square miles or twenty square leagues of a region of which the fertility surpasses anything that can be imagined." Particularly interesting was Marbois's description of the transportation difficulties in getting to the Oneida castle, which he claimed were even more "barbarous and wild than the Indians themselves," a common complaint that was to lead to state financing of roads in the 1790s and to place greater pressures on the Indians.[5] It was not surprising that the process of Oneida dispossession began in earnest less than one year after Marbois's visit and that the pulls over the next three decades were largely accentuated by the need to improve the state's transportation network to market agricultural and forestry products and salt. This process of dispossession was clearly aided by the divisions within the Oneida polity.

On October 11, 1794, Oneidas, at the urging of Timothy Pickering, came to a council with the federal commissioner to explain the roots of the great dissension occurring within the Indian community. Two Oneidas— Onondiyo, or Captain John, representing the sachems and Peter, representing the warriors—addressed Pickering although Peter's speech revealed little about the troubles occurring within the nation. Onondiyo's speech, however, explained much. He insisted, "Our minds are divided on account of our land."[6] Onondiyo was basically observing that, by the decade after the American Revolution, the Oneidas had become increasingly divided upon the merits of leasing or ceding lands to their alleged friends, whom they had hoped would act as supporters for them against the land companies or act as intermediaries and protectors with the Indians' enemies in Albany—most specifically Governors Clinton and Jay. Hoping to win the federal government's protection from state and land companies' actions, Onondiyo then tried to ingratiate himself with President Washington's remarkable American envoy:[7]

I am tender hearted and my mind is easily flattered and led away. I am willing to accommodate my brother of a white skin; and have always listened to their voices. The reason has been that if I thought they would not be pleased if I did not comply with their requests. And we comply because we wish to live in friendship with our brothers the white people. Brother, the United States planted a tree of peace for us, and desired that we would fit under the shade and smoke our pipes, and think of nothing but friendship. The path of peace was opened for us by the United States, and we were directed by our brother to walk in it. We have kept in the path with our brethren of the United States.

Even after Kirkland's death in 1808, Oneida service as loyal, faithful Indians continued. Oneidas and their "new appendages" the Stockbridge and Brothertown were among the most important Indian allies to the United States during the War of 1812. At the Battle of Sandy Creek on May 30, 1814, a force of approximately one hundred twenty Oneida riflemen helped trap and capture three British navy gunboats and smaller vessels containing Congreve rockets, forcing the British to lift the blockage of the major American shipbuilding center at Sackett's Harbor and eastern Lake Ontario.[8]

Although not the sole reason for Oneida factionalism in the period, Kirkland's presence contributed to the divisions and helped shape the Oneida world long after the American Revolution ended.[9] Besides his influence in bringing the Oneidas to the American side during the Revolutionary War, encouraging acculturation to white ways, and introducing Christianity, he reinforced already existing divisions within the community between warriors, mostly his supporters, and sachems. According to ethnohistorian Jack Campisi:[10]

Kirkland challenged the traditional beliefs of the Oneidas, and it is no coincidence that his followers came mainly from the ranks of the warriors. However, he did not cause factionalism; what he did was to introduce a doctrine that gave religious validation to the political reality that was already extant. Kirkland capitalized on this division and challenged the efficacy of the political structure by his insistence upon the rejection of Iroquois religious beliefs. In so doing, he attacked the symbolic basis of the political structure, thus weakening the position of the hereditary chiefs. Needless to say, they opposed Kirkland's religion and, by extrapolation, his politics. However, Kirkland's influence did not depend upon the support of the sachems but of the warriors who, by converting to the new religion, found a means of challenging the strictures and limitations of the Iroquois political system.

Thus, at the end of the American Revolution the pro-Kirkland warriors who had been allied with the Americans and who had become converted to Christianity largely resided at Oneida Castle, twelve miles south of the easternmost section of Oneida Lake; whereas the sachems and their supporters, now organized as the Pagan Party, resided at Oriskany (Old Oriske), eight miles west of present-day Rome, New York.[11]

Kirkland's career among the Oneidas had two stages. The first stage occurred before, during, and immediately after the American Revolution; Kirkland was seen, especially among the warrior element within the Oneidas, as their "friend" or "father." To historian James Ronda there was more to these designations "than just Iroquois courtesy in the air. The Oneida faithful saw Kirkland as a spiritual director, a guide in the midst of troubled times." His rigid message emphasized the notion of a solitary believer standing naked before an all-powerful, all-knowing angry God to be judged, in his lengthy unyielding hell-fire-and-brimstone sermons, which lasted hours at a time.[12]

Despite Kirkland's demanding New Light message some prominent Oneidas did, indeed, see the Presbyterian theologian as the right antidote for a growing dysfunctionalism in Oneida society. Kirkland's sermons

Samuel Kirkland
Courtesy of Hamilton College

stressed a complete reliance on farming and the abandonment of the demon rum, whose use had reached epidemic proportions among the Oneidas. At the centerpiece of Kirkland's thinking was education, which he believed could prepare the Indians for the Christian white world by erasing native ways and could serve the Indians as a survival skill enabling them to live in a hostile white world. Cooperating with Skenandoah and other influential Oneidas such as Laulence and Onondiyo, he pushed his "civilization plan." Thus, to some Oneidas such as Skenandoah, a former alcohol abuser, Kirkland offered a new level of self-respect.

Kirkland's significance is quite clear, easily seen upon examining the lives of two prominent Indians in this period: Good Peter and Skenandoah. The former, Agwelondongwas / Agwrondongwas or "Breaking of the Twigs," was a Bear Clan chief of the Oneidas. He was born around 1715 along the Susquehanna River. He was converted to Christianity by the missionary Elihu Spencer in 1748 at the upper Susquehanna village of Oquaga, a village of diverse refugee Indians under the watchful eyes of the Oneidas. It was at this time that Good Peter acquired both his Christian religious faith and his ability to read and write "fairly well." A strong advocate of temperance among his people, Good Peter by 1757 was preaching at Oquaga and at neighboring villages. Soon he was being referred to as the eloquent Dominie Peter, Peter the Priest, and Petrus the Minister and was carrying out the Christian message of Spencer and Gideon Hawley, who also taught and missionized at Oquaga in the 1750s.[13]

The New Light Christianity of the Great Awakening significantly affected these Indians, especially in its call for temperance. By 1765 Good Peter visited Reverend Eleazar Wheelock's mission school at Hanover, New Hampshire, asking the missionary to send teachers to the Oneidas and other Six Nations. Later Samuel Kirkland, Wheelock's first white student at the school, was dispatched to Oneida territory (after failing miserably as a missionary among the Senecas during a ten-month period in 1764–65).[14]

Good Peter as well as his friend and ally Skenandoah proved to be indispensable to Kirkland's missionary efforts. Good Peter later served as one of Kirkland's deacons, becoming an active, spellbinding Indian orator, preacher, and Christian missionary throughout Iroquoia. Although becoming somewhat disenchanted with Kirkland because of the missionary's support for Indian land cessions in 1788, Good Peter, with few options open to him and his people, still accompanied Kirkland on his official travels. Nevertheless, the Oneida continued to speak out as the most eloquent orator-defender of Indian land rights.

Just before his death Good Peter told Pickering that Governor George Clinton, who presented himself as protecting the Indians from the tentacles of land speculators, had tricked the Oneidas and that they had no intention of selling any lands in 1788. He insisted that the Indians would have leased "out a tier of townships, on the line of property, to any poor people of his state, who had no lands; and that we would do this on reasonable terms."[15]

Governor Clinton's strategy is revealed in a letter written as early as 1784. Clinton recognized Good Peter's high standing among the Oneidas, insisting to the state Indian commissioner, Peter Rykman, "You must also pay

*Good Peter (ca. 1715–1792), Agwelondongwas or Agwrondongwas
[Breaking of the Twigs], was a Bear Clan chief of the Oneidas.
Portrait by John Trumbull, ca. 1790.*
Courtesy of the Yale University Art Gallery

attention to, and flatter him [Good Peter] on account of his good sense and friendship to us." When Good Peter, too late, finally understood the governor's evil methods, he bemoaned, "After this transaction, the voice of the birds from every quarter, cried out—You have lost your country—You have lost your country!" The aged Oneida added that the alarm was sounded by a "white bird."[16]

With this difficult lesson learned, the venerable Good Peter attempted to educate United States Indian Commissioner Pickering about what had transpired and sought federal protection from New York State's avaricious actions. Unfortunately for the Oneidas, Good Peter, their great advocate, died in 1792. His hope, and that of Pickering, namely, that federal laws and new federal-Indian treaties—the Pickering Treaty of 1794 and the Oneida Treaty of 1794—would protect the Indians from New York State, proved to be worthless guarantees, totally ignored by omnipotent Empire State politicians such as Philip Schuyler, Good Peter's wartime "friend."

A second Oneida, Skenandoah, whose name meant "running deer," was the archetype of the "good Indian." Indeed, among his own people, he was known universally as "the good friend of the white man." Whether this was a derogatory designation is not altogether clear. Skenandoah, born into a Susquehanna (Andaste or Conestoga) Indian family around 1706, was later adopted by the Oneidas, rising to the role of war chief and later Pine Tree chief of the Oneida wolf clan. Skenandoah, described as a "tall, well-made and robust man," was known as a "brave and intrepid warrior" during his youth. He had tattoos on his chest and hands and apparently also had enormous ears. According to Oneida tradition told to William Beauchamp, the anthropologist and Episcopal minister at Onondaga, Skenandoah (also known as Shenandoah, Skenadoa, Skenandon, Skanondonagh, Skenondough, Skenandore, Johnko Skenando, John Skanondo, and many other variations of the name) had a religious transformation after an incident in Albany in 1755. He embarrassed himself at a treaty council when he became very drunk and found himself naked the following morning.[17]

His conversion to Christianity was complete when he met and fell under the influence of Samuel Kirkland in 1765. His unbridled friendship with Kirkland, a father figure to the Indian despite the missionary's younger age, lasted until Kirkland's death in 1808. This friendship was significantly to shape Oneida history and Iroquois and American histories as a whole.[18] Clergyman-anthropologist William Beauchamp writes: "In the Revolutionary War his [Skenandoah's] influence induced the Oneidas to take up arms in favor of the Americans. Among the Indians he was distinguished as the white man's friend."[19] Although he was later accused of serving the British during the war in part because he was the former father-in-law of Joseph Brant, the famed Mohawk war chief and British ally, Skenandoah apparently was one of the keys to the Oneida-American alliance in the Revolution.[20] Two incidents during the war illustrate his commitment and unabiding loyalty to Kirkland and the Americans. Beauchamp writes, "His vigilance once preserved from massacre the inhabitants at German Flats."[21] Secondly, his commitment to the Americans included being sent by General Schuyler to Fort Niagara on a special mission where he and his lifelong friend Good Peter were promptly imprisoned by British military authorities.[22]

After the war, nearly every prominent non-Indian visitor to the Oneida Country was taken to see the aging warrior, who by that time had become blind. To some white men in the post–Revolutionary War period Skenandoah became the "noble savage" incarnate, a symbol of the "genius" of the Indian character.[23] By 1810 he was described inaccurately by De Witt Clinton as "first chief of the Oneidas." Clinton then compared the impressive Oneida centenarian to an English monarch or to one of Queen Anne's famous Indian kings of a century earlier.[24]

Skenandoah, who by the 1790s was described as the "second chief" of the Oneidas, was to live in his declining years through the worst upheaval in his people's history. As in Good Peter's case, Skenandoah had few options, negotiating from a hand of weakness, not one of strength. Using an accommodationist approach to white land pressures, it is clear that Skenandoah agreed to piecemeal land cessions in a failed attempt to keep the whites from taking all of Oneida country, especially Oneida Castle. Faced with religious and political pressures from within the Oneida world that would spill over into internecine tribal violence in the last three decades of his life, Skenandoah's strategy was to fail miserably. In this regard the aged warrior used the *same* methods that the Oneidas had used since the crisis years of the 1770s: ingratiating himself with more powerful forces supported by his "father," the white missionary Samuel Kirkland. Always drawing support from his devout Christian faith, Skenandoah appealed for harmony within the terribly divided Oneida Indian community. On September 19, 1793, Kirkland wrote in his journal:[25]

Towards the close of the day, Schenando [Skenandoah], their second chief, addressed them in a very pathetic manner upon their present state, both in a religious and secular view; their declension in regard to religion, and their divisions and animosities in respect to their civil and political interest. He observed that it appeared to him the great God was about to give them up. He spoke for about three quarters of an hour, and very feelingly; often wept, which is a rare thing for him to do.

Yet his calls for unity and peaceful coexistence were largely ignored not only by his community but even by his own family. By 1796, although considered by many as "one of the best of the nation," Skenandoah had, as Belknap correctly observed, "little influence" among the Oneidas in the last decades of his exceptionally long life.[26]

Despite his remarkable life Skenandoah's insistence on cooperation with the white settlers and, undoubtedly, his frequent accession to land sales was to cost him his reputation among the Oneidas. According to a perceptive Polish traveler's account in 1805, Skenandoah's standing in his community had plummeted: "The King [Skenandoah] is a great friend of the white man and has thus incurred the animosity of the tribe. His power is limited to negotiations with the white man and to presiding in council; for the rest, he has not the least authority over his fellow tribesmen."[27] The great Oneida warrior had become a pathetic figure in his declining years, the archetype of "government chief," brought out to meet visiting dignitaries and needed to sign illegal state accords for Oneida land cessions. Yet Skenandoah's cooperation goes deeper than this. In effect, he had become psychologically and economically dependent on the whites, especially his surrogate father Reverend Samuel Kirkland.

Skenandoah's acceptance of the missionary's message offered him a way to free himself from the demon rum and the troubling world around him. Whatever the missionary advised him to do, Skenandoah, the faithful son, complied. Until Kirkland's death in 1808, Skenandoah followed his "father's" teachings. Kirkland's emphasis on hard work, self-discipline, and self-worth brought economic rewards as well. It also brought presents from influential whites such as New York State Governor Daniel Tompkins, who bestowed on Skenandoah an elegant silver pipe. Thus, those Oneidas more associated with the white man had clear economic advantages and lived in better housing than their "pagan" brothers. Skenandoah, for one, lived in a well-made house built in a Dutch style with a hearth on one side "with an open space all around and a kind of funnel above to let out the smoke." His residence, elaborate for an Oneida, was situated on the edge of the village commanding "an extensive and grand view all round."[28]

When Kirkland proposed his "Plan for Education of Indians," which emphasized teaching Oneidas using the English language, western methods of agriculture, and moral reform through Christian teachings, Skenandoah faithfully endorsed it. Besides ceding land for the Hamilton-Oneida Academy project (the predecessor of Hamilton College), Skenandoah and his fellow members of the Christian Party even went as far as writing to the

New York State Board of Regents and recruiting Onondaga and Seneca children from Buffalo Creek. They also petitioned federal authorities such as the powerful secretary of the treasury, Alexander Hamilton, Philip Schuyler's son-in-law, to support Kirkland's efforts in this regard.[29] It is little wonder that at Skenandoah's death in 1816, at somewhere between 96 and 106 years of age, the Oneida was buried on the grounds of Kirkland's Hamilton College next to the grave of his white father the missionary.[30]

Despite being unable to read and write English, Skenandoah's name appears on all the Oneida Indian land cessions of the 1780s and 1790s.[31] It also appears on the enormous 1793 twenty-one-year lease for more than 50,000 acres of land to Peter Smith, a business partner of John Jacob Astor. This lease comprised the towns of Augusta in Oneida County and Stockbridge, Smithfield, Fenner, and northern Cazenovia in Madison County. Smith, the father of the famous abolitionist Gerrit Smith, went so far as to name his first son Peter Schenandoah, after his alleged "friend." The 1795 state treaty with the Oneidas allowed for the purchase of Smith's leased tract. In the end, Smith later paid the state to obtain title to 22,300 acres of this "former" Oneida land.[32]

Smith's actions in this regard and the state's negotiations were aided by the nefarious Jacob Reed, a ne'er-do-well, intemperate Indian who constantly reported to Smith about the Oneida negotiating strategies and council positions. Reed had served as one of Kirkland's Oneida schoolmasters, along with another Smith collaborator, Ebenezer Caulkins, a white man. Reed also frequently served as a representative of and interpreter for the Oneidas throughout the 1790s.[33]

It would be too easy to suggest that Skenandoah was a "sell-out." It is clear that he was more willing to lease or cede Oneida lands than were most other Oneida leaders. Yet unlike other Indians of the period who were outrightly bribed, there is no evidence that indicates that he took direct payments for signing state land cessions, and thus, one cannot ascribe acquisitive values to this deeply religious man. Much of his adult life since the 1750s had been built on cooperation with the whites. A trusting man, his faith, his redemption from alcohol, his role as an intermediary between the Indian and non-Indian worlds, and his economic survival were determined by that cooperation, much like so many other Oneidas who became nearly totally dependent on outsiders. Besides, to blame this aged warrior would ignore that all factions at one time or another from 1785 onward accepted

Skenandoah's [Schenando's] Tombstone

Courtesy of Hamilton College

state money for land. The Skenandoah or the Christian faction was not alone in its concessions. Although the "traditionals" in the Pagan Party, the Cornelius or Doxtator Party, were initially against selling land to the state, they did accede in 1805 to the partition of the remaining Oneida reservation between themselves and the Oneidas of the Christian Party. In 1809, they did sign and acknowledge this partition while, at the same time, leasing their lands east of Oneida Creek, from Oneida Lake to Mud Creek—which flows into Oneida Creek to the south of the Genesee (Seneca) Turnpike—for an annual rent of 6 percent, based upon a value of $.56 per account and a state advance of $1,000.[34] Moreover, from 1827 onward to 1846, descendants of some of the original members of the Pagan Party, then known as the Orchard Party, sold land to the state in a series of illegal transactions.[35]

Just before his death in 1816, Skenandoah had come to realize what had befallen the Oneidas and that his strategy of cooperation with white friends had failed. He then described himself, as well as his leadership, as a hemlock tree with its top cut off.[36] Bemoaning the loss of Oneida country, he tried to explain what had happened:[37]

My warriors and my children! Hear!—It is cruel—it is very cruel! a heavy burden lies on my heart;—it is very sick. This is a dark day. The clouds are black and heavy over the Oneida nation; and a strange arm is heavy upon us, and our hearts groan under us. The graves of our fathers are destroyed, and their children are driven away. The Almighty is angry with us; for we have been very wicked; therefore his arm does not keep us. Where are the chiefs of the rising Sun? White chiefs now kindle their ancient fires! There no Indian sleeps but those that sleep in their graves. My house will soon be like theirs; soon will a white chief here kindle his fire. Your Scanando will soon be no more, and his village no more a village of Indians.

Skenandoah went on largely to blame New York State officials and "certain white men," rather than casting aspersions on any of the Oneida leadership, himself included. He insisted that alcohol made the Oneidas "mice for white men, who are cats. Many a meal have they eaten of you. Their lips are sweet, but their heart is wicked." After stating that "there are good whites, and there are good Indians" and that he loved "all good men," Skenandoah, Kirkland's surrogate son, once again put the fate of his troubled Indian nation in terms of devotion to Christianity: "Jesus, whom I love, sees all. His great day is coming, he will make straight; he will say to cheating whites and drinking Indians—'begone ye!—go! go! go!' Certainly, my children, He will drive them away." As a product of the Great Awakening, he hoped for the Second Coming of Christ to lead the Oneidas away from troubles.[38]

Instead, one year after Skenandoah's death, Eleazer Williams, a missionary product of the Second Great Awakening, showed up at Oneida, insisting that Zion was Wisconsin.

The strategy employed by the Oneidas in this period and the aging of its leadership were only two of many reasons why the Oneidas were unprepared for the foxes at the gates. Importantly, in the last decades of Skenandoah's life, a power vacuum occurred in Oneida leadership, one not solely attributable to Indian factionalism but caused by religious divisions. In the brief period between 1788 and 1795 the Oneidas lost four of their most powerful voices, including the remarkable Good Peter in 1792. The Oneidas at Old Oriske were led by Colonel Hongarry until his death in 1788. He was succeeded by [Peter] Oneyana or Beechtree (also called Captain Peter or Peter the Quartermaster of the Turtle Clan). Although Beechtree was present at both of the state negotiations with the Oneidas in 1785 and 1788, which he signed, he died before the key events of the mid-1790s. Moreover, Captain John (Onondiyo) died on September 12, 1795, three days before the New York State–Oneida accord of that year.[39]

The death of major Indian voices and the aging of others, besides Skenandoah, created a definite crisis in the Oneida community in the 1790s. Increasingly, the community was divided along religious lines. In the mid-1790s the Pagan Party was headed by Blacksmith (Silversmith), a nephew of Good Peter and the keeper of the standing stone, the symbol of the Oneida Nation. Belknap described Blacksmith and his beliefs:[40]

He informed us that the objects of his devotion were the rocks and mountains, which he believed were animated by some invisible Power, which had a superintendency over human affairs. To this invisible Power he addressed his devotions, and depended on it for success in hunting and in war. This had been his religion from his youth, and he had never failed of receiving answers to his prayers. He had always either killed his enemy or made him captive, and had generally good luck in hunting. Others, he said, paid the same devotion to the wind and to the thunder, believing them to be invisible powers, and put the same trust in them as he did in the rocks and mountains; and he regarded the Oneida stone as an image of the deity which he worshipped.

By the late 1790s the aged Blacksmith—Augweehstanis or Augharistonisk —was still leader of the non-Christian Oneidas. He was "aided" by Peter II or Pagan Peter, Good Peter's son, the chief "pagan" warrior, and a man known for his violent behavior, including his summary execution of witches within the Oneida community. From 1798 to 1805 the so-called Pagan Party was to undergo two major revivals that resurrected ancient rituals and brought many Christian Oneidas back to their traditional roots.[41]

In the autumn of 1798 a Mohawk prophet arose along the Grand River in Ontario. In his interpretations of his visions he claimed that the "Upholder of the Skies or Heavens" had been neglected by the Indians and that, as a result, the Iroquois faced epidemics, famines, and unpleasant days. He urged the revival of ceremonies that had been abandoned, such as the White Dog Ceremony.[42] In the past the Iroquois ritually strangled white dogs, usually two at a time, painted them with red spots, decorated them with ribbons and a wampum collar, and hung them upon a long pole. A few days later, the dogs were placed on a fire, a speech was recited, and tobacco was thrown into the fire as the dogs were consumed. They then took the roasted dogs off the fire, cut them into pieces, and ate part of them. The Oneidas, as did the Senecas in the past, held feasts involving dogs cooked in a soup before leaving on war parties. Later, hogs and deer were substituted for white dogs.[43]

The Mohawk prophet urged the substitution of deer for white dogs and emphasized "temperance, universal love, domestic tranquillity," and respect and sympathy for each other. He also advised the Indians to listen to their missionaries and follow the Bible's words and teachings. At least some of the Christian Oneidas were converted back to the traditional religion as a result of the Mohawk prophet's message and later that of Handsome Lake, a second and more influential prophet.[44]

Blacksmith and his nephew, Pagan Peter, revived the ceremony in 1799 and three dogs were sacrificed in very much the traditional manner previously described. Blacksmith then prayed:[45]

Come! Come! thou Upholder of the Skies, *gyanse* [i.e., fellow citizen, or cousin by the mother's side], and all the holy inhabitants of Heaven, who are your assistants— Come! Descend even to the offering, which is elevated. With this [i.e., the dog], you will make your vest or garment, and from the fire you will have a sweet savor, the seed of the plant which you gave our forefathers in the beginning. We thank thee that we yet live by thy guardianship. We now by this offering intreat thee to continue this protection to us. Give us a fruitful season, a plentiful harvest; defend us from pestilence, from hurricanes, thunder and lightning, from all serpents. Give us success in hunting, and if our liberties should be invaded, we depend upon you, fellow citizen, to animate and inspire our warriors with skill and courage to drive the enemy from our country with shame and loss. Do you our Great Captain march in front of our warriors, that aided by our prowess and skill they may always conquer their enemies.

According to missionary Kirkland, the sacrifice was the first of its kind among the Oneidas in thirty years. The missionary indicated that the Indians refrained from alcohol for ten days during the preparations and performance of this ceremony. The Oneidas subsequently performed a war dance followed by a social dance that lasted all night. The ceremony ended after the Iroquois Bowl Game (also known as the Peach Stone Game), a game of chance, was played the next day.[46]

The revival of this ceremony associated with war tells much about the Oneidas in this period. Good Peter and Skenandoah were not the only ones looking for answers in their acceptance of the word of Christ. Their "pagan" counterparts were also seeking answers in more traditional ways to deal with the crisis in Oneida society in the period. Kirkland saw nefarious intentions in this revival, blaming the Quakers and Reverend John Sergeant with placating the "pagan" elements among the Oneidas; the missionary, nevertheless, recognized the great appeal of this revival to a large number of Oneidas, the benevolence of the people involved, and the rich conversations that the ceremony engendered. Reading Kirkland's letters, one gets the overall impression that few Oneidas, most notably Nicholas Sharp and Peter Bread, were unaffected by these "pagan" doings.[47]

A second holy man, Handsome Lake, the Seneca prophet, also stirred Iroquoia in 1799 and 1800, changing it forever. Until his series of three visions, Handsome Lake was overshadowed by the political career of his younger half-brother, the Cornplanter. As a notorious drunkard before his visions, Handsome Lake scarcely played a central political role in the affairs of the Seneca Nation although he had been in attendance and had signed the ignominious agreement with Robert Morris, the Treaty of Big Tree, in 1797.

In June 1799 Handsome Lake lay ill, bedridden in his cabin. The Indians living at the old village on the Cornplanter grant had experienced much travail that spring, including drunken brawls, accusations of witchcraft, and even the execution of a witch who was blamed for the death of Cornplanter's and Handsome Lake's niece. Leaving his cabin at Cornplanter on June 15, Handsome Lake collapsed and was aided back to bed by his nephew Governor Blacksnake. Most Senecas believed that he was about to die. After two hours in a near-catatonic state witnessed by other Indians, Handsome Lake opened his eyes and began to recount a religious message that he had just had. His vision included three well-dressed messengers who had come to him with the Creator's commands. The prophet was to choose his sister and her husband as his medicine persons who were to join him and attend the Strawberry Festival. There the prophet was to preach the message of *Gaiwiio,* the Good Word; a message that condemned whiskey, witchcraft, love potions, and abortion. All wrongdoers had to confess and repent their wickedness or be punished.[48]

This first vision, later followed by two others, was to have a profound influence on the Iroquois who were faced with disaster in the aftermath of the American Revolution. In part, the origins of the Handsome Lake religion stemmed from the splintering of the Iroquois Confederacy, substantial Indian land loss, constant white land pressures, social disintegration as reflected in increased alcoholism and murder rates, and growing economic dependence on the non-Indian world.[49]

In the following months Handsome Lake had other visions, falling into trances and seeing many wonders and gaining insights relating to moral and social reform. He saw the punishment of wrongdoers: wife-beaters, drunkards, gamblers, witches, sinners. He traveled to the realm of the blessed, learning in this pleasant world how families among the Iroquois should live in peace in their own communities. Instructed by the sacred messenger who accompanied him on his spiritual journey, he was urged to continue to perform the Iroquois' religious ceremonial cycle.

In his third vision, which took place in 1800, he was commanded to write down the *Gaiwiio* to preserve it for all time and to carry the message to all the peoples of the Six Nations. Although Handsome Lake never preached among the Oneidas, the Good Word spread there. Handsome Lake combined his teaching with an emphasis on family values, condemning gossip, philandering, abortion, and alcohol, all of which were rampant at the time. He claimed to have received the Good Word from messengers of the Creator to advise his people, briefly summarized by the anthropologist Elisabeth Tooker:[50]

They said that the people should stop drinking, that the witches should confess and cease their activity, that the use of charms [i.e., charms employed in witchcraft] should cease, and that women should cease aborting themselves. These were the first four "words." Other messages included the admonitions that husbands and wives should not desert each other, that they should love each other and their children, and that they should not commit adultery. Children should be treated kindly and listened to; childless couples should adopt children of the wife's sister—if she had them. Old people unable to work should be helped by their grandchildren. Then the messengers said: if a visitor comes when the family is about to eat, the visitor should be invited to eat; children playing near the house should be invited to eat when those in the house are eating; orphans should be helped; the people should not gossip or spread evil reports; and people should not boast. The messengers also said that it was right that men cultivate lands as the white man did, build houses as he did, and keep horses and cattle as he did. At least some children should be sent to school to learn the white man's ways. People should help one another, should not steal, and should not perform dances in honor of the "totem animals" [i.e., should not perform the medicine society dances]. The messengers added, however, that the Creator has given four rituals—Feather Dance, Thanksgiving Dance, Personal Chant, and Bowl Game—which are to be performed. The Creator ordered that Thanksgiving ceremonies should be given at certain times. He also said there should be chiefs and that they should do good for the people.

The Seneca prophet also promoted men's participation in horticulture, which had been the traditional women's domain. The Oneidas such as Good Peter (and most Iroquois Indians from time immemorial) had viewed women with high regard: "Our Ancestors considered it a transgression to reject the Council of their Women, particularly the female Governesses. Our Ancestors considered them mistresses of the Soil. Our Ancestors said who bring us forth, who cultivate our Lands, who Kindles our Fires and boil our Pots, but the Women . . . they are the Life of the Nation."[51] Yet until the Age of Handsome Lake, only Skenandoah labored in the fields in the same manner as the women.[52]

Despite this radical departure the prophet was perceived by his contemporaries as a conservative, "attempting to restore and revitalize an existing system of beliefs and ceremonies that had been falling into disuse." Handsome Lake was a callback to an ancient faith, one that did not challenge the "old pantheon, the old annual calendar, the old myths, the old dream rites." He endorsed these traditions except for those that had been contaminated by alcohol or witchcraft.[53] In spite of this conservative message, however, he added strong warnings against any further alienation of Indian lands and land sales to whites as well as proscriptions against Iroquois warrior participation in another white man's war—both ignored by the Oneidas and other Iroquois Indians long before the prophet's death in 1815.[54]

Handsome Lake's message clearly contained Christian influences.[55] According to anthropologist Anthony F. C. Wallace, explicit "recognition of Christian theology is made in the code in his encounter with Jesus Christ, whom the prophet regarded as his counterpart among the whites. The images of heaven and, most particularly, hell seem clearly to have been based on a Christian model."[56] Indeed, the *Gaiwiio*'s acceptance among the Oneidas reflects this syncretization process. By 1805–6, the so-called "pagans" at Oneida "adopted the Christian sabbath, meeting in church from nine in the morning to four in the afternoon, when they required confession and absolution and made speeches."[57] To Oneidas faced with social disintegration and rampant alcoholism, Handsome Lake's messages proved appealing, even to Reverend Kirkland's Oneida helper, Doctor Peter, who spoke favorably of "the late revelations from the Seneka prophet, or man of God, as they stile him." Doctor Peter added: "He said the prophet enjoined the strictest temperance and sobriety upon all Indians, and commanded them to abstain from the use of ardent spirits, which was never made for Indians; and for any Indian to drink a single glass or one swallow would be a deadly sin if not repented of."[58] He concluded by stating that the Seneca prophet exhorted his followers to live in peace with "all mankind, white people as well as Indians." Stressing family values, the holy man "spoke upon the duties of husbands and wives and the great sin of divorce."[59] Although both "pagan" and Christian Oneida advocated temperance, the ravages of alcoholism continued to plague the community. The problem was, however, temporarily lessened with the introduction of the message of the Seneca prophet and the leadership of Henry Cornelius (Haunnagwasuke or "the little doctor") as head of the Pagan Party after 1800.[60] Later, in 1810 De Witt Clinton noted that the Pagan Party, which had grown considerably since 1798, had better morals "than those of the Christians," even though these Indians, according to Clinton, still practiced their "ancient superstitions" such as the White Dog Ceremony, which had been rejected by Handsome Lake, and devoted six days to their Midwinter Ceremony.[61]

The Oneidas thus were a hopelessly divided people during this post–Revolutionary War era. To complicate matters even further, a class system had apparently developed by this time. This was not only reflected in Skenandoah's elevated economic position but in other areas of the community, most notably in what became known as the French Party. François Marbois had noted the extensive French presence among the Oneidas as early as 1784, pointing out the presence of the former captive Nicholas Jordan, who had been born along the Somme River in France, among them. Jordan later married the daughter of an Oneida sachem who had been widowed. He was one of several Frenchmen married into the community who had considerable influence in tribal affairs in the 1780s and 1790s.[62]

Some Oneida, especially Kirkland's opponents, were swayed by another Frenchman, Peter Penet, a charismatic entrepreneur and merchant-trader from Nantes who had ingratiated himself with the Indians by invoking General Lafayette's hallowed name and that of the king of France, implying that he was in a quasi-official capacity as an envoy of Louis XVI to the Oneidas.[63] He also briefly instituted a Catholic mission among the Oneidas. Part of his early success was due to Penet's full exposure of the nefarious plans of John Livingston, who had convinced the Oneidas to lease the bulk of their lands to his enterprise, the New York Genesee Company of Adventurers, for 999 years.[64] In return for Penet's help in foiling this chicanery and in order to fulfill a dream that Penet allegedly had, this schemer obtained lands from the Oneidas totaling ten square miles at the state-Oneida "treaty" at Fort Schuyler in 1788.[65] Penet's initial success among the Oneidas is both intriguing and significant and demonstrates the nature and extent of the crises facing these Indians. It was no accident that Oneidas followed grand schemers such as Penet or, later, Eleazer Williams after the War of 1812, who both claimed French ancestry and promised "pie in the sky" tomorrow.

In 1789 Penet actually helped draft a plan of government for the Oneidas, which would have established a "grand council" for the community that would have mapped and surveyed their lands. Article VI of this proposal, one that drew initial support from various Oneidas including Beechtree, Blacksmith, and Skenandoah, specified emphatically:[66] "No man, woman or child, of the said Oneida nation, shall have it in his power, to sell one foot of land that shall fall to his or her lot or share, except it to be to one of their nation. All other bargains for such land shall be void and of none effect." Despite the appealing features of this proposal to a desperately divided Indian community, the Oneidas once again quickly split over Penet, his motives, and his character. His supporters, largely but not exclusively the opponents of missionary Kirkland, soon became known as the French Party. They included mostly members of the Pagan Party and wayward members of the Christian Party, including Atayataghronghta or Lewis Cook—the adopted son of Skenandoah, a Mohawk-African who had served the Americans faithfully during the Revolutionary War.[67]

Atayataghronghta may have financially benefited (as did Jacob Reed later) by the state-Oneida "treaty" of 1788 that provided for compensation to Penet and for the state's acquiring much of Oneida Country in 1788. John Tayler, the New York Indian commission's agent, wrote Governor George Clinton: "I have further promised to Louis [Lewis] a Reward when the

Treaty will be held at Fort Schuyler and have engaged him to return here [Albany] with the Messenger who is to come to Oneida from Buffalo Creek, and to render any other Assistance that will be required of him."[68]

The French influences went well beyond one Indian's scruples. Some Oneidas had long been enamored with the French and French culture. The well-educated Peter Otsiquette, dubbed "French Peter," an Oneida and an American hero, had served with Lafayette during the American Revolution and even went to visit the legendary nobleman in France after the war. While in Paris, he received three years of instruction in French, English, and German. He returned to Oneida and married an Oneida woman, but soon after died while on a visit to Philadelphia in 1792.[69] Otsiquette was not the only Francophile among the Oneidas. The continuous presence of French traders, not just Nicholas Jordan or Penet, who had married Oneida women, also had a direct effect on Oneida life and lands and not only among the Pagan Party. Angel De Ferriere, who had ties to Jan Lincklaen of the Holland Land Company, married one of the daughters of Lewis Denny (Dennie) and thus obtained substantial wealth and lands. In 1810 De Witt Clinton described the process. After living twelve years at Oneida and fathering three children, De Ferriere, being "a man of genteel manners, sensible, and well-informed," Clinton noted, "acquired a great influence over them, and has prevailed on them to confer on him donations of valuable land—which have been sanctioned by the State."[70]

This illegal transaction, dated February 16, 1809, was largely a land cession signed by the relatives of Lewis Denny, most importantly John (Jonathan) Denny, transferring "1700 acres of the best land—a great deal of it on the turnpike [Genesee Road]."[71] John Denny, largely responsible for this cession, was later described by Clinton as being "addicted to intemperance," and his children were "said to be the worst tempered of any in the nation."[72]

Clinton revealed another reason for this illegal transaction besides consanguinity and alcohol. Some Oneidas themselves, such as the Denny family, saw personal gains and were willing to cut deals at the expense of the nation. In 1810 Lewis Denny told Clinton that there were "hard times with the Indians" and that deer were scarce because of the rapidly expanding white settlements.[73] Thus, securing economic advantages for his daughter's faithful husband was like money in the bank. Individual family survival, it is clear, took precedence over Oneida national and cultural integrity in desperate times.

Indeed, long before 1809, individual components of the nation took precedence over Indian national interests. Despite periodic efforts to reconcile differences, the Oneida Indians agreed to divide their remaining Indian lands in 1805, with Skenandoah's Christian Party obtaining ownership of the southern portion of the tribal lands.[74] Thus, as De Witt Clinton noted five years later, the Oneidas were now "entirely separated in their territory, as well as in their God."[75]

Eventually, the splits within the Oneida Indian community widened. In 1816 and 1817 Eleazer Williams converted some members of the Pagan Party to Christianity and encouraged the remaining members of the Christian Party to change their religious affiliation from Presbyterianism to Episcopalianism. Williams's flock became known as the Second Christian Party. In 1826 some members of the Pagan Party were converted to Methodism, assuming the name of the Orchard Party. Despite this loss of membership, the Pagan Party maintained its existence by winning converts back periodically from both of the Christian parties. Under increasing pressured to migrate, by 1840 400 of the 578 Oneidas remaining in New York decided to sell their lands and leave the state. By 1843 the Oneidas retained two land bases in New York—approximately 190 acres at Orchard Park in Oneida County and 743 acres at Marble Hill in Madison County; however, in the same year, the New York State Legislature "permitted" the allotment of Oneida lands in severalty. Within eighty years the Oneida common land base had shrunk to thirty-two acres.[76]

In 1795 Samuel Kirkland's son, John Thornton, who later served as president of Harvard College, explained the origins of Oneida factionalism by noting its causes were "generally the contests of rival chiefs for pre-eminence, the sale and division of territory, and the intrigue and bribes of land-jobbers and traders."[77] Although accurate up to a point, what the future president of Harvard could not fathom was the size and shape of the outside forces contributing to Oneida factionalism that stretched from his father's sitting room in Clinton to all levels of New York State politics. No matter what the Oneidas did and no matter how divided they were, and they did have an extremely fractionated universe, their lands were going to be picked off parcel by parcel. No matter how observant of their traditional religion, accepting of the new message of Handsome Lake, or faithful to the Presbyterian, Episcopal, Methodist, or Catholic faiths, they had no chance to stem the tide. The process of Oneida dispossession and removal had been set in motion as early as the end of the American Revolution by powerful, so-called "friends" of the Indian, most notably the scion of New York politics, Philip Schuyler, the first great transportation magnate and great architect of the state's future.

CHAPTER 4

Trust Me

Self-serving "friends" of the Oneidas used their strategic positions to undermine the Indian land base from the mid-1780s on. Although the names of Jan Lincklaen, Peter Smith, Abraham Van Epps [Eps], and Abraham Wemple were more prominent on the leases and deeds of the time, Philip Schuyler was the major player in the events leading to the dispossession of these Indians. Aided and abetted by private speculators and land companies, the Federalist political establishment in the state, and by both Samuel Kirkland and James Dean, Schuyler systematically went about securing land concessions from the divided Oneida community. Realizing that the value of their lands (and that of their political allies and business partners in central New York) would skyrocket in value if transportation routes—canals and roads—made settlement attractive, Schuyler and his associates increasingly coveted Oneida country in a late-eighteenth-century version of "insider trading." At the center of Schuyler's activities was his involvement in the New York State–Oneida "treaty" of 1795, an accord that, although written about before, has not been fully examined by scholars. This state "treaty" and the subsequent accord of 1798 are keys to understanding the relationship of transportation to Indian dispossession in this era.[1]

Schuyler, undoubtedly, saw himself as being above the law. He, along with his son-in-law, Secretary of the Treasury Alexander Hamilton, dominated Federalist politics of the era, well beyond the state's borders. Another of Schuyler's sons-in-law, Stephen Van Rensselaer, was perhaps the richest New Yorker in the early republic. As United States senator throughout the postwar period, Schuyler's power was matched by few political figures in the new nation. At the end of the Revolution his great wealth was largely in lands in Saratoga, Cortlandt Manor, and Dutchess County, as well as in

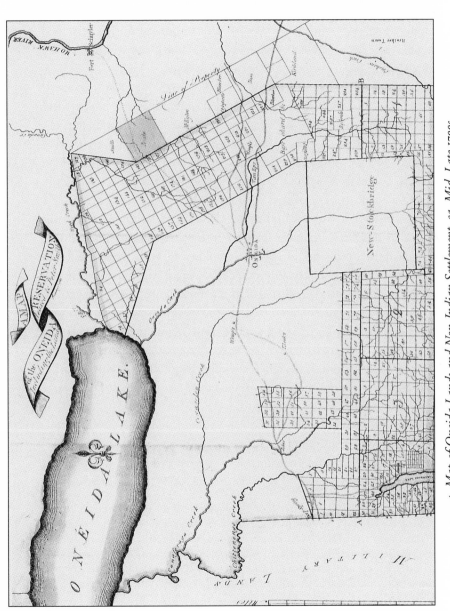

4. *Map of Oneida Lands and Non-Indian Settlement, ca. Mid–Late 1790s*

From Franklin B. Hough, comp., Notices of Peter Penet and His Operations among the Oneida Indians (1866)

banking and manufacturing in Albany and its environs. Throughout his life he took every opportunity to protect his interests and to advance his great family's fortune. By 1786 this New York scion, possibly taking a cue from his brother Peter (one of the New York Genesee Company of Adventurers), had secured large tracts in what later became downtown Utica, which, until the state-Oneida "treaty" of 1785, had been Indian lands.

Schuyler and his allies were aided by the activities of land surveyors, including John Cantine, Moses De Witt, John and Abraham Hardenbergh, and Benjamin Wright. De Witt surveyed and laid out the Oneida territory south from Oneida Castle to Binghamton obtained in the state-Oneida "accord" of 1785. Wright, later the head of the middle section engineering construction of the Erie Canal (and subsequently chief engineer of the entire New York State canal system), is most noteworthy. Long before becoming a "canawler," Wright was one of the major land surveyors laying out lots and towns in the former Oneida territory north and west of Oneida Lake (obtained from 1788 onward). He was employed by both Scriba and Smith throughout this period. His reports are filled with suggestions about rights-of-way and information gathered from the Indians about where to situate roads and the potential of resource development within the region. Many of these surveyors, drifting in and out of private service to land speculators, were employed in public service by De Witt's cousin Simeon, the surveyor-general of New York State. They attended treaty negotiations with the Indians, or, in the case of Cantine in the 1790s, served as a New York State commissioner negotiating with the Oneidas.[2]

State officials such as Governor George Clinton and Philip Schuyler constantly urged the Oneidas to trust them as the Indians' protectors. They frequently pointed to the provisions of the New York State Constitution adopted at Kingston on April 20, 1777. Article XXXVII reads as follows:[3]

XXXVII: AND WHEREAS it is of great importance to the safety of this state that peace and amity with the Indians within the same, be at all times and supported and maintained: AND WHEREAS the frauds, too often practised towards the said Indians, in contracts made for their lands, have, in divers instances, been productive of dangerous discontents and animosities: BE IT ORDAINED, that no purchases or contracts for the sale of lands made since the 14th day of October, in the year of our Lord one thousand seven hundred and seventy-five, or which may hereafter be made with or of the said Indians, within the limits of this state, shall be binding on the said Indians, or deemed valid, unless made under the authority and with the consent of the legislature of this state.

Later, at Fort Schuyler in 1788 Governor Clinton told Good Peter that the state's planned purchase of Oneida lands was aimed "to put a final stop to any future purchase of our lands but if we did not consent to his present purchase, we must never thereafter tell him of our being cheated out of any of our lands [e.g., by land speculators such as the Company of Genesee Adventurers] for he would not hear our complaints."[4]

Clinton and his political enemies, Governor John Jay and Schuyler, however, lusted after the rich inland empire of Iroquoia. They collaborated with key New York congressmen such as James Duane, the chairman of the Indian Committee of Congress. Duane, who was closely tied to, and aided by, Schuyler in his fact-finding, supported exacting concessions from the Iroquois after the Revolution. Duane, an advocate of state control over the Indians, cautioned Governor Clinton in 1784 not to adopt "the disgraceful system of pensioning, courting and flattering them as great and mighty nations" for fear that "we shall once more like the Albanians be their Fools and Slaves, and this Revolution in my Eyes will have lost more than half its value."[5]

Just as the Iroquois became entangled, much to their disserve, in the war of brothers between the colonists and Great Britain, the Indians became the victims of a battle within the American polity from 1774 on. The contest between federal authority and states' rights and between states themselves over each's claims to western lands became major outside factors shaping the Iroquois world in the fifteen years after the war. The most prominent statesmen of the Revolutionary era fought major battles over these two issues.

Throughout the early part of New York State history, state policymakers dealing with Indian affairs and their federal counterparts were speculators in western lands. Historian Reginald Horsman has correctly observed that these land speculators were on both sides of the national control–states' rights debate: "Those speculators who hoped to profit by state-granted lands opposed cession to the central government, whereas the speculators who had not gained recognition by the state governments pressed enthusiastically for the land cessions, hoping to gain a more favorable hearing from Congress."[6] Those advocates of the states' rights position over Indian affairs in New York included the most famous and powerful families, such as the Schuylers, Livingstons, and Van Rensselaers who stood to benefit most by Indian land title extinguishment.

According to historian Barbara Graymont, New York State Indian policy

in the American Revolutionary era was based on extinguishing "any claim of
the United States Congress to sovereignty over Indian affairs in the State of
New York"; on extinguishing "the title of the Indians to the soil"; and on
extinguishing the sovereignty of the Six Nations. Even before the end of the
war, these policies had been set in motion.[7] As early as October 23, 1779, the
New York State Legislature instructed the governor and four commissioners
to be mindful of New York's interests at the future peace negotiations with
the Indians.[8] In the same month, John Jay, later to serve as governor of New
York during key Oneida negotiations in the 1790s, wrote to Governor
George Clinton. Fearing Virginia's claims to western lands and the extension of federal authority over Iroquois lands conquered by the Continental
Army during the Sullivan-Clinton campaign, Jay urged Clinton to have
New York State assert quickly its claim to this area. Before the United States
could claim the Iroquois lands based upon conquest theory, Jay urged that
New York State assert its sovereignty in this region: "Would it not be proper
for New York to establish Posts in that Country, *and in every respect treat it
as their own.* In my opinion our State has had too much Forbearance about
these matters. Virginia, who has Claims and Rights under much the same
circumstances, manages differently" (emphasis mine).[9] Both Duane and Jay,
it is clear, were working in tandem to secure New York State control over
these Iroquois lands. They, along with Clinton, believed that Congress had
no right to interfere in New York affairs, which included state efforts to
negotiate and extinguish Indian title.[10]

Five months before the preliminary articles of peace were signed in 1783,
the New York State Legislature moved to expropriate Iroquois country,
except for lands occupied by Oneidas and Tuscaroras, for military bounty
lands. By March 1783 the New York State Legislature empowered the
Council of Appointment to appoint three Indian commissioners who
would, in conjunction with the governor, have control of Indian affairs and
to secure the rights of the Oneidas and Tuscaroras for their loyal service in
the American Revolution. One of the three appointed New York Indian
commissioners was Major Peter Schuyler, Philip's brother, who, through the
New York Genesee Company of Adventurers, attempted in the 1780s to
evade New York State's constitutional provision against private individuals
conducting land negotiations with the Indians without a license.[11]

The federal-state jurisdiction question soon came to the fore when

Congress called into question New York State's determination to use Iroquois country for military bounty lands. Nevertheless, the New York State Legislature continued to assert the state's sovereignty in Indian affairs within its "own borders." State officials such as Governor Clinton, who had depended on federal support during the American Revolution, now refused to cooperate with Congress on Indian matters. Importantly, the year 1784 marked two major negotiations with the Iroquois: one an inconclusive state negotiation, the second, the federal-Iroquois Treaty of Fort Stanwix. It is important to note that while the federal treaty negotiations were being conducted, sentries were posted to keep the New York Indian Commissioners Peter Schuyler and Peter Rykman away.[12] The federal commissioners later reported to Congress about the "great inconveniences from the conduct of the Governor of this state, in attempting to frustrate the treaty, and the consequent licentiousness of some of its citizens."[13]

Despite federal guarantees to protect the Oneidas and Tuscaroras at Fort Stanwix in 1784 the New York State Legislature, proposing to speed up white settlement, passed two laws in 1784 and 1785 to facilitate the "settlement of the waste and unappropriated lands" in the state and set up procedures to advertise and distribute Indian lands even before the state had bought title.[14] Previously, state officials had pointed out to the Indians that they were going to be treated fairly and that the Indians' land base would be respected. Governor George Clinton had made these promises in an address before the Indians at Fort Schuyler (Stanwix) on September 4, 1784:[15]

Brethren, we have been informed that some designing persons have endeavored to persuade you that we mean to take away your lands. This is not true. You must not believe it. We have no claim on your lands; its just extent will ever remain secured to you. It is therefore, the object of our present meeting to have metes and bounds thereof, precisely ascertained in all its parts, in order to prevent any intrusions thereupon.

Clinton gave further assurances, indicating that in order to prevent Indian-white disputes and conflict, the New York State Constitution provision forbidding Indian land sales to individuals without legislative permission would be enforced.[16]

In reality New York officials built a rising Empire State on profits from Indian land cessions. The Oneidas are a case in point. Between 1785 and 1838 these Indians lost their lands in New York State through a series of "treaties" despite being on the patriot side during the American Revolution, provisions in both the New York State and United States Constitutions, and congressional acts and federal treaty guarantees. Campisi has written:[17]

The [Oneida] factionalism permitted the New York State representatives to bargain one group against another, appealing to the vanity and desire for gain on the part of individual Oneidas. The state legislature, which had guaranteed protection against speculators, was dominated by the most unscrupulous land barons in America, the Hudson Valley aristocracy. What they really sought to protect were their rights to exploit. The trusted advisors of the Oneidas, men like Kirkland, Dean, Penet, and Eleazer Williams, were in the pay of the land companies and were anxious themselves to receive rich estates. Finally, as the supposed danger of an Indian uprising in New York State subsided, the federal government lost its need to placate the Indians.

In open defiance of congressional intent from 1783 onward, New York State continued to deal with the Indians as it pleased. While the federal government was attempting to keep the Iroquois at peace and keep them from joining an Indian war in the Ohio country through federal treaty making in the decade from Stanwix (1784) to Canandaigua (1794), New York State had designs on territorial aggrandizement. In this period the Iroquois status changed from independent or collective sovereignties on a large, viable agricultural land base tied to the religious ritual cycle to being dependent peoples boxed in on island reservations. Instead of the ancient Covenant Chain that bound Indian and white as equal partners, the Indian's world and power shrank. Land "purchased" by state "treaty" from Oneidas for fifty cents an acre was sold for seven to ten times its original purchasing price. Meanwhile, the state was encouraging the settlement of the central portion of the state. Madison County, which had fewer than one thousand settlers in 1800, had thirty-nine thousand by 1830. With the development of the Erie Canal, the Indians in central and western New York soon found themselves surrounded by whites who coveted their lands. By the 1830s and 1840s railroads further added to the rush for fertile lands.[18]

Nearly every political decision and treaty negotiation involving the Oneidas between 1785 and 1798 had Philip Schuyler's personal or family stamp of approval. Indeed, few New Yorkers before or since have had the power base of this major Federalist politico. Despite his outward appearances of friendship, patronlike support of Oneidas during the American Revolution, and longtime acquaintance with several key Oneidas Schuyler was a self-interested schemer and no friend of the Indians, be they "good" Oneidas or his "savage" enemies. In the summer of 1783 Schuyler wrote that the Indians would inevitably retreat westward once faced with massive white settlement in the vicinity of their territory. He insisted that the United States only take the land it needed from the Indians to satisfy its immediate interests, rather than perpetually to find itself fighting bloody and costly wars. To Schuyler, the simplest, cheapest, least distressing and violent, and most advantageous national policy was self-evident: "It will be or no obstacle to our future . . . for as our settlements approach their country, they must from the scarcity of game, which that approach will induce to, retire further back, and dispose of their lands." In his late-eighteenth-century version of manifest destiny he added that "they [will] dwindle comparatively to nothing, as all savages have done, who reside in the vicinity of civilized people and leave us the country without the expence [*sic*], trifling as it may be of a purchase."[19] Thus, Schuyler's view of progress, reminiscent of that of Christopher Colles, required rapid urbanization rather than a continued frontier setting, one that would better New York as well as America as a whole but, at the same time, would be best for his own pocketbook. In his scheme Indian councils were better alternatives than Indian wars; however, his vision for New York had no place for Indians, be they allies or not. In fact, as late as 1796, despite his family's support for Samuel Kirkland's Hamilton-Oneida Academy, Schuyler told the missionary Jeremy Belknap that there was little or no prospect of "civilization" among the Oneidas.[20]

Schuyler had had the longest contact with the Carrying Place and the Oneidas, one which began as early as the French and Indian War. Even before independence was declared, Schuyler had set his sights on occupying the strategic portage. Because Schuyler became Washington's commanding general of the Northern Department (besides being federal Indian commissioner during the early years of the war), his contacts with the Oneidas were quite extensive.[21] Schuyler had encouraged Oneida recruitment in the Patriot army and had frequently supplied these Indians during the desperate times of the American Revolution.[22] Fort Schuyler was the American outpost at Rome. When many Oneidas found themselves refugees of war during the later stages of the conflict, Schuyler appealed successfully to General Washington and financier Robert Morris for clothing and food supplies for these Indians.[23] While serving as one of the earliest United States Indian commissioners, treating with the Indians from the early days of the Revolution onward, he assured his loyal Oneida warriors that the Americans would long remember their contributions, that

"sooner should a fond mother forget her only son than we shall forget you."
He added that, once victory was achieved, the Oneidas would "then par-
take of every Blessing we enjoy and united with a free people your Liberty
and prosperity will be safe."[24] Thus, Oneida leaders such as Skenandoah
and Good Peter saw him as a valued ally while Oneida officers such as
Henry Cornelius, Hanyost, and Honyery Doxtator served Schuyler loyally
throughout the war. When peace was finally achieved, Schuyler, through
two Oneida intermediaries, Good Peter and Skenandoah, attempted to
bring the British-allied Iroquois back into the fold and helped arrange the
delivery of a peace offering, a bell, to the Continental Congress in July
1783.[25] Oneidas sought him out and saw the general as their protector and
patron. Indeed, to this day, Oneidas still bear Schuyler's name as both a
given name and a surname.[26]

Schuyler's familiarity with Oneida country and its vast economic potential was furthered by two other factors. First, at the end of the American
Revolution, he was appointed to the newly created post as New York State's
surveyor-general, a strategic position from which he resigned when he was
elected United States senator from New York State in 1783. Second, as senator he was actively involved in the grand design of federal Indian policy,
working with James Duane, a fellow New York Federalist, and other United
States Indian commissioners. As early as 1783, he came to the conclusion,
according to his biographer Don Gerlach, that it "would be 'advantageous'
if the tribes [Oneidas and Tuscaroras] could be persuaded to exchange their
lands for others 'more remote.'"[27]

Even though the Oneidas were given guarantees of United States recognition of their territory at the Treaty of Fort Stanwix in 1784, New York State
"acquired" the very next year at Fort Herkimer three hundred thousand
acres of Oneida lands, the present counties of Broome and Chenango, rich,
well-watered agricultural lands, for $11,500. In September 1788 at Fort
Schuyler the state "acquired" nearly five million acres of Oneida lands,
reserving three hundred thousand acres in Madison and Oneida Counties;
in return, the state paid the Oneidas $2,000 in cash, $2,000 in clothing,
$1,000 in provisions, and provided $500 to subsidize the building of grist
and sawmills. The state was also to provide an annuity of $600 to the
Indians. Importantly, one of the New York State negotiators at this "treaty"
(and later at the 1798 "treaty") was Egbert Benson—attorney general of New
York State, well-connected politician from Red Hook, associate of the

Holland Land Company, and Schuyler crony, allied to the Federalist establishment in the Hudson River valley.[28]

In this 1788 agreement, the Oneidas under their chief Good Peter, believing they were preventing land speculators such as John Livingston, Peter Schuyler, and their New York Genesee Company from defrauding them, signed an "instrument of cession" with New York State Governor George Clinton; the Oneidas viewed the action as a lease to the state in an effort to foil the speculators' nefarious efforts. Instead, state officials soon claimed that this agreement was an Oneida cession of much of their lands.[29] After this "agreement," Oneidas were increasingly reluctant to go to negotiate. When state officials no longer could get Indians to come to the treaty table, the state "granted power of attorney to a small segment of the tribe and then signed the agreement with those Indians in the name of all Oneidas."[30] This pattern was set in the so-called New York State–Oneida Treaty of 1795, which became the model for all Albany's efforts to dispossess the Oneidas for the next half-century.[31] Playing on the growth of divisions within the Oneida world, especially their religious splits, New York State officials, led largely by Federalist politicians, basically used a divide-and-conquer strategy that chipped away at the tribal land base, a conscious plan that furthered an overall economic program for the region and the state as a whole.

At the 1788 treaty grounds Elkanah Watson, a political ally of Benson and a business partner of Schuyler, had clearly spelled out his prediction that Oneida Lake would eventually be the center of a great transportation nexus with the salt industry as its basis. To Watson, when the "mighty canals" were developed, a vast central New York inland empire would result: "It will enter Ontario, and the other great lakes, and find its way down the St. Lawrence by Oswego, into Pennsylvania and the Chesapeake, up Seneca river to the head of Seneca lake, and by a portage (perhaps eventually a canal) of eighteen miles to Newtown, on the Susquehanna river, and through canals in contemplation, up Wood Creek and down the Mohawk river, into the Hudson." Watson's attitude toward the local Oneidas was clear. Despite coming into contact with Kirkland's good Indians, most notably the educated Peter Otsiquette, at the treaty grounds, the Albany banker and businessman, much like Schuyler later, insisted that it was folly to civilize the Indian as if he were a "bear."[32]

Watson was more than a racist schemer; he was a calculating opportunist, carrying out the principles of geographical prediction. With his Federalist ally and business partner, the omnipotent Philip Schuyler, a "friend" of the Oneidas, he was to put his business intuition into practice with the founding of two private transport companies in 1792–93: the Western Inland Lock Navigation Company and the Northern Inland Lock Navigation Company.[33]

The aim of the Western Inland Lock Navigation Company, the major predecessor of the Erie Canal, was to open navigable waterways from Albany west to Lake Seneca, and west northwest to Lake Ontario. The Northern Inland Lock Navigation Company, the second project, which soon failed, was designed to improve the waters between the Hudson and Lake Champlain. These shareholder companies were headed by Schuyler, and Watson served on the board of directors. Among the major investors were Egbert Benson; Robert Morris, the prominent Genesee speculator who later defrauded the Senecas at the Treaty of Big Tree in 1797; Theophile Cazenove, the major representative of the Holland Land Company, which also purchased shares in the Watson-Schuyler venture; Robert Troup, a leading attorney tied to the Phelps-Gorham land purchase, one of the Pulteney Associates, later attorney for both the Holland Land Company and Ogden Land Company and Hamilton's classmate at King's College; Stephen N. Bayard, leading merchant-capitalist and the largest purchaser of surveyor lots in the New Military Tract just west of the Oneida homeland; George Scriba, who along with Peter Smith was the largest investor in lands "acquired" from the Oneidas in 1785 and 1788; and other prominent New York City businessmen such as Nicholas Low, Daniel Ludlow, Melancthon Smith, and Thomas Eddy, a leading merchant and influential member of the Society of Friends. Represented also in this enterprise were Federalists Rufus King, the soon-to-be United States senator from New York; Goldsborough Banyar, Governor John Jay's son-in-law; and Jonas Platt, one of the most important promoters of central New York lands and one of the major advocates of the later Erie Canal project. Although the two companies were largely Federalist enterprises, De Witt Clinton himself was an investor, owning one share in the Western Inland Lock Navigation Company. Clinton's, Eddy's, and Platt's involvements are especially noteworthy. Clinton, Eddy, and Schuyler's son-in-law, Stephen Van Rensselaer, were three of the original seven appointees to the New York State Board of Canal Commissioners in 1810. Indeed, the rights to lands occupied by the Western Inland Lock

Navigation Company were eventually purchased by New York State at the behest of Platt and on the recommendation of the New York State Board of Canal Commissioners.[34]

Nathan Miller, a leading economic historian of the Empire State, has written that these investors saw their future profit in this venture capitalist experiment largely in "an increase in land values." Miller insisted, "Had Schuyler carefully examined the motives of many of the directors and stockholders, and possibly his own as well, he would have discovered that a large number of them considered the matter of dividends as purely incidental to the company's plans for the improvement of transportation." Miller added that these men "were speculators to whom the broad, unsettled stretches of land in western New York seemed like an untapped gold mine whose productivity would expand in proportion to the improvements wrought in transportation and communication linking the east and the west." The economic historian then calculated that fifteen of the thirty-six directors of the canal company "held lands which were likely to increase in value as a result of the canal company's improvements."[35] George Scriba, Schuyler's political ally (who had purchased a vast empire north of Oneida Lake and the Tug Hill upland, bounded by Lake Ontario in the east and the Oswego River on the west—a land base that was largely infertile and swampy in a not-so-temperate climate), saw the canal projects as his panacea, a way to make his undertaking pay off. Scriba, as did others, soon "took pains to advertise the fact that lands which he put up for sale were accessible to the company's system of inland communication."[36]

The connections among private land speculation, state transportation development, and Indian dispossession were especially clear by the early 1790s. Banyar's, Watson's, and Schuyler's efforts led to the passage by the New York State Legislature of "an act for establishing and opening lock navigations within the state," which in part subsidized this canal effort with state appropriations.[37] As early as 1793, the builders of the Western Inland Lock Navigation Company were trespassing on Oneida Indian lands, stripping the territory of its fallen timber along "Wood Creek, the stream which flows into Oneida Lake," and straightening the bounds of this water route "to the extent of shortening its length more than seven miles."[38] Thus, by the 1790s Schuyler began to see himself as the transportation magnate of the Empire State. Through geographical prediction he was now prepared for the challenge. With powerful connections to New York's major families based upon politics, economics, and consanguinity, and with "friends" among the Oneidas, Schuyler saw few impediments to his grand design.

Schuyler's actions were clearly aided and abetted not only by divisions within the Oneida polity but also by the actions of Kirkland and his long-time associate among the Oneidas, James Dean. In 1788 Kirkland allegedly told his flock that they should sell part of their lands, which led to his rejection by some former faithful Christian Oneida followers. By his presence at six illegal state treaties with the Cayuga, Oneida, and Onondaga from the mid-1780s to the mid-1790s, and in the negotiations for the gigantic Phelps-Gorham Purchase in 1788, the missionary gave a sense of moral legitimacy to these outright frauds and/or clear violations of federal supremacy in Indian affairs. Moreover, as Campisi has astutely observed, Kirkland encouraged the sale of Oneida lands to whites, which could "serve to offer a model of thrift and industry for Indians to emulate." Because he was convinced that Oneidas as a whole "would never become farmers unless forced to by the loss of land for hunting," the Presbyterian missionary could easily find it acceptable to serve the Oneidas on occasions as both a minister and a government representative, dealing with the likes of John Livingston or Oliver Phelps and Nathaniel Gorham.[39] But there were apparently other reasons for Kirkland's turnabout.

In 1790 the Oneidas and the State of New York granted Kirkland and his sons four thousand acres on the present site of Utica. Subsequently, after lobbying feverishly, Kirkland obtained an additional two thousand acres for his role in the Phelps-Gorham Purchase negotiations.[40] The pre–American Revolution Kirkland, who sincerely saw himself as the protector of his Oneida flock, leading them away from the fires of damnation, apparently compromised his principles under the pressures of family and mission financial exigencies and under his all-consuming passion to create the Hamilton-Oneida Academy. Although he remarried a woman of means after the death of his first wife in 1796, Kirkland in the early 1790s was increasingly desperate for money because of his substantial medical expenses and the extravagance of his profligate son George Whitfield, a land speculator.[41] It appears to be no coincidence that the missionary looked the other way when the Oneidas slowly were defrauded during this period. Increasingly dependent on outside sources for his mission, Kirkland was not going to risk his mission sinecure by criticizing Philip Schuyler, perhaps the most powerful New Yorker of the 1790s.

Kirkland's mind-set in the period 1788–95 was most affected by his obsession with creating the Hamilton-Oneida Academy and promoting his specific program of Indian education. Kirkland apparently never questioned the sources of his funding or the aims of the donors. He traded favors for donations and appointed "moneybags" to the board of trustees of his institution. Although he gave three thousand acres of the land he had obtained from the Oneida and most of his money, not drained away by his profligate son, to build the school, Kirkland clearly made "compromises" in the period after 1788 that alienated many of his flock.

In the late 1780s and 1790s Kirkland's relationship with Oliver Phelps, the major land speculator, raised eyebrows. From 1788 onward Kirkland attended land negotiations with the Senecas, adding his moral suasion, whereby Phelps furthered the building of his vast landholdings. Soon Phelps was writing Kirkland about the laying out of roads in the Phelps-Gorham lands. By November 1790 Iroquois Indians, including Cornplanter, accused Phelps, Kirkland, and Joseph Brant of altering deeds in favor of Phelps. Indeed, when the Hamilton-Oneida Academy was chartered in 1793 by the regents of the State of New York, Oliver Phelps was the largest financial contributor to the project![42]

The school and its founding illustrate much about Kirkland and his motives. In the same month the Hamilton-Oneida Academy was chartered, the nefarious Peter Smith asked Kirkland to do him a favor. Smith requested that Kirkland mention to Israel Chapin, the federal superintendent to the Six Nations, that "if any of the Indians should inquire, that you think they ought to be satisfied with the rents which I gave them as I should wish the Indians all to be satisfied."[43] It is little wonder that Smith, in the same month, matched Phelps's financial contribution to Kirkland's Hamilton-Oneida Academy. Indeed, the list of donors and trustees of the school in the early years illustrates much. Other donors included Jonas Platt and Moses De Witt, with Platt also serving as an original trustee of the school.[44]

Even more revealing were Kirkland's notes of 1792 in which he discussed his plan of education. Kirkland optimistically saw a bright future for the institution because of the support of the state's scion, Philip Schuyler: "The Honorable Philip Schuyler, Esq. of Albany, much approves of the plan, and says he will most cheerfully contribute his influence for carrying it into effect."[45] Hence, it was no mere coincidence that Kirkland named the school

Hamilton in honor of Schuyler's illustrious son-in-law. Less than three years later, when the school faced disaster because it needed to complete its only building, Kirkland asked Schuyler's other prominent son-in-law, Stephen Van Rensselaer, for the then exorbitant sum of one thousand to twelve hundred dollars, mortgaging him "three hundred acres of lands, including the Academy plot or lot of ground on which the Academy is erected." Insisting it was a sound investment, Kirkland, in the manner of later college hucksters, added that his institution was "better situated to be a means of diffusing useful knowledge, and enlarging the bounds of human happiness, and aiding the reign of virtue."[46]

Kirkland's fund-raising activities brought strong reactions from his long-time supporters among the Oneidas. Even his faithful "son," Skenandoah, and his Christian allies complained twice to the missionary society in Boston in 1794 and 1795 that Kirkland was frequently absent, ignoring his responsibilities, and not performing sermons or instructing the Indians.[47] Besides his fund-raising activities, Kirkland's absences were due to illness and failing eyesight caused by a twig that damaged one of his eyes while riding.

Kirkland's absences occurred at a critical time in Oneida history, namely the same eighteen-month period that Philip Schuyler plotted to get at the heart of Oneida territory. Unlike John Sergeant, the famous missionary to the nearby Stockbridge-Brothertown Indians, who questioned the actions of Peter Smith and the motives of state officials, warned of the dangers facing the Indians, and insisted that state and private land negotiations with the Oneidas violated federal laws, Kirkland remained silent. Through 1795 Sergeant wrote Timothy Pickering of his concerns, imploring him to do something to protect the Indians.[48] He was also critical of "the foibles of that worthy gentleman" Kirkland, whom he believed had lost touch with his Indian charges and had become through sheer folly too involved in building his school at the expense of his pastoral duties.[49] It appears that the charges against Kirkland's ministry were leveled by Sergeant himself and filed with the Boston missionary society.

Missionary Belknap, accompanied by Reverend Jedidiah Morse, came to investigate Kirkland's Oneida mission in 1796. The two visiting clerics dismissed most of the charges against the missionary but did find that Kirkland's school, the Hamilton-Oneida Academy, was largely defunct. Significantly, Belknap commented on Kirkland's holdings, indicating that the missionary to the Oneidas had a "large, handsome, new house, nearly finished," with thirty acres of wheat and corn and thirty head of cattle.[50] Although the Hamilton-Oneida Academy later made a slight comeback in the decade before Kirkland's death in 1808, only two Indians attended throughout this period. Four years after Kirkland's death the institution changed its name to Hamilton College and abandoned its original mission statement concerning its commitment to educating Indians.[51]

Schuyler's efforts at acquiring the Indian land base were further advanced by Kirkland's assistant, James Dean (1748–1843), the official interpreter at the 1795 treaty and at every state-Oneida land cession from 1785 to 1818! According to Sergeant, Dean was never completely trusted because upon entering Oneida country, he vowed never to seek land from these Indians, an oath he later violated many times over.[52] Dean, who learned to speak Oneida as a youth at Oquaga while working with the missionary David Avery, was active in Kirkland's religious efforts and worked as a silversmith among these Indians after being trained at Dartmouth College by the missionary Eleazar Wheelock. Later, Dean was a major in the American army and the Patriot Indian agent to the Oneidas during the American Revolution, serving as an intermediary between the two worlds. After the war, taking advantage of his unique position among the Oneidas, he had become involved in the schemes of the New York Genesee Company of Adventurers, who attempted to circumvent the restrictions on the private purchase of Indian lands without an expressed license from the New York State Legislature. In these hijinks he had allied himself with Peter Schuyler and the major speculators Robert Troup and John Livingston, "acquiring" the next year a two-mile tract in Westmoreland, New York, formerly Oneida territory.[53]

In the next quarter-century Dean parlayed his advantageous position into becoming a successful Federalist politician. He later served as a judge in Oneida County and as a state assemblyman. In 1810 his political enemy, De Witt Clinton, himself no friend of the Oneidas, hypocritically wrote that by ingratiating himself with the Oneidas, Dean had eventually "coaxed them out of large tracts of land."[54] Later, on March 14, 1816, in a revealing incident in Dean's life, the Federalist judge gave the eulogy at Skenandoah's funeral at Hamilton College, praising the Oneida as the "white man's friend" who "had profited by seeing civilized and polished society, and by mingling with good company in his better days." The trusting Skenandoah, it is clear, had been largely responsible for Dean's meteoric rise to fortune and fame in central New York.[55]

By the time the federal treaty with the Six Nations negotiated by Timothy Pickering was signed on November 11, 1794, which guaranteed Washington's protection against the state, the Oneida homeland had shrunk from five to six million acres of land to one-quarter of a million acres within Oneida and Madison Counties, with a central focus at Oneida Lake and Oneida Castle, approximately twelve miles south of the eastern end of the lake. Three weeks later, representatives from the United States and the Oneidas signed a second treaty of friendship, again with Timothy Pickering, whereby Washington recognized the important service of these Indians and the Stockbridge and Tuscarora, allies in the American Revolution, and awarded them compensation for "their individual losses and services" and provided moneys for mills and millers and for the construction of a church to replace "the one which was there burnt by the enemy, in the late war."[56]

Within ten months, state actions undertaken largely by Philip Schuyler were consciously and systematically to undo the actions of Timothy Pickering, the Indians' benefactor, and to set in motion a series of transactions that nearly rid the state of its entire Oneida Indian population. Despite his position as the United States senator from New York—a federal official—he furthered his own interests and, at the same time, flouted congressional laws, consciously violating the United States Constitution and the Federal Indian Trade and Intercourse Acts of 1790 and 1793, which required the presence of a United States Commissioner and/or prior federal approval of any and all land purchases from the Indians. Pickering knew about the state's intentions and warned Albany officials, including the newly installed Governor John Jay, about the illegality of negotiating with the Iroquois without federal approval. Pickering also secured an opinion from the attorney general of the United States, William Bradford, who maintained that Indian lands could not be purchased except by a treaty held under the authority of the United States.[57]

In 1793 state officials led by Simeon De Witt and John Cantine had earlier approached the Oneidas about new negotiations over land.[58] State plans for the construction of the Genesee Turnpike necessitated these deliberations with the Oneidas. In March 1793 De Witt noted in a report that the Oneidas expressed clear contempt over these deliberations and bitterness over past land dealings with the state. Acknowledging the cooperation of

Kirkland and Dean in trying to obtain "the object of the state," De Witt was, nevertheless, frustrated in his efforts to secure any more Indian lands. Beechtree (Captain Peter), one of the Oneida chiefs, forthrightly responded to De Witt's request, "You have been told that it is our determination not to sell or lease our lands." In the end, De Witt, blaming "evil-minded people" for giving the Oneidas bad advice, went back to Albany and reported his failed mission to Governor George Clinton.[59] It was to take an "old friend" of the Oneidas two years more to accomplish what De Witt and Cantine had failed to secure in 1793.

On February 27, 1795, a group of Oneidas recommended that the New York State Legislature appoint commissioners to treat with the Indians who were desirous of "making fresh disposal of some part of our land." Not surprisingly, one of the petitioners was Skenandoah and one of the witnesses attesting the document was Jacob Reed. The petitioners recommended the appointment of Philip Schuyler and James Dean as state commissioners because they insisted that "from our long acquaintance" they believed "them to be friends to us."[60] Instead, the legislature confirmed Schuyler, John Cantine, and David Brooks as state commissioners. Two weeks later, Israel Chapin indicated that "some white people in their vicinity have been making them [the Oneidas] offers for their land and a part of their chiefs wish to sell but the best part of them I believe are not desirous to do it hastily."[61]

In April 1795 Pickering was promoted to Washington's second secretary of war, succeeding Knox, leaving the way open for the appointment of Chapin to the post of superintendent of the affairs of the Six Nations. Pickering ordered Chapin "to protect the tribes under your superintendence from injury and imposition, which too many of our own people are disposed to practice upon them." He added that Chapin should provide for the tribes' comfort and improvement with "inviolate integrity and prudent economy"—possible because Pickering believed things were improved as the British were less of a threat than the previous year due to the Jay Treaty's ratification. Because of the great distance from the tribes to Chapin's headquarters at Buffalo Creek—more than two hundred miles—Pickering thought that Chapin could not adequately supervise the affairs of the Oneidas, Stockbridges, and Tuscaroras in central New York. Therefore, Pickering suggested that Chapin appoint someone in the vicinity of Oneida country to report back about the situation.[62] The distance from Buffalo Creek only exacerbated two existing problems: How was the federal government going to enforce the Federal Trade and Intercourse Act? And why should state officials, who knew this weakness, listen?

Because Schuyler and his partners had already trespassed on Oneida lands by making cuts for his channel and making other improvements along Wood Creek, he sought secure title through retroactive state approval for his past actions. In doing so he ignored the clear requirements set forth in the federal Trade and Intercourse Acts of 1790 and 1793. The temptation of getting the rich Oneida land base for himself and his cronies blinded him to the rule of law. To Schuyler, the New York State–Oneida "treaty" of 1795 provided both the means and opportunity to secure these goals. Importantly, Schuyler was strategically placed as one of the state commissioners to negotiate this land cession. His longtime acquaintances with the Oneidas was to serve him well through his dealings in 1795.

Schuyler's presence in the negotiations was deliberate. Both Indians and non-Indians knew that few outsiders had his standing among the Oneidas and Tuscaroras or had his knowledge about or overall experience with American Indians. For nearly forty years he had known Skenandoah and other prominent Oneidas of the day. On June 9, 1795, he wrote to Governor John Jay about his state assignment, which included treating with the Cayugas, Onondagas, and Oneidas, and about a wide variety of other Indian issues. In the letter he dismissed the "very extensive" claims of the Mohawks to lands west of Lake Champlain and the River Sorel and south of the Saint Lawrence River, which he termed "suspect" and ill-founded. Then he elaborated on his planned negotiations with the Onondagas, Cayugas, and Oneidas, asking for provisions for the conference and requesting the governor's attendance to aid Schuyler, David Brooks, John Cantine, and John Richardson in securing Indian approval. Lastly, Schuyler mentioned one caveat to Jay, namely his poor health. While on a visit to one of his daughters, the Albanian politico had been thrown out of his carriage when his horses bolted, damaging his ribs, causing him "not [to be] able to stir out of my room since." Despite his painful injury, Schuyler assured Jay that he would probably be able to travel to Onondaga by July 15.[63]

The state-Oneida "treaty" of 1795 was one of three that Philip Schuyler negotiated with the Iroquois in that year and can only be understood in conjunction with the two earlier agreements. On July 27, 1795, the Federalist secured Cayuga lands. Earlier, state officials, surveyors, and land speculators had been stymied in their efforts to secure Cayuga property because of the hardened stance of the Cayuga chief Steel-Trap and the intervention of Cayuga leaders from Buffalo Creek.[64] Schuyler in 1795 obtained Cayuga lands as far as Montezuma, New York, which contained rich salt deposits and which he needed for his canal scheme, the Western Inland Lock Navigation Company. But Schuyler was successful only after he threatened to seize all of the remaining Cayuga lands in New York State. The Cayuga chief, Fish Carrier, nevertheless, reserved some lands around Cayuga Lake for himself and for his community. Fish Carrier and the Cayuga leadership were able to hold on to this remaining parcel until 1807.[65] The day after the signing of the Cayuga-state agreement, Schuyler secured a "treaty" with the Onondaga.[66] This July 28, 1795, "treaty" must be seen in light of an early agreement made in March 1793.[67] Both of these agreements secured New York State's public ownership of the lands around Onondaga Lake and with it, once again, all of the salt deposits in its environs.[68]

Ten years later, Julian Ursyn Niemcewicz, a Polish aristocrat traveling to Niagara, wrote about the importance of the state securing this resource around Onondaga Lake from the Indians. Niemcewicz observed that the state salt "reservation" was leased to private individuals and that one hundred fifty cauldrons were making five bushels a day. "These sources are very rich. . . . It is of the most beautiful whiteness and of the best quality." After adding that there was a limitless supply of salt, the Pole remarked: "It is a real source of wealth for this country which, lacking this commodity, a prime necessity in preparing the many salt provisions for its sea voyages, was paying immense sums for it to foreigners."[69] Nevertheless, Niemcewicz also saw a downside to the operation, one that was to have an impact on the Indians, both Onondaga and Oneida, in the region:[70] "However, the extraction of this salt by heat from fires causes a consumption of wood which will end by devouring all the forests in the vicinity. Up to 100 cords are burnt in a day. Already all the neighboring woods have been devastated. In order to spare themselves the hardship of carting the wood, they lead the water by canals into the depth of the forests." Thus, by 1805, the development of the central New York salt industry required more forest lands, much of which were still in Indian hands or inaccessible in the Adirondacks because of limited transportation. Although fleets of Durham boats hauled tons of salt to Oswego and Schenectady, a vast improvement in transportation—such as canal building—could further the industry. Subsequently, a shift to true canal boats with the opening of the Erie Canal after 1825 was to provide a dramatic boost in transport capacity for salt.

Schuyler's "state treaty" of 1795 with the Onondagas must also be seen in the larger context of what had befallen these Indians. During the American Revolution Colonel Goose Van Schaick and his American forces destroyed the Onondaga villages along an eight-to-ten-mile swath, leading most Onondagas to flee to Fort Niagara and later to the Buffalo Creek Reservation. By the early 1790s only 25 percent of the four hundred Onondagas in New York State at that time were living in their central New York homeland while the remainder lived in Seneca country where the council fire of the Confederacy was rekindled.[71] By the early 1790s Onondaga lands had been reduced to less than a twenty-five-square-mile tract as a result of the creation of the New Military Tract and "state treaties" in 1788 and 1793. Because of the great salt rush, prominent New Yorkers began to push for the purchase of all Onondaga lands.[72] Besides the immense land loss, the Onondagas in 1793 had "agreed" to the following provision, one common in state "accords" of the period: "The People of the State of New York shall from time to time and all times forever hereafter have full power and authority to lay out and open roads through any part of the lands appropriated by the People of the State of New York to the use of the Onondagoes."[73]

On August 6, 1795, Philip Schuyler met with the sachems and warriors of the Oneida Nation. After moralizing about the evil effects of liquor among the Indians and advocating sobriety, Schuyler announced that his goal was to obtain land on the south side of Wood Creek to opposite Canada Creek on the eastern bounds of the Oneida Indian Reservation. Knowing full well that his negotiations required the presence of a federal commissioner to protect Indian interests—as required under the Federal Trade and Intercourse Acts of 1790 and 1793—and warned repeatedly by Chapin and Pickering about this requirement, Schuyler, nevertheless, proceeded with his negotiations.[74]

Captain John (Onondiyo), the Oneida chief, immediately responded to the presence of his old friend and patron. Addressing him as Brother Schuyler, Captain John asserted that his people had "always had reason to believe you have our welfare at heart." Recalling the Revolutionary War, the Oneida chief insisted that Schuyler in the past "had gave [*sic*] us good council and advised us to persevere to the end." The chief then stated that the Oneidas have "become poor and weak—we are nothing but a wreck of Bones! Our lands are almost all gone from us, for almost nothing" and that the nation was slowly becoming ashes. Once again playing the role of "good Indian," Captain John appealed to his former white patron, Schuyler: "It is true your doors have always been open to us and when we called upon you, you always gave us good advice." Captain John, who suggested to Schuyler that he had been warned by both Chapin and Pickering to be careful in state land negotiations, then noted that he was disappointed that Schuyler had not brought with him "an agent from the United States." Yet, the chief, who died suddenly three days before the treaty signing, nevertheless, maintained that the Oneidas were willing to sell lands if they received just value, were protected by their white patron in the future, and were guaranteed that their grievances would be dealt with by the state. The Oneida grievances included being denied equal access to fishing in and around Fish Creek. They also insisted that in order to protect their fishery, the north side of Oneida Lake, North East Bay, should be reserved for the Indians.[75]

During the negotiations other aspects of state-Indian relations were brought up. It is clear that the Oneidas negotiating the agreement were especially concerned with Peter Penet and his legacy. They appealed to Schuyler and the other commissioners to protect them from this type of trickery. The white backlash against the immense landholdings ceded to Penet by the Oneidas had led to increased Indian tensions with some of their neighbors, who sought similar "opportunities" to get at the Oneida land base.[76] Other issues besides Penet included the state's attempt to secure a "strip of land along the road between the deep spring" and Oneida Castle, which Albany was "desirous of obtaining for the purpose of improving" its roads. Still other concerns included the rewarding of Abraham Van Eps [Epps], referred to by the Oneidas as "our child," who "desired to obtain four square miles, two on each side of the [planned] road"; James Dean, "our good friend" who sought a one-mile-square parcel "adjoining Mr. Van Eps and west of [the property] of Mr. Bleeker" (another major speculator in Oneida lands); and Colonel Abraham Wemple, who sought one square mile in the vicinity.[77]

The Oneidas' requests did not interfere with Schuyler's own strategy. He was more concerned with securing concessions over the east side of Oneida Lake, the Fish Creek–Wood Creek region, which he needed to further his canal interests. He was also intent on securing lands through the southern end of Oneida Castle, which the state needed for the Genesee Turnpike and which land speculators lusted after as well.

On September 15, 1795, less than two months after the conclusion of state treaties with both the Cayugas and Onondagas, a group of Oneidas, armed with a state-provided power of attorney, signed an accord with the New York State Indian Commissioners. In it they "sold" to the state more than one hundred thousand acres of tribal lands for $2,952 payment and an annual payment of $2,952 to their "friend" Philip Schuyler. Going against the tribal sentiments expressed by Good Peter before his death not to cede any more land, this faction sold a portion of their land around Oneida Lake, the south and east side, but reserved the right to lake access and fish, and ownership rights to one-half mile sections along the north shore. Among the signatories of this cession was Skenandoah, the aged chief.[78]

Besides filing a detailed expense account for the Oneida and for the other two treaties, Schuyler sent a revealing report about these negotiations to the New York State Legislature. In it he explained the Oneidas' motivation for ceding land, which also included confirming grants to his Federalist allies, namely Dean, Van Eps, and Wemple. Schuyler claimed that the Oneidas had been "indebted" to Van Eps "in a considerable sum of monies" while the Wemples "afforded them [the Oneidas] very considerable pecuniary aid." Consequently, financial obligation to surrounding whites apparently led some Oneidas to cede lands from 1785 onward.[79]

Schuyler continued by citing two other reasons for Oneida land cessions. According to the New York scion, the Oneidas were once again attempting to be good, trusting Indians. They wanted to show their loyalty, adding that they made their cessions "in consideration of the many advantages derived" from their past relationships with the state, starting from the state's succor, arranged by Schuyler to the Oneida Indian refugees at Schenectady in the latter half of the American Revolution. Schuyler concluded that the Oneidas also came to the treaty table in 1795 "to prevent embarrassment in future negotiations," an ambiguous reference that possibly meant that the state and the Oneidas had to clear up outstanding unresolved issues, most specifically the state's assumption that it still had the right, despite Pickering's and the United States attorney general's contentions, to negotiate with the Oneidas *after* the federal Treaty with the Six Nations at Canandaigua and the federal Oneida Treaty of 1794.[80]

In open defiance of federal law, Schuyler's position was consistent from 1783 to 1795, namely, that Albany, not Washington, was supreme in all matters dealing with Indians and their lands. Drawing upon certain Indians' trust based upon Schuyler's wartime experiences with them, the former general was to undo this reciprocal obligation, dispossess the Indians, and, in the process, become the first great canal "pioneer" of the state. His vision was to make New York the Empire State but at a cost to his faithful allies, the Oneidas.

CHAPTER 5

Vision Quest

In the colonial and revolutionary eras, as well as in the early years of the American Republic, the waterway corridor from the Hudson River to the Great Lakes region remained essential to New Yorkers and to Americans as a whole. It was the only feasible passage other than the St. Lawrence River valley, which was controlled by the enemy British after the American Revolution. Hence, it was no coincidence that a retired military hero of the American Revolution, Philip Schuyler, envisioned the improvement of this corridor, which he believed would benefit the newly emerging settlements along the Mohawk frontier, meet the growing demands of new farmers and merchants alike, facilitate expansion west of Albany, and bring him added fame. It would also add to his family's vast political and economic fortunes.

After receiving its charter in 1792, the Western Inland Lock Navigation Company began improving Wood Creek by clearing fallen timber and debris out of the channel the following year. Thirteen short channels were cut to shorten and straighten the creek between Rome and Oneida Lake. According to transportation historian Philip Lord, Jr., in the next decade the company made Mohawk River improvements as well, deepening channels, removing boulders, and building a series of wing dams to raise the water level at several rapids between Little Falls and Schenectady. By 1795 the company had built a one-mile canal at Little Falls, which included five wooden lift locks, one guard lock, and a dam. Two years later, directly in the heart of traditional Oneida territory, the company constructed the Rome Canal, a 1.7-mile canal cut across the Oneida Carrying Place, connecting the upper Mohawk River with Wood Creek. The next year, it built the German Flatts Canal, a 1.1-mile canal used to bypass two dangerous rapids east of Herkimer along the Mohawk River. As Lord has further pointed out, in 1803 the company built four wooden locks in the shallow waters of Wood Creek to improve navigation between Rome and Canada Creek. Soon the Durham boat, twice as long with eight times the capacity of the bateaus of the era before the American Revolution, replaced the earlier outmoded river crafts. This innovation allowed for larger cargoes and, with it, expanded commercial activity, stimulating further the push for new, improved, and larger canal projects, most notably the Erie.[1]

Two years before the New York State–Oneida Treaty of 1795, construction crews began work on Schuyler's dream, the Western Inland Lock Navigation Company. From 1793 onward as many as four hundred workers began clearing obstacles from the Mohawk River and Wood Creek and constructing two miles of canal thirty-seven feet wide and four feet deep. Adding to the tensions between certain Indians and whites in the region were the activities of the land surveyors busy laying out the bounds of Peter Smith's vast lands. On May 12, 1793, Beechtree reported to Pickering that Colonel Honyere's sons, Jacob and Cornelius, and five other Oneida warriors had offered their services to kill Smith's surveyors.[2]

Tensions between Indians and whites involved in canal building and land speculation continued in the region even after the 1795 accord. In 1796 the Western Inland Lock Navigation Company attempted to hire twenty-five Brothertown Indians as construction workers on the Rome canal project. Only two came to work. They "worked two days at the lock, got their wages and went off without notice."[3] Later, on another occasion, Indians threatened non-Indian construction workers on Wood Creek by their "hostile disposition."[4] These outsiders were scarcely a welcome sight to the majority of the Indians in the region. Yet despite the opposition, within a brief time, two locks were completed at Rome, which opened navigation between the Mohawk River and Wood Creek.

Although he was first and foremost an entrepreneur, Schuyler's motives for securing the canal route through Oneida country were not merely pecuniary. In the last decade of his life he was unrelenting in his commitment to canal projects, even sacrificing his friendship with Elkanah Watson and his own health in the process.[5] It is true that his bold plan for a canal, which would open up lands from the Mohawk River to Cayuga Lake, would further his accumulation of wealth and power; however, it would also, he incorrectly believed, ensure his lasting fame as the great architect of the Empire State. In its short-lived existence the Western Inland Lock Navigation

Company's rudimentary water passage from Albany to Seneca Lake lowered carriage fees of transportation from one hundred dollars to thirty-two dollars per ton, and from Albany to Niagara by half.[6] The company carried substantial salt, wheat, furs, and lumber and was "principally ladened with European or Indian productions or manufactures."[7]

The Western Inland Navigation Lock Company became Schuyler's primary focus of attention when the Northern Inland Navigation Company, after making small improvements for navigation between Fort Edward and Lake Champlain and beginning work near Stillwater, dissolved its operations. Despite a periodic infusion of state moneys, the Western Inland Navigation Lock Company was always underfunded. Instead of designing an artificial river to ensure a steady and regulated water depth, the planners used the region's uncontrollable creeks and rivers, which naturally rose and fell based upon precipitation levels.[8] Moreover, the Western Inland Lock Navigation Company was constantly besieged by merchants for not clearing its passageway of obstructions, especially on Wood Creek. George Scriba, a proponent of and a stockholder in the project, wrote to the canal's board of directors that frustrated merchants as far as the Genesee country were complaining about having to unload and then reload their cargoes up to fifty times on a typical trip in order to maneuver their Durham boats around these obstructions, leading to costly delays. Scriba maintained that these merchants might turn to the turnpike, however bumpier and costlier, as an alternative due to these problems.[9]

The inland navigation companies also faced squabbles between Watson and Schuyler over management of the companies, political rivalries of Federalists and Clintonians, and charges of improprieties and even embezzlement against their directors. When Schuyler, himself accused of tyrannical tactics in managing the two companies, died in 1804, these canal experiments were already on the road to oblivion. Despite an outlay of four hundred thousand dollars in construction costs, the western company's revenues amounted to only ten thousand dollars in 1803.[10]

The Western Inland Lock Navigation Company suffered a slow death. Although operating after the War of 1812, the company faced continued financial exigencies. Moreover, the Western Inland Lock Navigation Company never did any work beyond Oneida Lake and by 1808 had surrendered all its rights west of that lake. In 1820 the company's accounts were finally closed and its property and lands sold off for the completion of the

Erie Canal, wholly controlled by the New York State Board of Canal Commissioners.[11] Ironically, Watson's and Schuyler's original vision fully materialized, appropriated by their political enemy, De Witt Clinton, who became famous as the master builder, the great canal builder of the Empire State! Thus, Watson's and Schuyler's plan for improved internal navigation, most notably the Western Inland Lock Navigation Company, was a short-lived but major venture capitalist experiment, becoming the rationale for much grander schemes, namely, the Erie Canal and the branch canal system of New York State.[12]

Despite their loyal service as the "good friends of the white man" the Oneida strategy of survival was to fail miserably. One year before Skenandoah's death, the First Christian Party surrendered to overwhelming pressures and "sold" four large parcels of the Oneida Reservation to New York State. This accord involved 562 acres along the highly prized and valuable Genesee (Seneca) Turnpike Road, which the state obtained for one dollar per acre. These Oneida lands included those occupied by Skenandoah's family and those of Lewis Denny.[13] Less than two years later, in 1817, the state's construction for the middle section of the Erie Canal began under the direction of Benjamin Wright. America's "Grand Canal," the Erie, was to make New York the premier state of the nation, economically and politically; however, it was also the death knell for the Oneidas. The Indians' homeland was seen as strategically important for individual, local, and state efforts at economic development, and, hence, to white policymakers even "good Indians" had to make sacrifices for the greater benefit of the state and nation as a whole in America's definition of progress.

Besides the Erie Canal project, the New York State Board of Canal Commissioners carried through on three other canal projects involving existing or former Oneida lands. The first was the Chenango Valley Canal. After concluding that the Hudson to Lake Erie grand canal route was feasible, the commissioners insisted that "it would not be difficult to extend this communication to the fertile vales watered by the Susquehannah and its wide spreading branches."[14] The first major lobbying effort to promote the canal occurred from 1823 onward, leading James Geddes, the well-known engineer of the Erie Canal, to survey and transmit a report on the canal's feasibility to the New York State Legislature in 1826. The project did not materialize at this time because of doubts about the sufficiency of water at the planned canal's summit, the likelihood of damage suits against the state for diverting water from mills, and questions related to costs of the project. New surveys were done in 1827–28 by David Thomas, Nathan S. Roberts, and Holmes Hutchinson (the latter a well-known canal engineer and speculator in Oneida Indian lands) and the construction of the canal was approved, but only after the intercession of Benjamin Wright and his formal endorsement of the project: "If a canal is to be made to connect the Erie Canal with the Susquehannah, the Chenango Valley ought to be the place of location for the first work."[15] A budgetary stalemate and concerns about water levels for the proposed canal delayed approval. Finally, as a result of coal fever—anthracite—the New York State Legislature finally authorized the construction of the Chenango Canal in February 1833.[16]

The Black River Canal, which extended northwestward from Rome, New York, proceeded from 1825 onward. The canal, its feeder, and canal extensions and river improvements were constructed from 1836 to 1861 at a cost of more than three million dollars and included 35.5 miles of canal, a ten-mile feeder, and 42.5 miles of improvements along the Black River in the Adirondacks. The region's vast lumber, its ample water supply, and the artificial waterway's proximity to British Canada all were reasons for its construction. Whitford has noted that the canal's advocates insisted "that such a canal would assist in securing the northern frontier, which could not be effectually done without a naval force on Lake Ontario, for which Sackett's Harbor was the most suitable station." Whitford added, "This argument was sustained by the fact that the amount paid for transportation of military stores through the Black River country [in the War of 1812] was believed to have exceeded two millions of dollars."[17]

To develop a third branch canal, the Oneida Lake Canal, which basically connected the lake with the Erie Canal and which was a greater eastern expansion of the earlier Schuyler-Watson plan, the Western Inland Lock Navigation Company, the state had once again to negotiate with the Oneidas. Only in 1832 did this project go forward, three years after the state "acquired" more Oneida lands in another nonfederally ratified agreement.[18]

Weakened, divided, and impoverished by the late 1820s, many Oneidas had already followed Eleazer Williams to Wisconsin. The lands sought by the state included two tracts, one of which it was to secure from the First Christian Party on October 8, 1829. This 1,692-acre tract lay on the south side of the Genesee Turnpike (then renamed the Seneca Turnpike) and west of Oneida Creek, an area that was still occupied by a sizable number of

Indians. These Indians, already planning to go to Green Bay, were "allowed" to remain on these lands in undisturbed possession until their soon-to-be relocation.[19]

Eventually, the Oneida Lake Canal opened and the Indians were removed. The canal, which was once the Old Oneida Lake Canal, a private venture that opened in 1835 at a cost of seventy-nine million dollars and was acquired by the state in 1841, was actually a 6.5-mile canal with 3 miles of feeder. The canal extended along two miles of Wood Creek and later four miles of Fish Creek. In 1867 a New Oneida Lake Canal was authorized. When completed in 1877 it ran a course of 5.3 miles; this second canal was abandoned one decade later.[20]

These canals did more than rid the state of most of its Oneida Indian population. The canals created a metropolitan corridor right to the Great Lakes, soon putting pressure on the Senecas and Indians farther to the west. American ideas of progress and nationalism soon became associated with the wonders of the Grand Canal. Historian Carol Sheriff has put this feeling best: "By following God's plan to build a water highway to the west, these leaders would lure enterprising settlers to a region where before only beasts and 'savages' roamed." Sheriff added, "By bringing with them not just their knowledge of God but also their commitment to 'free institutions,' these settlers would spread civilization westward. The notion would, in the 1840s, come to be called manifest destiny."[21] Thus, the vision of the great scion of early New York, Philip Schuyler, ended up becoming a national religious crusade by the 1840s, one that had no role for Indians except as foils for "American progress."

CHAPTER 6

Silent Partners

Almost two years to the day after Schuyler secured Oneida lands, Robert Morris—the legendary financier of the Patriot cause in the American Revolution—in a seemingly unrelated transaction, negotiated a treaty with the Senecas that extinguished Indian title to most of the Indian lands west of the so-called preemption line set in December 1786 at the Hartford Convention. At this Connecticut meeting, New York State and Massachusetts had attempted to resolve claims that could be traced back to the English Stuart kings and their royal land grants in America in the seventeenth century. Under provisions of their royal charters the two colonies were apparently granted the same western lands. At Hartford in 1786, the Empire State, in return for a recognition of its governmental jurisdiction in what is now the western part of New York State, ceded to Massachusetts the preemptive right to these lands, namely the right of first purchase from the Indians to more than six million acres of land (see map 5).

Massachusetts subsequently sold its preemption right to its huge tract to Oliver Phelps and Nathaniel Gorham. In November 1790 Morris bought 1.2 million acres of land lying between Seneca Lake and the Genesee River from Phelps and Gorham for eight cents per acre. In 1791 Morris successfully disposed of his easternmost township lands near Cazenovia and two patents near Rome in the historic Oneida territory. When Phelps and Gorham became increasingly burdened with financial difficulties and were unable to complete their purchase of the entire tract, Massachusetts sold the preemption right to the approximately four million acres west of the Genesee River to Morris at a bargain-basement price, which the land speculator-financier hoped to unload by reselling to the highest bidder.

On November 11, 1794, fearing the actions of these land speculators and

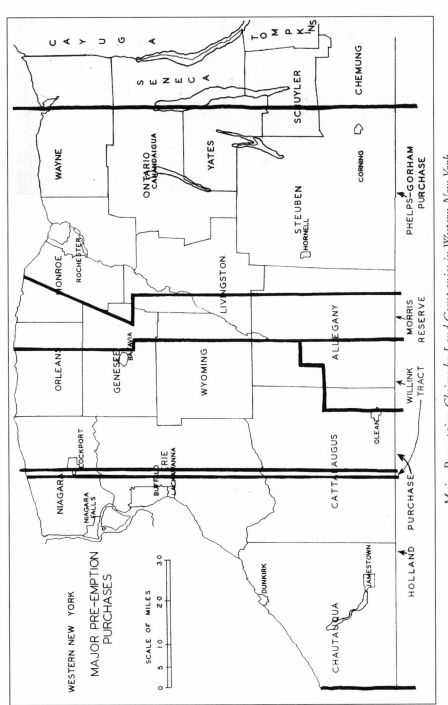

5. *Major Preemption Claims by Land Companies in Western New York*

From Records of the Indian Claims Commission, RG 279

their allies in the New York State Legislature, the Iroquois, most notably the Senecas, received assurances of territorial guarantees, friendship, alliance, and federal protection from United States Commissioner Timothy Pickering at Canandaigua, New York. This remarkable treaty included a federal receding of lands back to the Senecas and the Senecas recognizing federal control of their former lands in the Erie Triangle and farther west. After recognizing boundaries of the Seneca nation, the Pickering Treaty stated:[1]

> Now, the United States acknowledge all the land within the aforementioned boundaries, to be the property of the Seneka [*sic*] nation; and the United States will never claim the same, nor disturb the Seneka nation, nor any of the Six Nations, or of their Indian friends residing thereon and united with them, in the free use and enjoyment thereof: but it shall remain theirs until they choose to sell the same to the people of the United States, who have the right to purchase.

In the most recent analysis of the Pickering Treaty, ethnohistorians Jack Campisi and William A. Starna throw light on this remarkable accord with the Six Nations, most directly the Senecas. They insisted that "(1) it secured for the United States whatever title the Six Nations had to the Ohio Valley; (2) it returned to the Senecas the land they had lost at Fort Stanwix in 1784; and (3) it secured by treaty, which seemed a stronger assurance than legislation to the Six Nations, their reservations in New York, laid out in state agreements." In many ways it resolved longstanding issues that had never been resolved between the Iroquois, most notably the Seneca, and the federal government at the end of the American Revolution. The treaty was an "unconditional affirmation by the United States of the Six Nations' reserved lands." With a recent end to a bloody war with the Indians of the Ohio Valley and a continuing and menacing British presence as close as Fort Niagara, Pickering's treaty was much more than other Indian-white accords, as ethnohistorians Starna and Campisi have brought out, "without a doubt, a treaty between sovereigns." In agreeing to their permanent cession of the Erie triangle and the Ohio country claims, the Senecas, they thought, were getting something much more valuable to them, namely, federal confirmation of their primary lands in 1794 and federal protection from the lust of land companies and the speculators' state legislative allies. This treaty, then as now, "remains the primary basis for Iroquois assertions of sovereignty." Despite the virtuous intentions of Timothy Pickering, the treaty's "clear and unequivocal language, and its explicit guarantees, however, have afforded little protection or comfort" to the Senecas and other Iroquois from the

1790s to the present.[2] Within three years of the Pickering Treaty the Senecas were again faced with land pressures, once again from that Philadelphia shark, Robert Morris.

By the mid-1790s Morris found himself in severe financial difficulties, resulting in his sale of the preemption to individuals acting as trustees for four Dutch banking houses that had organized as a joint stock company, becoming known as the Holland Land Company; nevertheless, Morris had agreed to help these bankers extinguish Indian title. Morris, by then in bankruptcy, had to dispose of tens of thousands of acres of lands in the upper Genesee valley, which soon passed to his creditors, including the Wadsworth family.[3]

Fearing his creditors and debtor's prison, Morris sent his son Thomas with specific plans to negotiate with the Senecas at Big Tree, near today's town of Geneseo, New York. The elder Morris's strategy included outright bribery, the use of alcohol, and furthering factionalism among the Senecas, all of which proved effective in securing the speculator's goals. Thomas Morris and the Seneca leadership were joined at the treaty council by agents of the Holland Land Company; William Shepherd, a representative of the state of Massachusetts; and Jeremiah Wadsworth, the United States Indian commissioner. Despite the presence of a federal commissioner as required under the Trade and Intercourse Acts to protect Indian interests Wadsworth was scarcely an objective individual; he and his powerful family were among the largest speculators in Genesee valley lands!

When Red Jacket rejected Morris's proposals and covered the council fire, apparently ending all further negotiations, Thomas Morris, informed by Farmer's Brother that Red Jacket had exceeded his authority, then presented his father's proposals to a council of Seneca warriors and clan mothers. Like a smooth-talking flimflam man, Thomas Morris appealed to the women, whom he insisted truly understood the desperate conditions that the Senecas faced at the time, telling them that the "money that would proceed from the sale of their lands, would relieve the women from all the hardships that they then endured."[4] Faced with social disintegration caused by alcoholism and the increasing violence that resulted, the Seneca women declared themselves willing to cede land. Alcohol, cash payments, and promises of annuities were then made to win support for the treaty. Red Jacket, who had earlier labeled Robert Morris "the great eater with a big belly," received the largest payment of $600 and a $100 annuity, whereas Cornplanter received

$300 and a $250 annuity. Farmer's Brother, Young King, Little Billy, Little Billy's mother, and Pollard were also "awarded" annuities.[5]

Even though under the treaty the Senecas reserved some 310 square miles—approximately 200,000 acres—and their right to hunt and fish on the lands they ceded, the Indians, nevertheless, had surrendered most of their lands west of the Genesee River, a vast empire of millions of acres. In return, the Senecas were to receive one hundred thousand dollars, money which was to be invested and the interest distributed as an annuity.[6]

In effect the Treaty of Big Tree reduced Seneca country to eleven parcels of land. Six settlements were reserved for the Seneca on the Genesee River: (1) Canawaugus, in the environs of present-day Avon, Livingston County, New York; (2) Big Tree and (3) Little Beard's Town, on the west bank of the Genesee in the present town of Leicester, Livingston County; (4) Squawky Hill, north of the present-day Mount Morris, Livingston County; (5) Gardeau, or the "White Woman's [Mary Jemison's] Tract," on both sides of the Genesee River from the Town of Castile, Wyoming County, to south of Mount Morris, Livingston County; and (6) Caneadea, on both banks of the Genesee River in today's northern Allegany County, near Houghton, New York (see map 6).

Five other parcels were also reserved by the Seneca outside the Genesee Valley: (1) Buffalo Creek, 130 square miles, about 7 miles in width that included much of today's city of Buffalo and environs; (2) Tonawanda, along Tonawanda Creek, in Erie County; (3) Cattaraugus, up the north bank of Cattaraugus Creek and along Lake Erie in Erie and Cattaraugus Counties; (4) Allegany, along the Allegheny River in Cattaraugus County; and (5) Canadaway, along Lake Erie from Cattaraugus Creek south to Connondanerry Creek in Cattaraugus and Chautauqua Counties. Later, in 1801, as a result of an inadvertent omission in the Treaty of Big Tree, Oil Spring, a one-mile-square reservation between the Genesee and Allegheny River valleys, was added to Seneca landholdings at the behest of Handsome Lake, the Seneca prophet, and agreed to by Joseph Ellicott and the Holland Land Company.[7]

The events that transpired in September 1797 along the Genesee were directly related to those occurring 150 miles away in Oneida country. Despite his great wealth and power and his ability to secure initially a series of state subsidies for his Western Inland Lock Navigation Company project, Philip Schuyler needed allies, ones capable of underwriting his two massive

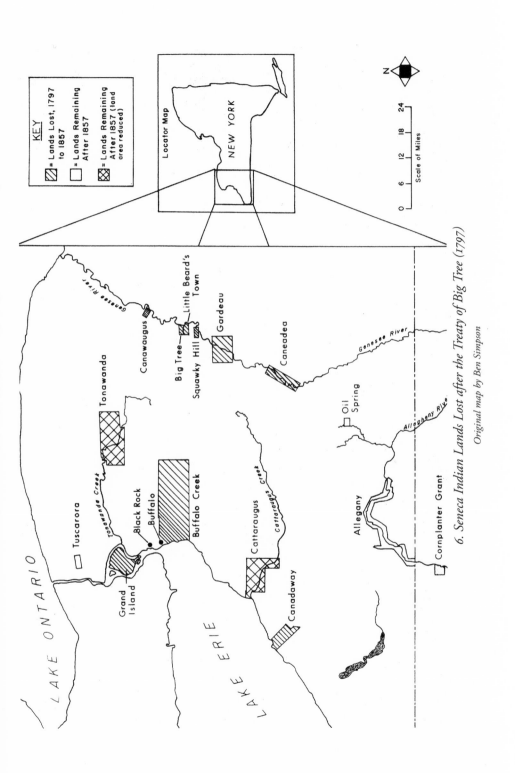

Locator Map

NEW YORK

N

0   6   12   18   24
Scale of Miles

LAKE ONTARIO

LAKE ERIE

Genesee River

Tuscarora

Tonawanda

Tonawanda Creek

Grand Island

Black Rock

Buffalo

Buffalo Creek

Cattaraugus Creek

Cattaraugus

Canadaway

Canawaugus

Big Tree

Squawky Hill

Little Beard's Town

Gardeau

Caneadea

Genesee River

Oil Spring

Allegany

Alleghany River

Cornplanter Grant

6. Seneca Indian Lands Lost after the Treaty of Big Tree (1797)

Original map by Ben Simpson

canal projects and his expensive vision for New York State.[8] These associates appeared in the 1790s in the form of foreign investors, the Holland Land Company, who, at the time, were collaborating with Schuyler's powerful Federalist ally, Robert Morris, in defrauding the Senecas of their lands in western New York.

The Holland Land Company's connection to Schuyler, the Oneida lands, and to the transportation projects is most revealing about New York State politics in the 1790s. Schuyler and Watson coveted foreign capital to cover the costs of canal building. In return, the Dutch bankers needed enabling legislation passed by Albany. Importantly, the Dutch bankers of the Holland Land Company were restricted in doing business in New York State. In the patriotic nationalism of the post–Revolutionary War era, Theophile Cazenove, the first agent-general of the company, initially failed in his efforts to legitimize the company's landholdings and to rescind the limits on aliens owning lands in New York State. Later, after hiring Alexander Hamilton as his legal advisor and investing in Schuyler's canal companies, Cazenove secured New York State legislation in 1796, allowing the Dutch bankers seven years to sell any and all of their lands.

Cazenove was aided by Schuyler's most trusted ally, Judge Egbert Benson, the Red Hook attorney and the former attorney general of New York State. Significantly, Cazenove saw Benson as his future successor as director of the Holland Land Company. Conveniently, by the early 1790s, Cazenove purchased state debt obligations of United States Bank stock and most of the pioneer canal companies, including Schuyler's two canal projects.[9] Later, Cazenove, not satisfied with "only" seven years to sell the Holland Land Company's lands in New York State, turned to Schuyler's political enemy, Aaron Burr, who blatantly went about bribing key legislators. The New York State Legislature eventually passed a bill allowing "aliens receiving lands during the three years immediately after the act was passed" to hold them "in perpetuity." With the Dutch bankers' acquisition of millions of acres of Seneca lands in 1797 at the federal Treaty of Big Tree and later in the federal Treaty of 1802, the Holland Land Company was now free to operate almost at will in the Empire State.[10]

The presence of Schuyler, Benson, Hamilton, and Burr in these seedy dealings was scarcely an accident. Whether Federalist or Democrat Republican, the politics of the time in New York State had little concern for ethics or ideology. In the words of the Federalist William Cooper, it was the age of

Egbert Benson
Courtesy of the New York State Library, New York State Museum, and Craig Williams

the "art of Hook and Snivey," namely, the art of trickery and deceit. Historian Alan Taylor has perceptively written that the best New York State politicians of the 1790s were all practical men relentlessly seeking office to expand their political and economic advantages, who presented their opponents as "crypto-aristocrats" who would corrupt the Republic, and who would do just about anything to win elections. Although the high ideals of republicanism were often espoused openly, the politics of "making interest" determined. In this combative setting it is little wonder that weak Indian communities fared badly.[11]

In February 1798 the New York State Legislature passed an act "Authorizing the Governor to Appoint Commissioners to treat with the Oneida Indians for the purchase of part of their lands." This act was aimed at encouraging road building and non-Indian settlements in central New York. It called for construction "as may be convenient for public roads and suitable settlements and accommodations."[12] On June 1, 1798, three New York State Indian commissioners—Egbert Benson, Ezra L'Hommedieu, and John Tayler, later governor of New York State—carried out the legislature's mandate. In this state "treaty," this time confirmed by the United States Senate, New York State "bought" more Indian lands, this time south of Oneida Lake, from a faction of Oneidas. Benson, the principal state negotiator, was aided by James Dean, who once again served as the official interpreter.[13]

Importantly, this cession allowed New York State to acquire the land it needed in what later became Madison County for the further development of its first state road, the Genesee Turnpike, bringing more traffic and more land pressures to Oneida country. The building of the road, which had already received state appropriations between 1794 and 1797, could not be completed in the region without these lands. Among the list of private stockholders in this Seneca Road Company, which extended to three miles west of Oneida Castle in 1801, were the "usual suspects": Peter Smith; Stephen Van Rensselaer, Philip Schuyler's other son-in-law; and the leading land speculators Oliver Phelps and Augustus and Peter Porter![14]

Benson's involvement in the 1798 state agreement with the Oneidas is no accident and was related to his Holland Land Company dealings. Opening up the former Seneca lands acquired at the Treaty of Big Tree the previous year could be accomplished only by acquiring the necessary piece of the puzzle—the transportation route connection—the state road that ran west from New Hartford to the Genesee. The ancient Seneca Trail, much of which became the state road, needed more land for improvement and had to be widened for wagons to carry great populations and commerce into Seneca country. Acquiring the Indian lands in the southern portion of Oneida Castle completed the master plan. Moreover, the lands of two Holland Land Company agents, Jan Lincklaen at the appropriately named Cazenovia and Gerrit Boon at Boonville, both west of the Oneida Indian territory, would rise in value with the completion of the transportation networks. It was no mere coincidence that the state-Oneida "treaty" of 1798 was ratified by the United States on exactly the same day that the august body confirmed both the Phelps-Gorham Purchase and the Holland Land Company land transactions with the Senecas![15]

The creation of this first state road spurred road building in and around and through Oneida Indian country. New roads soon abounded: the Hamilton and Skaneateles Pike, the Plainfield (Otsego–Madison Counties) Pike, and the Cherry Valley Pike from Madison to Morrisville, New York. Mail coaches, stagecoaches, and teamsters carrying freight became a frequent sight on Madison County's roads.[16] Yet the impact was not just locally in central New York State.

Western New York offered even greater opportunities than the central portion of the state; however, it was controlled by more recalcitrant Indians who had less trust than their Oneida "little brothers," in the white man's words. As the key access route to the Great Lakes, powerful New Yorkers such as Peter B. Porter, Schuyler's counterpart in the west, saw the great economic potential of the region. Two goals had to be accomplished, however, before the process could go forward: (1) the establishment of a permanent peace and a boundary settlement with British Canada; and (2) the building of a transportation system, with its central focus being the construction of the Erie Canal. Only when these two aims were achieved in 1825 did Albany officials focus their full attention on ridding themselves of their former enemies, the Senecas.

PART TWO

The Seneca Country: The Holy Grail

Buffalo in 1819

Courtesy of the New York State Library, New York State Museum, and Craig Williams

CHAPTER 7

The Lake Effect

The eminent New York State historian Blake McKelvey, former city historian of Rochester, labeled the Erie Canal "the mother of cities." Indeed, the
Erie Canal did create New York's urban metropolitan corridor. At its western end was the city of Buffalo. Although not principally a canal town but a
major Great Lakes port, the city's history, nevertheless, was directly tied to
the Erie Canal. According to McKelvey, "the lake boats would not have
docked there [Buffalo], not at least in such numbers, had it not been for the
Erie Canal over which most of their cargo was shipped to eastern markets."
Consequently, the city of Buffalo developed great warehouses and giant
grain elevators to store the unloaded produce from the West until canal
traffic and market conditions allowed for its transit eastward to Albany and
southward to the emerging metropolis of New York City. Incredibly, a village of one hundred houses—all but two of which were burned by the
British in the War of 1812—became one of the premier cities of the United
States by midcentury.[1]

Buffalo's rise differed from that of other cities in New York State's metropolitan corridor. Buffalo became America's great transshipment port, a key
in the early evolution of the United States' emerging economy. Grain-laden
vessels entered the city's harbor facilities—constantly being improved and
expanded upon from the 1820s—where they unloaded and picked up a
return cargo of merchandise and emigrants seeking their fortunes in the
West. The grain was then loaded onto boats for shipment east along the Erie
Canal to the Hudson River to the ports of the Atlantic coast. Thus, the city's
emergence was the result of its superior geographic position, at the junction
of Lake Erie and the outlet to the Erie Canal, combined with its superior
financial resources and business connections to New York City, which fueled

economic expansion. Importantly, the city's rise actually stemmed early from its greater assurance that Great Lakes vessels entering Buffalo harbor could secure a return cargo. By the 1830s these cargoes also included the manufactured products of the rising textile industry of Troy–Cohoes–New York City as well.[2]

Thus, a village that was largely "isolated from the main stream of commercial activity in 1816" was to emerge as the ninth largest city in the United States by the Civil War.[3] By 1839, 14 percent of the entire American wheat crop was transshipped from Buffalo. Ten years later, the percentage of the nation's wheat and flour transshipped was 25 percent of the nation's total supply. Even with competition from railroads from 1851 onward, by 1860 Buffalo transshipped 20 percent of all wheat raised in the United States. By 1852 grain receipts totaled $15.4 million. In one forty-eight-hour period, seventy vessels alone unloaded 230,000 bushels of wheat and flour at the granaries of Buffalo.[4]

Until 1826 the village was largely a narrow strip. Less than three miles wide, it bordered the Buffalo Creek Indian Reservation. The rapid growth of Buffalo depended on its extinguishment of Indian land titles to this immense reservation that bordered the city on the east and south. The Buffalo Creek Reservation, the nucleus of Seneca territory on the Niagara Frontier, was a rectangular plot of 128 square miles, 83,557 acres, which included some of the most fertile lands of Erie County (see map 7).[5] The existence of these federally recognized Seneca lands after 1798 limited the future commercial development of the city by preventing the exploitation of its strategic access to both the western Great Lakes and to the Atlantic coast ports. In addition, Senecas and other Indian residents here were all noncitizens and, hence, not taxpayers, restricting local non-Indian efforts for development.[6]

The establishment of Buffalo as a non-Indian settlement was largely the creation of Joseph Ellicott and the Holland Land Company who, in 1803–4, developed a bold plan for a village at the confluence of the Buffalo and Niagara Rivers and Lake Erie, which he labeled "New Amsterdam," a definite ploy to win support from his Dutch investors. Thus, right from the beginning, the future of Buffalo was largely dependent on its strategic geographical position as a major transportation nexus, much like the Oneida Carrying Place in central New York.

Ellicott's elaborate plans for Buffalo received support from Erastus

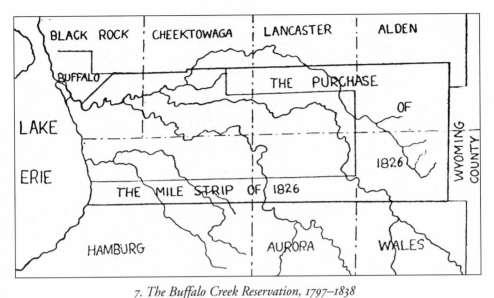

7. The Buffalo Creek Reservation, 1797–1838

Reprinted from Frederick Houghton, The History of the Buffalo Creek Reservation *(1920)*

Granger, a rising politico in western New York and a federal Indian agent for the Six Nations from 1804 to 1819. Granger, the cousin of Gideon Granger, Thomas Jefferson's postmaster general, had the right political connections to promote Ellicott's and the Holland Land Company's goals. Ellicott's political networking helped determine the location of new counties, county seats, towns, and villages in western New York. According to one historian, Ellicott even successfully negotiated a deal with the New York State Legislature "whereby the company was excluded from all school or road taxes."[7] These connections at times, however, did serve the interests of the Indians themselves. As a result of the Granger-Ellicott collaborative relationship, the Tuscarora Indians were "allowed" to purchase 4,329 acres of land, paying the Holland Land Company $13,722 for their reservation near Lewiston.[8]

It was, therefore, no coincidence that in 1810 Ellicott was appointed as one of the seven original members of the New York State Board of Canal Commissioners. For Ellicott, a genius, understood that canal building and road construction would only add to the value of the Holland Land Company holdings and make its lands more accessible and attractive to purchase by individuals (see map 8). Although frequently battling with Paul

Joseph Ellicott
Courtesy of Buffalo and Erie County Historical Society

Busti and other Holland Land Company directors about whether the company should donate lands to the state for canals and roads, Ellicott saw that if the canal were built, it would substantially increase the value of company holdings nearby many times over.[9]

In 1816 and 1817 Ellicott, joining De Witt Clinton, formed a temporary alliance with prominent citizens of Buffalo—Benjamin Caryl, Oliver Forward, Jonas Harrison, Reuben Heacock, B. W. Hopkins, Charles Townsend, and Samuel Wilkeson—countering the efforts of General Peter B. Porter who pushed Black Rock for the canal. Wilkeson, Townsend, and Forward were even willing to "pledge their individual property" to secure loans for harbor improvements to remove the sand bar and to straighten Buffalo Creek "so that it flowed westerly into the lake."[10] Importantly, it was

8. *Historic Map of Western New York Showing Seneca Indian Reservations*

Map by Joseph Ellicott and Holland Land Company (1804)

the same Oliver Forward, the United States Indian commissioner at the Treaty of 1826, who helped reduce the size of the Buffalo Creek Reservation by more than thirty-three thousand acres in a fraudulent agreement with the Senecas.[11]

From 1798 onward Ellicott envisioned the region between "Buffaloe and Tanawanta" as the future "grand emporium of the Western world."[12] His overall plan was designed to improve and form a modern harbor facility that would facilitate land sales by the Holland Land Company. He wrote Busti in May 1816, "That object has always been considered by me of primary importance to the agricultural and commercial prosperity of all those who inhabit the regions of the lake country, inasmuch as without a good safe harbor for vessels at or near the outlet of Lake Erie, from which with the lake the ingress and egress is without difficulty or detention, freight will be high in proportion to obstacles of this description vessels have to encounter." Although Ellicott saw this move as a way of furthering the mercenary interests of the Holland Land Company, he rationalized it by insisting that "general good" would result by the establishment of a "convenient and safe harbor" at the strategic eastern outlet of Lake Erie. He then elaborated on his extensive two hundred thousand dollar harbor construction project and his willingness "to unite with the enterprising citizens of Buffalo in all plans that appeared to me feasible."[13] Wisely, by May 1816 Ellicott deferred to De Witt Clinton, a fellow member of the New York State Board of Canal Commissioners, to lead the way as principal promoter of a "Grand Canal."[14] The New York State Board of Canal Commissioners reported in 1817, "It would be expedient to connect the west end of the great [Erie] canal with the water of Lake Erie, through the mouth of Buffalo creek." The report continued, "It is important to have at that end, a safe harbor, capable, without much expense, of sufficient enlargement for the accommodation of all boats and vessels, that a very extensive trade may hereafter require to enter and exchange their lading there."[15]

After the completion of the Erie Canal and its great initial success, Buffalo became the center of transshipment of goods between the lake and the canal. Increased facilities were required to accommodate the boom. According to Whitford, the "business of the canal soon reached such proportions that the great number of vessels engaged in traffic frequently congested the waterways terminating at Buffalo, causing vexations, delays, and consequent pecuniary loss to boatmen and merchants." In response, the common council of Buffalo, a city incorporated in 1831, took steps in 1833 to build new terminals and undertook plans for a new canal, the Main and Hamburg Canal, an extension of the Erie Canal. Four years later, through direct state intervention, this canal was completed. Eventually, through state, local government, and private efforts, the Clark and Skiller Canal and the Hydraulic Canal were completed as well as the Evans ship canal, the Erie basin, slips nos. 1, 2, and 3, the city ship canal, and several smaller branches of main canal channels.[16]

It is essential to note that the nucleus of Seneca territory along the Niagara Frontier was this same Buffalo Creek, a rectangular plot of 128 square miles, 83,557 acres, "the most fertile and most delightful of all the lands of Erie County," surveyed and laid out as a reservation in 1798 under the Treaty of Big Tree. Well watered by creeks—Buffalo Creek, Cayuga, and Cazenovia—the Seneca world was a rich forest-covered wilderness that provided for the needs of numerous refugees from the American Revolution. These included not only Senecas but all of the other Six Nations and other non-Iroquoian Indians. In 1792 Pickering noted that 331 Senecas were at Buffalo Creek, along with 215 Onondagas and 22 Cayugas.[17] By 1819, 686 Senecas, nearly 30 percent of all Senecas, resided at Buffalo Creek while 365 were at Tonawanda, 389 at Cattaraugus, 456 on the Genesee Reservations, and 597 at Allegany.[18]

The history of this reservation, which stretched on the west to only a few short blocks from the harbor of Buffalo, is central to Iroquois existence, not just Seneca life, after the American Revolution. When American Generals Sullivan and Clinton burned the Senecas' ancestral homes in the Genesee valley in a scorched-earth campaign ordered by George Washington in 1779, the Senecas fled westward to the safety of their British allies at Fort Niagara and other fortifications along the Niagara River. By the end of the American Revolution approximately two thousand Indians were living along the banks of Buffalo Creek, now in the present-day city of Buffalo, and along the Niagara River. The Senecas were joined by many Onondagas after American General Goose Van Shaiack burned their ten villages in central New York during the same conflict. Both Onondagas and Cayugas came in numbers when New York State began to use their territory as military bounty lands for payment of veterans after the American Revolution and after the "sale" of the Cayuga reservation on the northern end of Cayuga Lake in 1807, an action that was promoted by individual and state land, salt, and transportation interests.

Thus, Buffalo Creek, Seneca territory, became a refuge haven for displaced peoples, much like Iroquoia in the upper Susquehanna region, the Chenango valley, had been a half-century earlier for other Iroquoian and non-Iroquoian tribes: Tuscarora, Tutelo, Conoy, Munsee, Nanticoke, and so on.[19] Indeed, the Great Peace and Power, the Iroquois League, had from the seventeenth century operated in this manner to provide protection, secure adoptees and military allies, and establish a buffer against white settlement pressures.[20] While Joseph Brant was resurrecting the Iroquois Confederacy under Mohawk aegis at the Haldimand Patent along the Grand River in Lower Canada, the Senecas became the protectors of the League tradition in New York. The Confederacy's council fire was largely maintained throughout much of this period by Captain Cold (Ut-ha-wah), an Onondaga chief residing at Buffalo Creek. Importantly, Buffalo Creek became the ritual center of Iroquoian ceremonialism where the sacred wampum belts from the Onondagas were housed for their protection after the "whirlwind," the Seneca designation for what befell them in the American Revolution.[21]

Just as Buffalo Village was a planned site, one which was carefully selected by Joseph Ellicott, the Senecas reserving lands along Buffalo Creek at the Treaty of Big Tree in 1797 was also no accident. From the beginning the evolution of this multiethnic Indian community was purposeful. The reservation was well watered with the Buffalo, Cayuga, Cazenovia, and Seneca Creeks flowing through the communities, which, along with Lake Erie, provided limitless fishing possibilities. The land was also rich in white-tailed deer. Local black squirrel and pigeon, delicacies prized by the Iroquois, made their ways into Indian kettles.[22]

The soil of Buffalo Creek Reservation was especially fertile. The Indians cleared lands parallel to the creeks and raised traditional crops such as corn, beans, and squash, and other foodstuffs such as potatoes, oats, and rye. Gerald T. Hopkins, a Quaker representative visiting Buffalo Creek in 1804, described the land on which Red Jacket and Farmer's Brother was settled as "of superior quality" and stated that the Indians were making substantial "progress in agriculture, living in tolerable log houses, and have a number of cattle, horses and hogs." He observed that he had seen "many of them at work; they were preparing the ground for the plough by rolling logs, taking up stumps, etc."[23]

Captain Cold. Portrait by William Wilgus, 1838.
Courtesy of the Yale University Art Gallery

The reservation, before being overrun with trespassers who timber stripped, was a low plain forest world that included basswood, beech, hickory, maple, and walnut although giant hemlock and pine dominated. The abundance of basswood along the banks of the creeks provided the primary source for Iroquois False Faces used by their medicine societies at the Midwinter and other ceremonial times. Indeed, the reservation was designed *Dosyoua oo-sah Tiyoos-yo-wa,* meaning "at the place that abounds with basswood." The richness of wood supplies also provided the Indians with plentiful materials for the building of log cabins, which dotted the reservation.[24]

The Iroquois at Buffalo Creek lived in distinct neighborhoods, establishing separate settlements from the 1780s onward. They were largely concentrations of populations and dwellings along clearings, "scattered on the flats and terraces of the creeks." The dwellings were largely huts originally, followed by a plethora of log cabins and some frame houses, suggesting the emergence of class distinctions within the community.[25]

The first settlement at Buffalo Creek occurred in 1780 with the arrival of the Seneca chief, Old Smoke, his family and followers. The oldest village, referred to as the Seneca Village, was located at Seneca Street, Indian Church Road, and Buffam Street in what is today's town of West Seneca. Seneca leaders Farmer's Brother, Red Jacket, and Young King resided here. As early as the 1780s, eight other clusters of Seneca population were noted on this reservation. Later, perhaps as a result of the dispossession of the Senecas from Little Beard's Town in 1802, other villages or concentrations of populations developed. Jack Berry, a Seneca and interpreter from Little Beard's Town, established a settlement, "Jackstown," at Gardenville, New York; this and nearby Seneca population concentrations in "Turkeytown" and in Blossom, Elma, and East Elma were later the political base of Seneca chief Big Kettle, a leader of the Pagan Party in the 1820s to the 1840s.[26]

In Seneca Village the Indians had constructed a log council house before the War of 1812, about one hundred yards north of Little and Archer Streets in South Buffalo. By the 1820s two mission houses, a school, and a church were built in this main Seneca village, but, by that time, the village was largely divided into two neighborhoods: the "Pagan Village," or Red Jacket's Village; and the "Christian Village" along Pollard's Road headed by Captain Pollard and later Seneca chiefs Young King and Seneca White.[27]

As a refugee haven, other non-Senecas sought protection in Seneca territory. By the 1780s two Onondaga population clusters were at Buffalo Creek.

The Onondagas established their neighborhoods along Cazenovia Creek, in today's West Seneca, largely under the leadership of Chief Big Sky. By 1791 twenty-eight cabins were noted at the ford, one mile from Lower Ebenezer, and the Onondagas' council house was located on the east bank of the creek.[28] The Cayugas formed their community on the northern edge of the reservation along William Street and Cayuga Road in today's city of Buffalo.[29] Although the largest number of Indians were always Seneca, Onondaga, and Cayuga, refugees from Oneida, Munsee, Mahican, and many other Iroquoian and non-Iroquoian peoples made this reservation a true multicultural world. Unfortunately, this experiment in intercultural relations was a short-lived phenomenon because Buffalo was directly in the path of America's transportation revolution. While the Indians hoped to resurrect the Iroquois Great Law of Peace and Power in Seneca Country, Albany and Washington policymakers sought this strategic area as essential for both America's economic progress and national security at the same time. Thus, the "lake effect"—developing and expanding the village of Buffalo into the great transshipment center of the United States and, with it, the resolution of Anglo-American tensions—was to be the factor that drove both United States and New York State policies toward the Senecas in the first four decades of the nineteenth century.

The great architects of the Empire State—George Clinton, De Witt Clinton, John Jay, and Philip Schuyler—all saw New York's interests rising in the vacuum caused by the decline of Seneca power. In the 1780s state officials' interest in the engineering proposals of Christopher Colles for road and canal building to transform the "wastelands" of the western regions is indicative of this thrust. Before this could be put into effect, the Indian land titles, especially at Buffalo Creek which is the heart of part 2 of this book, had to be extinguished and the British threat in the northern and western regions of the state had to be removed. Although extinguishing Oneida title was the first step, the extinguishment of Seneca title was the second major piece of the puzzle.

The Iroquois world at Buffalo Creek was stirred by two major religious events from 1799 onward: (1) the visions and preaching of Handsome Lake and (2) the establishment of Protestant missions in their midst during the same period. The *Gaiwiio* soon spread to Buffalo Creek. By 1801 and after, Handsome Lake came annually to preach there. Although his message was to have an influence there, it was received by a smaller percentage than at

Allegany, Cattaraugus, and Tonawanda. His message of abstinence was undermined by several factors. Because of the proximity of Buffalo to the reservation and the ever-existing temptation of white settlers to sell whiskey to the Indians, alcoholism was to be more rampant there than at most other Seneca reservations—with the possible exception of those on the Genesee River. Even two of the more prominent Seneca chiefs at Buffalo Creek—Red Jacket and Young King—were frequently seen drunk and were viewed by community members as alcohol abusers. Perhaps hypocritically, Red Jacket preached abstinence. A political opponent of Handsome Lake, Red Jacket, according to Anthony F. C. Wallace, nevertheless, "supported a similar program of religious conservatism coupled with secular programs."[30]

The *Gaiwiio* was not the only new religious message accepted by Indians at Buffalo Creek in this period. In the early years of the nineteenth century the New York Missionary Society attempted to establish a school and mission at Buffalo Creek but with no success until 1811. By 1820 ministers of various denominations, such as Presbyterians and Baptists, preached on the reservation with a permanent mission school established by the New York Missionary Society. Quakers also established a presence here and remained until the period of removal. In 1821 the United Foreign Missionary Society sent a missionary to the reservation who eventually set up a mission church and school that lasted until the Indian removal from Buffalo Creek in the mid-1840s to Cattaraugus. This United Foreign Missionary Society joined the American Board of Commissioners for Foreign Missions in 1826, which ultimately came under the aegis of the Presbyterian Board of Missions.[31]

In 1811 Jabez Hyde, a teacher and agent of the New York Missionary Society, established the first school at the Buffalo Creek Reservation.[32] By 1817 the school consisted of thirty students. Hyde used a translator to teach and to get his students to write "simple discourses on parts of the Bible."[33] Although his efforts were successful in winning over key Senecas—including Captain Pollard—to allow his missionary efforts, he was replaced in 1821 by Thompson S. Harris, a missionary described as "tactless, fussy and officious, with little common sense, sympathy for his charges or fitness for his work."[34] Despite his limitations the membership of the Seneca Mission Church grew surprisingly, totaling forty-six congregants by 1828, including Seneca White. On August 19, 1829, the congregation dedicated their new church building. The following year the unpleasant Harris finally left his post.[35]

On November 9, 1831, Asher Wright assumed the directorship of the Seneca Mission. In sharp contrast to Harris, Wright was neither distant nor rude to his charges. He faithfully served the Senecas for fifteen years at Buffalo Creek until their removal to Cattaraugus in 1846 and continued as their Presbyterian missionary until his death in 1875. Wright and his wife Laura devised a writing system for the Seneca language, edited a newspaper—the *Mental Elevator*—in the Seneca language, and published the first hymnal in the Seneca language. Throughout his extraordinary life as a cleric he served as an educator, key adviser, scribe, important conduit between the Indians and the white establishment, and even as a determined champion of Seneca Indians and their lands.[36]

Despite tensions between Pagan and Christian followers, it would be simplistic at best to view Seneca divisions as simply originating from religious differences. Viewing the Christians as more willing to sign treaties, sell lands, or move west, and the Pagans as the opposite does not altogether conform to the reality of the 1820s and 1830s. Neither group held the moral high ground. Indeed, the Christian Party was blamed for the Seneca Treaty of 1826, whereas some of the traditional chiefs and warriors that later made up the Old Chiefs Party were blamed for the Treaty of 1838. Moreover, white missionaries such as Jabez Hyde and Asher Wright were at times greater defenders of Seneca land rights than were some of the Senecas themselves. With growing economic dependence and the payment of government annuities to certain select chiefs, the situation was ripe for manipulation and fraud. Into this setting came the major enemy of the Senecas, the Ogden Land Company, intent on separating the Indians from their lands from Buffalo eastward to the Genesee country. The Ogden Land Company was founded in 1810 by David A. Ogden, former New York City counsel to the Holland Land Company.

Pressures to relocate and to concentrate Indian populations in the state or to remove the Indians altogether from the state to various destinations in the West steadily increased. Even before the War of 1812, Robert Troup, the prominent attorney and one of the principal partners of the Ogden Land Company, was advocating Indian removal from New York to Arkansas or to a "spot in the Northwestern Territory, which the Government will be likely to grant them."[37]

Troup's background is most revealing. At the turn of the nineteenth century, he had been an early advocate of improving navigation on the Mohawk

River, becoming involved in the activities of the Western Inland Lock Navigation Company. He had also been an agent for the immense Pulteney landholdings. By 1816–17 Troup was allied with Canandaigua attorneys-entrepreneurs John Greig—another agent of the Ogden Land Company—and Gideon Granger, in promoting the building of the western section of the Erie Canal.[38]

For the next three decades the Ogden Land Company lobbied for this goal. Even before the fighting ended during the War of 1812, David A. Ogden wrote that the Indians "in the vicinity of Buffalo" had become "more depraved than any others to be found in the U.S." and that their situation "has become offensive to common decency." Ogden urged that the sale of their reservations be effected and that all the Iroquois should be concentrated on the Allegany Indian Reservation.[39]

In 1819 Ogden elaborated on his ideas in a letter to Secretary of War John C. Calhoun. Ogden insisted that the lands at Allegany were "sufficiently extensive as to all the purposes of cultivation for the accommodation of all the Seneca Indians." He pointed out that of all the Seneca reservations the Allegany was the "least liable to interference from the White Settlements, and must remain so, as the Allegany Mountains on each side are not calculated for improvement or cultivation and will present a constant barrier between the two populations."[40]

Ogden also petitioned President Monroe in 1819, once again seeking removal of the Senecas from New York State. Calling the Indians half civilized and half savage and completely debased in the vicinity of Buffalo, Ogden urged removal for the Indians' benefit and one "demanded by public sentiments." He insisted that the Indians were "becoming a heavy incumbrance, retarding the progress of cultivation and improvements and detracting from the public resources and prosperity." Despite their limited size, "little more than 2,000 souls," their extensive tracts totaled "220,000 acres of rich lands capable of giving support in profuse abundance to 50,000 of our citizens"; there "not one acre in a hundred" was cultivated or improved by the Indians. Because their lands were not taxed nor do the Indians "bear any part of the burden of roads and other objects of local improvement," Ogden insisted, they were in the way of the progress of the nation and even an impediment to national security: "These extensive tracts being situated principally along our western frontier, the acquisition of lands and [a] hardy white population in that quarter would appear moreover to be an object of immense importance to the United States." Because of their allegedly degraded condition, especially those in the vicinity of Buffalo, Ogden observed the Senecas were affecting "materially the growth of that important place."[41]

Ogden and his associates used a wide variety of methods to further their company's agenda. After the War of 1812, they discredited the missionary Jabez Hyde for his support of the Senecas' antiremoval stance. They also promoted the ambitions of Jasper Parrish as superintendent to the Six Nations when Erastus Granger's tenure came to an end; Parrish, in the pay of the company, later facilitated the transfer of Seneca lands to the Ogdens in 1826. In the same year as Ogden's petition to President Monroe, the land speculator, aware that Buffalo would probably be chosen as the western terminus of the Erie Canal after a preliminary determination in 1817, started buying up lands lying south and west of the Buffalo Creek Reservation to Lake Erie, anticipating both canal and harbor development.[42]

The Senecas faced other pressures besides the Ogdens' constant lobbying efforts. Senecas constantly complained about white trespassers and timber strippers on the reservation. When the Seneca chief Tommy Jemmy, a follower of the *Gaiwiio*, had carried out a tribal execution of Caughquautaugh, who had been convicted of witchcraft in 1821, local Buffalo residents reacted with horror at Seneca justice and demanded that Jemmy be punished, creating tensions between Indian and white in western New York. Local Buffalonians wanted Jemmy punished as a cold-blooded killer. Yet the Senecas, especially Red Jacket, defended the action as being tribal custom and tribal legal jurisdiction. The New York State Legislature then passed a law declaring that state courts had absolute jurisdiction over the reservations. Although Jemmy was eventually pardoned, the issue of state jurisdiction over Indians was raised for the first time, adding increased pressures on the Seneca polity.[43] The anti-Indian publicity surrounding the incident furthered the white perception of an overall negative Indian image—that the Indians were "superstitious savages" who practiced "antiquated" and "pagan" rituals.

Despite these negative portrayals of the Senecas in the period more perspicacious observers lauded the Senecas and understood the struggle they were facing. To George Catlin there were "no better people to be found than the Seneca Indians—none that are by Nature more talented and ingenious, nor any that would be better neighbors if the arts and abuses of white men and whiskey could be kept away from them." Despite Ogden's views, Catlin observed: "They have laid down their hunting habits and become efficient farmers, raising fine crops of corn, a great abundance of hogs, cattle, horses, and other necessaries and luxuries of life."[44] Catlin, the soothsayer, then accurately predicted the future for Red Jacket, whom he saw as a pathetic figure riddled by alcohol, and for the Seneca people: "Poor old chief—not all the eloquence of Cicero and Demosthenes would be able to avert the calamity, that awaits his declining nation—to resist the despoiling hand of mercenary white man, that opens and spreads liberally, but to entrap the unwary and ignorant within its withering grasp."[45]

The Senecas did not stand idly by and take the insults of David A. Ogden nor did they simply agree to the company's plans for Indian reconcentration and removal. Red Jacket insisted that a treaty made by one president is binding upon subsequent presidents. He frequently raised the guarantee of federal protection under the Pickering Treaty of 1794 as a defense against removal. Red Jacket, in a speech at a council at Buffalo Creek in July 1819, was eloquent in using this defense, not so subtly referring to the nefarious activities of the Ogdens: "At the close of that treaty it was agreed . . . that if any difficulties should occur, if any Monster should come across the chain of friendship, that we should unite as one to remove those difficulties, to drive away the Monster, we will, in such case, go hand in hand and continue the chain."[46] He continued by challenging David A. Ogden's racist assumptions about the Indians and questioned the land speculator's definition of progress and the government's right to tax the Indians:[47]

Brother. You told us, where the Country was surrounded by whites, and in possession of Indians, when it was unproductive, not liable to taxes, nor to make roads and other improvements, it was time to change. As for taxing of Indians, this is extraordinary. This was never heard of before, since the first settlement of America. The land is ours, by the gift of the Great Spirit. How can you tax it? We can make such roads, as we want, and we did so, when the land was all ours.

Brother. We are improving in our condition. See these large flocks of cattle! Look at those fences! These things were not seen formerly. We are surrounded by the whites, from them we can readily obtain cattle, and by what we procure from them we enlarge our improvements. Now that we are confined to small Reservations, we can readily make the roads we want, and assist in making public improvements. Look back to the first settlement of this Country, and after that, look at our present condition under the U.S. Under the British Govt. we continued our growth in numbers and in strength. What has now become of the Indians who extended themselves to the salt waters? They have become few and are driven back, while you

Red Jacket. Portrait by Robert W. Weir, 1828.

Courtesy of the New-York Historical Society

have been growing numerous and powerful. This land is ours from the God of Heaven. It was given us; we cannot make land. Driven back and reduced as we now are, you still wish to cramp us more & more. These lands are ours, given by the Heavenly Father. You tell us of a preemptive right; such men you say own one Reservation, such another. But they are all ours, ours from the top to the bottom. If Mr. Ogden should tell us he has come from Heaven, with the flesh on his bones as he now is, & say that the Heavenly Father has given him a title, we might then believe him.

Red Jacket then questioned Ogden's plan to concentrate the Indians at Allegany, a move that Ogden indicated was supported by President Monroe. The Seneca orator then insisted that Seneca treaties never provided for it and questioned whether the president had actually supported the move. Then the Seneca even stated that the president "must have been disordered in mind" to have ordered all the Indians' removal to Allegany.[48]

David A. Ogden's successors, Thomas L. Ogden and Joseph Fellows, continued their predecessor's efforts at extinguishing Seneca land titles but with a less confrontational style and with more success. They abandoned the option of concentrating the Indians in Allegany, but the company's agents, nevertheless, still adamantly advocated the wholesale removal of Indians from the state. After their failure to secure concentration or removal of the Indians in 1819, the agents of the land companies tried a new approach in the 1820s. They now tried direct cooperation with various missionary societies and governmental officials. They pushed the missionary emphasis on conversion, civilization, and education and presented these objectives as best served through Indian removal to a permanent abode in the West, much like the course pursued by the Indian missionary Eleazer Williams, who led the Oneidas to Wisconsin in this period and who was frequently cited as a model for other Indians.

On June 10, 1822, Ogden through attorney Troup assured Secretary of War Calhoun that he and other "proprietors of the Reservation"—a constant ploy in the letters that played down the Ogdens' speculative appetite—had no intention of obstructing the course of federal Indian policies "or to violate the rights, or to disturb the tranquillity of the Indians."[49] In a coordinated campaign, Troup, Thomas L. Ogden, and Peter Porter, operating in tandem for the interests of the company, castigated the Pagan Party and especially Red Jacket for opposing the government's "civilization" program, opposing missionaries, and refusing to sell more Seneca lands. Porter dubbed Red Jacket "a man of great talents, and a great intriguer," whose criticisms against Indian agent Jasper Parrish and interpreter Horatio Jones were unfounded and should be ignored.[50]

By 1823 the Ogden Land Company had indeed won with honey what it could not win with confrontation. Secretary of War Calhoun had agreed to allow them to send surveyors onto and to make a preliminary survey of the company's potential lands at Buffalo Creek, which the South Carolinian considered "as perfectly harmless to the rights and interests of the Seneca Nation, while it will be advantageous to the proprietors." Thus, even before treaty negotiations for the sale of Buffalo Creek, the Ogden Land Company was allowed to proceed with their survey "without further interruption."[51] The next year, Commissioner of Indian Affairs Thomas L. McKenney formally declared Red Jacket and his "pagan" followers "hostile to the interests and prosperity of the Six Nations" and further that no official federal government recognition be accorded them.[52] Thus, by 1825 there was a conscious governmental policy of undermining Red Jacket's leadership, which promoted the interests of private investors seeking to chip away at the still vast Seneca Indian land base in western New York.

To both private investors and New York State and federal leaders the expansion of Buffalo harbor (and the city as a whole) was only one major element of their formula to expand the Empire State to the West. Three other essential ingredients were necessary to encourage population growth and commercial development. The first element was a resolution of Anglo-American tensions. This was to come only after a bloody and destructive war on the Niagara Frontier. The second was to fix the international boundary to limit continued friction between the two countries. Under Article VI of the Treaty of Ghent of 1814, the Lake Erie–Niagara River–Lake Ontario–St. Lawrence River corridor was to be resolved by a Joint Mixed Boundary Commission, one which completed its work in 1822. Third, the route for the western section of the Erie Canal had to be finalized and its construction completed, essential components for both commercial and defensive considerations. Large-scale population moving into the western part of the state would lead to economic development and secure the territory against any and all threats from the British Lion in Canada.

In this thinking, rapid white settlement in the region based on commercial and agricultural attractiveness and the end of the British threat would ultimately and "inevitably" lead to the rise of the Empire State and, with it, the eventual removal of the Senecas. Before the final bell could be sounded in the making of western New York, private and state interests had to contend with the Senecas, who still controlled the rich farmlands eastward on the Genesee and still held forth at the great trade nexus between two of the eastern Great Lakes. To carry out private and public officials' definition of progress the Seneca world had to be undermined. No more determined representative of private land interests and Albany officialdom in this period was there than the Bashaw of Black Rock, Peter Buell Porter, who shaped the future of western New York and, with it, the Senecas.

CHAPTER 8

The Bashaw of the Border

Peter Buell Porter was the most influential white man in western New York dealing with the Iroquois in the first three decades of the nineteenth century. He was also one of the great proponents of transportation, namely, road and canal building and national defense. Much like Philip Schuyler in Oneida country, Porter on the surface presented himself as a friend of the Indians and served as the commander of Indian troops in wartime; however, in reality, he was one of the major state officials dispossessing the Senecas and, with it, one of the greatest promoters of the rise of western New York.

Born in Salisbury, Connecticut, on August 14, 1744, Peter Buell Porter was the son of Colonel Joshua Porter, a leading land speculator of southern New England. His older brother Augustus was an associate of Oliver Phelps in his land-jobbing activities and later served as a surveyor and agent for the Holland Land Company from the late 1790s onward. After Peter Buell Porter's graduation from Yale University in 1791, he attended law school at Litchfield, Connecticut. Subsequently, he moved to Canandaigua, New York, where he practiced law in this frontier community and entered local politics. Between 1797 and 1805 he held the position of clerk and, for one term, state assemblyman from Ontario County, which at the time included most of western New York. Although beginning his career as a Democratic Republican allied to Aaron Burr's Tammany Hall machine, Porter was the classic political opportunist, shifting affiliations frequently—from Burrite faction of the Democratic Republicans, to Clay "War Hawk," to Van Buren Bucktail, back to Democratic Republican during John Quincy Adams's administration, and then back to Clay and the Whigs.[1]

In 1810 Porter moved to Black Rock, then a village at the mouth of the eastern branch of the Niagara River three miles north of the village of

Peter B. Porter

Courtesy of the Buffalo and Erie County Historical Society

Buffalo. In the same year he was appointed by Governor Daniel D. Tompkins as one of the seven original members of the New York State Board of Canal Commissioners.[2] Because of the strategic location of the harbor at Black Rock, partly in Lake Erie and partly in the Niagara River, Porter lobbied for the village to become the end terminus for the planned Erie Canal. His arguments were aided by his gift for oratory, his boundless confidence, and his clear leadership skills. At Black Rock Porter established his firm—Porter, Barton and Company—which soon held a monopoly in the transportation business in the portage area below Niagara Falls and Fort Schlosser above the falls. His firm also became the dominant force in the salt trade from central New York to Lake Ontario and throughout western New York. His salt depot at Black Rock was vast, and his firm handled from fifteen thousand to eighteen thousand barrels of salt until the British destroyed the operation during the War of 1812.[3]

De Witt Clinton described the company's operations in 1810:[4]

The portage has been leased from the State by Porter, Barton and Co., and the principal article conveyed is salt; three yoke of oxen can carry twelve barrels of salt, and make one trip a day. There are twenty-two teams of various kinds employed in this portage. The distance from here to the falls is seven miles; to the outlet of the river into Lake Ontario, seven and a half miles. The whole length of [the] Niagara river, or rather the distance from lake to lake is thirty miles. There is a ferry between this place and Queenstown [British Canada], and the width of the river is one quarter of a mile.

Even before the Erie Canal, the salt, which largely came from the environs of the present city of Syracuse, was carried by bateau along the Seneca, Oswego, and Oneida Rivers to Three-River Point, near Cicero, and thence to Oswego. At Oswego, it was transshipped to larger lake craft to make the 160-mile water passage to Niagara. Porter and Barton had a monopoly at the Niagara portage between the lakes, so the company made a fortune before the War of 1812 because two-thirds of the salt exported from Oswego in 1810 made its way to consumers in the Ohio River valley.

Black Rock, the company's headquarters, was only a short distance from Lewiston, New York, the end terminus of the famous Ridge Road, the natural transportation link to the Genesee River valley. With the discovery of other salt supplies around the Montezuma marsh and near the Cayuga Reservation in the eastern Genesee region, Ridge Road became antiquated, with mule team traffic, and other roads and turnpikes needed to be developed. The Porter brothers first pushed the development of a toll road between Utica and Canandaigua and sought state subsidies for the project. Subsequently, the Porters fervently promoted the development of a canal to link eastern and western New York. Hence, it was no accident that in 1810 Porter was appointed as one of the original members of the New York State Board of Canal Commissioners.[5]

Porter's activities were also in land speculation. Because of his brother Augustus's early ties to the Holland Land Company, which at times hired him to undertake their surveys, Peter B. Porter had advanced knowledge and got in at the ground level on land purchases and on the company's plans for road development. When the Holland Land Company sold its preemptive right to Seneca lands to David A. Ogden in 1810, Porter soon became an associate of the new firm, the Ogden Land Company, and remained tied to its operations for the next fifteen years.

Before the War of 1812, Black Rock had largely outdistanced its rival Buffalo. Unlike Buffalo, the harbor at Black Rock was not impeded by sand bars, and dredging was not required to improve its existing natural advantages; consequently, the village had grown as the principal harbor at the eastern end of Lake Erie. By 1811 the New York State Assembly had designated Black Rock as the port of entry for the eastern end of Lake Erie during the navigation season. Yet its future was never completely secure because of the ever-existing presence of British forces close by, the ill-defined international boundary, and the existing Seneca claims to the islands in the Niagara River, most notably Grand Island, the massive land mass that divided the Niagara River into eastern and western branches and served as a buffer with British Canada. In the end it was none of these factors—all overcome by Porter's ability—that led to Black Rock's demise, but the frontier boom town's physical limitations: seven-knot currents in the Niagara River; crippling winter ice jams that choked the neck of the river; and dangers caused by frequent fog. By April 1853 the village of Black Rock, the former rival of Buffalo, was annexed by the city of Buffalo and disappeared as a separate entity. Thus, although Porter was able to deal with both the British and the Iroquois successfully from 1814 onward, he could never deal with the "lake effect," namely, the vicissitudes of western New York's climate and weather conditions.[6]

Porter understood that for Black Rock to emerge as the great metropolis of western New York, as the great depot of a future Erie Canal, it needed to develop its strategic position at the mouth of the eastern branch of the Niagara River. He sincerely believed that by acquiring the adjacent Indian-claimed islands in the Niagara River and by finally ending conflict with British Canada, the village would have a chance to rise to greatness. Before he could acquire these islands by purchase from the Senecas, the United States and Great Britain found themselves pitted in another major conflict that sent war scares all along the Niagara frontier (see map 9).

From 1809 to 1813 Porter served in Congress. There he promoted the interests of transportation, unsuccessfully advocating federal moneys for roads, canals, and other internal improvements. It was during his two-term

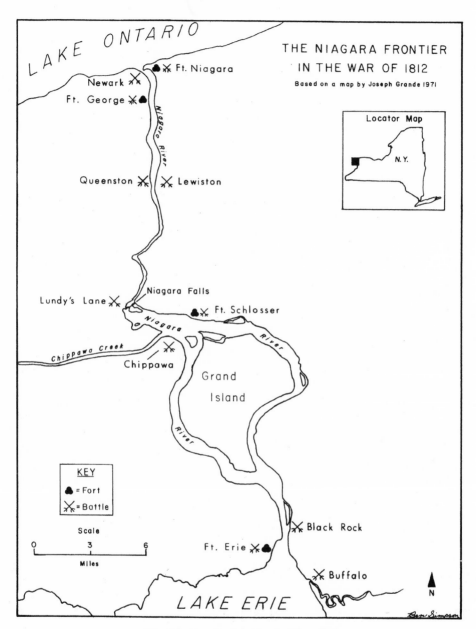

9. The Niagara Frontier in the War of 1812

Original map by Ben Simpson

congressional career that he became a leader of the "War Hawks," condemning British policies, especially their Orders in Council, which had pushed
the United States to employ the embargo, nonintercourse, and nonimporta-
tion acts to ensure its sovereignty and its rights to freedom of the seas. He
also condemned British impressment of American seamen into the British
navy; and British actions stirring up the Indians on the Great Lakes–Ohio
valley frontier. On November 29, 1811, Porter's House Committee on
Foreign Relations, less than three weeks after the Battle of Tippecanoe,
reported that the time had come when the United States "must now tamely
and quietly submit, or we must resist by those means which God has placed
within our reach." Hence, the leading political voice of western New York's
interests, an area that bordered British Canada, was now calling for armed
action. Besides, twisting the British lion's tail was always a successful political tactic that won votes for aspiring American politicians in non-Federalist
districts. For New York State to arise as a major force in the new nation, its
borders had to be secure. Porter's goal of making Black Rock and the
Niagara region as a whole a major center of commerce could be achieved
only by bringing permanent peace one way or another to the New York
frontier.

Porter, who did not seek reelection to Congress in the elections of 1812,
entered military service, where he distinguished himself and furthered his
political career. He became quartermaster-general of New York, serving in
the militia. In 1813 he was commissioned a brigadier general and authorized
by General John Armstrong, the American secretary of war, to raise a
brigade of volunteers and to merge them with a corps of Iroquois Indians.
Armstrong's response was conditioned by the fact that New York was one of
the most exposed fronts of the war and the state's officials were in panic,
faced with far superior British forces along a vast Canadian frontier boundary, inadequate roads to transport troops, and British control of the Great
Lakes.[7]

Despite opposition led by the followers of Handsome Lake against joining in another white man's war and attempts by the Six Nations on both
sides of the United States–British Canadian boundary to resolve differences
in council, the Senecas in New York joined the American side during the
War of 1812. In June 1812 the British and their Canadian Mohawk allies from
the Six Nations Reserve were reported to have taken possession of Grand
Island. The Senecas, seeing the islands in the Niagara River as their proper-

ty, debated their options. Red Jacket and Little Billy now urged Seneca participation on the American side.[8] Anthropologist Arthur C. Parker has claimed that Senecas of Neutral Indian Nation ancestry at that time also urged Iroquois alliance with the Americans because it meant not only war against the British and their allied Indians but also "it meant the defence of the graves of their [Neutral] forefathers" on Grand Island.[9]

Soon, through Porter's efforts, the Americans offered commissions to Farmer's Brother, an octogenarian and Seneca chief, and to Young Cornplanter, Henry O'Bail, the son of the famous Allegany Seneca chief. The Americans awarded commissions to at least sixteen other Senecas. In all six hundred Iroquois, not just Senecas, served the Americans in the War of 1812, with four hundred Iroquois, mostly Seneca, specifically assigned to the Niagara frontier and largely under General Porter's command.[10] The Senecas who served were not only racially distinct and had their own officers, such as Young King and Captain Pollard, but were also set apart as the Indian corps, often with very distinctive uniforms.[11]

After the British, with upward of four hundred men, crossed the Niagara River and sacked and burned Black Rock in July 1813, they proceeded south to Buffalo. Porter regrouped the American forces, including one hundred Indian troops, and helped drive the British back across the Niagara River. Porter, going against orders, then began a series of unauthorized incursions into Canada that quickly won him fame in local political circles as the hero of the Niagara frontier. In July 1814 General Jacob Brown and his United States force of 3,550 regulars, volunteers, and allied Indian warriors from New York, New Jersey, Pennsylvania, and New England, crossed the Niagara River and began a major assault on British Canada. On July 5, Brown's forces, in which Porter's contingent excelled, won a brilliant victory at the Battle of Chippawa against a British contingent that included Senecas and other Iroquois from the Six Nations Reserve along the Grand River. On the battlefield Porter's corps of Indians suffered one of the heavier casualty rates: nine were killed, four severely injured, four wounded, and ten were missing in action. Two days after the Battle of Chippawa, Porter led a force that helped recapture Fort George. In September 1814 Porter's men helped raise the siege of Fort Erie, later resulting in his promotion to major general and a special citation by Congress.[12]

By this time the pro-American Senecas had been joined by a contingent of Tuscaroras led by Solomon Longboard, who found their reservation along the Niagara River in the immediate path of the British invasion route into New York.[13] It should be noted that it was Porter's specific role to win support, especially from the Seneca at Buffalo Creek and the Tuscarora at Lewiston. Yet Iroquois support waned. Despite their initial participation in the war effort, Red Jacket and other Seneca leaders apparently cooled on participation with the Americans once the immediate threat to Seneca territory ended.[14] This was not to be the last time that Porter was to be frustrated by Red Jacket's actions. In the next fifteen years the great Seneca orator was to become Porter's great nemesis.

After the conclusion of the War of 1812, much of General Porter's attention was focused on rebuilding the devastated Niagara frontier, promoting the development of the Erie Canal, and fixing the international boundary between the United States and British Canada. As the great statesman-hero of the Niagara frontier with close ties to national leaders such as Henry Clay, Porter continued to dabble in politics, being reelected to Congress in 1814 and running unsuccessfully against De Witt Clinton for the governorship of New York State in 1817. A second defeat for Porter occurred in the same year when Buffalo was chosen as the western terminus of the Erie Canal instead of Porter's Black Rock, a decision that was not finalized until a meeting at the Eagle Tavern in Buffalo in 1822. Thus, for a five-year period, Porter had pressed on with his campaign to make Black Rock the seat of commerce of western New York. It was also precisely at this time, despite his earlier collaboration with the Iroquois during the War of 1812, that Porter increasingly became an advocate for the concentration of Iroquois away from the state's borders and even for total Indian removal from New York State. In this regard he allied himself politically and economically with David A. Ogden of the Ogden Land Company.

Porter's grand design for western New York went well beyond the village of Black Rock. For the hamlet to guarantee its future security, Porter believed, Indian-claimed lands in the Niagara River had to be extinguished through negotiations and the international boundary with Great Britain had to be set finally. Central to both concerns was Grand Island, the invasion route during the War of 1812 and the largest of several Seneca-claimed islands in the Niagara River. In 1810 De Witt Clinton wrote in his private canal journal:[15] "Grand Island is in our [United States] jurisdiction, and it contains 23,000 acres [in actuality 17,386 acres]. The Indian right is not extinguished, and the Indians will not tolerate any intrusions or trespassers on it. It is full of deer, owing to the absence of wolves and settlers. It is about twelve miles long, and its greatest breadth is six miles."

Grand Island and the other islands in the Niagara River have been associated with Seneca Indian history since the seventeenth century. Although centered from Canandaigua Lake westward to the Genesee country before Euroamerican contact, the Senecas expanded their influence and territory well westward and southward in the middle decades of the seventeenth century. Between the late 1630s and the mid-1670s they were able to expand their territory perhaps as much as threefold, defeating and absorbing other Iroquoian peoples. In 1638 they defeated the Wenros, who controlled the territory directly west of the Genesee River to the Niagara River; in 1651, they defeated the Neutrals who occupied Grand Island and other islands in the Niagara River; and in 1657, they defeated the Erie who occupied lands south of the present city of Buffalo and lands along Lake Erie.[16] In defeating these and other Indian communities, they absorbed these diverse peoples through an elaborate adoption process into a Seneca reality.

From the end of the seventeenth century right through the French and Indian War (Seven Years War), the entire Niagara River region was occupied by Senecas, mostly in temporary fishing and hunting camps. Although the Seneca resisted and opposed the growing European presence at nearby Fort Niagara at Youngstown, New York, they increasingly became dependent on this trade. According to ethnohistorian Donald H. Kent, the Senecas filled the vacuum caused by the defeat of these three Indian groups; located a temporary village at the mouth of the Niagara River; negotiated with both the French and English in this vicinity; worked in the employ of the French—from the building of Fort Niagara in 1726 to the end of the French presence in 1759; and frequently traversed this region, crossing the Niagara River into the Ontario peninsula in their hunting pursuits.[17] According to one local history, the Tonawanda Senecas continued to seek food sources and to hunt on Grand Island well into the nineteenth century.[18] Thus, it is little wonder that the Indian Claims Commission in its Finding of Fact in 1968 clearly indicated that the Niagara frontier and the Niagara River islands were Seneca country and that, from 1701 onward, both the French and English dealt with the Seneca "as the owners and controllers of the area."[19]

In 1763 a group of Seneca including Guyasuta, an uncle of Handsome Lake, proposed driving the English out of Iroquois country. These western

Seneca centered at Chenussio (Geneseo), not the entire Seneca Nation as a whole, soon became part of the famous Indian uprising known in history as Pontiac's War or Pontiac's Conspiracy. As anthropologist Anthony F. C. Wallace has written, this contingent of Seneca "struck perhaps the severest blows of the war, destroying the forts at Venango, Le Boeuf, and Presqu'Isle and at Devil's Hole almost annihilating two British detachments on the newly cut road along the cliff above the whirlpool at Niagara Falls." The Seneca war party of five hundred warriors ambushed a convoy of twenty-five horse- and ox-drawn wagons containing thirty-one British soldiers. When the company was reinforced by two other companies composed of eighty more men, these new forces were overwhelmed by the Seneca warriors. In all, seventy-two British soldiers "lay dead on the trail, scalped and stripped of their clothing."[20]

After the collapse of Pontiac's War, the British authorities demanded reparations for this "massacre." After summoning Senecas to Johnstown in August 1764, Sir William Johnson, the British superintendent of Indian Affairs, exacted a price from the "Chenussio [Geneseo] Indians." The cession of August 1764 came after a formal treaty of April 1764 that Johnson negotiated with the entire Seneca Nation after the French and Indian and Pontiac's Wars: "Parliamentary Articles of Peace, Friendship & Alliance, Entered Into Between the English, and the Deputies Sent from the Whole Seneca Nation, By Sir William Johnson Bart His Majesty's Sole Agent & Superintendent of Indian Affairs for the Northern Parts of North America, and Colonel of the Six United Nations Their Allies & Dependents Etc."[21] In both the April and August agreements of 1764, Johnson specifically served as the Crown's agent, not as an individual land speculator. In the accord of August 6, 1764, made by Johnson, Article V specifies the islands in the Niagara River:[22]

In addition to the grant made by the Chenussio Deputys to His Majesty at Johnson Hall, in April, of the Lands from Fort Niagara, to the upper end of the carrying place, beyond Fort Schlosser and four miles in breadth on each side of the River, the Chenussios now, surrender up all the lands from the upper end of the former Grant (and of the same breadth) to the Rapids of Lake Erie, to His Majesty, for His sole use, and that of the Garrisons, but not as private property, it being near some of their hunting grounds; so that all the Tract, of the breadth before mentioned, from Lake Ontario to Lake Erie, shall become vested in the Crown, in manner as before mentioned, *excepting the Islands between the great Falls and the Rapids, which the Chenussios bestow upon Sir Wm Johnson as a proof of their regard and of their knowledge of the trouble he has had with them from time to time.* All which the Chenussios hope will be acceptable to His Majesty, and that they may have some token of His Favour. (Emphasis mine)

This August 1764 "treaty" was a cession to the King of England by a portion of the Senecas, not all. When Sir William Johnson died in 1774, his will never contained mention of Grand Island or other Niagara River islands, proof that Johnson had subsequently transferred these lands to the Crown and that Great Britain's monarch had title to these lands although Seneca occupancy of Grand Island continued well into the nineteenth century.[23] Later, in 1790, the Cornplanter recalled the events surrounding the Seneca cession of 1764 when he was in council with President Washington in Philadelphia. Referring to Fort Niagara, Cornplanter maintained: "Sir William Johnson came and took that fort from the French, he became our Father and promised to take care of us and did so until you [Americans] were too strong for his King. To him we gave four miles round Niagara as a place of trade."[24]

In March 1783 the United States and Great Britain signed the Treaty of Paris, ending the American Revolution. Article II of the treaty appears to confirm United States jurisdiction to Grand Island:[25]

And that all Disputes which might arise in future on the Subject of the Boundaries of the said United States, may be prevented, it is hereby agreed and declared, that the following are & shall be their Boundaries, viz. . . . Thence along the middle of said River into Lake Ontario; through the Middle of said Lake until it strikes the Communication by Water between that Lake and Lake Erie; *thence along the middle of said Communication into Lake Erie, until it arrives at the Water Communication* between that Lake and Lake Huron. (Emphasis mine)

In the immediate aftermath of the American Revolution, the cession of 1764 involving Grand Island was alluded to by the Mohawk war chief, Joseph Brant. In the state negotiations at Fort Stanwix on September 10, 1784, Governor George Clinton asked representatives of the Six Nations for lands "in the Vicinity of Niagara and Oswego" to establish and settle boundary lines. Brant replied, specifically referring to the Niagara River cession of 1764:[26] "Brothers! You have particularly expressed your Wish to have Lands at Niagara and Oswego, for the Accommodation of your ancient Settlement of those Places. We have formerly ceded some Lands to the Government of the late Colony of New York *for the Use of the King. This already belongs to You by the Treaty with Great Britain*" (emphasis mine). Article III of the federal treaty of Fort Stanwix that followed on October 22, 1784, which forced large cessions of Seneca lands, never mentioned the Niagara River islands while defining the boundary between the United States and the Six Nations.[27] Moreover, in the federal-Iroquois treaties of 1784 at Fort Stanwix and 1789 at Fort Harmar and the New York State–Massachusetts accord of 1786, there is no specific reference or clear indication about the cession of 1764 or the ownership of the islands in the Niagara River. However, the Pickering treaty of November 11, 1794, with the Six Nations does refer to the islands in the Niagara River.[28] Article III of the treaty specifies that the land of the "Seneka Nation" is bounded as follows:[29]

Beginning on Lake Ontario at the northwest corner of the land they sold to Oliver Phelps, the line runs westerly along the lake as far as Oyongwongyeh Creek at Johnson's landing place, about four miles eastward from the Fort of Niagara; thence southerly up that creek to its main fork then straight to the main fork of Stedman's Creek which empties into the Niagara River above Fort Schlosser and then onward from that fork continuing the same straight course to that river. *This line from the mouth of Oyongwongyeh Creek to the River Niagara above Fort Schlosser being the eastern boundary of a strip of land extending from the same line to Niagara River which the Seneca Nation ceded to the King of Great Britain at a treaty held about thirty years ago with Sir William Johnson,* then the line runs along the River Niagara to Lake Erie; then along Lake Erie to the northeast corner of a triangular piece of land which the United States conveyed to the State of Pennsylvania as by the President's patent dated the third day of March 1792, then due south to the northern boundary of that state; then due east to the southwest corner of the land sold by the Seneca Nation to Oliver Phelps and then north and northerly along the Phelps line to the place of beginning on Lake Ontario. Now the United States acknowledge all the land within the aforementioned boundaries to be the property of the Seneka Nation and the United States will never claim the same nor disturb the Seneka Nation nor any of the Six Nations or of their Indian friends residing thereon and united with them in the free use and enjoyment thereof but it shall remain theirs until they choose to sell the same to the people of the United States who have the right to purchase. (Emphasis mine)

When interpreting the language of this treaty, it is essential to examine three specific pieces of correspondence. In each, Pickering stated his awareness of the 1764 cession and his belief that the United States now (1794) had sovereignty over the islands.[30] This interpretation of the Pickering treaty was also confirmed in the Indian Claims Commission's opinion in 1968, which found that the Six Nations recognized American "interest in the southern strip and in the islands" of the Niagara by this 1794 accord and that "any subsequent disposition of the lands by the Seneca would be under the protection of the Trade and Intercourse Act."[31] The former attorney for both the Seneca Nation and Tonawanda Seneca, George P. Decker, insisted that the Pickering treaty operated to release the Niagara shore above Stedman's Creek, thereby receding Grand Island to the Senecas. Pickering's Treaty, a unique accord, promised protection to the Senecas "subject only to the new privileges expressly stipulated in favor of the United States by Article 5 for land and water passageways and harbor accommodations."[32]

New York State's continuous efforts to buy Grand Island and the other islands in the Niagara River from the Senecas, a further indication that the state did not have title to them, had intensified in the years approaching the War of 1812. New York's questionable title was revealed in other ways. Despite an offer by land speculator John Livingston to buy these islands on February 4, 1793, no state action in this regard was taken.[33] The federal Treaty of Big Tree of 1797 and the two federal treaties of 1802 did not deal with Grand Island or the other islands in the Niagara River.[34] In one of the 1802 treaties the lands north of Buffalo Creek Reservation—the so-called New York Reservation lands—were ceded by the Senecas, but the treaty did *not* involve the Niagara River islands. By 1805 this shoreline cession was being laid out in lots; however, Grand Island was not.[35]

On March 19, 1802, the New York State Legislature authorized state officials to treat with the Senecas for a one-mile-wide strip along the Niagara River from Stedman's farm northward including Black Rock but did *not* specify acquisition of the Niagara River islands.[36] Despite this limited authorization New York State officials and representatives of the Holland Land Company pushed for a larger Seneca land cession involving the islands throughout the spring and early summer of 1802; nevertheless, the Senecas, after the debacle at Big Tree in 1797, refused to part with the islands, although they did finally agree to make a cession of the New York Reservation, namely, the shoreline. Red Jacket, the Seneca leader, addressing himself to John Tayler, the commissioner on the part of the United States and later governor of New York State, and to Governor George Clinton, specifically insisted:[37]

We propose to sell you the whole tract, with the reservation however of all of the islands [in the Niagara River]; the line to the edge of the water, but the use of the river to be free to you—We wish to reserve also the privilege of using the beach to encamp on, and wood to make fires, together with the uninterrupted use of the river for the purpose of fishing; And likewise the privilege of passing the bridge and the turnpike, when made, free from Toll, and of keeping a ferry service across the river—For the whole tract we ask $7500. We think this reasonable, and that in a few years it will refund you much more than this sum. (Emphasis mine)

On the next day, New York State concluded a land transaction with the Senecas. This August 20, 1802, agreement had a federal commissioner (John Tayler) present and the governor of New York State (George Clinton) and Seneca leaders (Red Jacket, Farmer's Brother, Young King, Pollard, and others) in attendance. This accord stated that the Indians "do sell, cede, release and quit-claim to the people of the State of New York, all that trust of land one mile wide on the Niagara River, extending from Buffalo to Stedman's Farm including Black Rock, *and bounded Westward by the shore or waters of said river*" (emphasis mine). Nowhere in the accord are the islands in the Niagara River specifically ceded. Importantly, the Seneca reserved the right to camp, fish, collect driftwood, and pass freely on bridges or on ferry and boat services, once established. Under this accord Jasper Parrish and Horatio Jones each received one-mile-square land cessions for their service. The legal giant Chancellor James Kent notarized the accord of August 20, 1802. The United States Senate approved this state agreement on December 30, 1802.[38]

Urged on by both Porter and the residents of Black Rock, Governor Daniel D. Tompkins clearly indicated his anxiety about the Niagara River islands and the ill-defined nature of the United States–British Canada boundary under the Treaty of Paris of 1783 in a letter to the American secretary of state on December 10, 1810:[39]

Numerous complaints have heretofore been made to me both by the inhabitants and by friendly Indians, of intrusions, and waste committed upon Grand & Navy Islands in the Niagara River, and upon Carlton Island, Grenadier Island, Buck Island, Grand Isle, and others in the St. Lawrence. Some of those Islands are of great value, and furnish important advantages for commerce, and eligible positions for military operations.

On the same day Governor Tompkins wrote a second letter to Congressman Porter, now the chairman of the House Foreign Relations Committee, further reflecting his concern about the ambiguity of the Treaty of Paris (1783). Tompkins, seeing war clouds on the horizon with Great Britain, reflected on the strategic and economic importance of these Great Lakes islands both to New York State and to the United States as a whole and urged final resolution by Congress:[40]

The Islands situated in the water communication between Lake Erie and the falls, (Grand Isle, Navy Isle &c.) and those which are in Lake Ontario and the St. Lawrence (Grenadier Island, Carlton Island, Buck Island, Long Island &c.) are of immense importance to this State, and the United States, as well on account of the

Daniel D. Tompkins

Courtesy of the New York State Library, New York State Museum, and Craig Williams

value of the soil and timber, as for the facilities they afford to commerce and their eligibility for military positions and operations.

On March 8, 1811, the New York State Legislature specifically authorized the governor to purchase the islands in the Niagara River from the Senecas. Governor Tompkins wrote Jasper Parrish, the subagent for the Seneca Indians, on April 11, 1811, attempting to facilitate negotiations with them for the purchase of the Niagara River islands.[41]

With a war with British Canada on the horizon, Tompkins's position on the Niagara River islands hardened by 1812. On February 12 he reported to the New York State Assembly Committee on Indian Affairs about a meeting he had had with a delegation of Seneca chiefs. Tompkins told them that in his estimation the Seneca cession to Sir William Johnson in 1764 and the Pickering treaty (1794) with the Six Nations denied the Seneca claim to the islands, that the Niagara River islands belonged to New York, but that he was willing to pay the Senecas for the islands. He insisted that New York State had no legal obligation to pay the Senecas but that state officials would do so to ensure friendship and amity with the Indians.[42] Yet in the same report Tompkins readily admitted, "The timber on Grand Isle, in Niagara River, *belonging to the Senecas* is some of the best in the vicinity" (emphasis mine).[43] The governor then revealed the increasing pressures on the Senecas caused by trespassers, namely, timber strippers, on the island.[44]

Tompkins's hardened view stands in sharp contrast with Seneca words and actions related to Grand Island. On September 16, 1810, the Seneca chief Little Billy addressed a Six Nations council at Buffalo Creek, telling the Indians that Governor Tompkins had inquired about a Seneca land sale of Grand Island to Sir John Johnson. Little Billy claimed that he had held three meetings and had interviewed the oldest chiefs about this matter. He insisted that there was "no recollection of any grant to Sir John [Johnson]. We view the islands as our own, and shall claim them." Little Billy recalled that Joseph Brant at Onondaga "produced a paper—16 years since." Once again the oldest chiefs were consulted, but "no one could tell anything about it." They then sent the paper back to Sir John Johnson.[45] Little Billy, addressing Erastus Granger, the federal Indian agent, further insisted: "We own all the islands. Do not wish at present to sell them, but remain as they are." Cornplanter reiterated Little Billy's sentiments to Granger, "He hopes the white people will not trespass on the islands and wishes me to prevent [them]."[46] Seneca determination to hold this territory was manifest in other ways, especially when they rallied when a British-allied force of Mohawks from Canada threatened an invasion of Grand Island in July 1812 and soon after these Senecas joined the American side in the War of 1812.

After the conclusion of the war and two months before the New York State–Seneca "treaty" in 1815 involving Grand Island, Governor Tompkins wrote Jasper Parrish about the details for negotiating an accord with the Indians. Tompkins once again insisted, "Although it is questionable whether these Indians have any title to the lands [islands in the Niagara River], yet I am willing (with a view to avoid any collisions, and to perpetuate the good understanding which at present exists between them and the government) to pay Twelve thousand dollars for the relinquishment of their right to all the Islands—This sum is to cover all the incidental expenses attending the purchase."[47]

On September 12, 1815, New York, with Congressman Porter serving as a "state commissioner," made an accord with the Seneca Nation relative to the islands in the Niagara River. The Senecas, fearing the loss of their remaining ten reservations, reluctantly agreed to the cession, made to their former military commander, General Porter. In return for a one thousand dollar payment and an annuity of five hundred dollars paid to the "Chiefs, Sachems and Warriors of the Seneca Nation of Indians," the Senecas, in this September 12, 1815, "treaty," "hereby sell, grant, convey and confirm to the people of the State of New York, all the islands in Niagara river between Lake Erie and Lake Ontario & within the jurisdiction of the United States." The Senecas also reserved "equal right and privileges with the citizens of the United States in hunting fishing and fowling in & upon the water on the Niagara river" besides the right to camp on the islands.[48]

Besides General Porter, the New York delegation "purchasing" the islands included Governor Tompkins and state commissioners Henry Crocheron, Samuel Younge, Rodger Skinner, Esec Cowan, Robert Tillotson, and Louis Livingston. Witnesses included Jasper Parrish, Horatio Jones, J. C. Brown, and L. Harrison. Among the Seneca signatories were Red Jacket, Little Billy, Pollard, Young King, Little Beard, and Captain Shongo.[49] With growing talk about concentrating Indian populations or removing the Iroquois from the state, the Seneca strategy appeared to be agreeing to piecemeal cessions of lands to delay or prevent these two disasters from happening. With the hovering shadow of the planned Erie Canal, which they knew would bring rapid changes and white population growth, the Indians had little choice but to concede the islands, lands that were less central to their cultural existence when compared to Buffalo Creek or to their other reservation communities.

At this September 12, 1815, accord, no federal commissioner was present at the negotiations and treaty council. Even the federal agent, Erastus Granger, was not present. There are no federal instructions about this land deal. Two of the witnesses to this deal were subagent Jasper Parrish and interpreter Horatio Jones, both of whom benefited significantly by Seneca land deals. Parrish and Jones, white men, had been captured as youths by the Senecas and had learned the Iroquoian languages and mores. They served as intermediaries between the white and Iroquois worlds from the late 1780s to the late 1820s. Jones received Seneca lands at the Little Beard's Reservation cession under one of the federal treaties with the Seneca in 1802, whereas Parrish received the 131-acre Squaw Island, one of the islands in the Niagara River at the foot of the Black Rock rapids, after the "treaty" of 1815 by a special act of the New York State Legislature in 1816.[50] General Peter B. Porter, along with his brother Augustus, themselves soon secured Goat Island in addition to other river properties. The motivating factors for this New York land deal were: (1) to secure a safe western border with British Canada after the War of 1812; (2) to further the development of Black Rock, Porter's residence, as an important site for the proposed Erie Canal; and (3) to further individuals', land companies', and New York State's land interests.[51]

With the "extinguishment" of Seneca title in the illegal agreement of 1815, Porter now turned to a second piece of the puzzle, namely, securing final British recognition of United States ownership of the islands in the Niagara River adjacent to Black Rock and the Niagara peninsula. The Treaty of Ghent, which ended the War of 1812 between the United States and Great Britain and which was signed on December 24, 1814, had provided a mechanism for settling the controversy over ownership of the Niagara River islands. The treaty was ratified by the United States Senate on February 17, 1815, and proclaimed by the president the next day. Article VI dealt with determining the meaning of the following language set forth in the Treaty of Paris of 1783: "along the middle of the said River into Lake Ontario, through the middle of said Lake until it strikes the communication by water between that Lake and Lake Erie thence along the middle of said communication into Lake Erie through the middle of said Lake until it arrives at the water communication into Lake Huron." The treaty provided for the appointment of two commissioners, one from the United States and one from Great Britain, to meet first in Albany and later elsewhere to determine ownership, among other things, of "the several Islands lying within the said Rivers, Lakes & water communications" to be "in conformity with the true intent of the said Treaty of one thousand seven hundred eighty three."[52] What ultimately resulted was the creation of the "Joint Mixed Boundary Commission," which formally reported in 1822 on Article VI of the treaty but which continued in operation until December 24, 1827, determining a multitude of boundary issues stretching across the immense United States–British Canadian boundary.[53]

As early as three days before the New York State–Seneca "treaty" of 1815, Secretary of State James Monroe wrote Porter:[54] "The President [Madison] taking into view your patriotic and useful services in the late war and entertaining a high opinion of your qualifications in other respects has appointed you one of the Commissioners for running the boundary line between the United States and the British provinces to the north as stipulated by the Treaty of Ghent." This letter was never received by Porter, but a copy was sent to him by Arch Campbell on September 28, 1815.[55] Porter finally received his official presidential appointment dated January 16, 1816.[56] By that time the former congressman, war hero, and agent of the Ogden Land Company was serving as New York's secretary of state.

Porter's appointment was a controversial one, leading to delays in his Senate confirmation.[57] Historian Frank Mogavero has clearly documented that some members of Congress questioned Porter's nomination because the general's entrepreneurial activities led to issues of conflict of interest:[58]

There were two reasons for this: first, Porter was a government contractor [salt] who supplied American army posts through the firm of Porter, Barton & Company, *and second, Peter and his brother Augustus had acquired the islands at the brink of Niagara Falls [in the New York State–Seneca "treaty" of 1815] which, being on the American-Canadian boundary would be under discussion by the Boundary Commission.* (Emphasis mine)

Finally, on November 18, 1816, Porter was sworn in as boundary commissioner.[59] Yet, throughout Porter's tenure as commissioner, charges of conflict of interest were leveled at him, especially concerning his business ties to David A. Ogden, the founder of the Ogden Land Company.[60]

Besides Porter, the United States contingent on this Joint Mixed Boundary Commission included Donald Fraser, the secretary; Samuel Hawkins (frequently at odds with Porter) and Major Joseph Delafield, who served as agents; Richard Delafield as draftsman; David P. Adams as astronomical surveyor; and William A. Bird (Porter's nephew and resident of Black Rock) and James Ferguson as assistant surveyors. The British contingent was first headed by John Oglevie, who died in 1819, and later by Anthony Barclay. John Hale served as agent, David Thompson as surveyor, and Dr. John Bixby and Alexander Stevenson as assistant surveyors.[61] Delafield's memoir is the more complete and revealing about both Mohawk and Seneca discontent and about their fears of losing their lands. The Senecas at Buffalo Creek in 1819 told the commission that the United States was supposed to protect them under the Pickering treaty (1794). Delafield was also rather frank about David A. Ogden's involvement in facilitating the workings of the commission.[62]

From their initial meeting at Albany, New York, this Joint Mixed Boundary Commission set forth certain guidelines about their individual and collective responsibilities and about their procedures for settling controversies. Both groups of surveyors were to proceed on their own. The entire border region was to be twice surveyed trigonometrically. Both governments' commissioners had to agree after the calculations made by each group of surveyors were compared. Maps were to be prepared in the winter months, and four sets of maps were drawn for each section, one set for each government and one for each commissioner. From the outset the commissioners agreed that no island would be divided in ownership even though by their rules the true boundary line would be the middistance from main shore to main shore. If the more sizable part of an island lay in the United States' half of a body of water, the United States would receive the island; if it lay mostly on the Canadian side of the waterway, it went to British Canada.[63]

I. Frank Mogavero, a historian and major authority on this Joint Mixed Boundary Commission, has described other methods the commission used to determine ownership of the islands:[64]

Another way of ascertaining ownership of an island was to determine the deepest channel or navigable channel as the case might be. If the navigable channel was found to be between the United States shore and the island, the island was given to Canada. On the other hand if the navigable channel was found to be between the Canadian shore and an island, the island went to the United States. If both channels could be used by ships the true channel would be that through which the greater volume of water flowed. When there were three or more channels, the one nearest to the whole body of water was taken provided that each party received a ship route. When there was no navigable channel the lands were to be equally divided.

The commissioners and their staffs dealt with issues related to the eastern regions—the St. Lawrence River and Lake Ontario (including making a decision negatively affecting Indians)—and with the assignment of Mohawk-claimed territory (Barnhart and other islands in the St. Lawrence River). By June 1819 the commission set their sights on the islands in the Niagara River. The commission held meetings on Iris Island (Goat Island) on June 4 and on Navy Island on June 14, 1819. Soon after these meetings, Grand Island was "awarded" to the United States along with all the other islands in the Niagara River except Navy Island. According to Mogavero, citing Bird's memoirs, the Joint Mixed Boundary Commission "found that the main channel of the Niagara River was the west branch of the river between Navy Island and Canada where the water was deeper, the current faster and the width greater than the east branch of the river."[65] 8,540,000 cubic feet of water passed through the east channel per minute, whereas 12,802,750 cubic feet of water passed through the west branch per minute. A check of the Niagara River at Black Rock above Grand Island indicated that 21,549,590 cubic feet of water flowed each minute.[66] Indeed, the commission actually violated its own rules by awarding Navy Island to British Canada.[67]

According to historian Mogavero, the decision to award Grand Island and the other islands except Navy Island to the United States was "a foregone conclusion" because of their proximity to the American shoreline.[68] William A. Bird's memoirs reveal how the decision over Grand Island was actually made. Assistant Surveyor Bird later recalled:[69]

The Commissioners came into the Niagara River with much the larger quantity of doubtful island territory on that [United States] side. There was therefore no hesitancy in appropriating Grand Island in the Niagara River to the United States. That island (other things being equal) would have been questionable, as the largest surface of water is probably on the American side, although the quantity of water is about three-fifths on the British side.

Although astronomy and mathematics have been cited as the reason for determining ownership of the islands, except for Navy Island, other forces were also at work. The presence of Porter, the leading entrepreneur of the Niagara frontier and the first citizen of Black Rock, as United States commissioner obviously did not hurt American chances to secure these islands. Moreover, compromise, not confrontation, was the British goal in the aftermath of war.[70] British policies in the post–War of 1812 setting were clearly designed to build amity and commerce with the United States, culminating in the Rush-Bagot Treaty of 1817 and British encouragement of John Quincy Adams's Monroe Doctrine of 1823.

New York State began efforts to assert its jurisdiction over Grand Island long before the Joint Mixed Boundary Commission made its final report on Article VI of the Treaty of Ghent. Governor De Witt Clinton wrote the New

York State Senate on March 11, 1819, that a number of families had settled on Grand Island since 1815 who "disclaim the authority of the state" and who may inflict "great injury on the public property" and "become a serious annoyance to that part of the country." In his message Clinton claimed that this situation on the island had worsened "since the extinguishment of the Indian title [by the state]" but admitted that the situation was largely *"because the jurisdiction over the islands in that river has not been settled under the treaty of Ghent"* (emphasis mine).[71] In response on August 13, 1819, the New York State Legislature enacted "An Act Authorizing the Removal of Certain Intruders from Grand Island in the Niagara River."[72] On December 9, 1819, a state force of 53 men began forcibly ejecting the "squatters" from the island. Seventy houses were burned and 150 men, women, and children were removed from the island in the five-day "mopping-up" operation that cost the state $568.99.[73]

Despite this state action New York State Surveyor-General Simeon De Witt, one of the major state officials dealing with the Iroquois in the period, whose office carried out cartographic surveys and administered state lands from the time of his appointment in 1784 to the 1830s, wrote Henry Livingston on April 15, 1820, "Nothing will probably be done with Grand Island in the Niagara River *till the boundary line between us and the British is settled which may not be done in some years from this*" (emphasis mine).[74]

In 1824 the state authorized a survey of Grand Island into farm lots. The next year, this survey was completed, and immediately these lots were put up for sale at the state land office in Albany. New York State sold the lots for $76,230. The largest purchaser of these lots was Mordecai Noah, a leading American Jew, former consul general of the United States in Tunis, and editor of the *National Advocate.* Noah believed that the nearby Seneca and Tuscarora Indians were the lost tribes of Israel and that creating a "great" city of "Ararat" on Grand Island was to lead to the redemption of the Jewish people and a Zion where his oppressed brethren could worship freely and live in peace. Despite the dream Noah's experiment was to fail miserably.[75]

On June 18, 1822, the Joint Mixed Boundary Commission's report under Article VI of the Treaty of Ghent was finalized and signed at Utica, New York. On July 24, 1822, Joseph Delafield formally presented this report to Secretary of State John Quincy Adams.[76] Ironically, the year of Porter's great achievement, the Joint Mixed Boundary Commission's report, was also the year of his greatest setback, the final decision to extend the Erie Canal from Black Rock to Buffalo, thus assuring the "Queen" City's supremacy.

Despite Porter's setback the general's personal and political fortunes did not wane. He remained, along with his brother Augustus, one of the richest men in the state, becoming involved in Niagara Falls water power development while maintaining major land and shipping interests. He later, as revealed in chapter 9, served as secretary of war, once again having a major impact on decisions affecting the Iroquois and other Indians. Although not a Jacksonian Democrat, he continued to push for frontier settlement and Indian removal beyond the Mississippi and for the extension of state laws and jurisdiction over the Indians.[77]

The long career of the "Bashaw of the Border," who died in 1844, was largely marked by his strong advocacy of the interests of western New York. His involvement in state and federal politics was also to be marked by an era of Iroquois decline. Thus, Porter's life clearly shows the connections between transportation, land interests, national defense, and the unmaking of the Iroquois world in the early republic.

CHAPTER 9

Genesee Fever

Besides the Seneca landholdings of Buffalo, Grand Island, and other Niagara River islands, and Allegany, Cattaraugus, and Tonawanda in the first decades of the nineteenth century, these Indians retained rich bottom lands along the west branch of the Genesee River valley. This aboriginal territory had been recognized as Seneca under Article III of the Pickering Treaty of 1794 and had been specifically reserved for these Indians under the Treaty of Big Tree of 1797. These lands were substantial, containing nearly one hundred thousand acres of the richest farmlands in New York State: (1) Canawaugus, a two-square-mile parcel on the west bank of the Genesee River west of the Town of Avon in Livingston County; Little Beard's Town and Big Tree, two, two-square-mile parcels each in Leicester on the west bank of the Genesee River opposite the Town of Geneseo, Livingston County; Squawkie Hill, a two-square-mile parcel in Leicester on the west bank of the Genesee River north of Mount Morris in Livingston County; Gardeau, or White Woman's Reservation, a twenty-eight-square-mile parcel on both sides of the Genesee River, half of which lies within the Town of Castile, Wyoming County, and stretched along the Genesee River northward (through much of today's Letchworth State Park) to just south of Mount Morris, Livingston County; and Caneadea, a sixteen-square-mile parcel on both sides of the Genesee River in the environs of the Town of Caneadea, Allegany County, New York.[1] The one-square-mile Oil Spring Reservation near Cuba, New York, in both Allegany and Cattaraugus Counties, appears to have been inadvertently left out during the Treaty of Big Tree negotiations.[2]

Even before the signing of the Treaty of Big Tree, land speculators and transportation interests began to eye these fertile lands. Substantial river transportation up the Genesee River had increased throughout the 1790s.

Later, after the War of 1812, entrepreneurs of the "Queen City" saw these rich lands east of Buffalo as alternate sources of grain when western Great Lakes and Midwest supplies were interrupted by famine or by war scares. Long before the 1830s, when Rochester's emergence led to bitter competition with its chief western New York rival, Buffalo, the lands south of Rochester's great canal depot were becoming attractive to land speculators and merchant capitalists.

From 1797 onward there had been attempts to rid this Genesee region of its Indian population. Ellicott, who surveyed the Seneca reservation boundaries in 1798 for the Holland Land Company, predicted that the Genesee valley would be rapidly settled by non-Indians if transportation could be improved. He wrote the directors of the Holland Land Company, "It is something to know that the Genesee River which is called and generally supposed to be a fine navigable stream, is like many others navigable in theory and conjecture only."[3] In a treaty of June 30, 1802, the Seneca sold the two-square-mile parcel of the Little Beard's Town to Oliver Phelps. A federal Indian commissioner was present, John Tayler, and the agreement was ratified by the United States Senate in 1803. Among the signatories were Cornplanter, Red Jacket, Young King, and Captain Pollard.[4]

Besides Indian opposition to selling their other lands in the region, there were major obstacles to Genesee development. The region had a reputation, partly undeserved, as being one of the least healthy areas of the state in which settlers were subject to a strange ague, commonly labeled "Genesee fever." Despite its singular designation the fever was perhaps a manifestation of three separate maladies: malaria, typhus, and typhoid fever. The fear of this "swamp fever" kept large-scale migrations to a minimum before the War of 1812. With increased public health awareness, improved drainage, and better sanitation, population in the region swelled from 1812 to 1840. Instead of being associated with disease, the term *Genesee fever* slowly became applied to the massive settlement of this rich agricultural region of the emerging Empire State.[5]

Even before canal transportation became the prime focus of boosters, private and public, road building became the central concern. To make the region more attractive to settlement, the Holland Land Company and, after 1810, the Ogden Land Company promoted road-building projects in the region. Ridge Road was improved and the Genesee Turnpike was built in stages from the 1790s to 1813. Other roads followed, laid out largely as a result of Ellicott's efforts. Ellicott concentrated his attention on building two major routes from the Genesee River to Buffalo: (1) the Middle Road, or Big Tree Road, which ran from Big Tree (Geneseo) to Lake Erie just south of the Buffalo Creek Reservation; and (2) the Buffalo Road, a section of the Genesee Turnpike between Batavia and Buffalo. In the first years of the 1800s Ellicott also initiated smaller projects such as the Oak Orchard Road from Batavia to Lake Ontario where he planned a trading post. He also connected the Big Tree Road with an already existing road built by Genesee land speculator Charles Williamson that connected southeastward to Bath and Painted Post. These efforts were followed by the Holland Land Company's subsidization of roads or road improvement along the entire New York State–Lake Erie frontier south of Buffalo and by Adam Hoops's efforts to extend roads in the southern Genesee region to connect with the Allegany River at Olean.[6]

Long before his appointment in 1810 to the New York State Board of Canal Commissioners, Ellicott also pushed canals as a way of making western New York attractive to non-Indian settlement. His survey maps and field books were employed in the first decade of the nineteenth century to determine the feasibility of developing the connection between the Genesee River and Lake Erie. He also promoted the possibilities of navigation along the Tonawanda Creek, Tonawanda Swamp, and through the Tonawanda valley as a whole. A hard-driven, determined fellow, Ellicott successfully battled with Porter over the site of the western terminus of the Erie Canal: Ellicott favored Buffalo (New Amsterdam) and Porter favored Black Rock. At other times, he came in direct conflict with his employer, Paul Busti, the chief agent of the Holland Land Company, over his elaborate and expensive efforts to promote roads and canals or to sell off Holland Land Company property to the state. Consequently, Ellicott must be considered the chief architect of the state's early development in the lands from the Genesee River to Lake Erie. Without his surveys, field books, town-site development projects, and especially his promotion of the regional transportation network, New York would not have emerged so rapidly as the Empire State.[7]

Another major obstacle for non-Indian development in the Genesee was the existence of nearly one hundred thousand acres of Seneca Indian lands in the region in 1797. Peace with Great Britain in 1815 and the renewed push for canal development in western New York brought new pressures to bear on the Seneca Indians living in Genesee country. Although Little Beard's

Town was lost in 1802, the Senecas did resist other efforts to dispose of their lands. As early as 1813 they had rejected all attempts to consolidate their populations onto the Allegany Indian Reservation. Now they were faced with a more determined and, perhaps, a more immoral foe, David A. Ogden, who had purchased the preemption rights to the Seneca reservations.[8]

In a deed in September 1810 the Holland Land Company conveyed their preemptive rights to the Cattaraugus, Buffalo Creek, Allegany, Tonawanda, Caneadea, and Tuscarora Reservations—196,335 acres—for fifty cents an acre with "all the estate, right, title, interest, property, claim and demand whatsoever" of the first parties, "subject only to the right of the native Indian, and not otherwise." The deed contained a covenant: "They, the first parties, are seized of an indefensible estate or inheritance of, in and to the above described premises, and are lawfully authorized to sell the preemption right of the reserved tracts above described."[9]

A former Federalist congressman and Holland Land Company attorney from New York City, David A. Ogden created a company that took the form of a "trust with twenty equal shares." Ogden held title to the land when obtained from the Senecas and "would receive 10 per cent of the proceeds from all sales." Among the shareholders were other members of the Ogden family—David A. Ogden, Thomas L. Ogden, Charles Le Roux Ogden, and Abraham Ogden—and Thomas and Aaron Cooper and Joshua Waddington.[10] On February 8, 1821, David A. Ogden transferred his preemptive right to Robert Troup, Thomas Ludlow Ogden, and Benjamin W. Rogers as trustees. This trust officially became known as the Ogden Land Company on February 8, 1821.[11] On December 19, 1829, Robert Troup, Thomas L. Ogden, and Benjamin W. Rogers, as the Ogden Land Company trustees, conveyed their interests to Thomas L. Ogden, Charles G. Troup, and Joseph Fellows. Right through the early 1840s, these individuals, together as the Ogden Land Company, attempted to rid New York State of its Indian populations.[12]

The Ogden Land Company was especially interested in expanding their holdings in two areas. They knew that the emerging metropolitan giant, Buffalo, needed lands to the east to expand, namely, lands held at the Buffalo Creek Reservation. They also saw the potential of the Senecas' Genesee River lands. Their action was furthered by growing Indian dependence, the pressures the canal created, and increasing white leasing of Seneca lands. As legal holders of the preemption right to all Seneca lands, the company's profits depended on getting the Indians to sell their lands to the company. Consequently, on the company's payroll from 1811 onward was Horatio Jones, the previously mentioned white captive and Seneca adoptee who helped negotiate most of the swindles of Seneca lands from the 1790s onward right down to 1826. Jellis Clute, who lived at Mary Jemison's Gardeau Reservation, also worked for the company and "facilitated" the transfer of the lands of the "White Woman" to the Ogdens between 1817 and 1826.[13]

By 1821 the three most powerful voices of the company and active "players" in securing Seneca lands were Troup; James S. Wadsworth, the largest land speculator in Livingston County and son of the founder of Geneseo; and the previously mentioned Peter B. Porter. They conspired with the Ogdens about the possibilities of securing the Senecas' Genesee lands and subduing "the opposition of Red Jacket."[14] Troup, it should be noted, represented the Ogdens at the time but was also an agent for the Pulteney Associates. He was one of the nation's leading attorneys and even had handled General Philip Schuyler's vast estate. By the mid-1820s he was also a promoter of land speculation in Indian lands in Georgia and lobbied for new roads to open up his holdings in Allegany and Steuben Counties to connect with the Erie Canal sixty miles away.[15] Even though he had withdrawn from company operations by the mid-1820s, Peter B. Porter as secretary of war did little to challenge how the Ogdens secured Seneca lands at the "Treaty" of 1826.[16] Later, Augustus wrote him about the economic opportunities provided by the company's securing three of the reservations—Squawkie Hill, Big Tree, and Canawaugus—because the surveyor–land speculator saw half of these lands as being "of the finest quality of cleared, high-cultivated Genesee flats" that could draw a resale price of one hundred dollars per acre! It should be noted that the Senecas ultimately received approximately fifty cents an acre for this "sale."[17]

When the Senecas rejected company and state urgings to sell their lands and to move west with the Oneidas and their missionary Eleazer Williams, the Ogden Land Company and its agents intensified their efforts to secure Seneca lands. They clearly played on the growing divisions within the Seneca world after the War of 1812 and not simply the religious divisions between Christian and "pagan." Although having a collective estate and a valued position as the protector of the Confederacy after the Revolution, the Senecas, nevertheless, had individualistic pulls that at times worked against their national interests. Each reservation had a set of chiefs whose political base depended on their abilities to keep the land companies at bay, but who at times were susceptible to outright bribery through annuity payments. With land and population pressures, increased social disintegration caused by alcohol, and economic dependence on the white world for survival, these local chiefs could be manipulated or enticed by outside forces. With fears of removal, a policy presented to them as "inevitable" at nearly every council, and with increased acculturative forces such as missionaries in their midst, it is easy to see how the land companies obtained leverage in certain Seneca communities after the War of 1812. Added to these pressures were political rivalries of powerful leaders, some of whom—such as Young King and Pollard—were even willing to make deals with the devil, the Ogden Land Company, to fight their Seneca enemy Red Jacket.

One of the reservations appears to have had more power and influence in the Seneca polity than the others. Buffalo Creek had more population and more standing as the ritual center. It was there that the Iroquois Confederacy met from the 1780s to the 1840s. To most Senecas in this period, the retention of Buffalo Creek had, for these reasons, greater priority. If and when the Senecas were pressured to cede lands, Buffalo Creek had to be maintained at all costs. Although land loss was to be avoided, the Senecas did place a priority on maintaining Buffalo Creek. Hence, although sharing a collective estate, the Senecas' individual interests at times worked against their national interest. Thus, the strategy of the Ogden Land Company was to promote these individualistic tendencies.

By the mid-1820s, through the efforts of Horatio Jones and Jellis Clute, the company began making "gifts" in 80 to 120-dollar payments to certain chiefs to entice them to sell Seneca lands. By the summer of 1825 T. L. Ogden had convinced the War Department to hold a treaty negotiation with the Senecas. President John Quincy Adams appointed Oliver Forward, a leading merchant and harbor promoter of Buffalo, who cooperated at every turn with the Ogden Land Company.[18]

Before the "treaty" of 1826, the Seneca lands at Gardeau, but not the other Seneca reservations, had been reduced in size. Gardeau or Gardow (*Ga-da-oh* or *Kau-tau* meaning "down and up," valley and hillside or bluff) was the White Woman's Reservation, occupied by Mary Jemison and forty-eight Senecas, mostly Jemison's family, by 1816.[19] Jemison was the famous girl captive, the "white woman of the Genesee."[20] At the urging of two enterprising white men—Micah Brooks and Thomas Clute—the New York State

Legislature passed a private bill on April 19, 1817, making Jemison a citizen of New York State and "confirming" her title to the Gardeau Reservation. Brooks, a congressman, was one of the founders of Livingston County and one of the earliest promoters of New York State's canal system. Thomas Clute was the brother of Jellis Clute, one of the main operatives of the Ogden Land Company. On April 23, 1817, in return for $3,000 and a mortgage to secure $4,286, the aged Jemison executed a deed of seven thousand acres on the east side of the reservation to the same Micah Brooks and Jellis Clute.[21] At the urging of John Jemison, Mary's son, Mary agreed, because of her advanced age and her inability to manage her property, to hire Thomas Clute as her guardian. In payment for his services Thomas Clute was given a great deal of land on the west side of the Gardeau Reservation. On August 24, 1817, Mary Jemison leased all of the remaining Gardeau Reservation, except for four thousand acres and Thomas Clute's lot, to Micah Brooks and Jellis Clute.[22] Jemison's words are revealing about this transaction:[23] "Finding their [Brooks and Clute] title still incomplete, on account of the United States government and Seneca Chiefs not having sanctioned my acts, they [Brooks and Clute] solicited me to renew the contract, and have the conveyance made to them in such a manner as that they should thereby be constituted sole proprietors of the soil."

By the winter of 1822–23 Mary Jemison agreed to sell Brooks and Jellis Clute all the Gardeau lands they desired, except for a tract "two square miles long, and one mile wide, lying on the [Genesee] river where I should choose it; and also reserving Thomas Clute's lot."[24]

On September 3, 1823, at Moscow, New York, in Livingston County, with Major Charles Carroll, a federal commissioner, present, Mary Jemison ceded all but two square miles (1,280 acres) to John Greig and Henry B. Gibson. Greig and Gibson obtained all of the Gardeau Reservation except the reserved two square miles, then in Genesee County and now in Wyoming County near Castile, New York, for $4,286, less than $0.30 per acre. Greig, a Scottish-born attorney from Canandaigua, was in the employ of the Ogden Land Company. Greig was, very much like Troup, amassing a fortune as a result of serving the land companies as their attorney. Before serving the Ogdens, his firm, Howell and Greig, had represented Thomas Morris, Phelps and Gorham, and the Pulteney Associates. He was also a major canal promoter and an urban developer of Rochester, owning significant real estate holdings in that city. By the time of his death in the 1850s, he had

John Greig
Courtesy of the Rochester Historical Society

vast holdings, mostly in the Genesee valley, totaling more than 30,000 acres of land. Among his clients and partners were Thomas Morris, the Phelps and Gorham, the Pulteney Associates, and the Ogden Land Company. Gibson, associated with Brooks and Jellis Clute, agreed to pay Jemison and her heirs and successors $300 a year forever. It should be noted that previously, in November 1818, Thomas Morris—Robert Morris's son involved with the Treaty of Big Tree in 1797—had conveyed to Greig the preemptive right to 9,769 acres of Gardeau. Five years later, in June 1823, Joseph Higbee, a trustee for one of Robert Morris's creditors, conveyed to Brooks and Jellis Clute 3,000 acres of Gardeau for $3,800.[25]

This land cession and others involving Gardeau Reservation were never submitted to or ratified by the United States Senate. In attendance at the treaty grounds in 1823 were United States Commissioner Carroll, Indian agent Jasper Parrish, and interpreter Horatio Jones. According to Mary Jemison, Nathaniel Gorham, the leading New York land speculator, and one Judge Howell, negotiated, "acted in concert with Maj. Carrol [*sic*]" and "upwards of twenty chiefs" signed this "treaty." It should be pointed out that as early as 1799 Horatio Jones had been involved in land schemes in the Genesee valley with Thomas Morris and Oliver Phelps, Gorham's business partner![26]

On February 17, 1824, Secretary of War John C. Calhoun, soon to be elected vice-president of the United States, wrote subagent Jasper Parrish of the Six Nations Agency that the "treaty" between John Greig and Henry Gibson and the Seneca Indians relating to the Gardeau Reservation did not need formal United States Senate approval because it was "considered in the nature of a private contract [that] does not require the special ratification of the Government as in treaties between the Indians and the United States." Calhoun added, "Consequently there is nothing to prevent its execution by the parties concerned, as soon as they may think it proper."[27] Later, on February 16, 1827, the commissioner of Indian Affairs wrote the secretary of war, indicating that the "treaty" of September 23, 1823, did not need Senate approval because it "was esteemed to be a useless ceremony; the President approving it only."[28]

By 1825 both Gibson and Greig had developed their plans for going after the remaining Seneca lands in the Genesee valley. Working closely with the Clutes and Jasper Parrish, also in the pay of the company, they pushed for the holding of new treaty negotiations. Until the fall of 1825, these negotiations remained on hold because the newly elected Adams administration had other priorities and the Indians themselves wanted to learn more about the new "Great Father" in Washington.[29]

The push for a new Seneca treaty entailing much of the tribal land base gained impetus in the late winter of 1826. On March 10, 1826, Congressman Garnsey of New York offered a resolution "proposing to instruct the Committee on Indian Affairs to inquire into the expediency of making an appropriation for holding a treaty with the Indians west of the Genesee River, in the State of New York." On March 10 and 11 the House of Representatives debated the merits and need to hold a Seneca treaty, but the discussion centered mostly on states' rights issues and whether states such as New York had jurisdiction over the Indians. Congressmen from New York, Georgia, and Connecticut mostly dominated the debate, discussing a variety of issues: whether there was even a need at all to appoint a special federal commissioner to treat with the Indians, the strange history of the preemption right to Indian lands in New York, and what Albany's position was on the matter. One congressman, in a prescient way, predicted, "Be assured that, whenever your Agent shall go there and propose such a sale, Red Jacket will be ready to meet him, and will drive him from his purpose by arguments which he will find it in vain to resist."[30] The same congressman wondered why a treaty was needed because neither Red Jacket nor the New York State Legislature had actually petitioned for it. Congressman Henry Storrs of New York's position eventually won. Referring to the Trade and Intercourse Acts, Storrs explained why a federal commissioner had to be appointed and was required under law:[31]

The resolution arises out of a statute passed by Congress, which makes it a penal offense for any person to purchase lands from any of the Indian tribes within the United States, without the consent of the United States. If the State of New York wishes to obtain lands held by the Indians, and which they are ever so willing or desirous to sell, she cannot do so without the presence of a Commissioner appointed by the United States, and the present resolution is only to inquire whether it is expedient to make an appropriation to enable a Commissioner on the part of the United States to attend and sanction a treaty between the State of New York and certain Indians in that State. Commissioners for this purpose have always been appointed.

On May 13, 1826, the House Committee on Indian Affairs issued a report, "To Hold a Treaty with the Seneca Indians." The report claimed that the majority of Senecas were "favorably disposed to the sale, of some parts of their land." It added that the Senecas were desirous of "civilization" because their lands "are mostly situated near flourishing villages." The report then concluded by recommending the appointment of a federal Indian commissioner to treat with the Senecas.[32]

Oliver Forward, who had been appointed as the federal commissioner to treat with the Seneca Indians at Buffalo Creek Reservation, had a clear objective. To Forward, a Buffalonian, the shrinking of the Buffalo Creek Reservation was his first priority, not the securing of Genesee lands. After all, the opening of the Erie Canal one year earlier made Buffalo real estate more attractive. The presence of a large Indian reservation stretching from near the Buffalo waterfront eastward for twelve miles retarded white efforts to expand the city. Any chipping away of this land base made Buffalo's emergence as a major metropolitan area and Great Lakes port more likely.[33]

In contrast, Red Jacket, the great orator, had his political base at Buffalo Creek. Although at times in his illustrious career he reluctantly agreed to land cessions (1797, 1802, 1815), none involved Buffalo Creek. The reservation not only was the seat of Red Jacket's power but was also the ceremonial center of the post–Revolutionary War Iroquois Confederacy. Hence, for Forward and Red Jacket alike—but for two distinct reasons—Buffalo was the Holy Grail.[34]

Despite this factor the Genesee was, nevertheless, the homeland of the Senecas and had special meaning for the people. Canawaugus, for example, was the birthplace of both Handsome Lake and the Cornplanter. Yet to the white settlers the Genesee country was to be a major center of agriculture, flour, timber, and canal transportation from the 1820s to the Civil War.[35]

On August 31, 1826, in a "treaty" held under the authority of the Untied States at Buffalo Creek with Oliver Forward present, the chiefs and warriors of the Seneca Nation reached agreement with trustees for the Ogden Land Company—Robert Troup, Thomas L. Ogden, and Benjamin W. Rogers—who were represented by their attorney, John Greig, the same fellow who had secured much of the Gardeau Reservation in the "treaty" of 1823. Nathaniel Gorham, a leading speculator in Indian lands, was appointed, once again as he had been in 1823, as a superintendent on behalf of the claims of the State of Massachusetts under the terms of the December 16, 1786, Hartford agreement.[36] Besides Forward, Phelps, Greig, and Seneca representatives, other in attendance included six interpreters, including Horatio Jones, who had served for more than three decades in this capacity, and Dr. Jacob Jemison (Jimeson), Mary Jemison's grandson and a trained physician who had attended Dartmouth College. Parrish, the Indian agent, who had served in various roles at treaty negotiations since 1788 and who had close ties to Porter and was in the pay of the Ogden Land Company, was also in attendance.[37]

At this "treaty" the Senecas ceded all of their remaining Genesee valley lands, including Big Tree, Canawaugus, and Squawkie Hill Reservations in Livingston County; the remaining two square miles at the Gardeau Reservation in Wyoming County; and the sixteen-square-mile Caneadea

Reservation in Allegany County. In addition, under this "treaty" the sizes of the Buffalo Creek, Tonawanda, and Cattaraugus Reservations were substantially reduced as well: Buffalo Creek by 36,638 acres; Tonawanda by 33,409 acres; and Cattaraugus by 5,120 acres. Thus, the Seneca land base was reduced by 86,887 acres. Among the Seneca signatories to this "treaty" were Young King, Pollard, Little Billy, Governor Blacksnake, Captain Strong, Seneca White, White Seneca, Henry Two Guns, Captain Shongo, Big Kettle, and Red Jacket, many of them with distinct motives for signing the agreement. Some chiefs, it is clear, defined their interests narrowly, namely, to protect their individual reservations and immediate interests, rather than to fight for the sanctity of all of the Seneca lands. Despite his signature on the "treaty" Red Jacket, for one, never truly supported the "treaty" and led the opposition to it until his death in 1830.[38]

The legal validity of the "treaty" of 1826 was questioned from the first by Red Jacket and his supporters. Even the anti-Indian New York State Assembly Committee to Investigate the "Indian Problem" of 1888, commonly known as the Whipple Committee, acknowledged in its final report in 1889, "This treaty [of 1826] was never ratified by the Senate of the United States, or proclaimed by the President, and the Indians have for a long time past claimed that the treaty was invalid for this reason."[39] According to the major article written on this "treaty" by Henry S. Manley, the former assistant attorney general of New York State, United States Indian Commissioner Forward "received money from Troup, the Ogden Land Company trustee, for unexplained expenses of the treaty." The Ogden Land Company also had Dr. Jacob Jemison on its payroll because the physician favored Indian land sales and pushed for Seneca emigration to the West. At least some of the chiefs who signed this 1826 "treaty" were apparently "bought off."[40] On July 20, 1827, Forward defended the practice: "Small annuities may have been allowed the principal chiefs, but the payment of such gratuities I believe has been practiced under every treaty with Indian tribes of this state since the organization of its government."[41] Because of the aged Red Jacket's unbending opposition to the "treaty," he was deposed as a Seneca chief on September 15, 1827, by the pro-treaty group. He was later reinstalled after a public outcry against the action.[42]

From the beginning, Forward's actions came under fire. Consequently, on January 30, 1827, he wrote President John Quincy Adams justifying his actions:[43]

The treaty was attended and executed by all the principals, and even minor chiefs of the tribe, with the exception of one or two, who were absent at the time. Dr. Jacob Jimison [Jemison], an educated native, also a young man of great worth, and of highly respectable literary attainments officiated as principal interpreter, and was employed by us as such, in consequence of the perfect knowledge which he possessed of the English, as well as of his native language [Seneca]. The proposals made by the agent of the proprietors, to the chiefs in council were fully explained to them and they were distinctly advised by us, that if a sale was made, it must be a voluntary act on their part, as they were at perfect liberty, to sell their lands or to retain them, as they should under the circumstances think expedient and proper.

Forward insisted that Red Jacket opposed the sale "of any of the Indian lands from commencement of negociations [*sic*]." Forward added that because of his attentiveness and the work of Jemison, Gorham, Parrish, and Jones, "no part of it [the 'treaty'] could have been misunderstood. Having been thus read, explained and declared to be satisfactory, it was executed by every one of the chiefs present."[44]

Red Jacket was joined by a "number of the Tonnewanta [Tonawanda Seneca] Indians" whom Forward claimed were not chiefs. Indeed, later in his letter, Forward insisted that the antitreaty forces at the Buffalo Creek council were largely outnumbered and were composed mainly of "a few of the indians [*sic*] who are scattered over the small reservations upon the Genesee River, and a part of the Tonnewantas [*sic*]."[45]

On February 16, 1827, Commissioner of Indian Affairs Thomas McKenney questioned whether Senate approval was even necessary on Indian treaties because the 1826 "treaty" had a federal commissioner present and, after all, "the President was the true guardian of Seneca interest." Nevertheless, President John Quincy Adams submitted the "treaty" to the Senate "for their advice and consent" on February 24, 1827.[46]

On May 19, 1827, Red Jacket and other prominent Senecas, including many of the earlier signatories of the "treaty" of 1826, appealed directly to President John Quincy Adams. Among those who signed this memorial were leading Tonawanda Senecas such as Jemmy Johnson and John Blacksmith. In it, these antitreaty Senecas insisted that "there are 2606 who are opposed to the sale of their lands, where on the other hand it has been ascertained that the number in favor are 430." The memorial went on to describe why Forward was appointed commissioner in the first place. It claimed that Forward was merely appointed "to save expenses of travel, he being at Buffalo and could attend to it without much trouble, whereas great expense would be incurred by sending a man all the way from the city of Washington." Forward only gave the Senecas two days to decide on whether they would sell land. The memorial further described how Red Jacket, fearing a trick, took his own interpreter with him rather than relying on Dr. Jemison whom he did not trust. The chiefs also decided to inform the Senecas on the other reservations about what was sought by Forward. Greig, of the Ogden Land Company, who arrived after Forward at the treaty grounds, then "told Red Jacket that he would have the land." Forward then "arose and informed the chiefs that it would be a very sorry thing to them if they did not sell their lands and continued saying the company [Ogden Land Company] will like it all the better for you to refuse to sell, and in that case you will not get one cent for your lands as you will be driven off them by the President of the United States." Soon after Parrish added a threat of removal "that if they did not sell it would be a serious thing for them" because the president had already appointed a set of commissioners "to go to the west and look out a tract of land for them."[47]

The memorial also claimed that Red Jacket was offered $260 to "convince" him to sell land while "other men of our nation" were offered and received $100. Parrish and Jones offered the "chief warrior" at Cattaraugus an annuity of $100 per year, and Jones offered a similar amount to one of the principal chiefs at Tonawanda, both of whom rejected the overtures to sell Seneca lands. The memorial castigated both Parrish and Jones, whom the Senecas had formerly trusted, but who had become "fattened" until their bellies hung over their knees. The Seneca memorial then called for the dismissal of Parrish and Jones and the appointment of future federal commissioners "living out of our immediate vicinity."[48] It also sought Adams's support for the retention of the Seneca lands lost in the "treaty" of 1826: "Your red children feel determined not to release their lands and possessions unless compelled to do so by our father's power which we are unable to resist, but we have every appearance that the hand of our father will not be raised against a handful of his suffering children."[49]

On September 13, 1827, the pro-treaty group led by Young King sent a memorial to President Adams, defending the actions of Forward, Parrish, and Jones, insisting that "there was no force, no threats, and no coercive language" used by the federal commissioner, agent, or interpreters. They chal-

lenged Red Jacket's veracity and his mental state. They claimed that Red
Jacket purposely overestimated the number of Indians "who are opposed to
the late treaty."[50] The memorial concluded:[51]

We would now request our Father the President to ratify the said Treaty, and to pay
no further attention to the communication of Red Jacket on the subject. Red Jacket
is an old man, his mind is broken, his memory is short, and he is devoid of truth.
He is not, and never has been the First Chief of our Tribe or our Nation. Young
King is and has been the first and Great Chief of the Seneca Nation.

Yet within the next three months as a result of a backlash against the "treaty"
of 1826 on the Seneca reservation communities, many of the Indians allied
with Young King reversed their position.

On December 28, 1827, Young King and his supporters sent a second
memorial to President Adams, now explaining the "real" reasons why they
put their names on the "treaty" of 1826. They indicated that they had
become "surrounded" by a growing number of "white settlements" and that
Forward had suggested "that if we [the Seneca] were more compact in our
settlements, it would give greater facility to our Father to attend to the wants
of his red children." Greig, the attorney for the Ogden Land Company, now
pictured as the real enemy, then informed the Senecas that if they "would
part with such a portion" of their lands, the company "should forever after
be left in quietness upon that subject. For these reasons we parted with a
portion, with a fixed resolution to keep the remainder for our posterity."[52]

On March 24, 1828, three Seneca Indians, including Red Jacket, accompanied by the secretary of war had an audience with President John Quincy
Adams at the White House. The Indians insisted that their lands should
"not be taken away from them, nor they compelled to remove to Green
Bay." They also urged President Adams to immediately replace Parrish as
their Indian agent because they "charged him with having defrauded them
of great part of their annuity, of receiving money from their adversaries
[Ogden Land Company], and generally disregarding the interest of those
whom he was bound to protect." The Senecas also beseeched the president
to appoint a special emissary to "investigate these charges, which they said,
could easily be proved."[53]

The United States Senate took up debate on the "treaty." On February 29
the Senate by a vote of twenty to twenty failed to ratify the "treaty."[54] John
C. Calhoun, the vice-president of the United States, did not break the tie,
although treaties, it should be noted, need two-thirds approval by the

Senate. Nor did Calhoun participate in the debate over the treaty. Until April 4, 1828, the Senate also placed an "injunction of secrecy" over deliberations over the "treaty" of 1826 with the Seneca. On that day the Senate passed the following ambiguous resolution:[55] "That by the refusal of the Senate to ratify the treaty with the Seneca Indians, it is not intended to express any disapprobation of the terms of the contract entered into by individuals who are parties to that contract, but merely to disclaim the necessity of an interference by the Senate with the subject matter." According to historian Francis Paul Prucha, the United States Senate was "torn between two provisions" of the federal Trade and Intercourse Act of 1802:[56]

one stipulated (following the act of 1790) that no purchase of Indian land was valid "unless the same be made by treaty or convention, entered into pursuant to the constitution," while the other authorized state agents, with the approval of the United States commissioners, to be present at an Indian treaty council and to deal with the Indians regarding compensation for claims to land extinguished by the treaty.

Prucha's contention does not appear to legitimize the so-called "treaty" of 1826 because all treaties, to be treaties, must be ratified by a two-thirds vote of the United States Senate. Prucha's contention is also a naïve one, which suggests that the senators simply had an interpretation "problem" dealing with this "treaty." The vice-president (Calhoun), the commissioner of Indian Affairs (McKenney), and the new secretary of war (Porter) were all clearly avoiding their federal trust responsibilities to protect the Seneca interests. Embarrassed by the revelations (1826–28) of fraud under the treaty and by Red Jacket's effective campaign to publicize the fraud, Senate action on the "treaty" came to a halt.

To his credit the president followed through with Red Jacket's request. On May 9, 1828, because of growing Indian and Quaker protest against the validity of the 1826 "treaty," the secretary of war appointed Richard Montgomery Livingston of Saratoga, New York, to investigate the events surrounding the 1826 "treaty." Livingston's report is both revealing and disturbing at the same time. The report was ironically sent on December 28, 1828, to Peter B. Porter, the newly appointed secretary of war. It clearly shows the fraud perpetrated at the "treaty." Livingston maintained that, until August of 1826, the Seneca chiefs "disputed about religion, but clung to the common object of retaining their lands." At no time from the founding of the Ogden Land Company in 1810 until ten days after the council of 1826 had been in session "were any of the chiefs, willing to convey any of their lands." The investigator then explained what had transpired to get Seneca "approval."[57]

Livingston reported that immediately after the War of 1812, the Ogdens gave five thousand dollars each to the government agent interpreter and one other interpreter in order to "influence" the Seneca to extinguish their title. "The Agents [probably meaning Parrish and Jones] thus retained were empowered to enlist in the service, by liberal . . . stipends for life, such as the chiefs as might be won." Until 1826 these efforts failed. The appointment of Forward to push a land transaction was done "without the solicitation or privity of the tribe." Forward then convened a council on August 11, 1826, employing arguments "addressed to the hopes and fears of the nation," implying that removal to the West was the only other option. "The terrors of a removal enchained their minds in duress," leading them to submit "to sell a part to preserve the residue."[58]

Livingston suggested several other ways Forward gained approval. He claimed that the Ogden Land Company proprietors and Forward had a secret rendezvous at Rochester before the council at which they perfected their strategy. Dr. Jacob Jemison, described by Livingston as a "civilized native," was "retained by the Proprietors." He and five others were hired as interpreters, but served the interests of the Ogden Land Company first and foremost. Livingston also pointed a finger at many of the chiefs, especially the Christian faction who resided around the Seneca Mission at Buffalo Creek, who had become dependent on federal annuities and other "rewards."[59]

Thus, largely because of the negative findings expressed in the Livingston report, the "treaty" of 1826 was never resubmitted to the United States Senate for its advice and consent. After the outpouring of support by reservation residents for Red Jacket's antitreaty stance in 1826 and the recantation by almost all of the chiefs who had agreed to the massive land sale, Red Jacket was politically rehabilitated; however, with the aged chief's death in 1830, Seneca resolve weakened and new fissures in the tribal polity erupted. By that time, the Senecas faced new threats largely aided by a national policy of forced Indian removal to the West, articulated by Andrew Jackson and his vice-president, Martin Van Buren, a New Yorker.

The treaties of 1823 and 1826, although fraudulent at their roots, were allowed to stand. Although they were later challenged in the courts of New York State in the 1890s, the legal obstacles to Indian land suits at the time made it impossible to obtain redress until monetary compensation was awarded the Senecas under the Indian Claims Commission in the late 1960s and early 1970s.[60] In the meantime, Genesee country became white man's territory with rapid settlement before the Civil War. Livingston County, formed from Genesee and Ontario Counties in 1821, had a population of 35,140 by 1840. Despite its split into several separate counties Genesee County's population rose from 12,588 to 59,587 from 1810 to 1840. Wyoming County was formed from Genesee in 1841, whereas Allegany County, in its present form, was established in 1856, after a series of annexations and cessions of land from 1806 onward.[61] Thus, it is clear that the Erie and its feeder canals facilitated the marketability and profitability of farming in a previously remote region.

Although technically it was to the west of the Genesee and closer to the upper Allegheny River, the Seneca's Oil Spring Reservation was directly affected by the same transportation and land pressures emanating from the state's metropolitan corridor. The push for the creation of the Genesee Valley Canal, an artificial river carrying the wheat of the Genesee valley to the flour mills of the great Erie Canal boom town of Rochester, directly affected the Senecas by the creation of Oil Spring Reservoir, now Cuba Lake. Despite these pressures the Senecas retained the majority of this reservation largely because of Governor Blacksnake, one of the extraordinary traditionalist leaders in their history.

CHAPTER 10

The Disciple

Despite the loss of more than eighty thousand acres in the Genesee River valley at the "treaty" of 1826, the Senecas did retain a small parcel between these lands and that of the Allegany Indian Reservation—the Oil Spring Reservation—which they continue to possess. Faced with canal-building proposals that threatened to lead to dispossession of the Indians from the entire reservation, the Senecas were able to counter many of these pressures. Although they were forced to cede acreage for the building of the Genesee Valley Canal project, the Senecas successfully withstood non-Indians' lobbying efforts and legal challenges to retain this reservation.

The Genesee Valley Canal was another artificial river that helped shape Iroquoia. Although the canal was short-lived, operating for only two decades, it, nevertheless, had a sizable impact on the Seneca Nation in the past and continues to have an impact on the Tonawanda Band of Seneca down to the present. The Oil Spring Indian Reservation, a holy spot in Seneca history, was situated along the canal's lower section, the land between the southern end of the Genesee River and the northernmost branch of the Allegany River, sacred Indian country associated with the early founding of the *Gaiwiio*, the Code of Handsome Lake.

The Oil Spring Reservation is a parcel of Seneca land one mile square, near Cuba, New York. Nearly two-thirds of the reservation is in Allegany County, and the rest is in Cattaraugus County. Even though the Oil Spring was not one of the Seneca lands reserved specifically in the 1797 Treaty of Big Tree, Seneca title to the land was later recognized by Robert Morris, Thomas Morris, and agents of the Holland Land Company, who reserved the one-mile tract for Handsome Lake, the Seneca prophet, as confirmed in a Joseph Ellicott–Holland Land Company map of 1801 and in a New York Court of Appeals case in 1860–61.[1]

The "spring" is "a natural flow of petroleum, which the Senecas used to gather and use for a liniment to treat rheumatic pains and old ulcers."[2] The earliest unequivocal citation in the historical record to the oil spring is in *Jesuit Relations* in 1656, "As one approaches nearer to the country of the cats [Erie Indians] one finds heavy and thick water, which ignites like brandy and boils up in bubbles of flame when fire is applied to it."[3] Until his death in 1815 Handsome Lake, according to anthropologist Anthony F. C. Wallace, viewed this land with special interest and as his personal domain, perhaps because of his practice as a shaman.[4]

The fame of the oil spring was increasingly publicized in the early years of the nineteenth century. Describing the Genesee country in 1804, Robert Munro observed: "Near the head of the Genesee River there is a remarkable spring, the water issuing from it being covered with a sort of oil, called by the Indian Seneca Oil, which is excellent for wounds and other medicinal uses."[5] More importantly, De Witt Clinton, while touring New York for the Board of Canal Commissioners in 1810, visited the oil spring, commenting, "Seneca Oil is procured from a spring in Olean, on the Allegany River, by dipping a blanket on the surface, which attracts the oil and then brushing it into a receiver."[6] Despite his mistakes in geography Clinton's 1810 memoir provided boosterism not only for canal development but also for Genesee Fever, a land rush of immense proportions. In his journal he stated unequivocally, "It is not perhaps too exaggerated to say that the worst lands in the western country [of New York State] are nearly equal to the best in the Atlantic parts of the state."[7]

Much of what happened to the Oil Spring Indian Reservation and environs after Handsome Lake's death in 1815 was the indirect result of the City of Rochester's emergence as a major metropolis. Nearly nonexistent in 1814, Rochester grew to more than thirty-six thousand people by 1850 (see table 3). Monroe County, which was not organized as a separate entity before the War of 1812, had more than sixty thousand residents by 1840.[8] Most of this growth was attributable to the completion of the Erie Canal just south of the city at Pittsford and its elaborate connections to the Irondequoit Creek and the Genesee River in 1822. By that date the Erie Canal extended from Little Falls to Rochester, 180 miles of inland navigation, resulting in a land and commercial rush in the Genesee.[9]

TABLE 3

Urban Growth in Central and Western New York State, 1814 and 1850

City	Year	
	1814	*1850*
Buffalo	1,060	42,261
Rochester	—	36,403
Syracuse	1,241	22,271
Utica	—	17,565

Source: Based on Noble E. Whitford, *History of the Canal System of the State of New York* (Albany, N.Y.: Brandon Printing, 1906), 1:914–19.

The area became a breadbasket overnight, producing substantial amounts of wheat. By 1840 Monroe County alone harvested one million bushels of wheat; Genesee, Livingston, Ontario, and Orleans produced a comparable harvest. Each of these counties and nearby Wayne County produced a substantial corn crop as well, with Monroe leading the way with more than four hundred thousand bushels by 1840.[10]

Rochester, situated in the greatest wheat-growing region of the state, became the leading granary of the Genesee. Other than Buffalo, it had more natural advantages than any other canal town because of its great access to both agricultural products and the extensive water power of the Genesee River. Thus, it was no coincidence that Rochester became the flour capital of the United States. As early as 1835, twenty-one water-powered mills were operating in the city. The ground flour was then packed into barrels and transshipped eastward by canal boats.[11]

Henry O'Reilly, a leading newspaperman and an early promoter of the city, wrote in 1838:[12]

The city is interested to a larger extent than any other in the carrying-trade of the Erie Canal—the great thoroughfare between the seaboard and the inland waters. About one half of the whole amount of stock in all the transportation lines on that waterway is owned or controlled by our citizens. Rochester is to the Canal what Buffalo is to the Lakes. Our staple product is remarkable for its quantity as well as quality. The celebrity of the Genesee wheat is increased by the skill with which it is here prepared for market. Rochester is already not merely the best, but the largest flour-manufactory in the world.

The city, which became the flower capital of the United States in the same period, also thrived on the lucrative lumber industry because rafts and logs could easily be floated down the Genesee River to the city's numerous sawmills. "The Water Power City," as it became known, became a boom town much like mining towns such as Denver, Helena, Sacramento, San Francisco, Seattle, and Tucson later in the trans-Mississippi West. Hence, it was no accident that the city fathers pushed for the expansion of transportation networks southward, hoping to secure trade as far as Pittsburgh and the Ohio River. They urged the creation of a Genesee Valley Canal to connect Rochester with the Allegheny River and beyond.[13] Their grandiose dream was best described by Noble E. Whitford:[14]

In the western section of the state, in the valley of the Genesee river, was an extensive tract of wonderfully fertile and productive land, having no means of access to the markets of the country. The Genesee river, which meets the Erie canal at Rochester, is separated from the Allegheny river at Olean by a very narrow divide. By constructing a canal across this divide and by canalizing the two rivers, an unbroken inland water communication would be afforded between all the important sections of New York State and the valleys of the Ohio, Mississippi, Missouri, Arkansas, Osage, Illinois, Wabash, Tennessee and Cumberland rivers, three-quarters of the entire territory of the United States. The dream of so extensive a line of internal communication appealed to the people of the Genesee valley as affording irresistible arguments for constructing a canal along this route.

By this time state efforts to develop a branch canal in the Genesee River were well underway. In 1813 the New York State Legislature declared the Genesee River to be a public highway. One decade later, the New York State Board of Canal Commissioners chose three potential routes for the construction of a Genesee valley canal, and in 1830 the New York State Legislature appropriated moneys for a survey. By 1836 the canal commissioners finally chose the Rochester to Olean route for construction of the canal.[15] An immediate sense of urgency gripped Rochester merchants about the need for rapid construction because they feared that the recently opened canal-rail connection between Philadelphia and Pittsburgh would threaten their ambitious plans of cornering north-south commercial routes to the Ohio River.[16] Greed and pork-barrel politics supplanted reality because the route chosen in 1836 was in hilly terrain, had scant water supply for canal purposes in the highlands near Mount Morris, and the construction costs of the venture (ultimately six million dollars, the second most expensive canal project in the history of New York State) proved much more than originally calculated.[17]

Pressures for a Genesee Valley Canal were also mounting in and around the Oil Spring Reservation in the years after the War of 1812. Because the region contained a significant growth of pine, oak, chestnut, beech, and maple, General Calvin T. Chamberlain established the first sawmill in the environs of the reservation. Chamberlain's family, as well as the Clarks, were the founding fathers of the region. They had purchased sizable holdings from the Holland Land Company adjacent to the Oil Spring Reservation. In 1822 the New York State Legislature incorporated the village of Oil Creek, which also included Clarksville and Genesee. In the same year a turnpike opened from Oil Creek to Olean. By the mid-1830s this village became a separate entity from Clarksville, taking the name of Cuba. At precisely that time General Chamberlain and Stephen Smith, the two founders of the village, along with other leading citizens of the region, met to organize the lobbying effort for a grand canal between the upper Genesee and the upper Allegheny Rivers. Construction in the southern section of the Genesee Valley Canal served as a catalyst and accelerated later developments along the canal. Cuba, now a town, reached 2,243 in population. With this growth came land speculators, land squatters, and timber strippers onto Seneca lands in the region.[18]

Soon after, one of the Clarks—Stanley—was elected to Congress from the area. A dabbler in Allegany and Cattaraugus Counties real estate, he and his partners, Benjamin Chamberlain and William Gallagher, soon became aware that the Oil Spring Reservation had never been reserved under any federal-Seneca treaty. At that time the three men's lands obtained from the Holland Land Company earlier were adjacent to the reservation. Clark, without Indian authorization, then went onto the Oil Spring Reservation, surveyed it, and claimed it for the three men. They then conveyed one-quarter of the reservation to Horatio Seymour, later governor of New York, Democratic candidate for the presidency in 1868, and major promoter of New York State's canal system. Another quarter, which included the oil spring itself, was conveyed in the mid-1850s to Philonus Pattison, who immediately cleared and fenced eighty acres, planted an orchard, and built a house.[19]

Central to the story of how the reservation was saved from these pressures is the life of the famed Indian leader, Governor Blacksnake.[20] Blacksnake was no ordinary chief. The famed Allegany Seneca was the nephew of both Cornplanter and Handsome Lake. Indeed, because Blacksnake's mother was the sister of these two prominent Indians, it should

Governor Blacksnake, In Thomas Donaldson, comp., *The Six Nations of New York.*

be emphasized that the relationship of mother's brother to sister's son is very significant in matrilineal societies such as the Senecas.[21] Down to the present day the Senecas consider Blacksnake among the nation's greatest leaders. His monument at the cemetery near Onoville on the Allegany Indian Reservation reads: "Devoted his later years to work among his people. *Absolutely honest and truthful* and enjoying the confidence of Indian and Pale-Face" (emphasis mine).[22]

Governor Blacksnake, the Chainbreaker—Tenh-Wen-Nyos—was born in the hamlet of Kendaia on Seneca Lake around 1753 and lived his early life at Canawaugus (today's Avon), New York. An impressive figure and orator, Blacksnake was a slim man slightly more than six feet tall. During the American Revolution he, as did most other Senecas, served the British Crown throughout the conflict. After the British defeat and the humiliating treatment of four of the Iroquois nations at Fort Stanwix in 1784, Blacksnake accompanied his uncle the Cornplanter on special missions to see General George Washington and members of the Continental Congress. He also attended the major Seneca councils and land negotiations with federal officials and land jobbers after the Revolution. When Blacksnake's home village of Canawaugus was included in the Phelps-Gorham Purchase of Seneca lands in 1788, he and his family moved to his uncle's lands, on the Cornplanter Tract, a few miles downriver from the Allegany Reservation.[23] Importantly, when Handsome Lake, the Seneca prophet, fell into his trance during his first vision on June 15, 1799, during the Seneca Strawberry Festival, Blacksnake, his nephew, was the first to rush to his side at his cabin.[24]

At Cornplanter, Blacksnake was converted to the new religion espoused by his uncle, Handsome Lake. Except for his military involvement in the War of 1812, Blacksnake remained true to the religion for nearly sixty years after his conversion in 1799–1800 and gave his uncle political support until Handsome Lake's death at Onondaga in 1815.[25] Handsome Lake's proscription against the sale of any more Indian lands appears to have had a special place in Blacksnake's thinking in the last years of his life.

Blacksnake, as a major supporter of his uncle, proselytized the new religion. During his uncle's life, Blacksnake served as an important advisor, the prophet's "privy counsellor."[26] Later, after Handsome Lake's death, the disciple helped institutionalize the *Gaiwiio* and by 1840 had formulated a specific version of the code "beginning with the account of the first vision" and mandating "twelve commandments prohibiting whiskey, witchcraft, love magic, divorce, adultery, premarital sex, refusal of the wife to live with her husband's parents, failure of parent to discipline unruly children, unwillingness to love all men, enmity, and gossip."[27]

After a dispute with Cornplanter in 1803, Handsome Lake, Blacksnake, and their followers moved from the Cornplanter tract to the Allegany Indian Reservation where they founded the community of Coldspring. For the remainder of his life the Chainbreaker resided 1.5 miles above Coldspring in a small frame house. When Handsome Lake began sanctioning the execution of witches, support for the prophet's message waned somewhat. Eventually, Handsome Lake left the Coldspring community for Tonawanda. Blacksnake, still a devoted follower of the Seneca prophet, stayed behind at Allegany where he remained until his own death in 1859.[28]

Blacksnake's long life spans almost the entire history of Seneca land loss. The Seneca chief bore witness to the rapid dispossession of his people from the time of the Treaty of Fort Stanwix of 1784, a negotiation he attended. From 1797 to 1826 he also attended the treaty councils during which land cessions were made; however, later in 1838, Blacksnake refused to place his name on a federal treaty ceding Buffalo Creek, remaining a holdout to the end. After being convinced by the Hicksite Quakers that his Allegany Indian Reservation could be returned only if he agreed to sign the Supplemental Treaty of Buffalo Creek of 1842, the elderly man of nearly ninety signed this so-called compromise treaty, which recognized the permanent loss of the Buffalo Creek and Tonawanda Indian Reservations. In 1848, as a result of a political upheaval, the so-called Seneca revolution, the old chiefs system of government was eradicated and a new elected republican form of government was installed.

Although Blacksnake and other Seneca chiefs at Allegany and Cattaraugus were swept out of power in 1848, one of the Chainbreaker's greatest moments was to occur several years later in the 1850s, even though he was well beyond one hundred years of age at the time. Seeing himself as the faithful disciple of his uncle Handsome Lake, Blacksnake protected the Seneca prophet's territory, namely the Oil Spring Indian Reservation, from being totally overrun by non-Indian trespassers-entrepreneurs taking advantage of state efforts to construct the Genesee Valley Canal. Even before that time the Seneca elder had foreseen Albany's master plan, canal development, for Seneca country.

As early as December 1835 Governor Blacksnake and other Seneca chiefs and warriors of the Seneca nation had made a thirty-year lease with "Irvine, Lowry, and Macomber one mile square on the Oil Spring Reservation in the county of Allegany 'with full power to search for any and all kinds of minerals or ore.'" This agreement went beyond Oil Spring Reservation; it also allowed for the company's construction of three mills, hydraulic works, and dams along the Allegheny River in Seneca country. In return Irvine, Lowry, and Macomber agreed to pay the Seneca four hundred dollars annually, promised to instruct the Indians in agriculture, and insisted the firm would prevent "any trespass committed by other individuals, such as cutting and carrying away timber." Seeing the potential of the proposed Genesee Valley Canal that might be compromised by this private agreement, the New York State Legislature rejected the Seneca petition to confirm this individual lease.[29]

Why the Seneca went to the New York State Legislature for confirmation of this lease is unclear. Perhaps, in the Age of Jackson Indians were reluctant to go to Washington to seek protection. At the time Washington officials were already planning for the removal of all the Iroquois Indians from New York State. Another possibility, a more likely one, is that the Indians were trying to delay or even stymie the building of the Genesee Valley Canal and were playing off private interests (Irvine, Lowry, and Macomber) against the New York State Board of Canal Commissioners. After all, the New York State Legislative Report maintained:[30]

By the terms of the contract, the leasees would have the entire control of the Allegany river, for a distance of about forty miles for the term of thirty years, which, in the opinion of your committee, is a power that should never be surrendered by the State, to any individual, or number of individuals, however respectable they may be, over a navigable river of so much importance as the Allegany, particularly when it is in contemplation to connect that river with our great commercial metropolis by splendid projects of internal improvement.

Should the projected improvements of this State be constructed, the Allegany river is destined to become the great thoroughfare from the city of New York to the valley of the Ohio and the Mississippi, and should the Legislature confirm the contract made by the Indians, they might thereby legalize a destruction of the navigation of that noble river, and have the sad consolation of knowing they had tied up their own hands for the space of thirty years, and given to a company of individuals what they would consider a *"vested right,"* and thereby prevent any further legislation on the subject. (Emphasis New York State Legislature Report)

The construction on the southern section of the Genesee Valley Canal began in 1839. Because of a major New York State budget crisis, the canal construction came to a halt in 1842. Construction resumed in 1846. As a result of the difficult hilly terrain and excessive cost of the project, final completion of the canal was delayed until 1858 (except for work on an 11-mile extension spur near Dansville). The canal, 128 miles long with 112 locks, connected the Erie Canal near Rochester to the New York and Erie Railroad at Olean, New York, a major railway that had opened in 1851.[31]

The Genesee Valley Canal had only a twenty-year history of use, 1858–78. Yet for the Senecas it led to court actions, federal hearings, congressional legislation, and contemporary land claims pursuits. From 1855 to 1861 the Seneca Nation fought to save the entire reservation from squatters. It began a major ejectment case, *Seneca Nation of Indians v. Philonus Pattison,* which ended up in the New York State Court of Appeals.[32] A second action was directed by the Seneca against Seymour, Gallagher, Chamberlain, and Clark for the northeast quarter of the Oil Spring tract. The reason why this action ended up in a state court is not altogether clear; however, it may be suggested that because of the political turmoil after the Seneca revolution of 1848 and the establishment of a new Indian republican elected government incorporated under New York State laws, the Seneca's attorney Daniel Sherman (later federal Indian agent) was scarcely concerned with Indian sovereignty issues. The case turned on evidence produced by Blacksnake.

The counsel for the defendants repeatedly attempted to challenge the Senecas' right to ownership of the Oil Spring Reservation because the lands had never been specifically reserved in any federal treaty. Yet in April 1857 Daniel Sherman, the attorney for the Senecas, produced a deposition by Blacksnake about the negotiations, which he had attended, relating to the Treaty of Big Tree of 1797. In it Blacksnake made clear that it was the intent of both the Senecas and the Holland Land Company to include these lands in the treaty, but they had been inadvertently omitted. Joseph Ellicott himself had surveyed the lands along with other Seneca parcels in 1798 and had produced a map indicating Seneca ownership of the property.[33]

On August 27 and 28, 1858, Governor Blacksnake appeared before Judge Cobb in Cattaraugus County Court and testified about his earlier deposition. Indicating he was one hundred eight years of age, he recounted his long and extraordinary life: his childhood on the Genesee, his involvement in the American Revolution, his appointment as chief, his five meetings with General Washington. He stated that he was well "acquainted with the Oil Spring Reservation" and that he had been frequently there long before the Treaty of Big Tree because the "Indians used the oil of the spring a good deal for medicine." He then described the negotiations for the treaty at Big Tree that he and other chiefs signed. After failing to recollect any talk there about the Oil Spring, he, however, noted that two or three years later, he noticed that the reservation boundaries had been marked: "The marks on the trees looked fresh and were the same as around the other reservations." Moreover, about a year or two after the Treaty of Big Tree, Blacksnake saw a map on which the Oil Spring Reservation was marked red like the others reserved under the treaty. He took the map from Ellicott, copies of which the Holland Land Company agent had made for all the Seneca parties to the agreement, and then filed it with the chief's other important papers in a chest underneath his bed.[34] The court found for the Senecas, and Pattison, Chamberlain, Clark, Gallagher, and Seymour were eventually ejected from the reservation after their appeals to the New York State Court of Appeals failed by 1861.

Despite this legal victory the Senecas faced more travail. The building of the Genesee Valley Canal, the second most expensive canal in New York State to construct, required the acquisition of land as a feeder for the canal. The Oil Spring Reservoir (Cuba Lake) was created in 1855 by the construction of a dam on Oil Creek, fifty-six feet high. In 1863 and then again in 1868 the New York State Legislature authorized the expansion of the spillway and the raising of the water level of Oil Creek Reservoir.[35] Before this 1868 take (and without federal or Indian approval), the New York State Board of Canal Commissioners expropriated forty-five acres of the Oil Spring Indian Reservation in the creation of the Genesee Valley Canal project. Charles Congdon indicated that "47 acres of reservation lands were affected, of which only 13.19 acres were appropriated for the reservoir, but certain other quantities were liable to be damaged and flooded, used for roads, spoilbanks, etc."[36]

New York State paid the Seneca attorney Daniel Sherman $1,319.04 on May 12, 1866, out of its Canal Fund for the flooding of Seneca lands before 1865, more specifically in 1858 and 1863.[37] Yet, apparently other Indian lands at Oil Spring were later appropriated by the New York State Board of Canal Commissioners, perhaps as long as six years after the state's final condemnation payment was made to the Seneca Nation. According to the secretary to the New York State Conservation Commission, writing in 1914, "About the year 1872 there was also acquired [by the state] 1.48 acres in the same reservation."[38] Although the state claimed that it subsequently, in 1927, received federal approval of the original "take" of 45–47 acres of land made *before* 1865, it never, before or since, had federal consent to the *later* "take."[39] Moreover, the state forester readily admitted in a 1913 report that the original state surveys done by the Genesee Valley Canal engineers "were very carelessly run. The chaining was very poor, and in transcribing from the field notes to the maps there were many errors," making it impossible to determine fully the boundary of the state property and the Indian lands.[40]

Because all these "takes" had been in clear violation of the federal Trade and Intercourse Acts—no federal commissioner was present and no United States Senate approval was secured—the New York State Legislature was obviously concerned about the legality of this taking of Indian lands. In 1867 at the New York State Constitutional Convention, the committee on the relation of the state to the Indians recommended the following be implemented:[41]

sec. 4. When the public exigency requires the use and occupancy of any of the lands or water privileges of the several Indian reservations for the construction of railways, common roads, bridges, manufacturing or other purposes, such lands or privileges should be so appropriated, and such tribe or nation holding such reservation shall receive a reasonable compensation thereof.

In 1868 and 1869 the New York State Canal Board and the New York State Legislature considered further compensation to the Seneca. The bill, "An act providing for the appraisal and payment of the damages to the Seneca Nation of Indians, caused by raising the banks of the feeder of the Oil Spring Reservation supplying water to the Genesee Valley canal," passed the New York State Senate and was reported favorably in the Assembly to the committee of the whole in 1869. No further record of this legislative action has been found.[42] Thus, even in its demise, the Genesee Valley Canal had an impact on the Seneca, one that bears directly on Indian land claims in New York State right down to today.[43]

The Oil Spring Reservoir, now known as Cuba Lake, an area of nearly sixteen hundred acres and the largest artificial body of water in the state when it was created, eventually became a leading pleasure resort. The nearby town of Cuba encouraged tourism, and the lake became famous for anglers from around New York State and from Pennsylvania. Thus, in effect, part of Oil Spring, Seneca holy ground, became a dammed playground for non-Indians. Indeed, tourism became a mainstay of the entire region that Handsome Lake and his disciple Blacksnake traversed and saw as their holy land. Even the old Caneadea Council House was eventually disassembled and sent up the Genesee Valley Canal. Later, it was reassembled by William Pryor Letchworth and placed near Mary Jemison's cabin at Letchworth State Park, the site of the old Gardeau Indian Reservation. Thus, some of the holiest spots in Iroquoia were now simply seen by non-Indians as fishermen's paradises or were becoming relics, "curiosities" to generate tourist dollars.[44]

In October 1872 before the council house was removed, many prominent Iroquois Indians gathered for the last time at Caneadea. One of the Senecas in attendance was William Blacksnake, Sho-noh-go-wah, the grandson of the famous Chainbreaker. The Indians solemnly recalled earlier councils at the site at a time when Seneca villages stretched in a line from the upper Genesee to the upper Allegheny.[45] While the last boats were moving down the Genesee Valley Canal, soon to be replaced by a new mode of transportation—the railroad—the Indians nostalgically looked back to the time of the disciple, who kept a watchful eye on the Seneca holy lands as a custodian of the prophet's domain. Although he was not altogether successful, Blacksnake's actions did help to define Oil Spring as Seneca Indian land, which it remains, except for some acreage underwater at Cuba Lake.

CHAPTER 11

The Bucktails Stop Here

As a result of the "treaty" of 1826, the Ogden Land Company obtained title to approximately thirty-three thousand acres of the Buffalo Creek Reservation, the southernmost and easternmost strips of Seneca lands; however, company officials' appetites were only whetted by the 1826 "accord." The quick rise of the city of Buffalo and its port facilities made T. L. Ogden and Joseph Fellows even more intent on getting at the Indian lands. By 1831 the city was formally incorporated. This instant city, only two decades after its burning by the British, was now seen as having limitless potential if and when Indian land rights to the Buffalo Creek Reservation could be extinguished. By the mid-1830s one tourist guide glowingly predicted a bright future for the Queen City: "Buffalo is a beautiful, flourishing city, at the outlet of Lake Erie, possessing the twofold advantages of a lake and canal navigation. The time is not far distant when it will rank with and rival any of the Atlantic cities."[1]

While these changes were happening locally in western New York, Indian policies were being transformed in Washington, D.C. Now state and private land and transportation interests were to be furthered by a shift in the nation's Indian policies as a whole. With the ascendancy of Andrew Jackson to the presidency and Martin Van Buren, the powerful New Yorker, to the vice-presidency in 1829, and the passage by Congress of the Indian Removal Act in 1830, a new national policy with regard to American Indians was to be articulated both at the federal and state levels. Instead of promoting Calhoun's carrot-and-stick approach to Indian removal, policymakers were now going to force the issue and allow local and state interests to lead the way. Thus, state officials increasingly determined the course and future of Indian populations within their limits, extended state jurisdiction, and made it nearly impossible for Indians to maintain themselves in their territories. By the 1830s the situation was ripe at the local, state, and federal levels to extinguish Seneca rights to the Buffalo Creek Reservation, the most sought after Indian real property in New York. This movement to get at the Seneca land base was to culminate with the Treaty of Buffalo Creek on January 15, 1838.

By 1830 the Ogden Land Company's aim of removing Indians from New York State piggybacked with the same growing feeling at state and national levels. In the past the land companies had at times allied themselves with Federalists, Jeffersonians, Burrites, and Clintonians to push for or secure their objectives. Now, they were to have powerful voices in Washington promoting what they had been urging for three decades. Indeed, in November 1828 the vice-president-elect, New York Governor Martin Van Buren—the former leader of the anti-Clintonian Bucktail faction in New York State politics after the War of 1812 and senator before becoming governor—was himself to be instrumental in the events leading up to and following the Buffalo Creek Treaty of 1838.

The Treaty of Buffalo Creek of 1838, largely the work of four New Yorkers from the eastern part of the state, is one of the major frauds in American Indian history, ranking in notoriety with the Walking Purchase of 1737 with the Delaware, the Treaty of Dancing Rabbit Creek of 1830 with the Choctaw and the Treaty of New Echota of 1835 with the Cherokee. The Treaty of Buffalo Creek permanently affected all of the Iroquois and the Stockbridge-Munsee as well. Besides the loss of the Seneca's Buffalo Creek Reservation (much of the present city of Buffalo), the treaty led to the removal of many Indians from the state. Within thirty years of this treaty more than one hundred thousand non-Indians had settled within the city's boundaries.

Under this fraudulent treaty consummated as a result of bribery, forgery, the use of alcohol, and other nefarious methods, the Seneca ceded all their remaining New York lands except the one-mile-square Oil Spring Reservation to the Ogden Land Company and relinquished their rights to Menominee lands in Wisconsin purchased for them by the United States. In return, the Indians accepted a 1,824,000-acre Kansas reservation set aside by the federal government for all the six Iroquois nations and the Stockbridge-Munsees. The Indian nations had to occupy these Kansas lands within five years or forfeit this reservation. For a total of 102,069 acres in New York, the Indians were to receive $202,000—$100,000 of which was to be invested in safe stocks by the president of the United States with the income earned to be returned to the Indians. The United States was also to provide the Indians a modest sum to facilitate removal, to establish schools, and to purchase farm equipment and livestock for their use.

The treaty had other far-reaching results. Some of the Indians on the Iroquois version of the "Trail of Tears" died en route to or in the Indian Territory of cholera, exposure, or starvation. In addition, the bitter in-fighting in tribal politics after the treaty's consummation eventually led to the creation of a new political entity, the Seneca Nation of Indians, in 1848. Moreover, the treaty led to a Quaker-directed campaign to restore the Indian land base in New York, resulting in the United States Senate's ratification of the Supplemental Treaty of 1842. The Seneca regained the Allegany and Cattaraugus, but not the Buffalo Creek and Tonawanda Reservations. Only in 1856 was the Tonawanda Band of Senecas finally "allowed" to purchase a small part of its reservation back from the Ogden Land Company. This land purchase and the confirmation of federal reservation status was acknowledged by the United States and the Tonawanda Band of Senecas in a treaty concluded the following year. American Indian claims under the Treaty of 1838 were not settled until the 1890s in a major United States Court of Claims award. Thus, in effect, the Treaty of Buffalo Creek was the basis of federal-Iroquois relations throughout much of the nineteenth century.[2]

Martin Van Buren and his cohorts saw the treaty and Indian removal as a way to build statewide political machinery, and, at the same time, create a national Democrat Party by supporting like-minded states' rights advocates in Alabama, Georgia, Mississippi, and other Southern states. Van Buren, a true mechanic, made the engine run and Indian removal a reality. Importantly, he was president of the United States at the time of the negotiations and the "ratification" of the Treaty of Buffalo Creek. As the "little magician of Kinderhook," he was also the creator of the first statewide political machine in the history of New York—the Albany Regency. After his election to the United States Senate in 1821, Van Buren organized this machine to gain and hold power and to extend his men's influence into every hamlet and county. Through discipline, organization, and communication and financed through a judicious distribution of offices to the faithful, Van Buren held his coalition together—however shakily at times—aided by the New York State Constitution of 1821, which placed a large portion of patronage in the hands of the governor and legislature.[3]

Van Buren personally chose a coterie of comrades in Albany, transferred power to them, and charged them with the responsibility of maintaining party discipline and control. These men, whose signature was wearing a buck's tail in their hats, included some of the leading figures of nineteenth-century New York State politics: Benjamin F. Butler, Erastus Corning, Edwin Croswell, John A. Dix, Azariah Flagg, William L. Marcy, and Silas Wright, Jr., just to mention a fair sampling. The group began as a holy alliance of office holders and office expectants in Albany in the early 1820s and blossomed into much more through a building of county organizations. Closing ranks after party caucus was essential. The ideal of a loyal party man, best idealized by Silas Wright, Jr., became a feature of the second party system. Designated party whips and other legislative leadership kept the cohesion. They shared party proposals and political strategy, gave advice relative to speeches and speech making, and viewed the concept of party as a positive good. The Albany Regency's system of rewards, patronage, stretched down to every village in the state and contributed to party loyalty. This small clique of friends used judgeships with abandon. The Regency also cultivated and groomed young men who showed promise for major responsibilities.

Much like the Ogden's, Van Buren's political allies saw the western region of the state as having limitless economic potential as a result of the opening of the Erie Canal. Although none of the major leaders of the Regency such as Van Buren, Croswell, or Wright seem to have profited directly from the dispossession of the Indians, they saw the issue in terms of true party men: office and votes; defense of loyal party members, however dishonest; a way to counter rising Whig politicos such as Millard Fillmore of Buffalo and William Seward of Auburn; and as a means to extend Democrat Party influence into western New York.[4]

Three New Yorkers from eastern New York—James W. Stryker, John F. Schermerhorn, and Ransom H. Gillet—all with close ties to Van Buren's Albany Democrat political establishment helped carry out the fraud. Stryker, born on Staten Island and a resident of Middletown and New York City for much of his life, was the subagent of the New York Agency. A graduate of Columbia University, Stryker had studied law with De Witt Clinton. He later rejected Clintonianism when he joined the Albany Regency in the mid-1820s. After faithfully serving the cause, he, in typical fashion, was rewarded with a county judgeship as a judge to the Court of Common Pleas in Erie County. At the same time he was appointed by Andrew Jackson as federal subagent for the New York Indians.[5]

On November 30, 1830, Secretary of War John H. Eaton conveyed Stryker's appointment as subagent "to aid the expected emigration of the New York Indians to Green Bay" and suggested that Stryker move to Buffalo.[6] In the next decade he built his connections by choosing key Indians as government interpreters, by recommending federal educational subsidies for certain cooperative Indians, and by outright bribery of Iroquois chiefs and warriors. As early as 1832 Stryker had laid out a specific removal plan in a letter to Secretary of War Lewis Cass.[7] In the same year Stryker's honesty had come into question because of discrepancies in Indian annuity accounts. In his defense the subagent blamed his predecessors and appealed for protection from his Regency benefactors, most notably Congressman Samuel Beardsley, a leading Jacksonian supporter in New York and a proponent of the Erie Railroad, which later was built through Iroquois lands.[8]

By November 1833 Stryker was pushing for full removal of Indians from the Buffalo Creek Reservation, which he insisted could be financed by the relinquishment of the Indians' claims to five hundred thousand acres of their so-called Green Bay lands. He also lobbied for the creation of an "exploring party" and for federal payment of three hundred dollars for each Indian delegate chosen.[9] By February 1834 he had already engendered such animosity that Indians petitioned the Jackson administration for his removal. The petitioners claimed that Stryker had misused tribal annuities, had the Indian interpreter on his private payroll, had "disturbed our peace and harmony," and even was being employed by the Ogden Land Company to get at the Indians' estate.[10] Yet, once again, Stryker's defenders—prominent Buffalo residents and key Regency men—came to his aid.[11] Charges against Stryker expanded in early 1835 to include "being friendly and supportive of deposed chiefs," failing to furnish supplies for official receptions, and being unprepared, not listening or not attending tribal council meetings.[12]

By the spring of 1836 Stryker was now ably assisted in his efforts at Indian removal by John F. Schermerhorn. After the return of a Schermerhorn-directed exploring party to the West in August 1837, Stryker conveyed the proremoval report to Secretary of War Joel Poinsett in most flattering terms. Stryker maintained that the proemigration party were "the most respectable and enlightened portion of our chiefs" and that removal was the most "liberal action of the government in behalf of their people." The subagent falsely conveyed the impression that the delegates were selected by the Indians based upon merit and not upon Schermerhorn's and his own dealings.[13] In the fall of 1837 Stryker wrote Commissioner Harris, claiming that treaty opponents were diminishing in number. It is also clear that by 1836–37 Stryker and the Ogden Land Company were collaborating, even at times suggesting the same names to the Indian office to aid in the negotiations with the Indians.[14]

Only after the Treaty of Buffalo Creek was concluded in January 1838 did the size of the "Stryker frauds" become fully known. In Senate Report no. 192 of September 9, 1850, after a thorough investigation of the facts by Congressman John Wales, the United States Government was judged responsible for the malfeasance of the Indian subagent. The Phelps-Gorham annuity fund disappeared from 1837 onward while under the subagent's control. Moreover, three years of stock dividends, 1837 to 1839, from the Troup-Ogden-Rogers agreement of 1826 had "vanished" while under Stryker's care. In addition, two New York State annuity payments, 1837 and 1838, from a treaty concluded in 1815 had disappeared while under the subagent's aegis. To make matters worse the "Indian woman Polly Jimeson" had entrusted her entire finances to Stryker for "safekeeping"; nevertheless, he had paid her back only $180 of more than $1,600. Stryker and his successors had also failed to pay annuities from 1837 to 1850. Finally, Stryker had deposited the 1838 federal annuity in Buffalo banks under the names of four chiefs; he later withdrew the money, distributing $117.50 and keeping $3,482.50 for himself. Besides the loss of their reservation at Buffalo Creek, Stryker had thus defrauded the Iroquois, primarily the Senecas, of $28,505.50 exclusive of interest payments![15]

Stryker remained "protected" until his death in 1851. As late as October 25, 1838, citizens of Erie County wrote Van Buren hailing Stryker for his "high character," "business talent," and "knowledge of Indian matters" and urged his reappointment in part because of "his long and active connection with the democratic [sic] party."[16] He and his Democrat associates spent much of their time plotting strategy to avoid prosecution. When Stryker was finally indicted in 1840, the Buffalo citizenry once again came to his aid.[17] This time William L. Marcy, the former Jacksonian governor of New York State, United States senator, and later secretary of war and secretary of state, rose to Stryker's defense. Writing to Secretary of War Joel Poinsett, Marcy indicated that "Judge S. [sic] has a great number of personal and political friends who feel solicitous that his case should not be disposed of before he has a chance for his defense." Although Marcy acknowledged personal ignorance of the facts in the case, the former governor expressed the views of associates who indicated Stryker's innocence.[18] Not surprisingly, Judge Horatio J. Stow, who presided over Stryker's court case in 1840, later acquitted the subagent. It is important to note that Stow was attorney for the Bank of Buffalo, which was tied to bribery contracts under the Treaty of Buffalo Creek. Despite pleas of infirmity and poverty, Stryker went on to establish his own magazine in the late 1840s and escaped further prosecution after his "trial."[19]

Perhaps next to Jackson and Van Buren themselves, no figure had more direct involvement in carrying out Indian policies in the 1830s than did John F. Schermerhorn, another eastern New Yorker. He was involved in treaty negotiations with twenty Indian nations, resulting in the removal of thousands of Indians from their homelands, "many of whom died or were killed as they were marched westward beyond the Mississippi River." The cleric was, according to his biographer, James Van Hoeven, "indirectly responsible for provoking the Seminole War" as well as factional conflicts within several Indian nations, including the Cherokees and Senecas. In fact, his machinations extended into the Van Buren administration and were still felt well after the clergyman's death in 1841. Van Hoeven has stated, "No appointed government official did more to implement Jackson's program of Indian removal in the field" than did Schermerhorn during the Jackson era.[20] Schermerhorn was also seen as "Jackson's man" by the Indians themselves. Oneidas forced to emigrate to Green Bay from New York by Jacksonian policies complained to Cherokee Chief John Ross "bitterly of Schermerhorn's past conduct towards them also" and Ross insisted *they feel as we* [Cherokee] *do,* in regard to Indian affairs generally" (emphasis Ross).[21] Less than one year later, the young Seneca Chief Maris Pierce referred to Schermerhorn sarcastically as that "certain notorious minister who preaches General Jackson's *humane* policy for the removal of the Indians now east of the Mississippi" (emphasis Pierce).[22]

Schermerhorn was a prominent Dutch Reformed minister from Schenectady and later Utica, New York. He was a descendant of one of the founders of Schenectady. The cleric had been a longtime admirer and supporter of Andrew Jackson, whom he had first met during the War of 1812. He was less tied to Martin Van Buren and the rising Democrat Party until

General Jackson's election to the presidency in 1828; nevertheless, it should be noted that Schermerhorn and Van Buren were both members of the Dutch Reformed Church in the capital district and that Van Buren was an uncle to one of Schermerhorn's close ministerial colleagues.[23] According to his biographer, "Drawing on these relationships, the prestigious legacy of his own family name in the Schenectady-Albany area, and his 'friendship' with Jackson, Schermerhorn apparently was able to gain entrée into the select circles of New York politicians."[24]

Schermerhorn's fanatical religiosity obscured other sides of his character. Dogmatically judgmental and uncompromising, the New York minister fervently backed Jacksonian removal policies and viewed political opponents as morally inept. Schermerhorn was also a slimy supplicant constantly badgering his political supporters for appointments to office. While serving as Jackson's ear to the missionary societies, he frequently sought his due rewards, not final judgment. Although his elaborate plan for the emigrant Indians included providing for eventual statehood and Indian representation in Congress, Schermerhorn was always careful to provide for his own financial needs at every turn. He speculated in Wisconsin lands while serving as a commissioner dealing with the Indians in the West and lobbied successfully for a two thousand dollar reimbursement in Article VIII of the Treaty of Buffalo Creek with the New York Indians, three months after he had been relieved of his negotiating duties![25]

Schermerhorn kept Jackson informed about the activities of the American Board of Commissioners for Foreign Missions, the Boston-based proselytizing society that opposed the president's Indian removal policies. He also transmitted news of the Indian Board for the Emigration, Preservation, and Improvement of the Aborigines of America, founded in 1829, whose "exclusive object" was to promote the federal government's Indian removal policies. Although Schermerhorn was not part of the leadership of the New York Indian Welfare Board (as it became known), his own Dutch Reformed Church was the driving force in this organization.[26]

Sincere humanitarian zeal, not the Schermerhorn variety, calling for Indian removal to the West to isolate the native from the greed, arrogance, and racism of the East has masked the crass intentions and harsh political realities of policymakers during this period. Although there were undoubtedly sincere good men associated with the cause of removal, the

Jackson–Van Buren administration used these men for their own political advantage.[27]

Because of his constant political badgering, Schermerhorn was eventually appointed to the Stokes Commission in 1832 as one of three commissioners who were required to examine the western region in an effort to obtain the necessary information to draft legislation to ameliorate existing tribal disputes over boundary lines and treaty obligations. In reality this Stokes Commission had as its chief aim the facilitation of further tribal removal to Indian Territory. It was to make recommendations for a plan for the improvement, government, and security of the Indians to the War Department intended to quiet critics of removal.

In 1832 and 1833 the three commissioners held councils and negotiated with the Cherokee, Chippewa, Creek, Miami, Osage, Ottawa, Potawatomi, Quapaw, Seminole, and Seneca-Shawnee nations.[28] It is important to note that Schermerhorn was judged by the Indians and his fellow commissioners as the "least compromising" of the three men, and his "manner and rhetoric was pedantic and less polite than his colleagues."[29] Although there were successes in convincing Indians to remove west, the Seminoles for one refused to accept the commission's findings and soon the Florida frontier erupted in a full-scale bloody conflict known in history as the Second Seminole War, 1835–42. The conflict resulted in the loss of more than fifteen hundred white soldiers and probably a greater number of Indian lives. One writer of the American frontier experience has specifically blamed Schermerhorn for tricking "touring Seminole chiefs at Fort Gibson into signing a document which could later be construed to represent a Seminole consent to migrate west, an expedient which presently precipitated the [Second] Seminole War."[30] Significantly, during his tenure as commissioner, Schermerhorn visited Buffalo Creek Reservation in March 1835 to discuss the possibilities of Seneca exploration of the West.[31] While being apprised of the situation in New York in 1835–36, the minister had another major responsibility to undertake for his commander-in-chief, Jackson, namely, the removal of the Cherokee Indians.

Schermerhorn's notoriety in history stems from being Jackson's emissary, the chief federal negotiator of the fraudulent New Echota Treaty of 1835. Threatening the Cherokees with reprisals if they rejected the treaty, Schermerhorn consciously played up divisions in Cherokee society with little concern for Indian cultural sensitivities. He saw John Ross in cosmic dimensions as the "Devil in Hell." Despite the Cherokee leadership's rejection of a removal treaty on previous occasions, Schermerhorn called a national council referendum. Although several hundred people attended and there were thousands of eligible voters in the Cherokee Nation, the vote at New Echota was only seventy-five to seven in favor of emigration. Schermerhorn fanatically defended the propriety of this questionable action and pushed for the treaty until its final ratification by the United States Senate in May 1836. Demographer Russell Thornton has estimated that perhaps as many as eight thousand Indians died on the Trail of Tears that resulted from the New Echota Treaty.[32] Gary Moulton, the editor of the John Ross Papers, has even suggested that "Schermerhorn's desire for success was prompted by his hope of attaining a personal reward from the Jackson administration, perhaps a government position in the future Indian state."[33]

The New York clergyman was soon rewarded for his "success" with the Cherokees by being appointed by Jackson, his benefactor, to serve as the commissioner to make a treaty of removal with the New York Indians. This appointment was especially significant because the Indians in the Empire State were one of the last major eastern indigenous populations who remained largely untouched by Jacksonian policies and therefore one that continued as a thorn to Washington policymakers. Yet by 1836 Schermerhorn had a political albatross around his neck, namely, that he was associated more than any other individual (outside of Jackson himself) with Indian removal policies. Political opponents of Jackson, such as Whig senators Henry Clay and Hugh Lawson White, frequently sniped at Jackson by attacking his special emissary Schermerhorn.[34]

Two weeks before the Senate vote on the New Echota Treaty in 1836, Schermerhorn was already lobbying to secure a position to negotiate a treaty for removal of the Iroquois Indians from New York. In fact, Schermerhorn had also been corresponding with members of the Seneca Indian emigration party! By July he had calculated how many Indians he had to remove from New York. Writing to his benefactor Andrew Jackson in the early fall of 1836, Schermerhorn referred to his past experience with the Cherokees but noted obstacles in his way in New York where he maintained that the majority of Indians were opposed to removal; nevertheless, he reassured Jackson about his commitment to secure the removal of New York tribesmen.[35] Schermerhorn also wrote the commissioner of Indian Affairs that he had "laid the foundations for the ultimate and speedy removal of the whole of the New York Indians, both those who reside at Green Bay and those who are still within this state."[36] What he had resolved upon was his strategy to isolate and divide the tribesmen by negotiating separately with each group. First, he was going to finalize agreements with the Oneidas, Mohawks, and Tuscaroras, then with the Stockbridges and Munsees, and finally with the remaining New York tribes.[37]

In the spring of 1837 the New York zealot announced that he was set to solve the thorny problem of the Ogden Land Company, the major speculators in Seneca lands, and their preemptive right to the lands occupied by the Indians. What Schermerhorn had apparently done was to exacerbate Indian divisions further by personally picking all the members of an Indian exploring party, thus bypassing the general councils of the Iroquois nations. When the exploring party—composed of proemigration Indians on the payroll of the federal government, Ogden Land Company, or the negotiators—filed their reports from August 1837 onward, it was little surprise that they defended their appointments as delegates. Although Schermerhorn had even apparently offended some of the proremoval party by showing them only certain western lands, they, nevertheless, largely defended the minister: "He [Schermerhorn] did not consider it necessary to hold a general council on the subject in as much as the very object in view might be defeated by delay."[38]

In October 1837 in three separate memorials Seneca, Oneida, and Onondaga chiefs protested Schermerhorn's actions. The Seneca protest argued that the minister had selected the exploring party himself and that these Indians "did not have any desire of again exploring the western country" because they wished to remain on their lands. They further insisted that Schermerhorn had violated the Pickering Treaty of 1794 and that negotiations between the United States and the Indians could only be transacted in "open council" with the Seneca leadership.[39] Because of increasing congressional criticisms of the minister and Silas Wright's desire to reward a protégé, Schermerhorn was "cut loose" by the Democrat administration and replaced by former Congressman Ransom H. Gillet as commissioner in late 1837.

Just before his dismissal, Schermerhorn had secured agreements from the Oneida, Mohawk, Tuscarora, Stockbridge, and Munsee by repeating his Cherokee formula, namely, by promoting internal chaos. Angered by War

Department officials' refusal to compensate him for negotiations with the Indians at Green Bay and for "expenses" incurred on one of the exploring parties to Indian Territory, Schermerhorn inserted the following provision into the Buffalo Creek Treaty:[40]

It is stipulated and agreed that the accounts of the Commissioner, and expenses incurred by him in holding a council with the New York Indians, and concluding treaties at Green Bay and Duck Creek, in Wisconsin, and in the State of New York, in 1836, and those for the exploring party of the New York Indians in 1837, and also the expenses of the present treaty, shall be allowed and settled according to former precedents.

Through Gillet's and Stryker's help, the New York cleric later received two thousand dollars under this provision, Article VIII, of the treaty.[41]

Although Stryker is usually given much of the blame for the Treaty of Buffalo Creek and his name is most associated with the frauds of the 1830s, Ransom H. Gillet, a former Democrat Congressman from Ogdensburg, was the single most important person in the securing of the treaty. Gillet, born in Columbia County, was the protégé of Senator Silas Wright, the leading Regency politician and close associate of Van Buren. Because of his status as a junior junto member and a rising star in Democrat politics, Gillet is a key figure in the period 1837–40. Despite his association with the nefarious negotiations, Gillet was rewarded from 1840 onward with a series of Democrat sinecures: solicitor of the treasury, assistant attorney general of the United States, solicitor of the United States Court of Claims. As a leading attorney his clients later included the noted Jacksonian, Amos Kendall. In later life he wrote books about American politics as well as a two-volume biography of Silas Wright; he also was viewed as a respected elder of the Democrat Party well into the 1870s.[42]

On May 10, 1836, Gillet and other prominent New Yorkers, who included Silas Wright and C. C. Cambreleng of the Albany Regency, sent a memorial to the commissioner of Indian Affairs, advocating a speedy removal of Indians from New York State: "Under the circumstances we think it a duty to some of our common constituents, as well as to the Indians themselves to ask that this government should make an effort to treat with them for the accomplishment of this desirable object." The Regency politicians pledged to do everything possible to get Congress to appropriate funds for removal during the coming sessions.[43] Sixteen months later Gillet was appointed commissioner to replace Schermerhorn to treat with the Indians. Admitting his lack of personal acquaintance with the Indians and Indian matters in general, Gillet dutifully accepted his appointment on October 29, 1837.[44] Taking his cue from his tutor Schermerhorn, whom he insisted was sympathetic to the Indians' plight, Gillet quickly came to the conclusion that the "Indians are not always accurate in their conclusions concerning what is most beneficial for them."[45]

Gillet was also apparently on friendly terms with the Ogdens. His residence was in the heart of the Ogden Land Company's domain— Ogdensburg. Gillet's appointment was even hailed by Thomas Ludlow Ogden. The patriarch land speculator expressed his "ready acquiescence in his [Gillet's] appointment."[46] Yet the direct connection between Gillet and Ogden remains elusive because later he criticized the company for delaying the treaty negotiations.[47]

Within three months Gillet had wrapped up the treaty negotiations. To escape criticism Gillet later blamed the illness of his Indian interpreter, the Ogden Land Company, his own lack of experience in negotiations, his lack of knowledge of relations between the Indians and the federal government, the arbitrariness of Schermerhorn, and the corruption of Stryker for the fireworks and scandals engendered by the Buffalo Creek Treaty.[48] Nevertheless, it is clear that Gillet was a loyal Democrat and had two protectors in the highest ranks of American government: Martin Van Buren and Silas Wright. He represented New York interests and saw increased state jurisdiction over Indians as a most desirable goal. He never criticized Schermerhorn or Stryker before the treaty was concluded in January 1838 and even had high praise for the negotiations.

One month after the signing, Gillet readily admitted that he was not certain that a majority of Onondaga chiefs had signed the document although he was unaware of "a single instance to my knowledge of a white man or an Indian objecting." He added that he was "informed by those who should know that several persons whose names appear on this paper as chiefs are not so in fact" although he insisted all the Senecas who signed the treaty were chiefs.[49] Gillet soon realized that the fraudulent aspects of the treaty negotiations and signings would lead to a political battle over ratification in the United States Senate as did Schermerhorn's New Echota Treaty of 1835. Thus, he suggested that Indian treaties, such as the one at Buffalo Creek, need not have majority consent by tribal councils before their official promulgation. To back up his claims to the validity of the treaty, he called up the endorsement of Nicholas Cusick, the well-known Tuscarora Revolutionary War veteran, friend of Lafayette, and hero of the early republic. Furthermore, Gillet added that he would be happy to counter "any remonstrance aimed to impinge on this transaction."[50] Despite Gillet's own admissions about questionable practices, he was politically rewarded and never faced the same criticisms directed at Stryker and Schermerhorn.

Protests against the treaty soon flooded Washington. Society of Friends branches in western New York, New York City, Baltimore, and Philadelphia charged irregularities, claiming the vast majority of the Indians opposed the treaty and that most of the chiefs, particularly the Senecas, had not signed it. On June 11, 1838, the United States Senate voted overwhelmingly to require the president to obtain a majority of Seneca chiefs' signatures of approval of the treaty in open and official councils. Van Buren directed Gillet to reconvene the Indian councils. Gillet obtained sixteen signatures at a council in August. By January 1839 Gillet claimed to have "secured" a total of forty-one endorsements of the treaty, which he presented as a majority of chiefs. Because of increasing criticism of Gillet and revelations about Stryker's shady financial dealings, Van Buren was forced to dispatch Secretary of War Poinsett to meet with the Indians in council and ascertain their views. Poinsett reported in October that the majority of Senecas were adverse to the treaty and that no majority approval in council could be obtained.[51]

Even after the incredible exposures of fraud, Van Buren, nevertheless, submitted the amended but questionable treaty of 1838 to the United States Senate on January 13, 1840. In his rambling message Van Buren insisted that the treaty was "alike beneficial to the Indians, to the State in which the land is situated, and to the more general interest of the United States." He elaborated by stating that removal presents the only prospect of preservation of the New York Indians and that it was "not only important to the tribes themselves, but to an interesting portion of western New York, and especially to the growing city of Buffalo, which is surrounded by lands occupied by the Senecas." Although he admitted that not all of the chiefs had affixed their signatures to the treaty and that perhaps as few as one-fifth had done so, he stated that the politics of the Six Nations had been disturbed by threats and intimidation. Importantly, Van Buren once again connected events in New York with the Southeast. He stated that the "late intelligence of the cruel murders committed upon the signers of the Cherokee treaty"— the assassinations of Ridge family members and Elias Boudinot—for signing the New Echota Treaty of 1835 had spilled over and was affecting the politics at Buffalo Creek. Because 1840 was a presidential election year and Van Buren was in political trouble, the Little Magician presented himself as a compromiser because of vocal Quaker opposition to the treaty. He asked the Senate to ratify the treaty except for the provisions related to the Senecas because he was convinced that "improper" means had been employed to obtain their assent.[52]

With his political fortunes in sharp decline from the Panic of 1837 onward, Van Buren turned to his reliable ally, Wright, to save the day on the treaty. Wright led the troops and in the process salvaged the political career of Gillet, his protégé. On March 25, 1840, Wright delivered a major speech advocating ratification of the treaty, including provisions relative to the Senecas. In it Wright traced the treaty negotiations, discussed the chiefs' actions, mentioned the nefarious bribery contracts, and defended Gillet's actions. Citing Henry A. S. Dearborn's report on the negotiations, Wright stated, "The conduct of Hon. Ransom H. Gillet, the commissioner of the United States, during the whole session of the council, has been such as to merit the confidence which had been reposed in him by the General Government, and to meet my entire approbation, *from the unwearied pains he has taken to fully, fairly, and clearly explain the provisions of the treaty*" (emphasis Wright). He went on to praise Gillet's thoroughness and earnestness in explaining the benefits of removal to the Indians. Recommending approval of the full treaty, Wright suggested that it was in the interests, pecuniary or otherwise, of all parties—the federal government, New York State, and the Indians themselves—to promote removal because even the great labor of philanthropists had not stemmed the tide and arrested the Indians' "downward and rapid march toward complete extermination." Picturing them as a vanishing race, Wright maintained that the Indians could only be protected from the contamination that surrounded them by their removal out of New York State to the West, which could only be accomplished by ratifying the Treaty of Buffalo Creek. He insisted that the treaty provisions were most generous to the Indians, adding, "Was ever an entire community so rich as these Indians will be in lands and money?" Putting most of the blame on the frauds of the Ogden Land Company, his former ally, and a few greedy white settlers, not the vast majority of Buffalonians surrounding the Indians, Wright concluded, "May I not hope I have succeeded in proving that it is within the power of the Senate to declare the assents of the Senecas to this treaty satisfactory, and thus to save them from a fate so certain and so sad?"[53]

On the same day as Wright's speech, the United States Senate voted on those amendments to the treaty, all of which ended with Vice-President Richard Johnson casting the decisive tie-breaking vote, even though a treaty needs a two-thirds vote by the Senate for ratification. Despite the treaty's questionable nature and growing splits within his own party on Indian removal policies, President Martin Van Buren officially promulgated the treaty on April 4, 1840. Although resistance and challenges to this treaty continued, the Indians were permanently removed from their unique lands at Buffalo Creek within the next seven years. Private, local, state, and national interests had finally achieved their long-desired goals, namely, lands to expand the Holy Grail—Buffalo, New York. By the time the dust settled in 1850, the Indians were no longer central to Buffalo's existence. The bustling port city, no longer Joseph Ellicott's minute village of New Amsterdam, had become part of America's rising empire, one built on a frontier legacy of Indian dispossession.

In spite of these actions certain issues remained unresolved, namely, whether federal and state officials would actually carry out this fraudulent treaty and whether the Senecas would have to abandon all their former treaty lands. Importantly, the Indians feared another Jacksonian Trail of Tears westward, one that would not only extinguish their title to lands in New York but might destroy them as a people forever.

CHAPTER 12

The Incorporation, 1838–1857

From January 1838 to the spring of 1842 the Senecas waged a relentless campaign to overturn the Treaty of Buffalo Creek of 1838. In May 1842 they agreed to another federal accord, the Supplemental Treaty of Buffalo Creek, one of only three federal-Iroquois agreements to allow for the return or repurchase of Indian lands.[1] This treaty, also known as the Second Treaty of Buffalo Creek, the Amended Treaty, or the Compromise Treaty, returned the Allegany and Cattaraugus Reservations to the Senecas but did not allow for the return of the Buffalo Creek and Tonawanda Reservations (see table 4). Another aspect of the Supplemental Treaty was Article IX, a unique but specifically narrow assurance by the federal government to intervene on behalf of the Seneca: "to protect such of the lands of the Seneca Indians, within the State of New York, as may from time to time remain in their possession from all taxes and assessments for roads, highways, or any other purpose until such lands shall be sold and conveyed by the said Indians, and the possession thereof shall have been relinquished by them."

The participants in the events of 1842 had different perceptions of what had transpired at the treaty council. Ambrose Spencer, the federal negotiator, believed that his mission had been totally satisfactory to all concerned and that there was never a fairer one entered into by the Indians.[2] Yet according to the Hicksite Friends' proceedings of the council, as many as sixteen of the fifty-five chiefs—fifteen chiefs from Tonawanda and Israel Jemison, a chief from Cattaraugus—rejected the federal-Indian accord.[3] In the Tonawanda protests over the treaty, the memorials indicated that about forty chiefs did not sign, but all of the emigration party chiefs and "some chiefs from Allegany and Cattaraugus and a few from Buffalo" did assent to the treaty.[4] Four years later the Tonawanda chiefs insisted, "by our national

TABLE 4

The Supplemental Treaty of Buffalo Creek, 1842
Principals: Ambrose Spencer, John Canfield Spencer

1. Returns Allegany and Cattaraugus, but not Buffalo Creek and Tonawanda Reservations
2. Article IX (re: taxation)

Whig Agenda	Seneca Agenda Majority view until May 1842) ⟶	Hicksite Friends Agenda ⟵
1. Follow fiscal conservatism, except for transportation agenda—promotion of canals, highways, railroads. 2. Promote economic development of western New York; see Ogden Land Company and other major land jobbers as creating political backlash and restricting real development. 3. Oppose further Indian removal, based on fiscal restraint and frontier politics. 4. Try to end Second Seminole War. 5. Encourage Indian "civilization" program: a. cheaper b. fits conciliation c. politically expedient d. alternative to Jacksonian policies e. makes Indians into taxpaying American citizens 6. Favor New York State jurisdiction.	1. Opposes Indian removal. 2. Oppose giving up any one of four reservations (Buffalo Creek, Allegany, Cattaraugus, and Tonawanda); reluctantly willing to make partial land cessions of each of four reservations. 3. Oppose land-speculating companies; see the Ogden Land Company as their primary enemy. 4. Oppose state taxation.	1. Opposes further Indian removal. 2. Favor end to Second Seminole War. 3. Encourage Indian "civiliza-tion" program: a. fits religious principles b. fits overall goal to transfer Indians into western-educated, self-sufficient, Christian farmers and taxpayers under American law and legal guarantees. 4. Favor New York State jurisdiction. 5. See economic development of western New York as "inevitable." 6. No mission at Tonawanda. 7. See traditional council of chiefs as "antiquated" system that must go. 8. Oppose Ogden Land Company and its methods.

laws it was, and still is, necessary that *all* of the chiefs should be of one mind; that they must *unanimously* agree to make a treaty, otherwise it cannot be made." They concluded, "In this fundamental law of the Iroquois, and of our nation, we at Tonawanda would have found protection."[5]

In their protests the Tonawanda chiefs saw a great injustice in 1842 and referred to the agreement as the "Compromised Treaty." Indeed, the chiefs were largely right in their assessment, except for their false assumption that the Ogden Land Company was once again behind the whole affair.[6] The major architects of the Treaty of 1842 were two New Yorkers: John Canfield Spencer, the secretary of war, and his illustrious father, Ambrose Spencer, the United States commissioner to treat with the Seneca. The two men allied themselves in the negotiations with three prominent representatives of the Hicksite Friends: Benjamin Ferris, Griffith Cooper, and, most importantly, Philip Thomas.

As late as April 1842, learning from their divisive past, the Senecas from all their communities had reached agreement among themselves that called for a reduction of the size of each of the four reservations, rather than surrendering any one. This agreement would have allowed approximately twenty acres per family use.[7] Even at the time of the treaty council in May, the Senecas believed that there would be negotiations over the retention of their lands. Instead, they were presented with a fait accompli. This fact was recognized by chiefs John Blacksmith and Jemmy Johnson at the treaty council in 1842: "The treaty [1838] was made before it was brought into council, and the present one [1842] was also made before it was brought here."[8]

Quite significantly, both the representatives of the Hicksite Friends and the Whigs—especially the powerful branch of the party in New York State that included Millard Fillmore, Hamilton Fish, Horace Greeley, William Seward, Thurlow Weed, and the Spencers father and son—received much of what they desired in the treaty. By consciously working with the Hicksites, the conservative Whigs wanted to extend New York State jurisdiction over Indians, save federal moneys, continue to develop state roads, canals, and railroads, ensure the future prosperity of Buffalo, and close the books on the much criticized, now discredited, and expensive Indian removal policies of the Jacksonian–Van Buren eras.[9] In effect, Albany was to become the new "Great Father" while the Hicksites were to have the primary responsibility to lead their Seneca charges to truth and salvation.

Much of the Seneca's positive image of the Friends in the contemporary period is largely based on the benevolent work of Joseph Elkinton and his Quaker School at Tunessasa in the nineteenth century and by the noble efforts of the Society in later fighting the Kinzua Dam in the late 1950s and early 1960s. It is clear that despite the Seneca image of the Friends, the Hicksite negotiators in the 1840s had a Whig-like agenda. They were also scarcely intent on minding their own business when it came to Seneca affairs. Both the Hicksites' and the Whigs' program was to absorb the Indians into the body politic in the most cost-efficient but most humane

Jemmy Johnson
Courtesy of Rochester Museum and Science Center

way. To both the Indians were to become taxpaying citizens of the state, but protected under law. Do-gooder Hicksites and conservative Whigs both saw the Indians as a vanishing race who had to be transformed carefully for their own good. They could not be left to their own "antiquated" political systems to negotiate a treaty in 1842 or to plan for their future. To the Hicksite Friends the Senecas had to be transformed for their own good because the Indians could not long endure the constant pressures of avaricious and morally corrupt whites. These Friends felt the Indians could not survive as separate enclaves in the dominant white world and must learn to cope with the larger society. Thus the Hicksite strategy, which at times became policy at the federal and state levels, was designed to bring "civilization" to the Senecas in order to absorb them into American society. Long before President Grant's peace policy after the Civil War or the founding of the Friends-dominated Indian Rights Association in the early 1880s, the Hicksite Friends, in response to Indian removal policies, developed what they considered a workable formula of assimilation. This Americanization process included: proselytizing on reservations to stamp out "pagan" influences, however different and less coercive the Quaker style was; instituting the white man's education, whether state or missionary directed; implementing United States citizenship; and, eventually, much later in the process, inaugurating Indian fee simple title, which had to be encouraged to instill personal initiative, allegedly required by the free enterprise system. The Hicksite Friends understood that the Indians were not yet ripe for the last part of the formula—land-in-severalty—because of the nefarious activities of the Ogden Land Company and the question of their preemptive right to Seneca lands.[10]

It is also significant to note that among the three major Hicksites at the negotiations was Philip Thomas, the philanthropist who later founded the Thomas Asylum (which later became the Thomas Indian School) in the 1850s. Thomas fit the Whig profile. The politically savvy Friend had been the president of the Merchants' Bank in Baltimore and a commissioner of the Chesapeake and Ohio Canal. He was also the founder and chairman of the Baltimore and Ohio Railroad, which by the time of the Civil War laid track to Buffalo and Rochester but also through the Allegany Indian Reservation at Salamanca.[11]

The Hicksites knew full well that the Buffalo Creek Reservation, one of their major missions, was now overrun with white squatters and timber strippers and had little chance of being returned to the Indians.[12] They also knew that, although losing this mission at Buffalo Creek, their overall "civilization" program for the Seneca was still on track. Quite significantly, the Friends had no mission at Tonawanda and had little influence there. The events of 1841 through 1843 also reveal that the Hicksite representatives had disdain for the traditional government, the Tonawanda Council of Chiefs.[13] Yet despite this Hicksite influence policies immediately before, during, and after the Treaty of 1842 were not set by them but by the Whig Party, that had first come to power in Albany in 1837 and in Washington in 1841.

Whig presidents William Henry Harrison and John Tyler were not simply carbon copies of the Jackson–Van Buren administrations. Times had changed and with them, Indian policies.[14] By 1842 in the Whig's diverse ranks were members who were outspoken boosters of western New York such as Fillmore, Albany leaders promoting state interests such as Seward and the two Spencers, and national party leaders such as Clay in Washington with longtime frontier racist attitudes toward Indians.[15] In Hicksite circles there was no more heroic figure than New England Whig Secretary of State Daniel Webster. It was Webster who had earlier opposed Indian removal policies and who first advised the Friends to seek a new federal-Seneca treaty to supplement the fraudulent one of 1838; in his typical conciliatory, legalistic manner—one appealing to the "people of the Inner Light"—Webster saw this new federal-Seneca accord as an alternative to a long, bitter, and costly struggle in the courts.[16]

The Whigs had taken advantage of criticisms of Jacksonian Indian policies despite the irony that William Henry Harrison was renowned as an Indian fighter and that John Bell, their first secretary of war, was the author of the Indian Removal Act of 1830. During the so-called Log Cabin presidential campaign of 1840, the Whigs bitterly blamed Jackson and Van Buren for the Second Seminole War, the most expensive Indian war in United States history, which claimed fifteen hundred American soldiers and cost the nation sixty million dollars. Hence, by 1842 forced removal of Indians was a discredited policy. The Second Seminole War, which started in 1835, continued unabated until 1842—precisely the year of the Seneca Supplemental Treaty of Buffalo Creek.[17] Much time during the presidency of Tyler was devoted to trying to secure "peace with honor" and to extricating the country from its Florida morass.

Importantly, Tyler's main "point man" in Washington working on securing peace in Florida in late 1841 and 1842 was John Canfield Spencer, a prominent attorney with offices in Canandaigua and Albany. Spencer's family interests were in ironworks, canal building, and in land, including some earlier financial dealings with the Holland Land Company. Although involved in land speculation himself, he and his father had little love for the crude practices of land jobbers such as Robert Troup, John Greig, and the Holland and Ogden Land Companies, whose actions they believed often retarded rather than promoted state economic policies. In the 1820s John Spencer had actually tried to overthrow Joseph Ellicott's control of the Holland Land Company and, in the mid-1830s, Spencer helped to challenge the company's claimed title to some of its empire. As conservatives and anti-Masons who feared social disorder, both Spencers, political opportunists to the core, knew that by their populist-styled attacks on the rich holdings of land companies, the Whigs could win votes from their Democrat enemies. In an age of antirent ferment they and other New York Whigs learned how to position themselves and to shift with the times. Thus, by 1840 John Canfield Spencer had become one of the major leaders of the Whig Party, both in and out of New York State.[18]

John Canfield Spencer's career sheds light on his later involvement in the drafting of the Supplemental Treaty of Buffalo Creek. After graduating from Union College, he served as private secretary to Governor Daniel D. Tompkins, as judge advocate general in western New York during the War of 1812, as district attorney for five western counties of New York after the war, as a United States congressman from 1817 to 1819, and as a member of the New York State Assembly, serving as Speaker in 1820.[19] Even more impressively, Spencer was the host for Alexis de Tocqueville and Gustave de Beaumont at his home on Canandaigua Lake on the Frenchmen's famous tour of the United States in 1831. Both de Tocqueville and de Beaumont had high praise for Spencer, favorably commenting about the American's expertise as an attorney, legislator, and legal editor and referring to him as one of the true intellectuals they had met in their travels.[20] According to historian George Wilson Pierson, Spencer's ideas permeated de Tocqueville's writings. Spencer firmly believed and de Tocqueville wrote that religion and moral order were necessary to ensure the basis of free institutions, although both men felt that all sects should keep directly out of politics.[21]

By the 1830s Spencer served as the secretary of state of New York and as superintendent of the Common Schools where he advocated the use of government moneys for the Christianization of the Indians. Appointed secretary of war in 1841, he advocated building up the Civilization Fund. To him, increasing appropriations and educating Indian youth bound them, much like "a new ligament," to the duties and obligations of civilized life.[22] He maintained that educating Indians was, in the words of historian Ronald M. Satz, "a wiser long-range investment than funds for military weapons."[23] It was these ideas that were quite attractive to his Hicksite allies in 1841–42.

By the early 1840s frontier folk in Missouri had also become vocal about the numbers of Indians who had been removed to the trans-Mississippi West. To them, moving more Indians to Indian Territory—fifty thousand had been removed by 1840—was unacceptable. With politicians such as the powerful Senator Thomas Hart Benton clamoring for American expansion in the 1840s, forcing more eastern Indians westward across the Mississippi did not make much sense. Even previously removed Indians objected to a new exodus of eastern tribes west.[24] Later, at the treaty council of 1842, this fact was not lost on the participants. Hicksite Benjamin Ferris observed that "strenuous exertions were made" to procure other lands for the Senecas in the west, "but there were so many difficulties laid in the way by the whites and Indians already located there, that the object was defeated."[25]

Scandals involving removal contracts also led the Whigs to reassess Indian policy. In 1841 Major Ethan Allen Hitchcock, later major general in the regular army, was appointed to investigate the frauds involving federal contracts in the supply of the so-called emigrant Indians, namely, those eastern Indians who had been removed to Indian Territory and who had been promised adequate supplies of provisions either during or after their removal. Hitchcock found widespread frauds in supplying the Five Civilized Tribes. His investigation covered the months from November 1841 to April 1842. Reporting directly to Secretary of War Spencer, Hitchcock's letters documented the frauds even while the Supplemental Treaty was being negotiated. The major's final report was filed on May 20, 1842, precisely the day the treaty was signed. Hitchcock's findings were slowly leaked to congressional critics of Indian policy and the public at large by the time of the official promulgation of the treaty in the summer of 1842.[26]

Whig Indian policy was shaped by several other factors. To be sure, their policy focused on "closing the books" on the Democrat era of Indian removal, which would save federal moneys. The year 1842 also marked a great Whig departure in both domestic and foreign affairs. The Whigs promoted an "open door" foreign policy and a domestic policy that stressed internal improvements, canals, railroads, and roads. Conciliation was both a foreign policy and a domestic policy objective aimed at promoting prosperity here and abroad. In 1842 Secretary of State Webster brought a resolution of the Maine boundary furthering commerce with Great Britain, the United States' most important trade partner but a feared neighbor in Canada. In 1842 Webster also furthered American economic interests by extending the Monroe Doctrine to Hawaii and by having the Massachusetts Whig diplomat, Caleb Cushing, sign the Treaty of Wangxia with China by which the United States gained the same rights on an unconditional most-favored nation basis that Great Britain had won in the much-detested Opium War.[27]

The Whig divergence with Jacksonian–Van Buren approaches toward the Indians is easily seen in examining the appointment of Ambrose Spencer as the federal commissioner to treat with the Seneca Indians in 1842. Spencer's appointment was no mere accident. Besides being the father of John Canfield Spencer, the secretary of war, Ambrose Spencer was literally the grand old man of New York State politics. Although a strong advocate of state jurisdiction over Indians, he was, nevertheless, a longtime opponent of forced removal and Jacksonian–Van Buren Indian policies. A man with dark, flashing eyes and the energy of two men, Spencer had significant previous experience in the adjudication of Indian matters.

Born in Salisbury, Connecticut, Ambrose Spencer attended Yale University, but was graduated from Harvard in 1783 at the age of eighteen! He became an attorney, practicing law in Claverack and Hudson, New York, and soon became a major player in the politics of Columbia and Albany Counties. He was elected as a Federalist candidate to the New York State Assembly in 1793 and to the New York State Senate two years later. In 1798 Spencer bolted the party and joined the Democratic Republicans of George Clinton and Thomas Jefferson. Indeed, on and off for the next three decades, Spencer was associated with and allied to the Clinton family. His second and third marriages were to De Witt Clinton's sisters. In 1802 Spencer became the attorney general of New York State, serving in this capacity until his appointment to the New York State Supreme Court two years later. In 1819 he became the presiding justice of this three-member court. After leaving the court, he practiced law in Albany and was elected the city's mayor in 1824. He later briefly served in Congress from 1829 to 1831, becoming one of the more vocal opponents of the Indian Removal Bill of 1830. After losing election, Spencer dabbled in politics and devoted much of his time toward outfoxing Martin Van Buren. Although first a Federalist and subsequently a Democratic Republican and Clintonian, Spencer, in the last nine years of his life until his death in 1848, served as grand old man of the Whigs, and, in fact, presided over the party's convention in Baltimore in 1844.[28]

Despite Spencer's advanced age in 1842—seventy-seven years old—the jurist had the makeup for his rough assignment in Seneca country. A strong-willed, self-confident man, he had little to prove or gain from his assignment. His son was already enshrined in Whig Party inner circles. One would ask why he even took this low-priority assignment.[29] Yet, in fact, Spencer was the most logical appointment that could have been made. In 1822, as the presiding justice of the New York State Supreme Court, Spencer rendered the decision in *Jackson v. Goodell,* involving the alienation of the lands of John Sagoharase, an Oneida Indian veteran of the American Revolution, who had been awarded bounty lands in the military tract in the Township of Junius, Seneca County, New York.[30]

Spencer's opinion in this case clearly shows his views on state power over Indians. Spencer insisted that the Indians were not aliens outside of state jurisdiction. He argued that these *"Indians* [emphasis Spencer] are born in allegiance to the government of this state, for our jurisdiction extends to every part of the state; they receive protection from us, and are subject to our laws." The New York jurist continued, "Indeed, our legislature regulates, by law, their internal concerns, and exercises entire and perfect control over them."[31] Spencer then clarified his position.[32]

We do not mean to say, that the condition of the Indian tribes, at former and remote periods, has been that of subjects or citizens of the state. *Their condition has been gradually changing, until they have lost every attribute of sovereignty, and become entirely dependent upon, and subject to our government. I know of no half-way doctrine on this subject.* We either have an exclusive jurisdiction, pervading every part of the state, including the territory held by the Indians, or we have no jurisdiction over their lands, or over them, whilst acting within their reservations. It cannot be a divided empire; it must be exclusive, as regards them or us; and the act referred to, as well as the actual state and condition of the Indian tribes within this state, shows that the jurisdiction is in the state, and, consequently, upon the principles of the common law, they must be citizens. (Emphasis mine)

Despite Spencer's opinion the decision was subsequently reversed by Chancellor James Kent.[33]

Although Kent differed with Spencer's views on state jurisdiction and citizenship of Indians, both men, as did most attorneys in the United States, became major opponents of Jackson–Van Buren forced Indian removal policies. After passage of the Indian Removal Act of 1830, Spencer joined Webster and Jeremiah Evarts, the secretary of the American Board of Commissioners for Foreign Missions, in a major effort. They sponsored the printing of the best congressional speeches opposing the act. In congressional debates Spencer defended the honor of New York opponents of Indian removal and helped refer their petitions to the House Committee on Indian Affairs. He even went so far as to advise the Cherokees delegation during their visit to Washington, strongly suggesting that the Cherokee bring their case before the United States Supreme Court by hiring William Wirt, the former attorney general under Presidents Monroe and Adams, as counsel to protect their rights. The Cherokee took the advice and the rest is history, *Cherokee Nation v. Georgia* (1831).[34]

Thus, in 1842 Spencer had long experience in Indian-related matters, much more than did the average federal negotiator. In his mind, as was true of the Hicksite Friends who negotiated with Spencer and his son, there was no contradiction between advocating citizenship for Indians and state jurisdiction over Indians and being against forced removal. With the backdrop of the Second Seminole War, Spencer received his formal instructions in February and March 1842. On February 17 Commissioner Crawford called Spencer's attention to the Indians' strong objections to the Treaty of 1838. Crawford indicated his hope that the new negotiations would be conducted in a "conciliatory spirit on all sides," calling the "proposed arrangement" "one of compromise." The commissioner added that Washington was concerned with two overriding factors: "[to keep] an already flourishing and still advancing portion of the Territory of New York from the encumbrance of Indian populations, and those Indians themselves from the temptations that surround them where there they now are." He then explained the interests of the Ogden Land Company in the negotiation and the presence of a Massachusetts representative at the treaty council. Significantly, Crawford, a holdover from the Jacksonian removal era, observed, "There is much more land embraced in small reservations than the Seneca can use." He then outlined the federal position, namely, that Buffalo should never be returned to the Indians, maintaining that the reservations nearest to the city would be the "most agreeable to the Senecas to yield." The commissioner added that the Indians "would thus be furthest removed from the vicinity of the whites and there will be the least interference with the progress of improvement of that important section of the state." Among other things, Crawford warned Spencer not "to depart from the provisions" of the Treaty of 1838 "except in respect to the Senecas and in reference to them only with the modification as to quantity of land to be ceded."[35]

Spencer's instructions in February are especially important in what they do not include. Nowhere did Washington specify the surrender of the Tonawanda Indian Reservation (Cattaraugus and Tonawanda are nearly equidistant from Buffalo), nor did federal officials even hint at discussions of the tax issue. Crawford also never gave his formal permission to allow the presence of Abram Dixon, a delegate of the New York State Legislature, who became a vocal participant in the treaty proceedings of April and May 1842. Dixon was an attorney, farmer, and New York State senator from Westfield in Chautauqua County, near the Cattaraugus Indian Reservation.[36]

Two weeks after Crawford's letter, Ambrose Spencer wrote the commissioner, clearly confirming that Tonawanda was not specified: "The principle and perhaps sole object of the [new] treaty as you represent is to enable Major Ogden and Fellows to reconvey to the Senecas all the lands ceded to them on the 15th of January, 1838, *except the Buffalo and some other portions of the lands ceded* [emphasis Spencer], on the principles stated in your letter." Spencer added that it was "inferable [that] most [Seneca] at present . . . do not intend to emigrate or at least only a part of them" and asked for further clarifications of his mission so he "might know precisely what is expected of me."[37]

Whig failures in Albany from 1837 to 1841 contributed to what was about to transpire in Seneca country. The party in its expenditures for canals had bankrupted the state after coming to power after the panic of 1837. The Whigs, in their typical style, had promised fiscal responsibility and the promotion of economic growth; however, in 1838 the Whig majority authorized forty million dollars for the subsidy of canal and railroad development in the state. Instead of rapid economic progress, the free-spending administration of Governor William Seward brought financial crisis. By 1841 the state debt had reached eighteen million dollars, much of it caused by the unnecessary and wasteful spending on the Genesee and Black River Canals authorized by the New York State Board of Canals. The massive program of construction was only half completed, resulting in a Democrat victory in

November 1841 as a result of the lack of public confidence in state securities, which fell to 20 percent under par.[38]

Before the Whig defeat, the New York State Legislature reacted to this budgetary crisis by looking for new avenues of taxation to pay for internal improvements. It saw its bailout from crisis in the unlimited potential of western New York with Rochester, the flour and later the flower capital of the United States, and the bustling Great Lakes port of Buffalo. Importantly, in both 1840 and 1841 the New York State Legislature attempted to extend its jurisdiction, including its taxing power, to Seneca country. These acts were the first of many others passed by state legislators on Indian-related matters during the next decade. In May 1840 the New York State Legislature passed "An Act in relation to the roads and bridges within the Allegany and Delaware Creek [*sic*] Reservations." The act gave the county boards of supervisors in Erie, Chautauqua, and Cattaraugus Counties the right to assess highway taxes on all lands within the Allegany and Cattaraugus Indian Reservations as they did neighboring non-Indian communities that "they may deem reasonable and necessary, to put the highways and bridges within said reservation in good repair."[39] The next year, the legislature passed "An Act authorizing the construction and repair of roads and bridges on the Indian lands in the Counties of Erie and Cattaraugus." The act authorized the county boards of supervisors in the two counties to survey and to construct roads across three of the Seneca communities: Buffalo Creek, Cattaraugus, and Allegany Indian Reservations. Significantly, the cost of these two-year road-building projects would be borne by the Indian residents of each reservation: five thousand dollars per year at Buffalo Creek and four thousand dollars per year at Cattaraugus and Allegany. If these taxes were not paid, the state comptroller "shall proceed to advertise and sell said lands in the manner now provided by law." The law gave the Indians an assurance of their continuing right of occupancy after tax foreclosure: "But no sale for the purpose of collecting said taxes shall in any manner affect the right of the Indians to occupy said land."[40] Hence, Article IX of the Supplemental Treaty of Buffalo Creek 1842 was without question a reaction to these two specific state acts, an effort to assuage the Indians over the loss of two of their reservations, not to exempt Indians from state taxation as a whole.

It is not surprising that Ambrose Spencer conducted himself in the manner he did during the councils discussing the treaty. On the second day of the council at Buffalo Creek, he proclaimed himself a New Yorker who was "proud of the way the Indians have always been respected" in the state. To him they "have been treated justly and humanely." Presenting the Supplemental Treaty as a "done deal" that had the total support of "your steadfast and benevolent friends, the Quakers," Spencer indicated it was impossible to save the Buffalo and Tonawanda Reservations because it "was found impracticable and inexpedient to insist on these requests." Perhaps attempting to force agreement, he pointed out firmly that the Treaty of 1838 was still binding and remained so even if the Senecas rejected the proposed Supplemental Treaty.[41]

On the next day Abram Dixon, a treaty participant by virtue of a New York State Senate resolution, repeated Spencer's line nearly word for word. Dixon then added something reminiscent of Spencer's opinion in *Jackson v. Goodell:* "You are under the protection of the laws of this state, and to a degree you are liable to their exactions and restrictions, like our own citizens." Dixon added, "Ours is a government of laws, and not of force."[42]

After drawing criticism from Chief Jemmy Johnson, Spencer insisted he had "restricted power" and, therefore, had "no power to negotiate at large." He continued by calling up the names of the benevolent William Penn and the Society of Quakers who had acted "in your behalf," secured the "very best terms they could possibly obtain for you," and helped prevent the necessity of forced Seneca emigration out of New York State.[43] Refusing to allow negotiations for twenty-five hundred acres of Tonawanda and unaware of—or unwilling to accept—Seneca tradition about unanimity and consensus in decision making, Spencer, on the fifth and final day of the council, insisted that majority ruled and that if a majority of chiefs, even proemigration chiefs, agreed to terms, the treaty was binding.[44] In his defense of the Supplemental Treaty, Spencer repeated the Hicksite line, namely, by being concentrated on the two reservations, "it will be much better for you—and your Friends, the Quakers, as I understand them intend to superintend, and offer succor, to educate you, and make you a much greater people than you are now."[45] After the vote, Chief Blacksmith, in an impassioned reaction, maintained that the 15 Tonawanda chiefs and 615 reservation residents were unanimously opposed to the agreement because they "love their children— they love their nation."[46]

Spencer's overall strategy was (1) to attempt to close the books on Indian removal—a policy that was too costly, politically untenable, and one that he had opposed for over a decade; (2) to cooperate with the Hicksites in order to silence their continued criticisms of Washington's Indian policies; (3) to develop inexpensive workable private arrangements, such as the Friends' work with the Senecas, to further the overall Indian civilization program; and (4) to maintain and to extend New York State jurisdiction over the Indians. As a proponent of state power over the Indians, he was unwilling to give a more specific federal commitment and unwilling to overturn the newly secured "right" of the state legislature to pass laws extending taxing power to Indian reservations. It may be suggested that to wrap up the negotiations as quickly as possible, Spencer included this narrowly defined assurance of federal intervention.

The three Hicksite Friends who negotiated the treaty with the Whigs were scarcely utopians or disinterested parties. Many of their sentiments paralleled the Whiggish politics of the times. They could easily agree with the Whigs that past Indian removal policies were a costly failure, that the Second Seminole Indian War in Florida was a stain against the national honor and had to be ended, and that a conciliatory approach to domestic and foreign policies was in the overall best interests of the United States. Their fervent support for Whig Indian policies gave moral legitimacy to the overall federal government "civilization" program. Through a carefully orchestrated campaign, the Hicksites drafted pamphlets and memorials, sponsored lyceum presentations, and held strategy meetings with the secretary of war and the governors of New York and Massachusetts.[47] They promoted their interests by "encouraging" the work of Maris B. Pierce, a Dartmouth-educated Cattaraugus chief who held the position of federal interpreter and who kept the Hicksites informed about Washington as well as Seneca doings. Ironically, the Hicksites made use of Pierce, a Seneca who would later be the spokesman of the Old Chiefs Party opposed to the Hicksite-sponsored Seneca Revolution of 1848. Yet Pierce also tried to use the Hicksites in 1841 and 1842. Pierce hoped that he and John Kennedy, Jr., would be "rewarded" for their personal efforts with an allotment of fifty acres at Buffalo Creek, a hope that never materialized. He became the most vocal Seneca speaker at lyceums and churches, stirring his white audiences, much in the manner of black abolitionists of the era.[48]

Pierce had been educated by Joseph Elkinton, an Orthodox Friend who ran the Quaker School at Tunessasa. Pierce had signed the original Treaty of

Maris B. Pierce
Courtesy of the Buffalo and Erie County Historical Society

Buffalo Creek of 1838, but he and others later claimed that he had reluctantly done so as a result of pressures from senior chiefs. Without question, he saw the advantages of serving as the Friends' Indian spokesman and as the federal interpreter throughout the fight over the Seneca Supplemental Treaty. Writing to federal officials including President Harrison in 1841, he frequently called on the Whig administration to reappoint the Hicksite Griffith Cooper, who was serving as temporary agent in New York, to a permanent post in the Indian Service.[49]

In February 1841 Pierce reported to the Friends that the Whigs appeared to be reluctant to spend money to carry out the Treaty of 1838. One month later, he appealed directly to President Harrison to reappoint Cooper as permanent Indian agent to thwart the activities of the Ogden Land Company. In April he wrote the War Department once again, promoting Cooper's reappointment and asking for a meeting with the secretary about a new treaty. In June Pierce praised the Quakers' efforts in presenting the Seneca "memorials and petitions on our behalf" and praised them for their efforts to counter the Seneca emigration party and the Ogden Land Company. In October he repeated his request about Cooper's reappointment. By December he had attended Hicksite-sponsored meetings in Boston and Albany about the need for a new treaty. At those occasions the Hicksites discussed the proposed treaty negotiations with Whig governors William Seward of New York and John Davis of Massachusetts.[50]

Two post-treaty memorials by the Tonawanda chiefs clarify the circumstances that transpired from December 1841 through March 1842. During the winter months the chiefs sent a delegation to a meeting in New York City conducted by the Hicksites. Much to their surprise and anger, the Quakers had already held negotiations with United States governmental officials. At the winter meeting the Tonawanda delegation was told to give their memorials of protest to the Friends, who would present them for them in Washington. The Tonawanda delegation was also strongly urged to return home because their continued presence might threaten the negotiation; however, the Indians were also informed that two or three delegates from each reservation would soon go to Washington to meet in council. Apparently, this did not occur. The Friends also told the Indians that the secretary of war would "send a man to hold a council with us."[51]

Ambrose Spencer was sent in May on a day determined by the Friends and government officials, not by the Indians. Instead of negotiations, "one of the friends arose and addressed the council stating that they had come for the purpose of explaining the compromised [sic] treaty. . . . And all that resided on the Tonawanda and Buffalo Creek Reservations should emigrate to the two remaining reservations."[52] Despite a vehement reaction by Israel Jemison, a chief from Cattaraugus, and the Tonawanda chiefs and a counterproposal "to give up a part of each reservation, reserving to each native that wished to remain twenty acres of land," the objections to the proposed treaty fell on deaf ears.[53] Jemison's proposal had been agreed on by the Seneca chiefs and conveyed to the secretary of war in early April.[54]

Even as late as the fifth day of the council, Samuel Gordon, a Cattaraugus chief who later signed the Supplemental Treaty, clearly explained that the majority of Seneca, both the chiefs and the people, wanted a compromise, but one based on remaining on their own reservations, however reduced in size by the terms of a new treaty. Gordon accurately predicted a bleak future if only two reservations remained: "They fear, if all are concentrated on two Reservations, there will be difficulties and jealousies among themselves. That is the main difficulty." He added, "Cannot they compromise so as to keep the same number of acres contained in the Cattaraugus and Allegany Reservations, divided among all the different Reservations?" Fearing that the Hicksite Friends had been criticized to the point of leaving the negotiations, Gordon begged "them to remain and not withdraw, but go on and assist in the negotiation."[55]

The collective views of the Hicksites—Cooper, Ferris, and Thomas—were set forth in the Hicksite proceedings of the councils of April and May 1842. They saw the Indians as a vanishing race who had to be led by the hand to civilization for their own good. Importantly, they did not see the loss of Tonawanda as a great tragedy, but a Friends opportunity to lead their charges to the "Inner Light." The three men also referred to the inevitability of Indian population decline and massive white population increases. The Hicksites indicated that from "the great water which lies toward the rising sun, to the great Mississippi, the father of rivers, a distance of almost one thousand miles, they [the Indians] have nearly all disappeared." Much like Troup's and Ogden's arguments earlier, the evil was increased by the Seneca's proximity to the city of Buffalo where Indians "are exposed to the pernicious examples and contaminating influences of wicked men, by which many of you have been corrupted, and others much injured." The Friends in attendance saw the solution as simple, namely, the Seneca had to consolidate their lands, reduced to fifty-two thousand acres (about one hundred acres per family in 1842), which would be "a quantity amply sufficient for every necessary purpose." Using a similar argument made by David A. Ogden after the War of 1812, they insisted that as a result[56]

the Indians will be more concentrated, and consequently more favorably situated for mental and moral improvement, as well as for the support of schools and other institutions for the advancement of science, and the formation of habits essential to a state of civilization, than they have heretofore been. In this concentrated state they will be accessible to their friends, and more open to the kindly influences of those who may believe it right to devote themselves to the amelioration of their condition.

One year after the conclusion of the Supplemental Treaty, the three Hicksite Friends arranged a meeting with Seneca leaders where Thomas and Cooper defended their actions. They insisted once again that the treaty of 1842 was the best that they could secure and that they had no agenda besides compassion for the Indians. Cooper insisted that the Hicksites never asked for money or lands nor "have we ever attempted to force our religion on you. You yourselves know, that we have never asked any thing of you, as a reward for our labor." Yet at the 1843 meeting the three Hicksites were already laying the groundwork for increased New York State jurisdiction and for the Seneca revolution of 1848 that overthrew the traditional chiefs system of government. For the first time in open council, the participants—Indian and white—openly questioned the continuing role of the chiefs and whether two-thirds of all adult males should decide on the alienation of lands. Discussions also included whether Indians should allot their lands. Equally important, the role of the state in Indian affairs was raised and whether the state should hold the remaining Indian lands in trust for the benefit of the Indians. After suggesting a trust deed, Thomas observed, "The only difficulty would be to get the state of New York to take the trust proposed; but we hope the state will be willing to extend its care and guardianship over you."[57]

Unlike the 1830s, no longer were the states or Washington viewed by the Friends as enemies of Indians intent on forcibly removing Indians westward. Indeed, now Indian removal was voluntary although Indians who had favored the 1838 treaty were in great disfavor and many sought to escape by going west. When a federal agent, Abram Hogeboom, showed up at Buffalo Creek in 1846 recruiting Indians to go to the Indian territory, he eventually convinced more than 190 Indians to leave, including many of the supporters of the 1838 accord: George Jemison, Thompson Harris, White Seneca, and the Cayuga leader, physician Peter Wilson. Within two years, more than eighty of these Indians perished as a result of disease and old age, including Thompson Harris and White Seneca. Eventually, half of the emigrants, including Peter Wilson, returned to New York.[58]

Instead of pushing removal, from the time of the Supplemental Treaty onward New York State officials, in moves supported by the Hicksites, attempted to extend their jurisdiction over the Senecas. In 1845 the state legislature passed "An Act for the Protection and Improvement of the Seneca Indians Residing in the Cattaraugus Reservations in this State." The act and its subsequent modification in a revised piece of legislation in 1847 clearly were influenced by the events of 1842 and by the legal doings of Ambrose Spencer. Under the guise of humanitarian reforms the New York State Legislature extended its jurisdiction. In 1845 Albany recognized the existence of the "Seneca Nation of Indians" as the government on the Allegany, Cattaraugus, and Oil Spring Reservations and awarded it the right to "prosecute and maintain in all courts of law and equity in this state, any action, suit or proceeding which may be necessary or proper to protect the rights and interests of said Indians and of the said nation, in and to the said reservations." In sharp contrast to Georgia and other states during the Indian removal eras the act allowed actions for damages suffered by the Indians "in common, or as a nation." With an obvious eye on Ambrose Spencer, one provision even allowed the governor to nominate, with the consent of the state senate, a person "who shall have been a counsellor in the supreme court of this state for three years or more, to be an attorney of the Seneca Nation of Indians." This person "shall from time to time advise the said Indians respecting controversies between themselves, and between them or any of them, and any other person." To satisfy the Friends and other prohibitionists, the act made it a crime punishable by law to sell or give any Seneca "spirituous liquor or any intoxicating drink." Other provisions of the legislation "granted" the Seneca peacemaker justices or a majority of them the right to call meetings of the chiefs of the Seneca to determine laying out lands for cultivation or other uses, to make by-laws for laying out roads and highways, and to regulate and protect their common lands. In an even more meddling way one provision allowed the non-Seneca Indians to reside on Seneca lands and to "enjoy the same privileges with them." Consequently, until 1862 Cayuga had voting rights in Seneca Nation elections.[59]

In 1847 new state legislation outlined Seneca voting qualifications and terms of office; described the specific duties and legal responsibilities of the peacemaker courts, treasurer, and clerk of the Seneca Nation; allowed for legal appeal to a jury of six chiefs; made it a state crime to offer false testimony in a tribal court; gave the chiefs the final say in assigning lands for cultivation; and provided individual Indians the right to sell timber on lands assigned to them but limited their rights elsewhere and set penalties.[60] Other legislation in this period dealt with the establishment of state schools for the Senecas, providing for the education of Indian youths at state normal schools, fixing the date of elections on the Cattaraugus and Allegany Indian Reservations, recognizing the new Seneca Constitution and republican form of government, and regulating the sale of alcohol.[61] In 1849 the New York State Legislature passed an "Act for the Benefit of Indians." It recognized Indian common law marriages and the right of Seneca peacemaker courts to marry Indians "with the like force and effect as if by a justice of the peace." Provisions 7 and 11 of the 1849 act tell the direction of state Indian policies in this period. Perhaps Hicksite inspired, Provision 7 "allowed" the Indian governments to divide their land to Indian individuals or families in "severalty and in fee simple, according to the laws of this state" but prevented the alienation of these lands "to any person other than the occupant, or his or her family." Provision 11 "allowed" the New York State commissioners of the land office to accept "such sums of money as such Indians may wish to put in trust with the state of New York" where it would be "vested in good and safe securities by the comptroller, or in stocks of this state bearing interest at the rate of six per cent."[62]

In sum, outsiders—Albanian politicians and Hicksite Friends—had carefully and systematically set their sights on transforming the Seneca world. Most of the Indians did not fully understand the implications of the events that had transpired at Buffalo Creek in 1842 and how the agenda had been set in Albany and Washington as well as in Baltimore, New York City, and Philadelphia. Pierce, for one, had no clue about the implications of the Supplemental Treaty. Pierce wrote his mentor, the Friend Joseph Elkinton, immediately after the agreement's signing in May 1842, labeling the accord "the best bargain they can make now."[63] Pierce and other Seneca nation chiefs came to realize how wise the Tonawanda leadership was in 1842, for, in fact, the Supplemental Treaty was not only about which lands the Senecas would retain after the travesty at Buffalo Creek in 1838. The state's men and the salvation seekers had now introduced a new agenda: Albany as "great father" working hand-in-hand with the missionary societies. The Supplemental Treaty of Buffalo Creek stands as a significant watershed in state-Indian relations that has been ignored by historians and anthropologists and misread by the Senecas. Instead of being hailed as an Indian treaty and used by contemporary Seneca to fight the state's tax authority, the accord should be dubbed, in fact, "the New York Whig–Hicksite Friend Compromise of 1842 that affected the Seneca."

Thus, by 1850 the Seneca world that had existed as a separate Indian reality in 1794 had been clearly incorporated into a New York State reality. That in many ways had been the result of massive settlement brought into Iroquoia by the transportation revolution. Buffalo, the Holy Grail, was firmly in New York's hands, confirmed in the legally ratified Supplemental Treaty of 1842. For the next decade Tonawanda Senecas lobbied, brought legal suit, and attempted to win support for the return of their reservation.[64] In 1857 in a federal treaty they "won" the right to "win" back by purchase a part of their old reservation, seventy-five hundred acres. In another "compromise" that was worked out for their alleged benefit, New York State, the new "great father," held these Seneca lands "in trust" for their new charges who, throughout the late nineteenth century, were administered by Albany officialdom through the New York State Board of Charities.[65] From nations federally recognized by Washington in 1794, they had now become incorporated as wards of the state, treated as if they were orphans or homeless peoples.

CHAPTER 13

Conclusion: The Iroquois Indians and the
Rise of the Empire State

The years between the end of the American Revolution and the Civil War dramatically transformed New York and made the state second to none. The state, which had a population of approximately 340,000 people in 1790, had nearly 3.5 million people by 1855, more than 10 percent of the entire population of the United States.[1] In part Albany's subsidization of canals and (to a lesser degree) road building led to the rise of this American behemoth. Between 1836 and 1856 the total tonnage and wealth of cargoes transported by the state canal system increased 300 percent. Grain, timber, salt, and people themselves were the major "products" transported. The state's collection of tolls on the Erie Canal between 1836 and 1856 increased by approximately 330 percent.[2] Moreover, out of this reality came the rise of a great metropolitan corridor between Albany and Buffalo that permanently changed the natural landscape and the lives of indigenous people.

While New York was emerging in the forefront economically and politically from the 1790s to the 1850s, the Iroquois largely found themselves on the defensive. Their population was largely stagnant or declined in the same sixty-year period. By the 1850s canals extensively traversed the Oneida country, bringing massive non-Indian population and creating an industrial reality. The Erie Canal extended through Utica, Whitestown, Rome, and Verona. The Black River Canal ran north from Rome along the Mohawk and Lansing Kil Valleys. The Oneida Lake Canal extended north from Rome to Wood Creek and along that waterway to its mouth. The Chenango Canal extended from Utica up the Oriskany Creek Valley through New Hartford, Kirkland, Marshall, and Augusta, connecting with the Susquehanna River at Binghamton. Thus, what remained of the traditional Oneida territory was simply a small tract of thirty-two acres, an island in the sea of white settlement. By the 1840s, faced with these pressures, most but not all Oneidas had "migrated" west to the vicinity of Green Bay, Wisconsin, or northwest to the environs of London, Ontario. In 1855 only 161 Oneidas were counted in the state census, in sharp contrast with the approximately 1,000 Oneidas living in Wisconsin in the same period.[3]

Almost destitute, these Oneidas in New York lived a hand-to-mouth existence on their remaining reservation lands along West Road near present-day Oneida, New York, or survived as allottees at nearby Marble Hill (see map 10). Others moved onto the Onondaga Reservation, intermarrying with Onondagas or existing in the shadow world as outsiders subject to the actions of their hosts. The former allies of General Washington, trusted advisers to General Lafayette, and devoted friends of General Schuyler now found themselves barely holding on to their cultural, economic, and political existence. Instead of being the dominant force of their Carrying Place, they were now aliens in their own land with fading memories of their heroic deeds at Oriskany and other battlefields. The classic *Gazetteer of New York State* published in 1860 described the Oneidas as "a small remnant of this once powerful nation" who "still live in the s.w. part of the [Oneida] town."[4] Hence, by the time of the Civil War to most New Yorkers the Oneidas had become like the dinosaurs, ancient curiosities, a "race" that had vanished from the state's landscape. Not only were their lands traversed by canals and state roads, their lands and the Seneca lands at Tonawanda were now crisscrossed by the statewide New York Central Railway system completed in 1861.

The Senecas, although occupying more than sixty-five thousand acres on four reservations by 1857, had lost a vast territory since the late 1790s: Big Tree, Buffalo, Caneadea, Cannadaway, Canawaugus, Gardeau, Little Beard's Town, Squawky Hill, and the islands in the Niagara River, most importantly Grand Island. Throughout this period the Seneca reservation population, which included many Cayugas, remained largely stagnant at 2,535 Indians in 1855 as a result of outmigration to Canada and Indian Territory and periodic outbreaks of epidemic diseases (see table 5).[5] After the sacred wampum was returned to Onondaga in 1847 when the Senecas were dispossessed of their Buffalo Creek Reservation, they were no longer the protectors of the Iroquois Council Fire. As a result of the events that occurred between 1838 and 1848, the Senecas were a divided people with the Seneca Nation, an

E A S T E R N   I R O Q U O I S

S E T T L E M E N T S

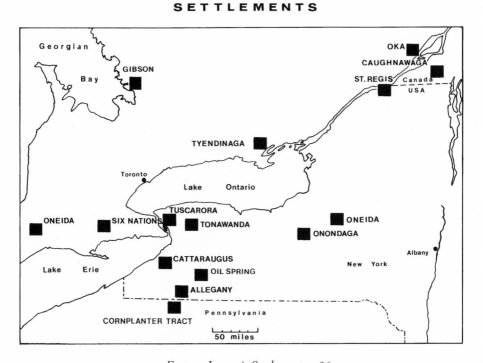

10. Eastern Iroquois Settlements, 1860

Map by Jo Margaret Mano from Laurence M. Hauptman, The Iroquois in the Civil War (1993)

elected system of government chartered under New York State law and apart from the Confederacy, maintaining control at Allegany, Cattaraugus, and Oil Spring, whereas the Tonawanda Seneca, a traditional government, remained a vital part of the Iroquois Confederacy.

By the 1850s Buffalo extended ten miles along the lakeshore and the upper part of the Niagara River, occupying an area of forty square miles. In 1853 under its new charter, Peter B. Porter's town of Black Rock was annexed and included within Buffalo's city limits. By 1855 Buffalo had a population of more than 74,214 people.[6] The *Gazetteer of New York State* described the city in 1860 as "densely covered with substantial warehouses and large stores, intermingled with factories, foundries, mechanics' shops and dwellings."

TABLE 5

Population of Iroquois Reservations, 1855

County	Individuals
Allegany	754
Cattaraugus	1,179
Oneida	161
Onondaga	349
St. Regis (Akwesasne)	413[a]
	845[b]
Tonawanda	602
Tuscarora	316
Total	4,619

Source: Derived from New York State, *Census of the State of New York for 1855,* comp. Franklin B. Hough (Albany, N.Y.: Charles Van Benthuysen and Son, 1857), 500.

    a. On U.S. side.

    b. On Canadian side.

The gazetteer concluded, "Buffalo has increased in wealth and population with the characteristic rapidity of the cities of the west."[7]

No longer a small outpost—with a few traders living among the Indians and threatened by the British presence along the Niagara frontier—Buffalo had become the ninth largest city in the United States. Its earlier Indian presence was now largely hidden, except for some place names, within the city's borders. By 1861 to most Buffalonians the impressive tomb memorial to the great orator Red Jacket in the city's Forest Lawn Cemetery symbolized the area's frontier past, a noble but vanishing one that had given way to factory smokestacks, lake steamers, and an immense granary. Indeed, by 1861, Buffalo, one of the nation's great transportation centers, already the major eastern Great Lakes port and Erie Canal terminus, was further tied to the greatest of Atlantic Coast cities, New York, even more solidly by the completion of the New York and Erie Railroad and the New York Central Railroad system.

Even before the decline of the canals, by the 1840s the iron horse had made its impact within Iroquoia. Some of its prominent men, indeed, were also associated with the Iroquois: Philip E. Thomas, the leading Quaker benefactor of the Iroquois and founder-president of the Baltimore and Ohio Railroad and member of the board of the Chesapeake and Ohio Canal; and

Lewis Henry Morgan, the Aurora-Rochester attorney for the railroads whose intellectual pursuits transformed anthropology.

The railroad's greatest effect was to be on the Allegany Indian Reservation. On June 28, 1850, the newly created Seneca Nation of Indians, still in political turmoil as a result of the Seneca revolution of 1848, leased a 145-acre right-of-way for $3,000 to the New York and Erie Railroad (later the Erie Railroad) for 11.66 miles of track through the Allegany Reservation. Although leasing of Indian lands required formal federal approval, this 1850 agreement was confirmed by the action of the New York State Legislature. The Erie Railroad, which had been chartered by the legislature in 1832, was to shape southwestern New York and state and Seneca politics well into the twentieth century. In April 1851 the Erie's last spike was driven into the track near Cuba, and the railroad was officially opened on May 14, 1851.[8] On August 20, 1863, while many Senecas were away fighting for the Union cause, the Erie Railroad leased an additional 23.85 acres for $2,385 for the "construction, occupancy, and maintenance" of its rail activities. According to one Salamanca historian, it "was this second deal which initiated the junction of the Erie Railroad and the Atlantic and Great Western Railroad at Salamanca, also laying the foundations for other villages which served as railroad depots."[9]

The railroad shaped Indian policy within the state of New York from 1850 to 1875. The railroad also transported significant numbers of people and resources and stimulated further entrepreneurial activities. During the Civil War James McHenry, an English iron magnate, and his friend and business associate, the Marquis of Salamanca (a Spanish loyalist who had made a fortune in investing and constructing railways throughout France, Italy, and Spain), extended the Atlantic and Great Western Railroad 369 miles from Salamanca, named after the marquis, to Dayton, Ohio. Between 1864 and 1866 the Atlantic and Great Western built a spur line south to Oil City, Pennsylvania, to take advantage of newly found petroleum fields. The Seneca Nation later approved a lease to the Buffalo and Pittsburgh Railroad. In each of these instances the railroads were to control their leased rights-of-way as long as they continued to operate. Four days after the surrender at Appomattox, Thomas Wistar of the Society of Friends reported that the railroads, which were now crisscrossing the Allegany Reservation, had six stations on Seneca lands and that fifty acres of tribal lands were being used by the railroads for depots, machine shops, and other buildings.[10] Thus, the town of Salamanca, 85 percent of which is on the Allegany Indian Reservation, and five other non-Indian communities—Carrolton, Great Valley, Red House, Vandalia, and West Salamanca—were settled by non-Indians between 1850 and 1875. The federal confirmation of these non-Indian "leases" to these so-called congressional villages in 1890 for ninety-nine years led to a contemporary dispute, the Seneca Nation–Salamanca lease issue, that was only resolved by a congressional act in November 1990.[11]

Despite the movement to incorporate the Iroquois into New York State's polity as a result of the Whig-Hicksite thrust of the 1840s, the call to remove Indians from the Empire State continued sporadically from the 1850s through the mid-1870s. In June 1855 Philip Thomas wrote George W. Manypenny, the commissioner of Indian Affairs, protesting the actions of "heartless" whites who were "determined to wrest from them [the Senecas] the land and drive them to destruction." Calling the Senecas a "cruelly wronged people," Thomas advocated federal intervention to protect the Indians. Despite this protest the New York State comptroller in Albany the following year initiated tax foreclosure proceedings on eleven hundred acres of the Cattaraugus Indian Reservation.[12]

Iroquois fears of being removed from their New York homeland continued unabated even after the formal Senate ratification of the Tonawanda treaty in 1857. Councillors of the Seneca Nation of Indians drew up a petition on June 2, 1858, insisting that the "council is strongly opposed to any commissioner being appointed on the part of the United States for the purpose of negotiating any treaty with the Seneca Nation respecting any proposed sale of their lands in the State of New York or elsewhere." The petition, which was forwarded to President James Buchanan and the Bureau of Indian Affairs, revealed that certain persons were circulating "petitions among our peoples" asking for negotiations encouraging emigration "in order to draw off our people from their present condition."[13] At approximately the same time Thomas further elaborated on the plan to rid New York of Iroquois Indians by "rapacious land sharks that are hovering about them." He added that these forces aimed to "find means to corrupt and secure the co-operation of certain unprincipaled individuals among the Indians" to effect their removal to Kansas.[14]

This movement for removal did not have the same appeal as it had had in Jacksonian America. Despite continued efforts by a small group of New

Yorkers, especially from the central and western regions of the state, to push this agenda, Iroquois removal was scarcely a viable option, especially after the Whig-Hicksite alternatives to removal in the 1840s. Making Indians taxpaying citizens of New York State became the avowed goal of Albany policymakers, one filled with the paternalistic rhetoric of humanely saving tribespeople both from the horrors of removal and, at the same time, from their own alleged "savagery." Indians had to be transformed for their own good through a careful process of "civilization."

New York State did not seek to simply incorporate the Indians and their lands into its polity, starting with the emerging canal era of the early 1790s. By the 1840s there was instead a clear design to "make over" the Indians. This makeover did not consist simply of Albany's aim to extend its jurisdiction over the Indians and the Indians' lands. In 1846 the New York State Legislature enacted a law providing for school buildings and annual appropriations for the education of American Indians on four of the reservations: Allegany, Cattaraugus, Onondaga, and St. Regis. Later, state-administered schools were specifically established at Shinnecock in 1848, Tonawanda and Tuscarora in 1855, Oneida in 1857, and Poospatuck in 1875.[15] One of the first enactments relating to American Indian education, passed in 1856, was entitled "An Act to facilitate education and *civilization* [emphasis mine] among the Indians residing within this state."[16] The attitudes of school superintendents and educators of Indian children can clearly be seen by examining any report of the superintendent of Public Education. In 1888 William L. Paxon, the school superintendent at Tonawanda, reflecting total cultural myopia about his Seneca charges, advocated "doing away with the system of reservations, dividing up the lands among them, and making them citizens subject to our laws" in order to make his students better educated and to "improve their condition generally."[17]

To make matters complete, after the Civil War, New York State created the Board of State Commissioners of Public Charities. This New York State Board of Charities, as it was known until 1929, had diverse functions. It administered poorhouses, institutions for the mentally and physically handicapped, "lunatic and idiot asylums," the Sailors and Soldiers Home, immigration "clearinghouses," and reformatories and orphanages to care for dependent children, including, after 1875, the Thomas Asylum for Orphan and Destitute Children, which operated on the Cattaraugus Indian Reservation. The New York State Board of Charities and its successors, the

Department of Social Welfare and now the Department of Social Services, was and still is the "lead agency" in the state carrying out programs to "its Indian citizens."[18]

Thus, American Indians, the state's first residents, ended up in a quasi-colonial status, dependent on the very people—Albany policymakers—who were responsible for dispossessing them. It is little wonder that the legacy of this colonial relationship in modern times has been the Iroquois land claims movement and that the lead community pushing these claims is the Oneidas, one of the two major foci of this book. Despite the feeling frequently expressed by Governor Mario Cuomo that the Indians were part of the "family of New York," most Iroquois Indians view Albany officials as colonial repressors. Governor George Pataki has only added fuel to the fire. His efforts to impose the collection of New York State sales taxes and his attempt to seal off the reservations by the deployment of New York State troopers in 1997 have only confirmed in the Indians' minds, whether true or not, that Albany policymakers believe the Indians will eventually disappear, that the "vanishing race" will eventually (as the Whigs believed in the 1840s) become solid, taxpaying citizens of New York State and no longer remain politically, culturally, and religiously separate Iroquoian peoples.

NOTES, BIBLIOGRAPHY, INDEX

NOTES

BECHS	Buffalo and Erie County Historical Society, Buffalo, N.Y.
Coll.	Collection
CU	Columbia University, Butler Library, New York, N.Y.
DHI	Francis Jennings et al., eds. *Iroquois Indians: A Documentary History of the Six Nations and Their League.* 50 microfilm reels. Woodbridge, Conn.: Research Publications, 1985.
DRCNY	Edmund B. O'Callaghan and Berthold Fernow, eds. *Documents Relative the Colonial History of the State of New York.* 15 vols. Albany, N.Y.: Weed, Parsons, 1853–87.
Hav.	Haverford College, Magill Library, Haverford, Pa.
HC	Hamilton College, Clinton, N.Y.
HRR	Haviland Record Room, New York Yearly Meeting of Friends, New York, N.Y.
ICC	Indian Claims Commission
M	Microcopy
MHS	Massachusetts Historical Society
MR	Microfilm reel
MSS	Manuscript collection
NA	National Archives, Washington, D.C.
NYHS	New-York Historical Society, New York, N.Y.
NYPL	New York Public Library, Special Collections Division, New York, N.Y.
NYSA	New York State Archives, Albany
NYSL	New York State Library, Manuscript Division, Albany
OHA	Onondaga Historical Association, Syracuse, N.Y.
OIA	Office of Indian Affairs
RG	Record Group
SHSW	State Historical Society of Wisconsin, Madison
SNI	Seneca Nation of Indians
Stat.	*United States Statutes at Large*
SU	Syracuse University, George Arents Research Library, Bird Library
UR	University of Rochester, Rush Rhees Library
VC	Vassar College, Poughkeepsie, N.Y.
Whipple Report	New York State Legislature. Assembly. Doc. no. 51, *Report of the Special Committee to Investigate the Indian Problem of the State of New York.* Appointed by the Assembly of 1888. 2 vols. Albany, N.Y.: Troy Press, 1889.

1. INTRODUCTION: DITCHES, DEFENSE, AND DISPOSSESSION

1. William L. Stone, *Narrative of the Festivities Observed in Honor of the Completion of the Grand Erie Canal,* in *Memoir, Prepared at the Request of a Committee of the Common Council of the City of New York, and Presented to the Mayor of the City, at the Celebration of the Completion of the New York Canals,* comp. Cadwallader D. Colden (New York: W. A. Davis, 1825; reprint, Ann Arbor: Univ. Microfilms International, 1967), 293–96; Ronald E. Shaw, *Erie Water West: A History of the Erie Canal, 1792–1854* (Lexington: Univ. Press of Kentucky, 1966), 184–91, 405; Russell Bourne, *Floating West: The Erie and Other American Canals* (New York: W. W. Norton, 1992), 124–26; Robert G. Albion, *The Rise of New York Port* [1815–60] (New York: Charles Scribner's Sons, 1939), 86–87.

2. Shaw, *Erie Water West,* 184–91, 405.

3. Quoted in Stone, *Narrative of the Festivities,* 293–96.

4. The most comprehensive history of the canal era in New York still is Noble E. Whitford, *History of the Canal System of the State of New York,* 2 vols. (Albany, N.Y.: Brandow Printing, 1906). Besides the works cited in n. 1 above, I have found the following helpful: Carol Sheriff, *The Artificial River: The Erie Canal and the Paradox of Progress, 1817–1862* (New York: Hill and Wang, 1996); and Ronald E. Shaw, *Canals for a Nation: The Canal Era in the United States, 1790–1860* (Lexington: Univ. Press of Kentucky, 1990). See also the classic, George Rogers Taylor, *The Transportation Revolution, 1815–1860* (New York: Rinehart, 1951).

5. John R. Borchert, "American Metropolitan Evolution," *Geographic Review* 57 (1967): 301–33. I have also benefited from the following: D. W. Meinig, *The Shaping of America: A Geographical Perspective on 500 Years of History,* 2 vols. (New Haven, Conn.: Yale Univ. Press, 1986 and 1993); and James E. Vance, Jr., *Capturing the Horizon: The Historical Geography of Transportation Since the Transportation Revolution of the Sixteenth Century* (New York: Harper and Row, 1986).

6. Shaw, *Erie Water West,* 263.

7. Jack Campisi, "Ethnic Identity and Boundary Maintenance in Three Oneida Communities" (Ph.D. diss., SUNY Albany, 1974), 97.

8. Walter R. Kuehnle, *Supplemental Appraisal of Lands in Western New York: Lands Ceded to or Exchanged with the United States by Seneca Nation and Tonawanda Band of Seneca Nations* [1802–12], 18, Dockets no. 342A, B, C, E, F, 368, 368A, ICC, RG 295, NA. This manuscript-report, defendant's exhibit no. V-175, was prepared for the United States Department of Justice. For this region see William Wyckoff, *The Developer's Frontier: The Making of the Western New York Landscape* (New Haven, Conn.: Yale Univ. Press, 1988); William Chazanof, *Joseph Ellicott and the Holland Land Company: The Opening of Western New York* (Syracuse, N.Y.: Syracuse Univ. Press, 1970); Orasmus Turner, *History of Phelps and Gorham's Purchase* (Rochester, N.Y.: William Alling, 1851); and idem, *Pioneer History of the Holland Purchase of Western New York* (Buffalo, N.Y.: George H. Derby, 1850). Seventeen hundred Indians lived in western New York in 1795 according to a Holland Land Company census (22).

9. See tables 1 and 2.

10. U.S. Bureau of the Census, *Eighth Census of the United States: Mortality and Miscellaneous Statistics,* [1860], xviii. For the rise of Buffalo see David A. Gerber, *The Making of an American Pluralism: Buffalo, New York, 1825–1860* (Urbana: Univ. of Illinois Press, 1989), 3–62; Mark Goldman, *High Hopes: The Rise and Decline of Buffalo* (Albany, N.Y.: SUNY Press, 1983), 21–71. For Rochester see Blake McKelvey, *Rochester on the Genesee: The Growth of a City* (Syracuse, N.Y.: Syracuse Univ. Press, 1973).

11. See, for example, Joseph Ellicott, *Holland Land Company Papers: Reports of Joseph Ellicott,* ed. Robert W. Bingham (Buffalo, N.Y.: Buffalo Historical Society, 1941), 1:142–48, 330–31. The Buffalo Historical Society subsequently changed its name to the Buffalo and Erie County Historical Society.

12. Ibid., 2:35. For more on Ellicott's road construction efforts see Paul D. Evans, *The Holland Land Company* (Buffalo, N.Y.: Buffalo Historical Society, 1924), 275–87; Wyckoff, *Developers Frontier,* 78–82; Chazanof, *Joseph Ellicott,* 80–93.

13. William W. Campbell, ed., *The Life and Writings of De Witt Clinton* (New York: Baker and Scribner, 1849), 114, 117. Evans, *Holland Land Company,* 275 passim. Kuehnle, *Supplemental Appraisal,* 25–28. There is a need for a major modern history of New York roads. For early studies see Oliver W. Holmes, "The Turnpike Era," in *History of the State of New York,* ed. Alexander C. Flick (New York: Columbia Univ. Press, 1934), 257–93; Archer B. Hulbert, *Historic Highways of America,* vol. 12, *Pioneer Roads and Experiences of Travelers* (Cleveland, Ohio: Arthur H. Clark, 1904), 97–142; Joseph A. Durrenberger, *Turnpikes: A Study of the Toll Road Movement in the Middle Atlantic States and Maryland* (Valdosta, Ga.: Southern Stationary Printing, 1931), 55–56, 61–62. Besides the Ellicott reports, see also Wyckoff, *Developers Frontier,* 53–54, 58–59, 63, 74, 78–82, 101–2, 105, 140–41, 155, 186; and especially Chazanof, *Joseph Ellicott,* 80–93. For Red Jacket's appeal see his speech of August 19, 1802, in Paul Reilly Collection on Indian Land Claims, ICC, Box 41, Doc. no. 12, SUNY, Buffalo (also on MR 6); see also Jacob Taylor to De Witt Clinton, 1802, NYSL.

14. Benjamin Wright Journal, 1816, Erie Canal Village, Rome, N.Y., copy in historical survey, New York State Museum. I thank Craig Williams of the New York State Museum for bringing this entry to my attention.

15. Whitford, *History of the Canal System,* 1:654–58. For this so-called state treaty see New York State Legislature, Assembly, Doc. no. 51, *Report of the Special Committee to Investigate the Indian Problem of the State of New York.* Appointed by the Assembly of 1888 (Albany, N.Y.: Troy Press, 1889), 1:291–97 (hereafter cited as the *Whipple Report*).

16. Whitford, *History of the Canal System,* 1:708–27, 1010–15. Charles Congdon, *Allegany Oxbow: A History of Allegany State Park and the Allegany Reserve of the Seneca Nation* (Little Valley, N.Y.: Straight Publishing, 1967), 197–205. New York State Board of Land Commissioners, *Proceedings of the Commissioners of the Land Office for the Year 1924* (Albany, N.Y.: J. B. Lyon, 1924), 109–12.

17. Vivian C. Hopkins, "De Witt Clinton and the Iroquois," *Ethnohistory* 8 (Spring 1961): 113–43; 8 (Summer 1961): 213–41. The list of canal commissioners can be found in Whitford, *History of the Canal System,* 2:1130–31.

18. Evans, *Holland Land Company*, 201–2; Scott Anderson, "Land Speculation and the Formation of Capital and Class in Central New York" (paper presented at the Conference on New York State History, June 7, 1996, SUNY, New Paltz), 9.

19. These connections can easily be seen in the relationship of Joseph Ellicott to De Witt Clinton: see Ellicott to Clinton, Jan. 19, 1816, De Witt Clinton MSS, 6:44; Feb. 25, 1816, 6:51; Mar. 25, 1816, 6:60–63, MR 2; Apr. 16, 1817, 7:14; Apr. 25, 1817, 7:15; Mar. 6, 1818, 8:17; Mar. 18, 1818, 8:21; Apr. 2, 1818, 8:27; June 29, 1818, 8:48, MR 3, CU; Clinton to Ellicott, Apr. 4, 1816, 17:292–93; Feb. 16, 1817, 18:35–36; June 18, 1818, 19:136–37, MR 5, CU. In his letter of February 16, 1817, Clinton discussed how the development and improvement of Buffalo harbor would further land development as far south as Chautauqua County. Clinton himself had more than dabbled in Genesee Valley lands—fifty thousand acres—in the 1790s: Clinton to Oliver Phelps, De Witt Clinton MSS, Nov. 30, 1795, 16:39; Dec. 8, 1795, 16:39–41; Mar. 24, 1796, 16:52; Nov. 13, 1796, 16:75; Nov. 24, 1797, 16:174–75, MR 5, CU.

20. Besides the Chazanof, Evans, and Wyckoff books, which describe the Porters' activities, see Campbell, *Life and Writings of De Witt Clinton*, 122, 155, 182–83; Frank H. Severance, ed., Buffalo Historical Society *Publications* 7 (Buffalo, N.Y.: Buffalo Historical Society, 1904), 229–360; and Turner, *Pioneer History*, 611–16. For Peter B. Porter's career see chap. 8.

21. Walter W. Ristow, "Introduction," in Christopher Colles, *A Survey of the Roads of the United States of America, 1789*, ed. Walter W. Ristow (Cambridge, Mass.: Belknap Press, Harvard Univ. Press, 1961), 1–29. For Simeon De Witt see Walter W. Ristow, *American Maps and Mapmakers* (Detroit, Mich.: Wayne State Univ. Press, 1985), 73–83.

22. Christopher Colles, *Proposals for the Speedy Settlement of the Waste and Unappropriated Lands on the Western Frontiers of the State of New York, and for the Improvement of the Inland Navigation Between Albany and Oswego* (New York: Samuel London, 1785), 6.

23. Ristow, "Introduction," 21–29.

24. Ibid.

25. Christopher Colles, *Proposal of a Design for the Promotion of the Interests of the United States of America, Extending Its Advantages to All Ranks and Conditions of Men by Means of Inland Navigable Communication of a New Construction and Mode* (New York: Samuel Wood, 1808), 4–5.

26. Biographical information about Watson can be found in Winslow C. Watson, *Men and Times of the Revolution; or, Memoirs of Elkanah Watson* (New York: Dana, 1856).

27. Journals of Elkanah Watson, Sept. 1788, in Elkanah Watson MSS, NYSL.

28. Journals of Elkanah Watson, Sept. 1788, in Elkaneh Watson MSS, NYSL.

29. Journals of Elkanah Watson, Sept. 1791, in Watson MSS, NYSL. Watson, Bayard, and Van Cortlandt were three of the largest speculators in New Military Tract lands. Others included Moses De Witt, the cousin of Simeon De Witt, New York State surveyor-general; John Tayler, the negotiator of the federal-Iroquois treaties of 1802 and later governor of New York State; and Major Abraham

Hardenbergh, the co-head surveyor (with Simeon De Witt) of New Military Tract lands. According to geographer Scott Anderson in his brilliant paper delivered at the New York History Conference in June 1996 at SUNY, New Paltz, Hardenbergh and Moses De Witt, two of the most aggressive land speculators, "played a critical role in the routing of the Genesee Road and Seneca Turnpike" through Hardenbergh's brother John's lot, "assuring the prosperity of his brother's family." Anderson, "Land Speculation."

30. Journals of Elkanah Watson, Sept. 1791, in Elkanah Watson MMS, NYSL.

31. Ibid.

32. Elkanah Watson, *History of the Rise and Progress, and Existing Condition of the Western Canals in the State of New York* (New York: D. Steele, 1820).

33. Quoted in Watson, *Men of the Revolution*, 412.

34. Shaw, *Erie Water West*, 15, 21. For Schuyler see chap. 5.

35. Whitford, *History of the Canal System*, 1:33–37.

36. Albert Gallatin, *Report of the Secretary of the Treasury on the Subject of Public Roads and Canals, 1808* (Washington, D.C.: R. C. Weightman, 1808; reprint, New York: Augustus M. Kelley, 1968).

37. Campbell, *Life and Writings of De Witt Clinton*, 72, 75, 77–78, 84, 95, 105, 122, 139–40, 159, 182–83.

38. Ibid., 61–62, 130, 159, 167, 171, 204.

39. Ibid., 61–62, 122, 155, 186–91. For an excellent revisionist work on Clinton see Craig Hanyan, *De Witt Clinton and the Rise of the People's Men* (Montreal: McGill-Queen's Univ. Press, 1996).

40. Laurence M. Hauptman, *The Iroquois Struggle for Survival: World War II to Red Power* (Syracuse, N.Y.: Syracuse Univ. Press, 1986), chaps. 8 and 9.

41. Campbell, *Life and Writings of De Witt Clinton*, 205–66. For more on Clinton's views see David Hosack, comp., *Memoir of De Witt Clinton* (New York: J. Seymour, 1829).

42. For Calhoun as secretary of war, see Merrill D. Peterson, *The Great Triumvirate: Webster, Clay and Calhoun* (New York: Oxford Univ. Press, 1987), 84–95; John Niven, *John C. Calhoun and the Price of Union: A Biography* (Baton Rouge: Louisiana State Univ. Press, 1988), 58–101; Roger J. Spiller, "John C. Calhoun as Secretary of War, 1817–1825" (Ph.D. diss., Louisiana State Univ., 1977), especially on Indian policy, 178–243; John C. Barsness, "John C. Calhoun and the Military Establishment, 1817–1825," *Wisconsin Magazine of History* 50 (Autumn 1966): 43–53.

43. Meinig, *Shaping of America*, 2:339.

44. W. Edwin Hemphill, ed., *The Papers of John C. Calhoun* (Columbia: Univ. of South Carolina Press, 1967), 3:341–55. For Calhoun's views on transportation policies, see Forrest G. Hill, *Roads, Rails, and Waterways: The Army Engineers and Early Transportation* (Norman: Univ. of Oklahoma Press, 1977), 7–36.

45. Hemphill, *Papers of John C. Calhoun*, 3:667–69, 4:475, 6:723, 7:103–4, 8:425. For Ogden's outwardly racist views see also Francis Jennings et al., eds., *Iroquois Indians: A Documentary History of the Six Nations and Their League*, 50 microfilm

reels (Woodbridge, Conn.: Research Publications, 1985) (hereafter cited as *DHI*): Ogden to Bishop Hobart, Dec. 14, 1814, MR 45; and Ogden's memorial to President Monroe, 1819, MR 46.

46. Hemphill, *Papers of John C. Calhoun*, 4:160, 576–77; 3:350–51. See also his letter to Clay on Jan. 15, 1820, ibid., 4:576–77.

47. See, for example, ibid., 3:11, 78, 90. For a good discussion of Calhoun's Iroquois policies, especially the secretary of war's efforts to find western lands for the Indians, see Spiller, "Calhoun as Secretary of War," 206–26.

48. Hill, *Roads, Rails, and Waterways*, 8–10.

49. Hemphill, *Papers of John C. Calhoun.*

50. Jedidiah Morse, *A Report to the Secretary of War of the United States on Indian Affairs, Comprising a Narrative of a Tour Performed in the Summer of 1820 for the Purpose of Ascertaining, for the Use of the Government, the Actual State of the Indian Tribes in Our Country* (New Haven, Conn.: S. Converse, 1822), 16, 24–27, apps. A, 1–6; I, 62–64; M, 75–89.

51. Hemphill, *Papers of John C. Calhoun*, 5:160.

52. Ibid., 9:421–30.

53. The records reveal that most of the claims were by Oneidas and Senecas. Justin Ingersoll to Enos T. Troup, Mar. 4, 1830, New York State Library, Manuscript Division, Albany (hereafter cited as NYSL). New York State Board of Canal Appraisers, *Digest of Claims from 1818 to 1858* (Rochester, N.Y.: A. Strong, 1858), 499, 598; New York State Board of Canal Appraisers, *Digest of Claims During the Years 1858, 1859, and 1860* (Albany, N.Y.: Weed, Parsons, 1861), 139–40; New York State Board of Canal Appraisers, *Digest of Claims from 1866 to 1870,* Inclusive (Albany, N.Y.: Argus, 1870), 11, 113.

54. William H. Armstrong, *Warrior in Two Camps: Ely S. Parker, Union General and Seneca Chief* (Syracuse, N.Y.: Syracuse Univ. Press, 1978), 41, 44, 50, 53, 56.

55. Richard H. Schein, "A Historical Geography of Central New York: Patterns and Processes of Colonization on the New Military Tract, 1782–1820" (Ph.D. diss., Syracuse Univ., 1989), 271–73.

2. THE ONEIDA CARRYING PLACE

1. Jan [John] Lincklaen, *Travels in the Years 1791 and 1792 in Pennsylvania, New York and Vermont: Journals of John Lincklaen, Agent of the Holland Land Company* (New York: G. P. Putnam's Sons, 1897), 780; Timothy Pickering Census of the Six Nations, 1792, found in Jasper Parrish MSS, Vassar College, Poughkeepsie, N.Y. (hereafter cited as VC).

2. Jack Campisi, "Oneida," in *Handbook of North American Indians,* vol. 15, *The Northeast,* ed. Bruce G. Trigger (Washington, D.C.: Smithsonian Institution, 1978), 481–90; idem, "Ethnic Identity and Boundary Maintenance," 193–211, 262–67; and idem, "The Oneida Treaty Period," in *The Oneida Indian Experience: Two Perspectives,* ed. Jack Campisi and Laurence M. Hauptman (Syracuse, N.Y.: Syracuse Univ. Press, 1988), 48–64. For Williams's actions see, for example, General Albert E. Ellis, "Some Accounts of the Advent of the New York Indians into Wisconsin,"

Wisconsin Historical Collections 2 (1856): 415–49; Reginald Horsman, "The Origins of Oneida Removal to Wisconsin, 1815–1822," in *An Anthology of Western Great Lakes Indian History*, ed. Donald L. Fixico (Milwaukee: American Indian Studies Program of the University of Wisconsin, Milwaukee, 1987), 203–32. Although there are numerous articles on the life of Eleazer Williams, a missionary of Mohawk descent who "claimed" to be the "Lost Dauphin" of France, there is no *adequate* scholarly biography of this major figure in Oneida history. For the early pressures on the Oneidas after the American Revolution, see the excellent summary article by Barbara Graymont, "New York State Indian Policy after the Revolution," *New York History* 58 (Oct. 1976): 438–74.

3. Franklin B. Hough, comp., *Proceedings of the Commissioners of Indian Affairs Appointed by Law for the Extinguishment of Indian Titles in the State of New York* (Albany, N.Y.: Munsell, 1861), 1:45–47.

4. T. Wood Clarke, *Utica: For a Century and a Half* (Utica, N.Y.: Widtman Press, 1952), 5–9, 16–30.

5. See the 1741 map in Cadwallader Colden, *The History of the Five Nations Depending on the Province of New-York in America* (1727–47; paperback reprint, Ithaca, N.Y.: Cornell Univ. Press, 1964), xviii–xix.

6. John F. Luzader, Louis Torres, and Orville W. Carroll, *Fort Stanwix* (Washington, D.C.: National Park Service, 1976); Lee Hanson and Dick Ping Hsu, *Casemates and Cannonballs: Archeological Investigations of Fort Stanwix, Rome, New York* (Washington, D.C.: National Park Service, 1975); William A. Starna, "The Oneida Homeland in the Seventeenth Century," in *The Oneida Indian Experience: Two Perspectives,* ed. Jack Campisi and Laurence M. Hauptman (Syracuse, N.Y.: Syracuse Univ. Press, 1988), 9–22.

7. Hanson and Hsu, *Casemates and Cannonballs,* 6–7.

8. Quoted in Harry F. Jackson, *Scholar in the Wilderness: Francis Adrian Van der Kemp* (Syracuse, N.Y.: Syracuse Univ. Press, 1963), 88.

9. Paoli Andreani, "Travels of a Gentleman from Milan," in *In Mohawk Country: Early Narratives of a Native People,* ed. Dean Snow, Charles Gehring, and William A. Starna (Syracuse, N.Y.: Syracuse Univ. Press, 1996), 322.

10. Friedrich Rohde, "Journal of a Trip from New Jersey to Oneida Lake," in *In Mohawk Country: Early Narratives of a Native People,* ed. Dean Snow, Charles Gehring, and William A. Starna (Syracuse, N.Y.: Syracuse Univ. Press, 1996), 377.

11. Journals of Elkanah Watson, Sept. 1788, Sept. 1791, Elkanah Watson, MSS, NYSL; Campbell, *Life and Writings of De Witt Clinton,* 61–62, 72, 75, 77–78, 84, 95, 105, 118; Jeremy Belknap, *Journal of a Tour from Boston to Oneida, June 1796,* ed. George Dexter (Cambridge, Mass.: John Wilson, 1882), 21, 25–26.

12. Jackson, *Scholar in the Wilderness,* 88.

13. Ibid., 89.

14. Belknap, *Journal,* 26.

15. John Taylor, "On a Mission Through the Mohawk and Black River Country in the Year 1802," in *In Mohawk Country: Early Narratives of a Native People,* ed. Dean Snow, Charles Gehring, and William A. Starna (Syracuse, N.Y.: Syracuse Univ. Press, 1996), 367.

16. Lewis Henry Morgan, *League of the Ho-de-no-sau-nee or Iroquois,* paperback reprint, ed. William N. Fenton (New York: Corinth Books, 1962), 420. For more on Oneida Castle see J. N. B. Hewitt, "Ganowarohare," in *Handbook of American Indians North of Mexico,* ed. Frederick Webb Hodge (Washington, D.C.: Bureau of American Ethnology *Bulletin* 30, 1907), 1:487.

17. D. W. Meinig, "Geography of Expansion, 1785–1855," in *Geography of New York State,* ed. John H. Thompson, rev. ed., paperback (Syracuse, N.Y.: Syracuse Univ. Press, 1977), 148.

18. E. B. Tustin, Jr., "The Development of the Salt Industry in New York," *New-York Historical Society Quarterly* 33 (1949): 40–46; Joseph Hawley Murphy, "The Salt Industry of Syracuse: A Brief Review," *New York History* 30 (July 1949): 304–15; W. Freeman Galpin, "The Genesis of Syracuse," *New York History* 30 (Jan. 1949): 19–32; Blake McKelvey, "The Erie Canal: Mother of Cities," *New-York Historical Society Quarterly* 30 (Jan. 1951): 54–71.

19. *United States Statutes at Large* (hereafter cited as *Stat.*), 1:137–38 (July 22, 1790); 414 U.S. 661 (Jan. 21, 1974); 470 U.S. 226 (Mar. 4, 1985). For the history of Oneida land claims see George C. Shattuck, *The Oneida Indian Land Claims: A Legal History* (Syracuse, N.Y.: Syracuse Univ. Press, 1991); and Hauptman, *Iroquois Struggle for Survival,* chap. 10.

20. William Bradford (U.S. attorney general) to Pickering, June 16, 1795; Pickering to Israel Chapin (U.S. Indian agent), June 29, July 23, Aug. 26, 1795, *DHI,* MR 43, NYSL.

21. See *Stat.,* 470 U.S. 226.

22. William L. Riordan, comp., *Plunkitt of Tammany Hall,* ed. Terence J. McDonald (New York, 1905; reprint, New York: Bedford Books of St. Martin's Press, 1994), 49–50.

3. THE GOOD INDIANS AT THE CROSSROADS

1. Campisi, "Ethnic Identity and Boundary Maintenance," 101.

2. Timothy Pickering to Henry Knox (secretary of war), May 2, 1792, Timothy Pickering MSS, MR 62, MHS. For the Oneidas in the war see Barbara Graymont, "The Oneidas and the American Revolution," in *The Oneida Indian Experience: Two Perspectives,* ed. Jack Campisi and Laurence M. Hauptman (Syracuse, N.Y.: Syracuse Univ. Press, 1988), 31–42; idem, *The Iroquois in the American Revolution* (Syracuse, N.Y.: Syracuse Univ. Press, 1972), 234. See *The Balloting Book and Other Documents Relating to Military Bounty Lands in the State of New York* (Albany, N.Y.: Packard and Van Benthuysen, 1825), 140, 180 (Town of Junius "awards" of Cayuga lands to Oneidas for military service). Apparently, they or their heirs sold these military bound lands, a total of eight lots totaling three thousand acres, on May 26, 1809, for twenty-three thousand dollars. L. P. Gillett Deed, New York Surveyor-General's Land Papers, ser. 2, A40167, Box 12, folders 81B, 83B, 94A, NYSA. For more on Oneida military service in the American Revolution see Lyman C. Draper, "Notes from Oneida Indians, Oct. 30–Nov. 2, 1877," Lyman C. Draper Collection,

Frontier Wars Papers, 11C, State Historical Society of Wisconsin, Madison (hereafter cited as SHSW).

3. Walter Pilkington, ed., *The Journals of Samuel Kirkland* (Clinton, N.Y.: Hamilton College, 1980), 132, 134, 148 n. 1, 159; Patrick Frazier, *The Mohicans of Stockbridge* (Lincoln: Univ. of Nebraska Press, 1992; Bison Books paperback, 1994), 237–38.

4. In 1668 Father Bruyas, who lived among the Oneidas, reported that two-thirds of the Oneida population was made up of Algonquins and Hurons "who have become Iroquois in temper and inclination." Reuben G. Thwaites, ed., *The Jesuit Relations and Allied Documents* (reprint, New York: Pageant Books, 1959), 51:123.

5. Francois Marbois, "Journey to the Oneidas (1794)," in *In Mohawk Country: Early Narratives of a Native People,* ed. Dean Snow, Charles Gehring, and William A. Starna (Syracuse, N.Y.: Syracuse Univ. Press, 1996), 300–317.

6. Timothy Pickering, Account of Captain John's Speech of Oct. 11, 1794, *DHI,* MR 43, NYSL.

7. Ibid.

8. For the Oneidas in the War of 1812 see Abstract of Pension Applications, War of 1812, Claimant nos. 9,997–10,006, 10,566, New York State Division of Military and Naval Affairs, NYSA. Draper, "Notes from Oneida Indians," Draper MSS, 11U, SHSW. I thank Dr. Carl Benn of the Fort York Historic Site for information about the Iroquois in the War of 1812. For the Oneida involvement in the Battle of Sandy Creek see Donald R. Hickey, *The War of 1812: A Forgotten Conflict* (Urbana: Univ. of Illinois Press, 1989), 185; J. Mackay Hitsman, *The Incredible War of 1812* (Toronto: Univ. of Toronto Press, 1965), 185–86.

9. James Ronda, "Reverend Samuel Kirkland and the Oneida Indians," in *The Oneida Indian Experience: Two Perspectives,* ed. Jack Campisi and Laurence M. Hauptman (Syracuse, N.Y.: Syracuse Univ. Press, 1988), 23–30; Christine Patrick, "Samuel Kirkland: Missionary to the Oneida Indians" (Ph.D. diss., SUNY, Buffalo, 1992).

10. Campisi, "Oneida," 482–83.

11. Campisi, "Oneida Treaty Period," 60.

12. Ronda, "Reverend Samuel Kirkland," 23–24, 29.

13. Pilkington, *Journals of Samuel Kirkland,* 43–44 n. 9; Lincklaen, *Travels,* 68–69; Colin Calloway, *The American Revolution in Indian Country: Crisis and Diversity in Native American Communities* (New York: Cambridge Univ. Press, 1995), 112–13; Richard Smith, *A Tour of the Hudson, the Mohawk, the Susquehanna and the Delaware in 1769,* ed. Francis W. Halsey (paperback reprint edition and retitled from the 1906 original, *A Tour of Four Great Rivers,* Fleischmanns, N.Y.: Purple Mountain Press, 1989), 133–34. Calloway misidentified Good Peter's clan as eel. There is *no* eel clan then or now among the Oneidas. For more on Good Peter see also Draper, "Notes from Oneida Indians," Draper MSS, 11U, SHSW.

14. James Dow McCallum, ed., *The Letters of Eleazar Wheelock's Indians* (Hanover, N.H.: Dartmouth College, 1932), 25, 79–80; Pilkington, *Journals of Samuel Kirkland,* xvii–xviii; Ronda, "Reverend Samuel Kirkland," 24–25.

15. Good Peter to Timothy Pickering, early April 1792, Pickering MSS, MR 60, MHS. Good Peter remained on close terms with Kirkland, defending him and accompanying him to official meetings. See Good Peter speech, Mar. 1792, Pickering MSS, MR 62, MHS. For Good Peter's relationship to Skenandoah, see Good Peter to Pickering, early April 1792, cited above.

16. Good Peter to Pickering, early April 1792, Pickering MSS, MR 60, MHS. For more on this extraordinary Oneida see Hough, *Proceedings of Commissioners of Indian Affairs,* vol. 1. Pilkington, *Journals of Samuel Kirkland,* 129–30, 142–44, 159, 199–201, 215–22, 231; Graymont, "New York State Indian Policy," 454–55; J. David Lehman, "The End of the Iroquois Mystique: The Oneida Land Cession Treaties of the 1780s," *William and Mary Quarterly* 47 (Oct. 1990): 536–40.

17. Skenandoah's obituary can be found in the *Utica Patriot and Patrol,* Mar. 19, 1816, 4. Hough, *Proceedings of Commissioners of Indian Affairs,* 1:87–88; Pilkington, *Journals of Samuel Kirkland,* 48; Campbell, *Life and Writings of De Witt Clinton,* 187–88; Belknap, *Journal,* 20; William Beauchamp, "Johnko' Skeanendon" (The hemlock), in "St. Regis Indians and Five of the Six Nations," William Beauchamp MSS, bound vol. 3, Box 15, item 184, 51–53, NYSL; "Instances of Indian Genius" (1816), SHSW, reprint of an article from the *Commercial Advertiser;* William W. Campbell, *Annals of Tryon County* (Cherry Valley, N.Y.: Cherry Valley Gazette Printers, 1880), app., 233–36.

18. Pilkington, *Journals of Samuel Kirkland,* 34, 217–18, 263–70, 289–98, 305–6, 311–15, 323–39, 344, 349, 356–57, 368, 375–86, 393–99, 407, 415–20.

19. Beauchamp, "Johnko' Skeanendon," Beauchamp MSS, item 184, 51–53, NYSL.

20. Graymont, *Iroquois in the American Revolution,* 53. Indeed, Brant married two of Skenandoah's daughters: Margaret and, after she died, her sister, Susanna. The accusations against Skenandoah can be found in the Draper MSS, 11U, SHSW.

21. Beauchamp, "Johnko' Skeanendon," Beauchamp MSS, item 184, 51–53, NYSL.

22. Timothy Pickering to Henry Knox, May 2, 1792, Samuel Kirkland MSS, no. 148b, Hamilton College, Clinton, N.Y. (hereafter cited as HC). Graymont, *Iroquois in the American Revolution,* 225–35.

23. See chap. 3, n. 17.

24. Campbell, *Life and Writings of De Witt Clinton,* 187–88.

25. Pilkington, *Journals of Samuel Kirkland,* 264.

26. Belknap, *Journal,* 21–22. Belknap's conclusion about Skenandoah's limited power appears accurate. For a different conclusion about Skenandoah's continuing influence (as late as 1799) see Pilkington, *Journals of Samuel Kirkland,* 315.

27. Julian Ursyn Niemcewicz, "Journey to Niagara, 1805," ed. Metchie J. E. Budka, *New-York Historical Society Quarterly* 74 (Jan. 1960): 95.

28. Belknap, *Journal,* 21–22. See also Niemcewicz, "Journey to Niagara, 1805," 95. For his silver pipe see Campbell, *Life and Writings of De Witt Clinton,* 187–88.

29. Oneida Indians [Skenandoah et al.] to the Regents of the State of New York, Apr. 27, 1793, Kirkland MSS, no. 159b, HC; from Representatives of the Oneida

Indians to Alexander Hamilton, Jan. 15, 1794, in *The Papers of Alexander Hamilton,* ed. Harold C. Syrett et al. (New York: Columbia Univ. Press, 1969), 15:642.

30. See the photographic plate of Skenandoah's tombstone at Hamilton College.

31. See *Whipple Report,* 234–52.

32. An original copy of this Peter Smith 1793 lease and affidavit can be found in Peter Smith MSS, Syracuse University, George Arents Research Library, Bird Library (hereafter cited as SU).

33. For Reed's dealings with Smith see Jacob Reed to Peter Smith, Apr. 7, Oct. 19, 20, 1792; Jan. 5, Feb. 22, Mar. 11, May 9, 1793; Ebenezer Caulkins to Peter Smith, May 10, 1793, Peter Smith MSS, Box 1, SU. Beauchamp, "Jacob Reed" (Atsiskta), in St. Regis Indians and Five of the Six Nations, Beauchamp MSS, item 238, 57, NYSL; Pilkington, *Journals of Samuel Kirkland,* 153 n. 76. Good Peter apparently did not trust Reed: "We have another [Jacob Reed] who can never fix his attention." Good Peter to Timothy Pickering, early April 1792, Pickering MSS, MR 60, MHS.

34. *Whipple Report,* 269–72; Hough, *Proceedings of Commissioners of Indian Affairs,* 1:198 n. 1.

35. *Whipple Report,* 269–72; Hough, *Proceedings of Commissioners of Indian Affairs,* 1:198 n. 1. Arlinda Locklear, p.c., June 12, 1997. Locklear is the attorney for the Oneida Indians pursuing their land claims.

36. Hough, *Proceedings of Commissioners of Indian Affairs,* 1:88n.

37. Speech of John Scanandon (Skenandoah) from article in *Niles Register,* Oct. 12, 1816, *DHI,* MR 45, NYSL.

38. Ibid.

39. Beauchamp, "Beech Tree—Peter Oneyana," Beauchamp MSS, item 203, 54–55, NYSL; Pilkington, *Journals of Samuel Kirkland,* 153 nn. 79–80. "Capt. John, Oneida Chief," *Charleston Gazette* (South Carolina), Oct. 17, 1795, Draper MSS, 11U, SHSW.

40. Belknap, *Journal,* 21, 23–24. Silversmith and Blacksmith were apparently the same Oneida. Field notes, June 1997.

41. Samuel Kirkland to Alexander Miller, May 24, 1800, Samuel Kirkland MSS, no. 211c, HC; Pilkington, *Journals of Samuel Kirkland,* 360–65.

42. Kirkland to Miller, May 24, 1800, Kirkland MSS, no. 211c; Pilkington, *Journals of Samuel Kirkland,* 360–65; Elisabeth Tooker, "The Iroquois White Dog Sacrifice in the Later Part of the Eighteenth Century," *Ethnohistory* 12 (1965): 129–40.

43. Besides the Tooker article cited in n. 42, for more on the White Dog Sacrifice see Anthony F. C. Wallace, *The Death and Rebirth of the Seneca* (New York: Alfred A. Knopf, 1969), 299. Robert F. Berkhofer, Jr., *Salvation and the Savage: An Analysis of Protestant Missions and American Indian Response, 1787–1862* (reprint, New York: Atheneum, 1976), 131–32. For the White Dog Sacrifice see Harold Blau, "The Iroquois White Dog Sacrifice: Its Evolution and Symbolism," *Ethnohistory* 11 (1964): 97–119; William N. Fenton, "Northern Iroquoian Culture Patterns," in *Handbook of North American Indians,* vol. 15, *The Northeast,* ed. Bruce G. Trigger (Washington, D.C.: Smithsonian Institution, 1978), 316; and idem, *The Iroquois Eagle Dance: An*

Offshoot of the Calumet Dance (1953; paperback reprint, Syracuse, N.Y.: Syracuse Univ. Press, 1991), 104–7.

44. Tooker, "Iroquois White Dog Sacrifice," 132–33; Wallace, *Death and Rebirth of the Seneca,* 299, 309.

45. Quoted in Tooker, "Iroquois White Dog Sacrifice," 133.

46. Ibid., 146. Kirkland to Miller, May 24, 1800, Kirkland MSS, no. 211c; Pilkington, *Journals of Samuel Kirkland,* 360–65.

47. Kirkland to Miller, May 24, 1800, Kirkland MSS, no. 211c.

48. The literature on the origins of the Handsome Lake Religion is too vast to cite in its entirety. For a synopsis see Anthony F. C. Wallace, "Origins of the Longhouse Religion," in *Handbook of North American Indians,* vol. 15, *The Northeast,* ed. Bruce G. Trigger (Washington, D.C.: Smithsonian Institution, 1978), 442–48.

49. Wallace, *Death and Rebirth of the Seneca,* 149–236.

50. Elisabeth Tooker, "On the New Religion of Handsome Lake," *Anthropological Quarterly* 41 (1968): 187–200.

51. Hough, *Proceedings of Commissioners of Indian Affairs,* 279–80.

52. Graymont, *Iroquois in the American Revolution,* 291.

53. Wallace, "Origins of the Longhouse Religion," 447.

54. Handsome Lake attempted to keep the Indians out of the War of 1812. See Erastus Granger to Jasper Parrish, Oct. 24, 1812, Parrish MSS, VC.

55. Wallace, "Origins of the Longhouse Religion," 447. These influences can be traced to visiting Quakers. For Friends-Seneca connections in the age of Handsome Lake see Halliday Jackson, "Halliday Jackson's Journal to the Seneca Indians, 1798–1800," ed. Anthony F. C. Wallace, *Pennsylvania History* 19 (1952): 117–46, 325–49; George Snyderman, ed., "Halliday Jackson's Journal of a Visit Paid to the Indians of New York (1806)," *Proceedings* of the American Philosophical Society 101 (Dec. 1957): 565–88; Halliday Jackson, *Civilization of the Indian Natives* (Philadelphia: Marcus Gould, 1830); Merle H. Deardorff and George Snyderman, "A Nineteenth-Century Journal of a Visit to the Indians of New York," *Proceedings* of the American Philosophical Society 100 (Dec. 1956): 582–612.

56. Quoted in Wallace, *Death and Rebirth of the Seneca,* 308–9.

57. Ibid.

58. Pilkington, *Journals of Samuel Kirkland,* 413.

59. Ibid.

60. Ibid., 370 n. 10. Julia K. Bloomfield, *The Oneidas,* 2d ed. (New York: Alden Bros., 1907), 117. Cornelius Haunnagwasuke, the Little Doctor, was chief at Oriske and fought at the Battle of Oriskany in the American Revolution and in the War of 1812, dying in 1831 at the age of one hundred. Abstract of Pension Applications, War of 1812, Claimant no. 10,002 (Henry Cornelius), New York State Division of Military and Naval Affairs, NYSA.

61. Campbell, *Life and Writings of De Witt Clinton,* 187. Clinton claimed that the Christians outnumbered the non-Christians by one hundred in 1810. In 1797 the Quaker missionary Joseph Clarke estimated that the Oneida population in central New York was six hundred souls and that their land base was twelve square miles.

Clarke, *Travels among the Indians, 1797* (Doylestown, Pa.: Charles Ingerman, Quixott Press, 1968), postscript.

62. Marbois, "Journey to the Oneidas," 307–8.

63. Lafayette felt a keen responsibility to his Oneida warriors during the American Revolution because he had helped recruit them: "Whenever the army needed Indians, or there was any business to be conducted with those tribes [Oneidas and Tuscaroras], they always had recourse to the influence of M. de Lafayette, whose necklaces and words the Indians respected." Stanley J. Idzerda, ed., *Lafayette in the Age of the American Revolution: Selected Letters and Papers, 1776–1790* (Ithaca, N.Y.: Cornell Univ. Press, 1977), 1:247.

64. Franklin B. Hough, *Notices of Peter Penet of His Operations among the Oneida Indians* (Lowville, N.Y.: privately printed paper read before the Albany Institute, 1866), 3–24; Hough, *Proceedings of Commissioners of Indian Affairs,* 1:152n; 2:346, 352, 354.

65. *Whipple Report,* 239.

66. Hough, *Notices of Peter Penet,* 25.

67. Beauchamp, "Lewis Cook," Beauchamp MSS, item 344, 62, NYSL Hough, *Notices of Peter Penet,* 19 n. 3; Pilkington, *Journals of Samuel Kirkland,* 233 n. 3.

68. Hough, *Proceedings of Commissioners of Indian Affairs,* 1:39 nn. 140–41.

69. Beauchamp, "Peter Otsiquette," Beauchamp MSS, item 216, 55, NYSL; Watson, Journals of Elkanah Watson, Watson MSS, Sept. 1788, NYSL; Lincklaen, *Travels,* 69.

70. Campbell, *Life and Writings of De Witt Clinton,* 190–91.

71. *Whipple Report,* 266–69.

72. Campbell, *Life and Writings of De Witt Clinton,* 191.

73. Ibid.

74. Berkhofer, *Salvation and the Savage,* 131–32; see *Whipple Report,* 259–63.

75. Campbell, *Life and Writings of De Witt Clinton,* 187.

76. Berkhofer, *Salvation and the Savage,* 132; Campisi, "Ethnic Identity and Boundary Maintenance," 94–132; Campisi, "Oneida Treaty Period," 60–62.

77. John Thornton Kirkland, "Answer to Queries," Massachusetts Historical Society, *Collections* 4 (1795): 71.

4. TRUST ME

1. Jack Campisi, "New York–Oneida Treaty of 1795: A Finding of Fact," *American Indian Law Review* 4 (Summer 1976): 71–82. Campisi's well-documented article shows the illegality of the treaty because there was neither a federal commissioner present nor United States Senate ratification. Campisi, however, does not mention all the forces at work, Schuyler and the transportation and land interests involved in this dispossession.

2. Benjamin Wright to George Scriba, July 20, 1793, Dec. 14, 1796, Sept. 20, 1797, George Scriba MSS, Box 2; Dec. 19, 1802, Mar. 20, 1804, July 13, 1807, Scriba MSS, Box 3, NYSL, MSS Div., Albany; Wright to Peter Smith, Dec. 25, 1813, Dec. 13, 1815, Peter Smith MSS, SU; Wright to Nicholas Low, Mar. 4, 1797, Benjamin

Wright MSS, Box 1, Folder 1, NYSL; Wright to Schuyler, May 12, July 15, 1802; June 26, Oct. 8, 1803, Philip Schuyler MSS, MR 3, NYPL. For the actions of the Hardenberghs, see William Hardenbergh to Moses De Witt, Oct. 5, 1791, which is critical of Timothy Pickering and discusses the leasing of the Cayuga Indian Reservation, De Witt Family MSS, Box 2, Folder, Correspondence, Oct. 1791; John Cantine to Moses De Witt, De Witt Family MSS, Box 2, Folder, Correspondence, Sept. 1–15, 1791, SU. Cantine was one of three New York State commissioners who negotiated with the Oneidas in 1795. *Whipple Report,* 244–49. For Moses De Witt, Abraham Hardenbergh, and other surveyors see the previously cited paper by Scott Anderson, "Land Speculation."

3. The Constitution of the State of New-York, Apr. 20, 1777, reprinted in New York State Constitutional Convention, *Reports of the Proceedings and Debates of the New York Constitutional Convention, 1821* (New York: Da Capo Press, 1970), 19.

4. Good Peter to Timothy Pickering, early April 1792, Pickering MSS, MR 60, MHS.

5. Hugh Hastings, ed., *The Public Papers of George Clinton* (Albany, N.Y.: Oliver Quayle, 1904), 8:328–32.

6. Reginald Horsman, *The Frontier in the Formative Years, 1783–1815* (New York: Holt, Rinehart and Winston, 1970), 30–31.

7. Graymont, "New York State Indian Policy," 440.

8. Ibid., 443.

9. Richard Morris, ed., *John Jay: The Making of a Revolutionary: Unpublished Papers, 1745–1780* (New York: Harper and Row, 1975), 2:659–60.

10. Graymont, "New York State Indian Policy," 442–43.

11. Ibid., 444–45.

12. Ibid., 449–51.

13. Quoted in ibid., 451.

14. Ibid., 453.

15. Hastings, *Public Papers of George Clinton,* 8:354.

16. Ibid., 355. See n. 2.

17. Campisi, "Ethnic Identity and Boundary Maintenance," 93–94.

18. Ibid., 94–102.

19. Philip Schuyler, "Thoughts Respecting Peace in the Indian Country," July 29, 1783, Philip Schuyler MSS, MR 7, NYPL. Throughout 1783 Schuyler, Washington, and Duane corresponded about the "Indian question." See George Washington, *The Writings of George Washington,* ed. John C. Fitzpatrick (Washington, D.C.: U.S. Government Printing Office, 1938), 27:133–37.

20. Belknap, *Journal,* 5. For Belknap's final report see "The Report of a Committee of the Board of Correspondents of the Scottish Society for Propagating Christian Knowledge Who Visited Oneida and Mohekunuh Indians in 1796," Massachusetts Historical Society, *Collections,* 1st ser. (Boston: Samuel Hall, 1798), 5:12–32.

21. Luzader, Torres, and Carroll, *Fort Stanwix,* 3–26; Hanson and Hsu, *Casemates and Cannonballs,* 6–13.

22. Don R. Gerlach, *Proud Patriot: Philip Schuyler and the War of Independence, 1775–1783* (Syracuse, N.Y.: Syracuse Univ. Press, 1987), 212, 303, 336–38, 347, 350,

418–20, 429, 441, 463, 478, 504, 506. Graymont, *Iroquois in the American Revolution,* 242–43.

23. Washington, *Writings of George Washington,* 11:284–85, 364, 384–85; E. James Ferguson, ed., *The Papers of Robert Morris* (Pittsburgh, Pa.: Univ. of Pittsburgh Press, 1975–77), 2:169–71, 256–57, 273–74; 3:188–91, 194–97. John Thornton Kirkland Notes, Feb. 1795, Draper MSS, 11U, SHSW.

24. Quoted in Calloway, *American Revolution in Indian Country,* 286. Skenandoah and Good Peter delivered a bell on behalf of the British Indians, July 1783, Philip Schuyler MSS, MR 7, NYPL.

25. Graymont, "Oneidas and the American Revolution," 31–42.

26. Laurence M. Hauptman, Oneida Field notes, 1977–96.

27. Gerlach, *Proud Patriot,* 514. See also Worthington C. Ford et al., eds., *Journals of the Continental Congress* (Washington, D.C.: U.S. Government Printing Office, 1922), 24:501 n. 1; 25:680–95.

28. For the federal Treaty of Fort Stanwix of 1784, see 7 *Stat.,* 15 (Oct. 22, 1784); for the state accords of 1785 and 1788, see *Whipple Report,* 234–43.

29. Hough, *Proceedings of Commissioners of Indian Affairs,* 1:45–47.

30. Campisi, "Oneida Treaty Period," 54.

31. *Whipple Report,* 243–49; Campisi, "New York–Oneida Treaty of 1795," 71–82.

32. Watson, Journals of Elkanah Watson, Watson MSS, Sept. 1788, NYSL.

33. Whitford, *History of the Canal System,* 1:25–47; Nathan Miller, "Private Enterprise in Inland Navigation: The Mohawk Route Prior to the Erie Canal," *New York History* 31 (Oct. 1950): 398–413; and idem, *The Enterprise of a Free People: Aspects of Economic Development in New York State During the Canal Era, 1792–1838* (Ithaca, N.Y.: Cornell Univ. Press, 1962), 18–29, 43–44, 72; Shaw, *Erie Water West,* 15–20, 31–32, 51, 56.

34. List of Stockholders and List of Directors, Western Inland Lock Navigation Company, Philip Schuyler MSS, Boxes 5 and 6, NYPL. See also Dixon Ryan Fox, *The Decline of Aristocracy in the Politics of New York, 1801–1840,* ed. Robert V. Remini (reprint, New York: Harper Torchbook, 1965), 151–57.

35. Miller, "Private Enterprise in Inland Navigation," 403. See idem, *Enterprise of a Free People,* 18–29, 43–44, 72.

36. Miller, "Private Enterprise in Inland Navigation," 403, 411 n. 24.

37. Whitford, *History of the Canal System,* 1:29–37.

38. Ibid., 1:37.

39. Hough, *Proceedings of Commissioners of Indian Affairs,* 1:141; Campisi, "Ethnic Identity and Boundary Maintenance," 80–81.

40. Samuel Kirkland to Governor of New York State and Commissioners of Indian Affairs of New York State, Dec. 18, 1788, Kirkland MSS, no. 111b, HC. See also H. J. Lennox, *Samuel Kirkland's Mission to the Iroquois* (Chicago: Univ. of Chicago Libraries, 1935), 13; and Campisi, "Ethnic Identity and Boundary Maintenance," 80–81; cf. Ronda, "Reverend Samuel Kirkland," 23–30.

41. For Kirkland's lands and financial exigencies see Samuel Kirkland to John Thornton Kirkland, Sept. 30, 1795, Kirkland MSS, 189–93, 279–80, HC; Campisi, "Ethnic Identity and Boundary Maintenance," 93–94. Pilkington, *Journals of Samuel Kirkland,* 122, 189–93, 279–80.

42. Petition of Gorham and Phelps, Feb. 7, 1789, Kirkland MSS, no. 113a; Oliver Phelps to Samuel Kirkland, Nov. 14, 1790, Kirkland MSS, no. 130c; "List of Donors to Hamilton-Oneida Academy," Apr. 1793, Kirkland MSS, no. 159e, HC.

43. Peter Smith to Samuel Kirkland, Apr. 29, 1793, Kirkland MSS, no. 159d, HC.

44. "List of Donors to Hamilton-Oneida Academy," Apr. 1793; "Trustees of Hamilton-Oneida Academy to New York State Board of Regents," Nov. 12, 1792, Kirkland MSS, no. 154a, HC.

45. Samuel Kirkland notes discussing his "Plan of Indian Education," 1792, Kirkland MSS, no. 143b, HC.

46. Samuel Kirkland to Stephen Van Rensselaer, Feb. 24, 1795, Kirkland MSS, no. 176c, HC.

47. "John Skannondogh" (Skenandoah) et al., To the Commissioners for Propagating the Gospel among the Natives of America, Jan. 29, 1794, Kirkland MSS, no. 164d, HC; Oneida chiefs to Peter Thacher (Boston missionary society), July 25, 1795, Kirkland MSS, no. 181c, HC.

48. John Sergeant to Timothy Pickering, Jan. 3, 1795, Kirkland MSS, no. 175a, HC; Sergeant to Pickering, Apr. 26, 1795, Kirkland MSS, no. 178b, HC; Sergeant to Pickering, Oct. 20, 1795, Kirkland MSS, no. 184a, HC.

49. Sergeant to Kirkland, Jan. 3, 1795. For the charges against Kirkland see Peter Thacher to Samuel Kirkland, Apr. 11, 1794, Kirkland MSS, no. 167a, HC.

50. Belknap, *Journal* (1796), 19.

51. Pilkington, *Journals of Samuel Kirkland,* 279–80.

52. Sergeant to Kirkland, Jan. 3, 1795, Kirkland MSS, HC.

53. Hough, *Proceedings of Commissioners of Indian Affairs,* 1:27–28; Campisi, "Ethnic Identity and Boundary Maintenance," 94; Calloway, *American Revolution in Indian Country,* 17; Graymont, *Iroquois in the American Revolution,* 59, 336; Graymont, "New York State Indian Policy," 439–74.

54. Campbell, *Life and Writings of De Witt Clinton,* 61–62.

55. Campbell, *Annals of Tryon County,* 230–32.

56. The two federal treaties can be found in Charles J. Kappler, comp., *Indian Affairs: Laws and Treaties* (Washington, D.C.: U.S. Government Printing Office, 1903–41), 2:34–35.

57. Timothy Pickering to Israel Chapin, Aug. 26, 1795; William Bradford to Pickering, June 16, 1795, *DHI,* MR 43, NYSL; Pickering to John Jay, July 16, Sept. 1, 1795, John Jay MSS, CU.

58. Simeon De Witt Report on Council with Onondaga, Oneida, and Cayuga Indians, Mar. 11, 1793, New York State Land Records, 2d ser., A 4016 Book 21, 120, NYSA; John Cantine and Simeon De Witt Report on Proceedings with Onondaga, Oneida, and Cayuga Indians, 1793, *DHI,* MR 42, NYSL.

59. De Witt Report, Mar. 11, 1793, NYSA.

60. Speech of Oneida Indians to New York State Assembly and Senate, Feb. 27, 1795, *DHI,* MR 43, NYSL.

61. Israel Chapin letter to ? [unknown correspondent], Mar. 10, 1795, *DHI,* MR 43, NYSL.

62. Timothy Pickering to Israel Chapin, Apr. 6, 1795, *DHI,* MR 43, NYSL.

63. Philip Schuyler to John Jay, June 9, 1795, John Jay MSS, CU.

64. *Whipple Report*, 224–28. For Cayuga resistance to state efforts to secure lands around Cayuga Lake see Moses De Witt, *Journal*, no. 2, 47–54, Moses De Witt MSS, Box 6, Folder, Surveying Records M. 12 Journals, Cayuga and Onondaga Counties, 1789, SU.

65. Moses De Witt to New York State Legislature, ?, 1794, Moses De Witt MSS, Box 6, Folder, Legal Records, Petition . . . to buy Onondaga Reservation, SU.

66. *Whipple Report*, 199–203.

67. Ibid., 195–99.

68. Nearly every major New York State entrepreneur was involved in salt speculation. They included the following major speculators in Indian lands: Moses De Witt, Asa Danforth, Elkanah Watson, and Peter B. Porter. See Campbell, *Life and Writings of De Witt Clinton;* Tustin, "Salt Industry in New York," 40–46; Niemcewicz, "Journey to Niagara, 1805," 95; Murphy, "Salt Industry of Syracuse," 304–15; Galpin, "Genesis of Syracuse," 19–32.

69. Niemcewicz, "Journey to Niagara, 1805," 96–97.

70. Ibid.

71. Harold Blau, Jack Campisi, and Elisabeth Tooker, "Onondaga," in *Handbook of North American Indians,* vol. 15, *The Northeast,* ed. Bruce G. Trigger (Washington, D.C.: Smithsonian Institution, 1978), 495–96.

72. *Whipple Report*, 190–99.

73. Ibid., 242–49.

74. See chap. 4, n. 57; and Timothy Pickering to Israel Chapin, Jr., Apr. 6, May 22, June 29, July 3, 1795; Chapin to Pickering, May 6, May 22, June 13, Oct. 9, 1795, Henry O'Reilly MSS, Box 11, Western Mementoes Papers, NYHS; Washington, *Writings of George Washington,* 34:250–51.

75. Philip Schuyler et al. to Brothers, Sachems, and Warriors of the Oneida Nation, Aug. 6, 1795; Notes of Aug. 6, 1795, Council with Oneidas, Aug. 8, 1795, Philip Schuyler MSS, MR 7, NYPL.

76. See chap. 4, n. 75; John Schenando (Skenandoah) et al. to New York State Commissioners, Aug. 16, 1795, Philip Schuyler MSS, MR 7, NYPL.

77. Draft of Oneida Treaty Council negotiations, Sept. 12, 1795, Philip Schuyler MSS, MR 7a, NYPL.

78. *Whipple Report*, 242–49.

79. For Schuyler's expenses see Philip Schuyler MSS, Box 2, Folders 23–25, Financial Documents, NYSL. The commissioners received five thousand pounds to cover their expenses. For the Schuyler, Cantine, and Brooks report, see *Report of Agents Appointed to Negotiate a Purchase of Lands,* July 6–Sept. 15, 1795, *DHI,* MR 43, NYSL. Schuyler did provide cash payments to prominent Oneidas including Skenandoah, who received fifteen dollars. The largest of the nine payments were to "White Hongarry," who received thirty dollars. These were scarcely "bribes," unlike the large payments made by Robert Morris to the Seneca chiefs at the Treaty of Big Tree (1797), which were more than twenty-five times larger and which could be considered payoffs. "List of Payments/Presents to the Oneidas made by M. General Schuyler and G. W. Edwards," Sept. 1795, Philip Schuyler MSS, MR 7a, NYPL.

80. Schuyler, Cantine, and Brooks, *Report of Agents Appointed to Negotiate a Purchase of Lands,* July 6–Sept. 15, 1795, *DHI,* MR 43, NYSL.

5. VISION QUEST

1. Philip Lord, Jr., *Heading West* (Albany, N.Y.: New York State Museum, 1991). This excellent brochure summarizes New York State's early transportation efforts and especially the Western Inland Lock Navigation Company.

2. Whitford, *History of the Canal System,* 1:36–37. Beechtree (Peter Oneyanha) to Timothy Pickering (Brother Caneghsade), May 12, 1793, Pickering MSS, MR 62, MHS.

3. I thank Philip Lord, Jr., for access to the following document: William Weston to Philip Schuyler, Sept. 14, 1796, New York State Department of Education, Records of the Division of Historical and Anthropological Services, Cultural Education Center, Albany (original in Philip Schuyler MSS, NYPL).

4. Shaw, *Erie Water West,* 19.

5. Ibid.; Syrett et al., *Papers of Alexander Hamilton,* 21:91–92, 93n, 105, 196; 25:586; 26:19, 20n, 36, 137–38.

6. Shaw, *Erie Water West,* 17–18.

7. Ibid., 18.

8. Whitford, *History of the Canal System,* 1:38–47.

9. George Scriba, "Report to the Directors of the Western Inland Lock Navigation Company, 1805," Scriba MSS, vol. 29, Letterbook, 1798–1805, 217–32, NYSL.

10. Julius Rubin, "An Innovating Public Improvement: The Erie Canal," in *Canals and American Economic Development,* ed. Carter Goodrich (New York: Columbia Univ. Press, 1961), 22–23.

11. Miller, "Private Enterprise in Inland Navigation," 408–10; Shaw, *Erie Water West.*

12. Whitford, *History of the Canal System,* 1:654.

13. *Whipple Report,* 280–83.

14. Whitford, *History of the Canal System,* 1:672.

15. Ibid., 1:676: David Thomas and Benjamin Wright collaborated on the Erie Canal project as well. See Wright to Thomas, Oct. 16, Nov. 16, 1820, David Thomas MSS, NYSL. Holmes Hutchinson worked with the Seymour family (Horatio and Henry) as a surveyor; he was directly involved with laying out lots on the "former" Oneida Indian Reservation. [Aug. 13, 1838] Holmes Hutchinson MSS, Box 2, Folder 26, Oneida Reservation, NYSL.

16. Whitford, *History of the Canal System,* 1:678–80.

17. Ibid., 1:506–7.

18. Ibid., 1:654–57; *Whipple Report,* 293–95.

19. Whitford, *History of the Canal System,* 1:654–57; *Whipple Report,* 293–95. For the deplorable conditions among the Oneidas in 1831 before their removal to the West see Patrick Shirreff's Erie Canal traveler's account in Clayton Mau, ed., *The Development of Central and Western New York* (New York: Du Bois Press, 1944), 336:

To the English traveler, these "descendants of the original owners of the soil have been gradually deprived of their birthright; and although Greenbay [*sic*] is 1000 miles from their old habitations, the white man in progress of time will envy their possessions, and the poor Indian will retire still farther to the west, if drunkenness and other vices acquired from the whites, do not exterminate the race."

20. Whitford, *History of the Canal System,* 1:659–71.

21. Sheriff, *Artificial River,* 35. See John Disturnell, *A Gazetteer of the State of New York* (Albany, N.Y.: privately printed, 1842), which further confirms this point (405–6).

6. SILENT PARTNERS

1. 7 *Stat.,* 44 (Nov. 11, 1794).

2. Jack Campisi and William A. Starna, "On the Road to Canandaigua: The Treaty of 1794," *American Indian Quarterly* 19 (Fall 1995): 467–90.

3. Norman B. Wilkinson, "Robert Morris and the Treaty of Big Tree," *Mississippi Valley Historical Review* 40 (Sept. 1953): 257–78; Barbara A. Chernow, "Robert Morris: Genesee Land Speculator," *New York History* 58 (Apr. 1977): 195–220; *Whipple Report,* 105–34; Wallace, *Death and Rebirth of the Seneca,* 179–83. The best study of the Holland Land Company, its origins, operations, and history, is still Paul D. Evans, *Holland Land Company* (1924).

4. Thomas Morris, "Account of the Treaty of Big Tree," Henry O'Reilly Collection of Western Mementoes, NYHS.

5. See chap. 6, n. 1. Robert Morris wrote to his son Thomas and Charles Williamson on Aug. 1, 1797: "Some dollars may be promised before the Treaty and paid when finished to the amount of $500 or $600, or if necessary $1000 to the chiefs. Captain Joseph Brandt [*sic*] although not belonging to the Seneca Nation, yet being an influential character, he must be satisfied for his services and at reasonable terms as possible, after the Purchase is made." Skivington Coll., Box 26, Folder 1, University of Rochester, Rush Rhees Library (hereafter cited as UR).

6. Ibid.

7. Ibid.

8. Shaw, *Erie Water West,* 16. The Western Inland Lock Navigation Company received quarterly payments of five thousand dollars each from New York State in 1798. Receipts can be found in New York State Comptroller Records, File, Western Inland Lock Navigation Company, Onondaga Historical Association, Syracuse, N.Y. (hereafter cited as OHA).

9. For the connection of Hamilton and Schuyler to Benson and Morris see Mrs. Alexander Hamilton [Elizabeth Schuyler] to Philip Schuyler, Feb. 2, 1794, Philip Schuyler MSS, Box 1, Folder 19; Philip Schuyler to Robert Morris, Mar. 29, 1796, Philip Schuyler MSS, Box 1, Folder 20, NYSL. It is important to note that Morris, at the time of Schuyler's request for political help concerning internal navigation in New York State, was president of the boards of directors of the Pennsylvania Canal Conference, once again showing the connections between land speculation and transportation! Syrett et al., *Papers of Alexander Hamilton,* 21:91–92, 105, 195–96; Chazanof, *Joseph Ellicott,* 68–69.

10. Shaw Livermore, *Early American Land Companies: Their Influence on Corporate Development* (reprint, New York: Octagon Books, 1968), 206–7; Miller, "Private Enterprise in Inland Navigation," 406–8; Evans, *Holland Land Company,* 77, 208–10.

11. Alan Taylor, "The Art of 'Hook and Snivey': Political Culture in Upstate New York During the 1790s," *Journal of American History* 80 (Mar. 1993): 1371–96.

12. *Laws of New York,* chap. 23, Feb. 26, 1798.

13. *Whipple Report,* 249–52.

14. List of shareholders, Dec. 9, 1801, "Seneca Road Co." File, New York State Comptroller Records, OHA.

15. See chap. 6, n. 10.

16. Durrenberger, *Turnpikes,* 58–59; Oliver Wendell Holmes, "Turnpike Era," 5:267–72; L. Ray Gunn, *The Decline of Authority: Public Economic Policy and Political Development in New York, 1800–1860* (Ithaca, N.Y.: Cornell Univ. Press, 1988), 36–37.

7. THE LAKE EFFECT

1. McKelvey, "Erie Canal," 5–71.

2. Marvin A. Rapp, "The Port of Buffalo, 1825–1880" (Ph.D. diss., Duke Univ., 1947), 1–33. See also Gerber, *Making of an American Pluralism,* 3–39; Mark Goldman, *High Hopes,* 21–55.

3. John G. Clark, *The Grain Trade in the Old Northwest* (Urbana: Univ. of Illinois Press, 1966), 118.

4. Ibid., 111–22, 280–85.

5. For the Buffalo Creek Reservation see Frederick Houghton, *The History of the Buffalo Creek Reservation,* Buffalo Historical Society *Publications* 24 (Buffalo, N.Y.: Buffalo Historical Society, 1920), 3–181; and Faith E. Karas, "Material Culture on the Buffalo Creek Reservation, 1780–1842" (Master's thesis, SUNY, Buffalo, 1963).

6. Gerber, *Making of American Pluralism,* 4–5.

7. Goldman, *High Hopes,* 46.

8. Chazanof, *Joseph Ellicott,* 75–76.

9. See chapter 1 of this book. See also Chazanof, *Joseph Ellicott,* 157–80. Frank H. Severance, ed., *The Holland Land Company and Canal Construction in Western New York: Buffalo–Black Rock Harbor Papers, Journals and Documents,* Buffalo Historical Society *Publications* 14 (Buffalo, N.Y.: Buffalo Historical Society, 1910), 62–63; Shaw, *Erie Water West,* 64.

10. Rapp, "Port of Buffalo," 11–21.

11. See chap. 9.

12. Ellicott, *Holland Land Company Papers,* 1:53.

13. Severance, *Holland Land Company and Canal Construction,* 44–45.

14. Shaw, *Erie Water West,* 65–80.

15. Quoted in Whitford, *History of the Canal System,* 1:588.

16. Ibid., 1:589–90.

17. Timothy Pickering, Indian Census of 1792, in Jasper Parrish MSS, VC.

18. New York State Legislature, Assembly, Doc. no. 90, Mar. 4, 1819, *Report Relative to Indian Affairs, DHI,* MR 46, NYSL.

19. Laurence M. Hauptman, "Refugee Havens: The Iroquois Villages in the Eighteenth Century," in *American Indian Environments,* ed. Christopher Vecsey and Robert W. Venables (Syracuse, N.Y.: Syracuse Univ. Press, 1980), 128–39.

20. Daniel K. Richter, *The Ordeal of the Longhouse: The Peoples of the Iroquois League in the Era of European Colonization* (Chapel Hill: Univ. of North Carolina Press, 1992), 8–74.

21. Graymont, *Iroquois in the American Revolution,* 259–96.

22. See Marlene Johnson, comp., *The Iroquois Cookbook,* 2d ed. (Tonawanda Indian Reservation: Peter Doctor Memorial Fellowship Foundation, 1989).

23. "Visit of Gerard T. Hopkins: A Quaker Ambassador to the Indians Who Visited Buffalo in 1804," in Buffalo Historical Society *Publications* 6, ed. Frank H. Severance (Buffalo, N.Y.: Buffalo Historical Society, 1903), 219.

24. Houghton, *Buffalo Creek Reservation,* 64.

25. Ibid., 117–20; Karas, "Material Culture," 59–61.

26. Karas, "Material Culture," 54–59; Houghton, *Buffalo Creek Reservation,* 116; Henry R. Howland, "The Seneca Mission at Buffalo Creek," in Buffalo Historical Society *Publications* 6, ed. Frank H. Severance (Buffalo, N.Y.: Buffalo Historical Society, 1903), 127–28.

27. See chap. 7, n. 26.

28. Houghton, *Buffalo Creek Reservation,* 116.

29. Ibid.

30. Wallace, *Death and Rebirth of the Seneca,* 298, 301, 309–10.

31. Thomas S. Abler and Elisabeth Tooker, "Seneca," in *Handbook of North American Indians,* vol. 15, *The Northeast,* ed. Bruce G. Trigger (Washington, D.C.: Smithsonian Institution, 1978), 509–11. For the missionary accounts at Buffalo Creek see Frank H. Severance, ed., Buffalo Historical Society *Publications* 6 (Buffalo, N.Y.: Buffalo Historical Society, 1903), 165–380.

32. Jabez Backus Hyde, "A Teacher among the Senecas: A Narrative of Rev. Jabez Backus Hyde, 1811–1820," in Buffalo Historical Society *Publications* 6, ed. Frank H. Severance (Buffalo, N.Y.: Buffalo Historical Society, 1903), 239–74.

33. Houghton, *Buffalo Creek Reservation,* 143–44.

34. Ibid., 147.

35. Thompson S. Harris, "Journals of Rev. Thompson S. Harris, Missionary to the Senecas, 1821–1828," and "Register of the Seneca Mission Church, 1823–1848," in Buffalo Historical Society *Publications* 6, ed. Frank H. Severance (Buffalo, N.Y.: Buffalo Historical Society, 1903), 281–380.

36. William N. Fenton, "Toward the Gradual Civilization of the Indian Natives: The Missionary and Linguistic Work of Asher Wright (1803–1875) among the Senecas of Western New York," *Proceedings* of the American Philosophical Society 100 (1956): 567–81; and Thomas S. Abler, "Protestant Missionaries and Native Cultures: Parallel Careers of Asher Wright and Silas T. Rand," *American Indian Quarterly* 26 (Winter 1992): 25–37.

37. Robert Troup to Jasper Parrish, Aug. 24, 1810, *DHI,* MR 45, NYSL.

38. Shaw, *Erie Water West,* 16, 21, 59, 102, 107–8, 116–21. For more on Troup see Wendell E. Tripp, Jr., "Robert Troup: A Quest for Security in a Turbulent New Nation, 1775–1832" (Ph.D. diss., Columbia Univ., 1973), 228–38.

39. David A. Ogden to Bishop J. H. Hobart, Dec. 14, 1814, *DHI,* MR 45, NYSL.

40. Hemphill, *Papers of John C. Calhoun,* 3:669.

41. David A. Ogden Memorial to President of the United States [Monroe], 1819, *DHI,* MR 46, NYSL.

42. See chap. 8. Hemphill, *Papers of John C. Calhoun,* 3:188, 255, 295, 301, 336. Rapp, "Port of Buffalo," 1–33.

43. Houghton, *Buffalo Creek Reservation,* 121.

44. George Catlin, *Letters and Notes on the North American Indians,* ed. Michael M. Mooney (reprint, New York: Clarkson N. Potter, 1975), 8, 14, 18, 50, 312–15.

45. William H. Truettner, *The Natural Man Observed: A Study of Catlin's Indian Gallery* (Washington, D.C.: Smithsonian Institution Press, 1979), 216.

46. Joseph Delafield, *The Unfortified Boundary,* ed. Robert McElroy and Thomas Riggs (New York: privately printed, 1943), 236.

47. Ibid.

48. Ibid., 237.

49. Hemphill, *Papers of John C. Calhoun,* 7:158.

50. Ibid., 7:276–77.

51. Ibid., 7:476.

52. Ibid., 9:25.

8. THE BASHAW OF THE BORDER

1. For Porter's career see Joseph A. Grande, "The Political Career of Peter Buell Porter, 1797–1829" (Ph.D. diss., Notre Dame Univ., 1971); and I. Frank Mogavero, "Peter Buell Porter: Citizen and Statesman" (Ph.D. diss., Univ. of Ottawa, 1950). For information about the Porter family, especially Peter Buell Porter's brother Augustus, see Buffalo Historical Society *Publications* 7 (Buffalo, N.Y.: Buffalo Historical Society, 1904): 229–322.

2. Campbell, *Life and Writings of De Witt Clinton,* 28.

3. Rapp, "Port of Buffalo," 13–14.

4. Campbell, *Life and Writings of De Witt Clinton,* 122–23.

5. Ibid., 78, 94–95, 114; Grande, "Political Career of Peter Buell Porter," 7–8.

6. Rapp, "Port of Buffalo," 13–14.

7. Quoted in Robert H. Brown, *The Republic in Peril: 1812* (New York: Columbia Univ. Press, 1964), 55–56.

8. For a recent treatment, see Carl Benn, *The Iroquois in the War of 1812* (Toronto, Ont.: Univ. of Toronto Press, 1998). For a good portrait of the confused state of affairs of the American military on the Niagara frontier in the first year of the war see J. C. A. Stagg, *Mr. Madison's War* (Princeton, N.J.: Princeton Univ. Press, 1983), 230–53. The Iroquois debate whether to join the Americans in the War of 1812 can be traced in Charles M. Snyder, ed., *Red and White on the New York Frontier: A*

Struggle for Survival, Insights from the Papers of Erastus Granger, 1807–1819 (Harrison, N.Y.: Harbor Hill Books, 1978), 55–81.

9. Arthur C. Parker, "The Senecas in the War of 1812," *Proceedings* of the New York State Historical Association 15 (1916): 78–90.

10. Ibid.

11. Ibid.

12. Grande, "Political Career of Peter Buell Porter," 62–69. For the Battle of Chippawa see John Brannan, comp., *Official Letters of the Military and Naval Officers of the United States During the War with Great Britain in the Years 1812, 13, 14, 15* (Washington, D.C.: Way and Gideon, 1823), 368–73. For a list of Iroquois pensioners who served in the war see New York State Adjutant-General's Office, comp., *Index of Awards: Soldiers of the War of 1812* (Baltimore, Md.: Genealogical Publishing, 1969), 563–73. For a portrait of the Iroquois in Canada's involvement in the war see Benn, *The Iroquois and the War of 1812,* and Carl F. Klinch and James J. Talman, eds., *The Journal of Major John Norton* (Toronto, Ont.: Champlain Society, 1970), 336–67. For a negative view of Indian participation, except for Oneida involvement at Sandy Creek (184–86), see Hitsman, *The Incredible War of 1812,* 188–205.

13. For the Tuscarora involvement see Elias Johnson, *Legends, Traditions, and Laws of the Iroquois, or, Six Nations and History of the Tuscarora Indians* (Lockport, N.Y.: Union Print and Publishing, 1881), 167–71.

14. Snyder, *Red and White,* 55–56.

15. Campbell, *Life and Writings of De Witt Clinton,* 134.

16. For a general history of the island see Robert W. Bingham, "The History of Grand Island," in *Niagara Frontier Miscellany,* ed. Robert W. Bingham, Buffalo Historical Society *Publications* 34 (Buffalo, N.Y.: Buffalo Historical Society, 1947), 59–78. Richter, *The Ordeal of the Longhouse,* 63, map. The archaeology of Grand Island indicates a Neutral Indian presence before Seneca conquest: Marian E. White, "A Reexamination of the Historic Van Son Cemetery on Grand Island," Buffalo Society of Natural Sciences, Anthropology Contributions, *Bulletin* 24 (1968): 1–48. See also Frederick Houghton, "Report on Neuter [*sic*] Cemetery, Grand Island, N.Y.," Buffalo Society of Natural Sciences *Bulletin* 9, no. 3 (1909): 376–85; Audrey J. Sublett, "Osteological Analysis of the Van Son Site," Buffalo Society of Natural Sciences, Anthropology Contributions, *Bulletin* 24 (1968): 49–66.

17. Donald H. Kent, "Historical Report on the Niagara River and the Niagara River Strip to 1759," in *Iroquois Indians II. Commission Findings: Indian Claims Commission* (New York: Garland Publishing, 1974), 173–74.

18. H. Perry Smith, *History of the City of Buffalo and Erie County* (Syracuse, N.Y.: D. Mason, 1884), 1:429.

19. 20 Indian Claims Commission 177 at 194. Findings of Fact decided Dec. 30, 1968, found in *Iroquois Indians II. Commission Findings: Indian Claims Commission,* 388.

20. Wallace, *Death and Rebirth of the Seneca,* 115–16.

21. Edmund B. O'Callaghan and Berthold Fernow, eds., *Documents Relative to*

the Colonial History of the State of New York (Albany, N.Y.: Weed, Parsons, 1853–87) (hereafter cited as *DRCNY*), 7:621–23.

22. Ibid., 8:652–53.

23. Sir William Johnson's Will recorded in Supreme Court of Judicature, Record of Wills Proved at Albany, 1799–1829 (Record of Wills no. 4), 35–48, ser. J0041, NYSA.

24. *American State Papers: Documents, Legislative and Executive of the Congress of the United States,* Class 2, *Indian Affairs,* 1832–34. (Washington, D.C.: Gales and Seaton, 1832–61), 1:140.

25. 8 *Stat.,* 80–83 (Sept. 3, 1783).

26. Hough, *Proceedings of Commissioners of Indian Affairs,* 1:57.

27. Ibid., 1:60.

28. 7 *Stat.,* 15 (Oct. 22, 1784); *Whipple Report,* 107–8; 7 *Stat.,* 33 (Jan. 9, 1789).

29. 7 *Stat.,* 44 (Nov. 11, 1794). For more on the treaty, see Campisi and Starna, "On the Road to Canandaigua," 467–90.

30. Timothy Pickering to Henry Knox, Nov. 12, 1794, Timothy Pickering MSS, MR 60, MHS. Quoted in William L. Stone, *The Life and Times of Sa-Go-Ye-Wat-Ha, or Red Jacket: Being the Sequel to the History of the Six Nations* (reprint, Albany, N.Y.: Joel Munsell, 1866), 475–77. Pickering to Knox, Dec. 26, 1794, Pickering MSS, MR 62, MHS.

31. 20 Indian Claims Commission 177 at 181. Opinion of the Commission, Dec. 30, 1968, found in *Iroquois Indians II. Commission Findings: Indian Claims Commission,* 375.

32. See George P. Decker's legal argument "Trace of Title of Seneca Indians," in U.S. Congress, House of Representatives, Committee on Foreign Affairs, Hearings on H.R. 2498, 11756, 16542, 16547, and 16587: Diversion of Water from the Niagara River, July 15, 1914, 63d Cong., 2d sess. (Washington, D.C.: U.S. Government Printing Office, 1914), 26–27.

33. New York State, Secretary of State, *Calendar of New York Colonial Manuscripts, Indorsed Land Papers, 1643–1803,* ed. Edmund B. O'Callaghan (reprint, Harrison, N.Y.: Harbor Hill Books, 1987), 908.

34. 7 *Stat.,* 601 (Sept. 15, 1797); 17 *Stat.,* 70 (June 30, 1802); 7 *Stat.,* 72 (June 30, 1802); *Whipple Report,* 214–15.

35. *Whipple Report,* 214–15. The treaty was approved by the Senate on December 31, 1802. U.S. Congress, Senate, *Journal of the Executive Proceedings of the Senate* [1789–1828] (Washington, D.C.: Duff Green, 1828), 1:427–28. Map of Niagara Frontier showing shoreline subdivision lots but Grand Island not subdivided, 1805, map A, draw 7, no. 88, Buffalo and Erie County Historical Society, Buffalo, N.Y. (hereafter cited as BECHS).

36. *Laws of New York,* chap. 47 (Mar. 19, 1802), 73–75.

37. Red Jacket's speech to governor found in Paul Reilly MSS, Box 41, Doc. 12, MR 6, SUNY, Buffalo. The original of this document is in Records of the New York State Legislature, Legislative Assembly Papers, vol. 40, 393–404, NYSA.

38. *Whipple Report,* 214–15. For the United States Senate's approval see U.S. Congress, Senate, *Journal of the Executive Proceedings,* 1:427–28.

39. Hugh Hastings, ed., *Public Papers of Daniel D. Tompkins, Governor of New York, 1807–1817* (Albany, N.Y.: J. B. Lyon, 1902), 2:303–9.

40. Ibid., 2:339–40.

41. *Laws of New York,* chap. 37 (Mar. 8, 1811), 50–51.

42. Hastings, *Public Papers of Daniel D. Tompkins,* 2:480–81.

43. Ibid., 2:483.

44. Ibid.

45. Erastus Granger's notes on Little Billy's speech of Sept. 16, 1810, in Snyder, *Red and White,* 40.

46. Ibid.

47. Daniel D. Tompkins to Jasper Parrish, July 10, 1815, Parrish MSS, A00-461, BECHS. The original of this letter is missing from the Buffalo and Erie County Historical Society. I found a photocopy in the records of the Seneca Nation of Indians.

48. *Whipple Report,* 211–13.

49. Ibid.

50. See chap. 9. See also William N. Fenton, *The Great Law and the Longhouse: A Political History of the Iroquois Confederacy* (Norman: Univ. of Oklahoma Press, 1998), 629. Parrish and Jones were *also* involved in the 1826 "treaty" defrauding the Seneca. For undeserved praise of these two men see Buffalo Historical Society *Publications* 6, ed. Frank H. Severance (Buffalo, N.Y.: Buffalo Historical Society, 1903), 493–546. For Jones's involvement in the 1797–1802 doings and his reward, see ibid., 501–4; and 7 *Stat.,* 72 (June 30, 1802). For Parrish's payment (Squaw Island) for the 1815 state "treaty," see *Laws of New York,* chap. 63 (Apr. 5, 1816), 65–66. See also Daniel D. Tompkins to New York State Senate, Feb. 21, 1816, *DHI,* MR 45, NYSL.

51. For the Seneca pressures from the land companies see Chazanof, *Joseph Ellicott;* Wyckoff, *Developer's Frontier;* Turner, *Pioneer History;* Evans, *Holland Land Company;* and A. M. Sakolski, *The Great American Land Bubble* (New York: Harper and Bros., 1932).

52. 8 *Stat.,* 218 (Dec. 24, 1814).

53. For an excellent synopsis of the commission see I. Frank Mogavero, "The Joint Mixed Boundary Commission under the Treaty of Ghent" (paper delivered at the sixth College Conference on New York History, D'Youville College, Buffalo, N.Y.). Printed copy found in New York State Library, Albany.

54. James Madison to Peter B. Porter, Sept. 9, 1815, copy attached to letter of Arch Campbell to Porter, Sept. 28, 1815, Peter B. Porter MSS, E-1, MR 6, BECHS.

55. Campbell to Porter, Sept. 28, 1815, Porter MSS, BECHS.

56. Mogavero, "Joint Mixed Boundary Commission."

57. Henry Clay to Peter B. Porter, Feb. 10, 1816, Porter MSS, BECHS.

58. Mogavero, "Joint Mixed Boundary Commission," 5.

59. Ibid.

60. See, for example, Peter B. Porter to John C. Spencer, Apr. 16, 1818, Porter MSS, E-22, MR 6, BECHS.

61. For the primary documents of the commission see Delafield, *Unfortified*

Boundary; William A. Bird, "Reminiscences of the Boundary Survey Between the United States and the British Provinces," in Buffalo Historical Society *Publications* 4 (Buffalo, N.Y.: Buffalo Historical Society, 1896), 1–14.

62. Delafield, *Unfortified Boundary,* reveals much about Seneca discontent and fears of losing their lands, which they had believed were protected under the Pickering treaty (215–43); about the Mohawks and the boundary question (137–62); and about David A. Ogden and the Ogden Land Company's "interest" in and cooperation with the Joint Mixed Boundary Commission (157, 160, 218, 231–38).

63. Bird, "Reminiscences of the Boundary Survey," 1–14; Mogavero, "Joint Mixed Boundary Commission," 8–10.

64. Mogavero, "Joint Mixed Boundary Commission," 9.

65. Ibid., 14.

66. Bird, "Reminiscences of the Boundary Survey," 8.

67. Mogavero, "Joint Mixed Boundary Commission," 16.

68. Ibid., 16.

69. Bird, "Reminiscences of the Boundary Survey," 7–8.

70. For a Canadian perspective on the boundary settlement see Joseph Bouchette, *The British Dominions in North America or a Topographical and Statistical Description of the Provinces of Lower and Upper Canada* (London: Longman, Rees, Orme, Brown, Green and Longman, 1832), 1:15–26. Bouchette was the surveyor-general of Lower Canada.

71. Charles Z. Lincoln, ed., *Messages from the Governors* (Albany, N.Y.: J. B. Lyon, 1909), 2:995.

72. *Laws of New York,* chap. 228 (Dec. 9, 1819), 302–3.

73. Bingham, "History of Grand Island," 65–69; Merton M. Wilner, "Grand Island, Independent State," *York State Tradition* 17 (Spring 1963): 27–28.

74. Simeon De Witt to Henry Livingston, Apr. 15, 1820, Simeon De Witt Folder, De Witt Family MSS, Tompkins County Historical Society, Ithaca, N.Y.

75. Bingham, "History of Grand Island," 65–69. For this early Zionist experiment see Lewis F. Allen, "The Founding of the City of Ararat on Grand Island by Mordecai M. Noah," in Buffalo Historical Society *Publications* 1 (Buffalo, N.Y.: Bigelow Bros. for the Buffalo Historical Society, 1879), 305–7.

76. 8 *Stat.,* 274–77 (June 18, 1822). Delafield, *Unfortified Boundary,* 61 n. 187; Mogavero, "Joint Mixed Boundary Commission," 20–21.

77. Grande, "Political Career of Peter Buell Porter," 284–87, 302–7. Ronald Satz, *American Indian Policy in the Jacksonian Era* (Lincoln: Univ. of Nebraska Press, 1975), 4.

9 . GENESEE FEVER

1. 7 *Stat.,* 44 (Nov. 11, 1794); 7 *Stat.,* 601 (Sept. 15, 1797). Ellicott, *Holland Land Company Papers,* 1:51, 87–89. Lockwood L. Doty, *History of Livingston County, New York* (Geneseo, N.Y.: Edward L. Doty, 1876), 59–103.

2. See chap. 10.

3. Ellicott, *Holland Land Company Papers,* 1:66.

4. 7 *Stat.,* 72 (June 30, 1802). The treaty was ratified by the Senate on Feb. 7, 1803, and proclaimed by the president on the same day.

5. Paul D. Evans, "The Frontier Pushed Westward," in *History of the State of New York,* vol. 5, *Conquering the Wilderness,* ed. Alexander C. Flick (New York: Columbia Univ. Press, 1934), 164. See the elaborate preparations to guard against disease made by De Witt Clinton in 1810; Campbell, *Life and Writings of De Witt Clinton,* 101–2.

6. Chazanof, *Joseph Ellicott,* 80–93; Evans, *Holland Land Company,* 275–87.

7. Whitford, *History of the Canal System,* 1:61; Severance, *Holland Land Company and Canal Construction,* 51, 63, 73, 75, 76, 126, 127, 128, 138. See also Chazanof, *Joseph Ellicott,* 157–80; Evans, *Holland Land Company,* 287–89.

8. The best portrait of the Ogden Land Company, its origins and its operations, is Mary Conable, "A Steady Enemy: The Ogden Land Company and the Seneca Indians" (Ph.D. diss., Univ. of Rochester, 1995).

9. *Whipple Report,* 134–41.

10. Conable, "Steady Enemy," chap. 1.

11. *Whipple Report,* 172–83.

12. Ibid., 183–89. Besides Conable's work, for the schemes of the Ogden Land Company see Henry S. Manley, "Buying Buffalo from the Indians," *New York History* 28 (July 1947): 313–29; Society of Friends (Hicksite), *The Case of the Seneca Indians in the State of New York* [reprint of three Quaker pamphlets dated 1840, 1841, 1872] (Stanfordville, N.Y.: Earl M. Coleman, 1979).

13. Conable, "Steady Enemy," chap. 1.

14. See, for example, Peter B. Porter to T. L. Ogden, June 14, 1823, Porter MSS, MR 4, BECHS.

15. Robert Troup to John Greig, Mar. 16, 1826, Skivington Collection, A. 562, Box 1, Correspondence, Jan.–Mar. 1826, UR; "Gen. Schuyler's estate," Notebook, 1803, 3, Robert Troup MSS, Box 13, NYPL; Masterton Ure to Robert Troup, Aug. 4, 1825, Robert Troup MSS, Box 13, Folder 4, Pulteney Estates, NYPL. Box 13, Folder 2, of Troup's MSS at the NYPL are with Joseph Fellows, his partner. For Troup's estate, which included former Indian lands, see Box 2, Folder 7, Troup MSS, NYPL.

16. Henry S. Manley, "Red Jacket's Last Campaign," *New York History* 31 (Apr. 1950): 149–68.

17. Augustus Porter to Peter B. Porter, Sept. 29, 1826, Porter MSS, MR 4, BECHS.

18. Conable, "Steady Enemy," chap. 2.

19. Doty, *History of Livingston County* (1876), 61.

20. James E. Seaver, comp., *A Narrative of the Life of Mrs. Mary Jemison,* ed. and foreword by George H. J. Abrams (1824; reprint, Syracuse, N.Y.: Syracuse Univ. Press, 1990), xiii. Idem, comp., *A Narrative of the Life of Mrs. Mary Jemison,* ed. June Namias (1824; paperback reprint, Norman: Univ. of Oklahoma Press, 1992), 33.

21. For more on Brooks see Shaw, *Erie Water West,* 67, 400; Whitford, *History of the Canal System,* 1:65; Lockwood R. Doty, *History of the Genesee Country* (Chicago: S. J. Clarke Publishing, 1925), 597–98.

22. Seaver, *Mrs. Mary Jemison* (1990 reprint), 119–24.

23. Ibid., 122. See also Lockwood L. Doty, *History of Livingston County,* vol. 2 (Jackson, Mich.: W. J. Van Deusen, 1905), apps. 4 and 6.

24. Seaver, *Mrs. Mary Jemison* (1990 reprint), 123.

25. Thomas Morris to John Greig, Oct. 2, 1805; Archibald Kane to Greig, Jan. 15, 1807; Joseph Ely to John Greig, Oct. 26, 1807; Howell and Greig to Henry Remsen, Nov. 25, 1808; Greig to Ebenezer Wood, Mar. 17, 1821 (notarized date, Apr. 28, 1821); John V. Henry to Greig; Gideon Granger to John Greig, Oct. 3, 1821; Greig to Thomas Morris, Sept. 8, 1826, Skivington Collection, Box 1, UR. For the Greig-Morris connection see Skivington Collection, Box 17, UR. For Greig's connections to canals and to the Ogden agenda see Joseph Fellows to Greig et al., June 6, 1836; Humphrey Howland to Greig, Sept. 13, 1836; T. L. Ogden to Greig, Feb. 15, 1836; Greig to James Stryker, Jan. 25, 1833; L. R. Lyon to Greig, Oct. 12, 1836; Fellows to Greig, May 1, 1837; Memorial of John Greig, Nov. 1837–Dec. 1, 1837, Skivington Collection, Box 2, UR. For Greig's vast fortune see "Abstract of the Real Estate, Jan. 1, 1850," John Greig—List of Property and Estate, Skivington Collection, Box 25, UR. Doty, *History of Livingston County* (1905), 2:apps. 4 and 6. A portrait of Greig can be found in Lockwood R. Doty, *History of the Genesee Country,* vol. 1.

26. Oliver L. Phelps to John Henry, Sept. 13, 1799, Skivington Collection, Box 1, UR. Francis Paul Prucha, *American Indian Treaties: The History of a Political Anomaly* (Berkeley and Los Angeles: Univ. of California Press, 1994), 144–45. Charles J. Kappler prints it as an "unratified" treaty in Kappler, *Indian Affairs: Laws and Treaties,* 2:1033–34.

27. John C. Calhoun to Jasper Parrish, Feb. 17, 1824, *DHI,* MR 46, NYSL.

28. *American State Papers, Indian Affairs,* 2:868.

29. Henry Gibson to John Greig, Skivington Collection, Box 1, UR.

30. U.S. Congress, *Register of Debates in Congress,* House of Representatives (Mar. 10–11, 1826), 1598–1609.

31. Ibid., 1604.

32. U.S. Congress, House of Representatives, Committee on Indian Affairs, Report no. 209: *To Hold a Treaty with the Seneca Indians,* 19th Cong., 1st sess., May 13, 1826, Serial set 142.

33. Rapp, "Port of Buffalo," 11–17.

34. See chap. 7.

35. See Neil Adams McNall, *An Agricultural History of the Genesee Valley, 1790–1860* (Philadelphia: Univ. of Pennsylvania Press, 1952).

36. *Whipple Report,* 144–50.

37. For Dr. Jacob Jemison see William N. Fenton, ed., "Answers to Governor Cass's Questions by Jacob Jameson, a Seneca (ca. 1821–1825)," *Ethnohistory* 16 (Spring 1969): 113–19.

38. Manley, "Red Jacket's Last Campaign," 149–62; *Whipple Report,* 23, 147–49.

39. *Whipple Report,* 23.

40. Manley, "Red Jacket's Last Campaign," 150–56.

41. Quoted in ibid., 153.

42. Ibid., 155.

43. Oliver Forward to the president of the United States, Jan. 30, 1827, OIA, Records of the Six Nations Agency, M234, MR 832, RG 75, NA.

44. Ibid.

45. *American State Papers, Indian Affairs,* 2:866.

46. Ibid., 868.

47. Memorial of Red Jacket and Seneca Chiefs and principal men to president of the United States, May 19, 1827, Oliver Forward MSS, BECHS.

48. Ibid.

49. Ibid.

50. Young King et al. Memorial to Our Father the President of the United States, Sept. 13, 1827, OIA, Records of the Six Nations Agency, M234, MR 832, RG 75, NA.

51. Ibid.

52. Young King et al. Memorial to Our Father the President of the United States and to the Secretary of War, Dec. 28, 1827, OIA, Records of the Seneca Agency in New York, M234, MR 808, RG 75, NA.

53. Charles Francis Adams, ed., *Memoirs of John Quincy Adams* (Philadelphia, Pa.: J. B. Lippincott, 1875), 7:484–85.

54. U.S. Congress, Senate, *Journal of the Executive Proceedings,* 3:601 (Feb. 29, 1828).

55. Ibid., 3:603 (Apr. 4, 1828).

56. Prucha, *American Indian Treaties,* 144–45.

57. Richard Montgomery Livingston Report to Secretary of War Peter B. Porter, Dec. 25, 1828, OIA, Records of the Seneca Agency in New York, M234, MR 808, RG 75, NA.

58. Ibid.

59. Ibid.

60. *Seneca Nation v. Christie [Christy],* 126 N.Y. 122 (Apr. 14, 1891); 28 Indian Claims Committee 12.

61. U.S. Census of 1810, 1820, 1830, 1840, 1850; J. H. French, comp., *Gazetteer of the State of New York* (Syracuse, N.Y.: R. Pearsall Smith, 1860), 168–77, 320–28, 380–87, 710–21; Whitford, *History of the Canal System,* 1:914–19.

10. THE DISCIPLE

1. For the Treaty of Big Tree see Kappler, *Indian Affairs,* 2:app., 1027–30; *Seneca Nation v. Philonus Pattison,* Records of the New York State Court of Appeals, vol. 487, case 1 (1860–61), NYSL. The special status of the Oil Spring Reservation has been misinterpreted ever since. See, for example, C. C. Royce, comp., *Indian Land Cessions in the United States,* Bureau of American Ethnology, *18th Annual Report, 1896–1897,* part 2 (Washington, D.C.: U.S. Government Printing Office, 1899), 660; Thomas Donaldson, comp., *The Six Nations of New York,* Extra Census Bulletin of the Eleventh Census [1890] of the United States (Washington, D.C.: U.S. Census Printing Office, 1892), 28; Wallace, *Death and Rebirth of the Seneca,* 183.

2. Wallace, *Death and Rebirth of the Seneca,* 182.

3. *Jesuit Relations* 43 (1656): 259–61.

4. Wallace, *Death and Rebirth of the Seneca,* 182, 266, 269, 280, 300, 324.

5. Robert Munro, "Description of the Genesee Country," *DRCNY,* 2:1176.

6. Campbell, *Life and Writings of De Witt Clinton,* 204.

7. Ibid., 194.

8. See table 2.

9. Shaw, *Erie Water West,* 123–30.

10. McKelvey, *Rochester on the Genesee,* 44–50; and idem, *Rochester: The Water-Power City, 1812–1854* (Cambridge, Mass.: Harvard Univ. Press, 1945),˙ 6, 72, 112, 203; McNall, *An Agricultural History of the Genesee Valley,* 124–27, 183–200.

11. See chap. 10, n. 10.

12. Henry O'Reilly, *Sketches of Rochester* (Rochester, N.Y.: William Alling, 1838), 31.

13. See chap. 10, n. 10, and especially Whitford, *History of the Canal System,* 1:708–27.

14. Whitford, *History of the Canal System,* 1:708.

15. Ibid., 1:709–13.

16. McKelvey, *Rochester on the Genesee,* 44.

17. Whitford, *History of the Canal System,* 1:708–27, 1010–14; 2:1030–36.

18. Turner, *Pioneer History,* 538–39; John S. Minard, *History of Allegany County* (New York: W. A. Ferguson, 1876), 813–15; idem, *The Indian Oil Spring* (Gowanda, N.Y.: privately printed, 1901), 3.

19. Minard, *Indian Oil Spring,* 4.

20. The best biographical treatment of Governor Blacksnake is the introduction and notes provided in Thomas S. Abler, ed., *Chainbreaker: The Revolutionary War Memoirs of Governor Blacksnake as Told to Benjamin Williams* (Lincoln: Univ. of Nebraska Press, 1989). For more on Governor Blacksnake see Lyman C. Draper, "Visit to Cold Spring, Cattaraugus County—Governor Blacksnake," Feb. 10–20, 1850, Draper MSS, 4S, SHSW.

21. Abler, *Chainbreaker,* 2–3.

22. Laurence M. Hauptman, Seneca Field notes, 1971–97.

23. Abler, *Chainbreaker,* 16–43, 151–62, 203–6.

24. Wallace, "Origins of the Longhouse Religion," 15:445–46.

25. Wallace, *Death and Rebirth of the Seneca,* 240–41, 285–95.

26. Ibid., 289.

27. Ibid., 334–35.

28. Ibid., 335.

29. New York State Legislature, Assembly, Doc. no. 168 (1836), 1–4.

30. Ibid.

31. Whitford, *History of the Canal System,* 1:708–27, 1010–15; Robert J. Rayback, ed., *Richards Atlas of New York State,* rev. ed. (Phoenix, N.Y.: Frank E. Richards, 1965), 50.

32. *Seneca Nation of Indians v. Philonus Pattison* (1861). Transcript of court proceedings and testimony at the Cattaraugus County Court in 1857–58 can be found

in Map Book Indian Reservation Cattaraugus County Courthouse, Little Valley, N.Y. A copy of Blacksnake's map and papers are also filed there. For a discussion of this case and for the Horatio Seymour reference see Congdon, *Allegany Oxbow*, 197–202; Donaldson, *Six Nations of New York,* 28–29; Daniel Sherman, "The Six Nations" speech delivered before the Chautauqua Society of History and Natural Science, Jamestown, N.Y., on January 29, 1885 (Cleveland, Ohio: W. W. Williams, 1885), 4–8.

33. See chap. 10, n. 32.

34. Ibid.; *Seneca Nation v. Philonus Pattison.*

35. Whitford, *History of the Canal System,* 1:708–27, 1010–15; interview with Robert Stapf, director of the Bureau of Land Management, Office of General Services, July 22, 1996, Albany, N.Y.

36. Congdon, *Allegany Oxbow,* 205.

37. The New York State treasurer's records for May 12, 1866, indicate that the New York State "Canal Fund" paid out in 1865 to "D. Sherman Atty $1,396.04." New York State Archives, ser. A0005, Records of the New York State Treasurer, Register of Payments, vol. 176 (Oct. 1864–Sept. 1865), 312. For more on this transaction see Congdon, *Allegany Oxbow,* 205; and New York State Board of Land Commissioners, *Proceedings of the Commissioners,* 109–12.

38. Albert E. Hoyt to Delbert P. Snyder, Aug. 13, 1914, Records of the Seneca Nation of Indians (hereafter cited as SNI), 4, Sen. Seneca Nation of Indians 3.1D (4), documents produced by New York State Office of Parks, Recreation, and so on (loose).

39. For the 1927 federal statute see *Stat.,* 44, pt. 2 (Jan. 5, 1927), 932–33.

40. F. A. Gaylord, "Report on State Land in the Vicinity of Cuba Lake, 1913," Records of the SNI, 4, Sen. Seneca Nation of Indians 3.1D (4), documents produced by New York State Office of Parks, Recreation, and so on (loose).

41. New York State Constitutional Convention, *Documents of the Convention of the State of New York, 1867–1868* (Albany, N.Y.: Weed, Parsons, 1868), 5, Doc. no. 168 (Jan. 21, 1868), 167–68. See also Charles Z. Lincoln, comp., *The Constitutional History of New York* (Rochester, N.Y.: Lawyers Cooperative Publishing, 1906), 2:389–90.

42. New York State Board of Canal Appraisers, *Digest of Claims from 1866 to 1870,* 113; New York State Legislature, *Senate Journal* for 1869, 288–91, 442–43, 562–65, 604–5; New York State Legislature, *Assembly Journal* for 1869, 562–63, 634–35, 1180–81, 1414–15.

43. For the later history of the Genesee Valley Canal and the Seneca land claim see New York State Board of Land Commissioners, *Proceedings of the Annual Report of the Board of Land Commissioners for 1924* (Albany, N.Y., 1924), 109–12. In 1927 New York State convinced the Congress to retroactively confirm the state's "take" of Indian lands at Oil Spring between 1858 and 1865 in what is popularly known as the "Seneca Conservation Act." At the present time litigation is pending on Seneca claims to lands at Oil Spring condemned by the state.

44. Henry R. Howland, *The Old Caneadea Council House and Its Last Council Fire* (Perry, N.Y.: Comfort Craftsmen, 1932), 34–40 (supplement about Letchworth).

45. See the original edition of Howland's "The Old Caneadea Council House and Its Last Council Fire," in Buffalo Historical Society *Publications* 6, ed. Frank H. Severance (Buffalo, N.Y.: Buffalo Historical Society, 1903), 97–123.

II. THE BUCKTAILS STOP HERE

1. Robert J. Vandewater, *The Tourist Pocket Manual for Travelers on the Hudson River, the Western Canal and Stage Road to Niagara Falls* (New York: Harper and Bros., 1834), 64–65.

2. For the text of the treaty see Kappler, *Indian Affairs,* 2:502–12. See also Henry S. Manley, "Buying Buffalo from the Indians," 313–29. For another view of the treaty see Prucha, *American Indian Treaties,* 202–7.

3. For the Albany Regency see Michael Wallace, "Changing Concepts of Party in the United States: New York, 1815–1828," *American Historical Review* 74 (Dec. 1968): 453–71; Robert V. Remini, "The Albany Regency," *New York History* 39 (Oct. 1958): 341–55. Kalman Goldstein, "The Albany Regency: The Failure of Practical Politics" (Ph.D. diss., Columbia Univ., 1969). For Van Buren's role in New York State and national politics see Donald B. Cole, *Martin Van Buren and the American Political System* (Princeton, N.J.: Princeton Univ. Press, 1984); James C. Curtis, *The Fox at Bay: Martin Van Buren and the Presidency* (Lexington: Univ. of Kentucky Press, 1970); Robert V. Remini, *Martin Van Buren and the Making of the Democratic Party* (New York: Columbia Univ. Press, 1959); John Niven, *Martin Van Buren: The Romantic Age of American Politics* (New York: Oxford Univ. Press, 1983); Major L. Wilson, *The Presidency of Martin Van Buren* (Lawrence: Univ. Press of Kansas, 1984). Recently, Craig Hanyan has actually suggested that the "new politics" of Van Buren were largely originated by his political foe, De Witt Clinton. See Hanyan, *De Witt Clinton,* 3–20, 46–54, 68–69.

4. For the connection between the rise of the Democrat Party and the issue of Indian removal see Ronald N. Satz, *American Indian Policy,* 19–31; David J. Russo, *The Major Political Issues of the Jacksonian Period and the Development of Party Loyalty in Congress, 1830–1840,* in Transactions of the American Philosophical Society, 62, pt. 5 (Philadelphia, Pa.: American Philosophical Society, 1972); and, especially, Richard E. Ellis, *The Union at Risk: Jacksonian Democracy: States' Rights and the Nullification Crisis* (New York: Oxford Univ. Press, 1987), 25–32.

5. Manley, "Buying Buffalo from the Indians," 313–27; *Genealogical Record of the Stryker Family,* 55–57; *The Stryker Family in America,* 101–2; pamphlets on file, NYSL, genealogical collection, Albany.

6. John H. Eaton to James W. Stryker, Nov. 30, 1830, OIA, M234, Records of New York Agency Emigration, 1829–51, MR 597, RG 75, NA.

7. Stryker to Lewis Cass, Nov. 27, 1832, OIA, M234, MR 597, RG 75, NA. Thomson Harris, a Seneca, was a frequent supplicant/sycophant on Stryker's payroll. See Stryker to Herring, Jan. 22, 1835; Report of Exploring Party, Dec. 26, 1837, OIA, M234, MR 597; Petition of Pro-Removal Chiefs and Headmen of Seneca Nation to Our Father the President of the United States, Sept. 13, 1827, OIA, M234, MR 832; Thomson Harris to Herring, Jan. 20, Oct. 14, 1835, Feb. 19, 1836; Thom-

son Harris to Cass, Dec. 27, 1834, Mar. 2, 20, Nov. 26, 1835; Thomson Harris to Millard Fillmore, Dec. 27, 1834; Thomson Harris to C. A. Harris (commissioner of Indian Affairs), Jan. 23, 1837; Fillmore to Cass, Jan. 12 and 15, 1835; Stryker to Thomson Harris, Dec. 19, 1833, OIA, M234, MR 583, RG 75, NA. Nathaniel T. Strong, a Seneca who was also on Stryker's payroll, attended Yale University and, along with Harris, served as an official interpreter at councils at Buffalo Creek. For Strong see N. T. Strong to Herring, Oct. 24, 1835; Stryker to Herring, Oct. 14, 1835; Six Nations Petition to Cass, Feb. 3, 1835, OIA, M234, MR 583, RG 75, NA. For both see Manley, "Buying Buffalo from the Indians," 315; and Thomas S. Abler, "Factional Dispute and Party Conflict in the Political System of the Seneca Nation (1845–1895): An Ethnohistorical Analysis" (Ph.D. diss., Univ. of Toronto, 1969), 91–104.

8. Stryker to Elbert Herring (commissioner of Indian Affairs), Feb. 21, Apr. 14, May 29, July 13, and July 26, 1832; Stryker to D. Kurtz (acting commissioner of Indian Affairs), Sept. 11, 1833; Stryker to Samuel Beardsley, Jan. 11, 1833, OIA, M234, Records of the Six Nations Agency, 1824–32, OIA, M234, MR 832, RG 75, NA. For Beardsley's support of the Erie Railroad see *Albany Argus,* May 21, 1836, 1.

9. Stryker to Herring, Nov. 12, 1833, OIA, M234, MR 832, RG 75, NA.

10. "Indian Petitions for Removal of James Stryker," Feb. 5, 1834, OIA, M234, MR 832, RG 75, NA.

11. See the petitions by the local Democratic Party in support of Stryker to Lewis Cass, Oct. 8, 14, and Nov. 2, 1835, OIA, M234, Records of the New York Agency, 1834–39, OIA, M234, MR 583, RG 75, NA; to Cass, Oct. 7 and 18, 1834, OIA, M234, MR 832, RG 75, NA.

12. "Seneca and Cayuga Complaints Against Stryker," Petition to Cass, Jan. 30, 1835, OIA, M234, MR 583, RG 75, NA. Stryker was able to extricate himself. See minutes of the Buffalo Creek Council of July 21–23, 1835, OIA, M234, MR 583, RG 75, NA.

13. Stryker to Joel R. Poinsett, Sept. 9, 1837, with Report of the Exploring Party to the President of the United States, Aug. 5, 1837, OIA, M234, MR 583, RG 75, NA.

14. Stryker to Poinsett, Sept. 9, 1837; Stryker to C. A. Harris, Oct. 11, Nov. 17 and 27, 1837; Thomas Ludlow Ogden to C. A. Harris, Dec. 4, 1837, OIA, M234, MR 583, RG 75, NA.

15. U.S. Congress, *Senate Report no. 192,* 31st Cong., 1st sess. (Sept. 9, 1850).

16. Citizens of the County of Erie in the State of New York to Martin Van Buren, Oct. 25, 1838, OIA, M234, MR 583, RG 75, NA.

17. Gillet to Stryker, Aug. 3, 1839, OIA, M234, MR 583, RG 75, NA; H. W. Rogers et al. to President of the United States, Feb. 21, 1840, OIA, M234, MR 584, RG 75, NA.

18. William L. Marcy to Joel R. Poinsett, MR 584, RG 75, NA.

19. Manley, "Buying Buffalo from the Indians," 315. For Stryker's successful attempts to avoid prosecution or testifying before congressional committees see U.S. Congress, *Senate Report no. 31,* 30th Cong., 1st sess., especially Doc. nos. 18 and 37, which are Stryker's defense of his actions to congressional investigator T. B. Stoddard in 1846–47.

20. The best analysis of Schermerhorn's career is James W. Van Hoeven, "Salvation and Indian Removal: The Career Biography of Rev. John Freeman Schermerhorn, Indian Commissioner" (Ph.D. diss., Vanderbilt Univ., 1972), 8–9, 104–5.

21. Gary Moulton, ed., *The Papers of Chief John Ross* (Norman: Univ. of Oklahoma Press, 1985), 1:573–74.

22. Maris Pierce speech of July 4, 1838, Maris Pierce MSS, BECHS.

23. Van Hoeven, "Salvation and Indian Removal," 98–105.

24. Ibid., 105.

25. Ibid., 106–23, 239, 262–64.

26. Ibid., 113–15. See also Francis Paul Prucha, "Thomas L. McKenney and the New York Indian Board," *Mississippi Valley Historical Review* 48 (Mar. 1962): 635–55.

27. Prucha, "Thomas L. McKenney," 651–52.

28. Van Hoeven, "Salvation and Indian Removal," 118–23. For Schermerhorn's involvement with the Miamis see Robert A. Trennert, Jr., *Indian Traders on the Middle Border: The House of Ewing, 1827–1854* (Lincoln: Univ. of Nebraska Press, 1981), 45–49; and Bert Anson, *The Miami Indians* (Norman: Univ. of Nebraska Press, 1970), 197–98.

29. Van Hoeven, "Salvation and Indian Removal," 138, 150.

30. Dale Van Every, *Disinherited: The Lost Birthright of the American Indian* (New York: Avon Books, 1966), 218. For the Second Seminole War see John K. Mahon, *History of the Second Seminole War, 1835–1842* (Gainesville: Univ. Press of Florida, 1967). Mahon, in an earlier article, refused to accuse the Stokes Commission of fraud but did insist that the Seminoles did not regard the treaties negotiated in 1832 and 1833 as fair and that their refusal to abide by these agreements led to war. Mahon, "Two Seminole Treaties: Payne's Landing, 1832, and Fort Gibson, 1833," *Florida Historical Quarterly* 41 (July 1962): 1–21.

31. Van Hoeven, "Salvation and Indian Removal," 138, 150.

32. Ibid., 205–6. See also Gary E. Moulton, *John Ross: Cherokee Chief* (Athens: Univ. of Georgia Press, 1978), 67–86. The historian Ralph Gabriel has gone so far as to describe Schermerhorn as "the sanctimonious glove concealing the fist of that uncompromising hater of Indians, Andrew Jackson." Gabriel, *Elias Boudinot, Cherokee, and His America* (Norman: Univ. of Oklahomas Press, 1941), 145. The Schermerhorn-Ross "war" can be traced in Moulton, *Papers of Chief John Ross,* 1:346 passim.

33. Moulton, *John Ross,* 67–68.

34. Satz, *American Indian Policy,* 51–56.

35. John F. Schermerhorn to Andrew Jackson, Oct. 29, 1836, OIA, M234, MR 583, RG 75, NA; Schermerhorn to (Commissioner of Indian Affairs) Herring, May 5, 1836; Schermerhorn to Indian Office, July 12, 1836, Jan. 10, 1837, OIA, M234, MR 583, RG 75, NA.

36. Schermerhorn to C. A. Harris (new commissioner of Indian Affairs), Oct. 27, 1836, OIA, M234, MR 583, RG 75, NA.

37. Report of Exploring Party to the President of the United States, Aug. 5, 1837, OIA, M234, MR 583, RG 75, NA; Report of Exploring Party, Dec. 26, 1837; and

"List of Expenses Advanced by Schermerhorn to . . . Exploring Party Indians," June 14, 1838, OIA, M234, MR 583, RG 75, NA.

38. Report of Exploring Party to the President of the United States, Aug. 5, 1837, OIA, M234, MR 583, RG 75, NA; Report of Exploring Party, Dec. 26, 1837; and "List of Expenses Advanced by Schermerhorn to . . . Exploring Party Indians," June 14, 1838, OIA, M234, MR 583, RG 75, NA.

39. (Protest of) Seneca Chief (Big Kettle et al.) to President of the United States, Oct. 16, 1837, OIA, M234, MR 583, RG 75, NA. See also (Protest of) Oneida Chiefs (Moses Schuyler et al.) to Our Father the President of the United States, Aug. 17, 1837; and (Protest of) Onondaga Chiefs (Captain Frost, Abraham La Fort et al.) to Great Father, Aug. 11, 1837, OIA, M234, MR 583, RG 75, NA.

40. Kappler, *Indian Affairs,* 2:502–12.

41. Van Hoeven, "Salvation and Indian Removal," 264–65.

42. Much of the background on Gillet is from two boxes of his papers in the New York State Library Manuscript Division in Albany. See also Goldstein, "Albany Regency," 185; and John Garraty, *Silas Wright* (New York: Columbia Univ. Press, 1949), 89, 340–41. Gillet's own writings include: *The Life and Times of Silas Wright,* 2 vols. (1874); *Democracy in the United States* (1868); *The Federal Government; Its Officers and Their Duties* (1872). He was also long active in the Jacksonian Association.

43. Silas Wright et al. (includes R. H. Gillet, C. C. Cambreleng, William Seymour) to Indian Office, May 10, 1836, OIA, M234, MR 583, RG 75, NA.

44. Gillet to Joel Poinsett (secretary of war), Oct. 29, 1837; Gillet to Commissioner Harris, Nov. 9, 1837, OIA, M234, MR 583, RG 75, NA.

45. Gillet to Commissioner Harris, Nov. 26, 1837, OIA, M234, MR 583, RG 75, NA.

46. T. L. Ogden to Commissioner Harris, Dec. 4, 1837, OIA, M234, MR 583, RG 75, NA.

47. Gillet to Commissioner Harris, Jan. 13, 1838, OIA, M234, MR 583, RG 75, NA.

48. Gillet, "Autobiography," Box 5, Folder 10, Ransom H. Gillet MSS, NYSL; Gillet to Commissioner Harris, Feb. 27, 1838, OIA, M234, MR 583, RG 75, NA.

49. Gillet Report, Feb. 27, 1838, OIA, M234, MR 583, RG 75, NA.

50. Ibid. Nicholas Cusick to Gillet, Jan. 1838, and Cusick et al. to the Senate and House of Representatives, Oct. 3, 1838, Special Case File 29, RG 75, NA.

51. Fred L. Israel, ed., *The State of the Union Messages of the Presidents* (New York: Chelsea House, 1967), 1:490–91; Society of Friends (Hicksite), *The Case of the Seneca Indians in the State of New York;* Manley, "Buying Buffalo from the Indians," 325–26; Abler, "Factional Dispute and Party Conflict," 94–100; James D. Richardson, comp., *A Compilation of the Messages and Papers of the Presidents* (Washington, D.C.: U.S. Government Printing Office, 1899): 3:561–66.

52. Richardson, *Messages and Papers,* 3:561–66.

53. *Congressional Globe,* 26th Cong., 1st sess. (Mar. 25, 1840), 352–58. Gillet later reprinted this speech in his biography of Wright. For Dearborn's account see Henry A. S. Dearborn, *Journals of Henry A. S. Dearborn,* Buffalo Historical Society

Publications 7, ed. Frank H. Severance (Buffalo, N.Y.: Buffalo Historical Society, 1904), 35–235.

12. THE INCORPORATION, 1838–1857

1. 7 *Stat.*, 586 (1842). The treaty was signed on May 20, 1842, and was promulgated by President John Tyler on August 26, 1842. The other treaties that allowed for the return or repurchase of land are the Pickering treaty (1794) and the Tonawanda treaty (1857).

2. Ambrose Spencer to General John Armstrong, May 25, 1842, Rokeby Collection, NYHS.

3. Society of Friends (Hicksite), Executive Committee of the Yearly Meetings, *Proceedings of an Indian Council Held at the Buffalo Creek Reservation, State of New York, Fourth Month, 1842* (Baltimore, Md.: William Wooddy for the Executive Committee of the Yearly Meetings, 1842), 72–74. Despite its title it should be noted that the council included proceedings through May 20, 1842.

4. Tonawanda Protest (Jemmy Johnson, John Blacksmith, et al.) to Governor William H. Seward, June 4, 1842, William H. Seward MSS, Box 18, Folder, "Seneca," UR; Tonawanda Protest (Jemmy Johnson, John Blacksmith, et al.) to Secretary of War, June 17, 1842, *DHI,* MR 49, NYSL.

5. "From the President [Polk] of the United States Communicating a Petition of the Tonawanda Band of Seneca Indians, praying that steps may be taken to abrogate the treaties of 1838 and 1842," U.S. Congress, *Senate Doc.* 273, Ser. Set 474 (1846).

6. See chap. 12, n. 4.

7. Ibid.; Maris B. Pierce to John Canfield Spencer, Apr. 9, 1842, Records of the New York Yearly Meeting, Haviland Record Room, New York Yearly Meeting of Friends, New York, N.Y. (hereafter cited as HRR).

8. Society of Friends (Hicksite), *Proceedings of an Indian Council,* 72.

9. The New York Whig Party needs major historical research and study. I have learned much about Whigs in the following: Daniel Walker Howe, *The Political Culture of the American Whigs* (Chicago: Univ. of Chicago Press, 1979); Thomas Brown, *Politics and Statesmanship: Essays on the American Whig Party* (New York: Columbia Univ. Press, 1985). Most of the biographical studies of New York Whigs are outdated or inadequate.

10. For Friends' relations with the Seneca see Hugh Barbour et al., eds., *Quaker Crosscurrents: Three Hundred Years of Friends in the New York Yearly Meetings* (Syracuse, N.Y.: Syracuse Univ. Press, 1995), 97–99, 316. Lois Barton, *A Quaker Promise Kept: Philadelphia Friends' Work with the Allegany Seneca, 1795–1960* (Eugene, Ore.: Spencer Butte Press, 1990). Rayner W. Kelsey, *Friends and the Indians, 1655–1917* (Philadelphia, Pa.: Associated Committee of Friends on Indian Affairs, 1917), chaps. 5 and 6. For more critical studies of the Friends see Diane Rothenberg, "The Mothers of the Nation: Seneca Resistance to Quaker Inter-vention," in *Women and Colonization: Anthropological Perspectives,* ed. Mona Etienne and Eleanor Leacock (New York: Praeger, 1980), 63–87; Thomas S. Abler, "Friends, Factions and the Seneca Nation Revolution of 1848," *Niagara Frontier* 21 (Winter

1974): 74–79. Berkhofer, *Salvation and the Savage,* 56, 72–84, 104, 135–37. For other studies of the Friends among the Seneca, see Frank H. Severance, "The Quakers among the Senecas," in Buffalo Historical Society *Publications* 6, ed. Frank H. Severance (Buffalo, N.Y.: Buffalo Historical Association, 1903), 165–68; and Joseph Elkinton, "The Quaker Mission among the Indians of New York State," in Buffalo Historical Society *Publications* 18 (Buffalo, N.Y.: Buffalo Historical Association, 1914), 169–89.

11. For more on Thomas see Albro Martin, *Railroads Triumphant: The Growth, Rejection, and Rebirth of a Vital American Force* (New York: Oxford Univ. Press, 1992), 250; Fenton, "Gradual Civilization," 567–81.

12. See the subagents' reports for the New York Indians, S. Osborn to T. Hartley Crawford, Feb. 21 and Mar. 1, 1842, OIA, Records of the New York Agency, M234, MR 584, NA.

13. Society of Friends (Hicksite), *Proceedings of an Indian Council,* 59.

14. Satz, *American Indian Policy,* 265–78.

15. For Clay's racism toward Indians see Charles Francis Adams, ed., *The Memoirs of John Quincy Adams,* 7:89–90. Ironically, because of his opposition to Cherokee removal, he was praised by Indians! See Robert V. Remini, *Henry Clay: Statesman for the Union* (New York: W. W. Norton, 1991), 315.

16. Webster's role can easily be seen in *Whipple Report,* 28–29.

17. For the Second Seminole War see Mahon, *Second Seminole War;* James W. Covington, *The Seminoles of Florida* (Gainesville: Univ. Press of Florida, 1993), chaps. 4 and 5. For the Indian issue in the political campaign of 1840 see Robert G. Gundersen, *The Log-Cabin Campaign* (Lexington: Univ. of Kentucky Press, 1957), 94.

18. John Canfield Spencer was later secretary of the treasury and a failed Whig nominee to the U.S. Supreme Court in 1844. There is much evidence of his financial doings in his correspondence with his brother-in-law, John Townsend, an Albany iron magnate, in the Townsend Collection, NYSL. On the Spencer family's dealings with the Holland Land Company see John C. Spencer to Gentlemen [John Townsend, Benjamin Hale, et al.], July 10, 1822, DC13209, NYSL; and Evans, *Holland Land Company,* 344–45, 374–78, 384–85. For an excellent study of Spencer's anti-Masonry see Elizabeth B. Haigh, "New York Antimasons, 1826–1833" (Ph.D. diss., Univ. of Rochester, 1980), 239–326.

19. Haigh, "New York Antimasons," 237–44. Haigh's dissertation is an excellent one that deserves publication. More information of Spencer can be found in Trennert, *Indian Traders,* 103, 106–9, 122.

20. Alexis de Tocqueville, *Journey to America,* trans. George Lawrence, ed. J. P. Mayer and A. P. Kerr (Reprint, Garden City, N.Y.: Doubleday, Anchor Paperback, 1971), 11, 16, 201–3.

21. George Wilson Pierson, *Tocqueville and Beaumont in America* (New York: Oxford Univ. Press, 1938), 215–16. Spencer wrote the preface for the second edition of de Tocqueville's *Democracy in America.* Alexis de Tocqueville, *Democracy in America,* trans. Henry Reeve, with preface and notes by John C. Spencer (New York: Adlard, 1838), 286–87. Haigh, "New York Antimasons," 298–99.

22. Quoted in Satz, *American Indian Policy,* 267.

23. Ibid. Interestingly, Spencer had been challenged by Whig Millard Fillmore, the chairman of the House Ways and Means Committee in 1841, for detailed justification for his (Spencer's) proposal to expend more money for Indian education. Spencer, as a good Whig type, argued that spending more federal money in the short run was actually cost efficient in the long run. Ibid., 265–68.

24. Ibid., 211–36, and Satz, "Thomas Hartley Crawford," in *The Commissioners of Indian Affairs, 1824–1977,* ed. Robert M. Kvasnicka and Herman Viola (Lincoln: Univ. of Nebraska Press, 1979), 24–25.

25. Society of Friends (Hicksite), *Proceedings of an Indian Council,* 30.

26. Ethan Allen Hitchcock, *A Traveler in Indian Territory: The Journal of Ethan Allen Hitchcock,* ed. Grant Foreman (Cedar Rapids, Iowa: Torch Press, 1930), 10–14, 69, 71, 78, 80–82, 89, 101, 111, 142, 145, 150–56, 169–70, 175, 179, 186, 193–94, 197, 205–7, 215, 219, 227–29, 249–54; W. A. Croffut, *Fifty Years in Camp and Field: Diary of Major-General Ethan Allen Hitchcock* (New York: G. P. Putnam's Sons, 1909), 154–62, 172–73. For Hitchcock's later reporting on the genocide committed against the Indians in northern California in the 1850s see Laurence M. Hauptman, *Between Two Fires: American Indians in the Civil War* (New York: Free Press, 1995), 9.

27. For Whig diplomacy and the Canadian boundary see Howard Jones, *To the Webster-Ashburton Treaty* (Chapel Hill: Univ. of North Carolina Press, 1977); Kenneth R. Stevens, *Border Diplomacy* (Tuscaloosa: Univ. of Alabama Press, 1989).

28. There is no full-scale biography of Ambrose Spencer. Some biographical materials were found in the *Dictionary of American Biography,* the *Biographical Directory of Congress, 1789–1949,* in Spencer and Townsend family correspondence in NYSL, in Haigh's study of anti-Masonry, and in the writings of Jabez Hammond.

29. Although Tyler spoke highly of John Canfield Spencer, Ambrose Spencer viewed President Tyler as "radically unfit for the place he occupies." Ambrose Spencer to General John Armstrong, Dec. 28, 1841, MSS no. 13490, NYSL. For Tyler's view of John Canfield Spencer see Lyon G. Tyler, *The Letters and Times of the Tylers* (Richmond, Va.: Whittet and Shepperson, 1885), 2:397–98.

30. 20 *Johns* 188 (1822).

31. Ibid.

32. Ibid.

33. 20 *Johns* 693 (1823). In this case, in an earlier one *(Jackson v. Wood),* and in his *Commentaries* Kent helped predict Marshall's decisions in the Cherokee cases. The chancellor argued that because of their state of "dependence," the Indian tribes within the territorial jurisdiction of the government of the United States must have the right to protection, that the United States had the "exclusive right of extinguishing the Indian title by possession," and that the "Indian possession is not to be taken from them, or disturbed without their free consent, by fair purchase, except it be by force of arms in the event of a just and necessary war." James Kent, *Commentaries on American Law* (1826; reprint, New York: Da Capo Press, 1971), 3:311–12.

34. Joseph C. Burke, "The Cherokee Cases: A Study in Law, Politics, and

Morality," *Stanford Law Review* 21 (Feb. 1969): 506–8, 511, 506 n. 31. Jeremiah Evarts, *Cherokee Removal: The "William Penn" Essays and Other Writings,* ed. Francis Paul Prucha (Knoxville: Univ. of Tennessee Press, 1981), 16 (introduction by Prucha).

35. T. Hartley Crawford to Ambrose Spencer, Feb. 17, 1842, *DHI,* MR 49, NYSL.

36. Dixon was there because on January 29 and February 24, 1841, both houses of the New York State Legislature petitioned the Congress to investigate the circumstances involving the Treaty of Buffalo Creek of 1838 and to determine whether it had been voluntarily assented to by the Seneca. New York State Legislature, *Assembly Journal,* 64th sess., 1841 (Albany: Thurlow Weed State Printer, 1841), 222, 408.

37. Ambrose Spencer to T. Hartley Crawford, Mar. 1, 1842, *DHI,* MR 49, NYSL.

38. Shaw, *Erie Water West,* 315–35.

39. *Laws of New York,* 63d sess., chap. 254 (May 9, 1840), 26–27.

40. *Laws of New York,* 64th sess., chap. 166 (May 4, 1841), 134–36.

41. Society of Friends (Hicksite), *Proceedings of an Indian Council,* 42.

42. Ibid., 50.

43. Ibid., 61. See also 40, 44, 51, 60, 72.

44. Ibid., 37–55, 61–62, 68–69, 72.

45. Ibid., 62.

46. Ibid., 73–74.

47. An extraordinary Hicksite publication was *The Case of the Seneca Indians in the State of New York.*

48. Howard A. Vernon, "Maris Bryant Pierce," in *Indian Lives: Essays on Nineteenth and Twentieth Century Native American Leaders,* ed. Raymond Wilson and L. George Moses (Albuquerque: Univ. of New Mexico Press, 1985), 19–39.

49. For Pierce's opposition during the deliberations of the Treaty of Buffalo Creek (1838) see Dearborn, *Journals,* 92, 136. For one of Pierce's speeches against the Treaty of Buffalo Creek of 1838 see M. B. Pierce, *Address on the Present Condition and Prospects of the Aboriginal Inhabitants of North America with Particular Reference to the Seneca Nation* (speech at the Baptist Church in Buffalo, N.Y., Aug. 28, 1838) (Buffalo, N.Y.: Steele's Press, 1838). For Pierce's agenda (and John Kennedy, Jr.'s), see Pierce to John Canfield Spencer, Apr. 9, 1842, Records of the New York Yearly Meeting, HRR.

50. Maris B. Pierce to Abraham Bell, Jan. 29, Dec. 10, Dec. 18, Dec. 28, 1841; Pierce to Jacob Harvey, Feb. 19, June 18, 1841, Apr. 19, 1842; Pierce to John Canfield Spencer, Apr. 9, 1842, Records of the New York Yearly Meeting, HRR. Pierce to T. Hartley Crawford, Jan. 15, 1842; Pierce and Henry Two Guns to William Henry Harrison, early March, Mar. 6, 1841; Pierce to John Bell, Apr. 14, 1841; Pierce et al. to Daniel Kurtz, Oct. 1, Oct. 11, 1841, OIA, Records of the New York Agency, M234, MR 584, NA.

51. Tonawanda Protest to Secretary of War, June 17, 1842; Tonawanda Protest to Governor William H. Seward, June 4, 1842.

52. Society of Friends (Hicksite), *Proceedings of an Indian Council,* 6.

53. Tonawanda Protest to Secretary of War, June 17, 1842; Society of Friends (Hicksite), *Proceedings of an Indian Council,* 27–28.

54. Pierce to John Canfield Spencer, Apr. 9, 1842, Records of the New York Yearly Meeting, HRR.

55. Society of Friends (Hicksite), *Proceedings of an Indian Council,* 60–61.

56. Ibid., 5–6, 11–12.

57. Society of Friends (Hicksite), Executive Committee, *Report of the Proceedings of an Indian Council at Cattaraugus in the State of New York, 1843* (Baltimore, Md.: William Wooddy, 1843), 11, 13, 16.

58. "Results of Emigration," *Mental Elevator* 13, Dec. 24, 1846, 111; Frank H. Harris, "Neosho Agency, 1838–1871," *The Chronicles of Oklahoma* 43 (1965): 35–58. William C. Sturtevant, "Oklahoma Seneca-Cayuga," in *Handbook of North American Indians,* vol. 15, *The Northeast,* ed. Bruce G. Trigger (Washington, D.C.: Smithsonian Institution, 1978), 537–43; Abler and Tooker, "Seneca," 511; "Muster Roll," Maris B. Pierce MSS, Box 2, BECHS.

59. "An Act for the protection and improvement of Seneca Indians, residing on the Cattaraugus and Allegany Reservations in this State," *Statutes of the State of New York,* chap. 150 (May 8, 1845), 146.

60. *Statutes of the State of New York,* chap. 365, 464 (Nov. 15, 1847), 464.

61. *Statutes of the State of New York,* chap. 300, 432 (Apr. 12, 1848), 432; chap. 378 (Mar. 27, Apr. 11, 1849), 530, 721; chap. 89 (Mar. 23, 1850), 140; chap. 45 (Apr. 1, 1846), 50; chap. 420 (Apr. 11, 1849), 576.

62. "An Act for the benefit of Indians," *Statutes of the State of New York,* chap. 420 (Apr. 11, 1849), 576.

63. Maris B. Pierce to Joseph Elkinton, May 31, 1842, Records of the Philadelphia Yearly Meeting of Friends, HRR. Even as late as February 21, 1849, in utter disbelief, Pierce wrote Elkinton that the commissioner of Indian Affairs told "me that the *Society of Friends* are in favor of it [the new republic—the Seneca Nation of Indians]. I wish to be informed if this is true among the Society of Friends in your city Philadelphia who have laboured so much for the Senecas." Pierce to Elkinton, Feb. 21, 1849, Pierce MSS, BECHS.

64. See, for example, Chiefs and Warriors of the Tonawanda Reservation to Governor Silas Wright, Nov. 9, 1846, MSS no. 12842, NYSL. For the Tonawanda Seneca's legal action see Armstrong, *Warrior in Two Camps,* 32–60. For the case see *Fellows v. Blacksmith,* 19 Howard 366.

65. For the Tonawanda treaty see 11 *Stat.,* 729 (Sept. 24, 1857).

13. CONCLUSION: THE IROQUOIS INDIANS AND THE RISE OF THE EMPIRE STATE

1. New York State, *Census of the State of New York for 1855,* comp. Franklin B. Hough (Albany, N.Y.: Charles Van Benthuysen and Sons, 1857).

2. French, *Gazetteer,* 54–57.

3. *Census of the State of New York for 1855.*

4. French, *Gazetteer,* 469 n. 4.

5. *Census of the State of New York for 1855.*

6. Ibid.

7. French, *Gazetteer,* 284, 288.

8. Thomas E. Hogan, "City in a Quandary: Salamanca and the Allegany Leases," *New York History* 55 (Jan. 1974): 84; Laurence M. Hauptman, "The Historical Background to the Present-Day Seneca Nation–Salamanca Lease Controversy: The First Hundred Years, 1851–1951," Working Paper no. 20, Fall 1985, Nelson A. Rockefeller Institute of Government, reprinted in Christopher Vecsey and William A. Starna, eds., *Iroquois Land Claims* (Syracuse, N.Y.: Syracuse Univ. Press, 1988), 101–22.

9. Hogan, "City in a Quandary," 84.

10. Thomas Wistar, "Report of the Committee on the Civilization and Improvement of the New York Indians," *Friend* 38, June 10, 1865, 325.

11. I have previously written about the Salamanca lease affair in *The Iroquois in the Civil War: From Battlefield to Reservation* (Syracuse, N.Y.: Syracuse Univ. Press, 1993), chap. 9; and in my *Iroquois Struggle for Survival: World War II to Red Power,* chaps. 2–4. I was the expert witness giving oral and written historical background before the United States Senate Select Committee on Indian Affairs and the United States House Subcommittee on Interior and Insular Affairs in September 1990. The bill that was passed—the Seneca Nation Settlement Act of 1990—was signed into law by President Bush on Nov. 3, 1990. For a summary of these events, see my "Compensatory Justice: The Seneca Nation Settlement Act," *National Forum* 71 (Spring 1991): 31–33.

12. Philip E. Thomas to George W. Manypenny, June 6, 1855; Marcus H. Johnson to George Manypenny, Nov. 25, 1856, with attached notice of a sale of land for taxes, Oct. 10, 1856, signed by Harvey Baldwin, New York Agency Records, OIA, M234, MR 588, RG 75, NA; Nathaniel Starbuck to "Respected Friend," Mar. 12, 1856, and Philip E. Thomas to George T. Trimble, Amos Willetts, and William C. White, Nov. 20, 1856, Papers and Letters Relating to the Work of the Joint Indian Committee of Four Yearly Meetings, 1835–63, File 21, 1856–57, New York Yearly Meeting, HRR.

13. Petition of the Councillors of the Seneca Nation to the President of the United States, June 2, 1858, New York Agency Records, OIA, M234, MR 589, RG 75, NA.

14. Fragment of a letter written by Philip E. Thomas, 1858 or 1859, New York Agency Records, OIA, M234, MR 589 (plate 0089), RG 75, NA.

15. Ruth A. Birdseye, *Indian Education in New York State, 1846–1953/1954* (Albany, N.Y.: New York State Department of Education, 1954). This is an informational handout distributed by the New York State Department of Education since it was first prepared by Ruth Birdseye in the mid-1950s.

16. Ibid.

17. New York State Department of Public Instruction, *Thirty-fourth Annual Report,* 1888 (Albany, N.Y., 1888), 765.

18. See my discussion of this agency in Hauptman, *Formulating American Indian Policy in New York State, 1970–1986* (Albany, N.Y.: SUNY Press, 1988), 70–75.

BIBLIOGRAPHY

ARCHIVAL RECORDS AND MANUSCRIPT COLLECTIONS

Allegany County Courthouse, Belmont, N.Y.
  Oil Spring Reservation, land records and maps
American Philosophical Society, Philadelphia, Pa.
  Fenton, William N., MSS
  Parker, Ely S., MSS
  Speck, Frank G., MSS
Buffalo and Erie County Historical Society, Buffalo, N.Y.
  Forward, Oliver, MSS
  Granger, Erastus, MSS
  Holland Land Company, MSS
  Indian Collection
  Parker, Arthur C., MSS
  Parker, Ely S., MSS
  Parker, Isaac Newton, MSS
  Parrish, Jasper, MSS
  Pierce, Maris B., MSS
  Porter, Peter B., MSS
  Potter, Heman, MSS
Cattaraugus County Courthouse, Little Valley, N.Y.
  Map Book: Indian Reservations
  Transcript of case with testimony, *Seneca Nation v. Philonus Pattison*
Columbia University, Butler Library, New York, N.Y.
  Clinton, De Witt, MSS
  Jay, John, MSS
  Morris, Gouverneur, MSS
Erie Canal Village, Rome, N.Y.
  Benjamin Wright Journal, 1816 (copy in New York State Museum, Albany)
Hamilton College, Clinton, N.Y.
  Kirkland, Samuel, MSS
Haverford College, Magill Library, Haverford, Pa.
  Elkinton, Joseph, Papers, Journals
  Friends, Society of Indian Committee of the Society of Friends, 1757–1896
Records of the Philadelphia Yearly Meeting.
  Records of the Tunesassa Boarding School
Haviland Record Room, New York Yearly Meeting of Friends, New York, N.Y.
  Records of the Genesee Yearly Meeting of Friends

Records of the New York Yearly Meeting of Friends
Historical Society of Pennsylvania, Philadelphia
  Etting Family, MSS
  Gratz Family, MSS
  Wayne, Anthony, MSS
Library of Congress, Washington, D.C.
  Jackson, Andrew, MSS
  Morris, Gouverneur, MSS
  Morris, Robert, MSS
  Troup, Robert, MSS
  Van Buren, Martin, MSS
  Wadsworth Family, MSS
Massachusetts Historical Society, Boston
  Pickering, Timothy, MSS
Miscellaneous Manuscript Collections
  Holland Land Company Archives (Frederica Safran, comp.), microfilm publications housed at State University of New York, Fredonia
  Indian Claims Commission, Expert Testimony on Dockets no. 342 A, B, C, E, F, 368, 368 A (microfiche)
  Jennings, Francis, et al., eds. *Iroquois Indians: A Documentary History of the Six Nations and Their League.* 50 microfilm reels. Woodbridge, Conn.: Research Publications, 1985
National Archives, Washington, D.C.
  Cartographic Records, College Park, Md.
  Correspondence of the Office of Indian Affairs. Letters Received, 1824–81. M234, RG75.
      Green Bay Agency, 1824–80, microfilm reels 315–16
      Neosho Agency, 1831–75, microfilm reels 530–37
      Records of the New York Agency
      Emigration, 1829–51, microfilm reel 597
      Records of the New York Agency, 1829–80, microfilm reels 583–96
      Seneca Agency in New York, 1824–32, microfilm reel 808
      Six Nations Agency, 1824–34, microfilm reel 832
  Office of the Secretary of War. Letters Received by the Secretary of War Relating to Indian Affairs, 1800–1823. M271. Microfilm reels 1–4
  Records of the Indian Claims Commission. RG279
  Records Relating to Indian Treaties
      Documents Relating to the Negotiation of Ratified and Unratified Treaties . . . , 1801–69. T494
      Microfilm reels 1, 2, 4, 6, 8
      Ratified Indian Treaties, 1722–1869. M668
      Microfilm reels 2, 3, 9, 12
  Special Case File 29 (Re: Treaty of Buffalo Creek of 1838 and Kansas Claims)
New-York Historical Society, New York, N.Y.
  King, Rufus, MSS
  Morris, Thomas, [Account of the Treaty of Big Tree], MSS

Ogden, Alfred, MSS
O'Reilly, Henry, MSS [Western mementos]
Rokeby Collection
Troup, Robert, MSS
New York Public Library, Special Collections Division, Albany
Morse, Jedidiah, MSS
Schuyler, Peter, MSS
Schuyler, Philip, MSS
Troup, Robert, MSS
New York State Archives, Albany
Records of the Division of Military and Naval Affairs
Abstract of Muster Rolls, War of 1812
Office of the New York State Surveyor-General, Land Office Records, ser. 1 and 2
Records of Indian Deeds and Treaties, 1748–1847
Records of the New York State Canals
Account books for the Genesee Valley Canal, 1843, 1863
Canal damage awards by canal appraisers
Canal System Survey Maps (Holmes Hutchinson Maps), 1832–43
Description of lands appropriated for the Genesee Valley Canal, 1839–82
Estimates for the Genesee Valley Canal, 1851–55
Minutes of the Board of Canal Commissioners
Miscellaneous payments made for work done on the western division of the
    Erie Canal and the Genesee Valley Canal
Original maps and surveys for the Erie Canal (Geddes Map), 1817
Petitions and appeals to the canal board
Records of land appropriations and damage records relating to the Genesee
    Valley Canals, 1843–47
Western Inland Navigation Company damage assessments and reimburse-
    ments, 1820
Records of the New York State Court of Appeals
Seneca Nation v. Christy
Seneca Nation v. Philonus Pattison
Records of the New York State Legislature. Assembly Papers. Indian Affairs
Records of the State Comptroller's Indian Annuity Claims, Receipts and Related
    Documents, 1796–1925
Records of the State Treasurer (Comptroller's office), 1864–66
Records of the War of 1812, Certificates of Claims by War of 1812 Veterans
New York State Bureau of Land Management, Albany
Minutes of the New York State Board of Land Commissioners, nineteenth-
    century minute books
New York State Library, Manuscript Division, Albany
Banyar, Goldsbrow, MSS
Beauchamp, William, MSS
Bleecker, Harmanus, MSS
Bliss Family, MSS
Cayuga County, N.Y., Survey Map . . . formerly the Cayuga Reservation, MSS

Clinton, De Witt, MSS
Deardorff, Merle, MSS
Fish Family, MSS
Genesee Land Company Papers
Gillet, Ransom, MSS
Great Western Turnpike, MSS
Holland Land Company, MSS
Hough, Franklin Benjamin, MSS
Hutchinson, Holmes, MSS
Livingston Family, MSS
Ogden land Company Record Book, 1811–82
Parker, Arthur C., MSS
Phelps-Gorham, MSS
Schoolcraft Population Census of Indian Reservations, 1845
Schuyler Family, MSS
Scriba, George, MSS
Seymour, Horatio, MSS
Stillman, Lulu, MSS
Tayler, John, MSS
Thomas, David, MSS
Townsend Family, MSS
Troup, Robert, MSS
Van Buren, Martin, MSS
Van Rensselaer Family, MSS
Visscher, Bastinen, MSS
Wadsworth Family, MSS
Watson, Elkanah, MSS
Wright, Benjamin, MSS
Oneida Nation of Indians of Wisconsin, Oneida, Wis.
  WPA Oneida Folklore and Language Project Stories
Onondaga Historical Association, Syracuse, N.Y.
  Beauchamp, William, MSS
  New York State Comptroller Records (Albany Papers)
  Vertical Files
Rochester Public Library, Rochester, N.Y.
  Fellows, Joseph, MSS
  Pulteney Associates, MSS
St. John Fisher College, Rochester, N.Y.
  Decker, George P., MSS
Seneca Nation of Indians, Salamanca, N.Y.
  Records of the Department of Justice, Seneca Nation of Indians
State Historical Society of Wisconsin, Madison
  Draper, Lyman C., MSS
State University of New York, College at Buffalo
  Reilly, Paul G., MSS. [Indian Claims Commission]

Swarthmore College, Friends Historical Society, Swarthmore, Pa.
  Records of the Baltimore Yearly Meeting of Friends
  Records of the Indian Committee (Hicksite) of the Philadelphia Yearly Meeting
    of Friends
      Indian Concerns Subcommittee
      Minutes
      Miscellaneous Records
Syracuse University, Bird Library, George Arents Research Library, Syracuse, N.Y.
  De Witt Family, MSS
  Smith, Peter, MSS
Tompkins County Historical Society, Ithaca, N.Y.
  De Witt Family, MSS
University of Rochester, Rush Rhees Library, Rochester, N.Y.
  Morgan, Lewis Henry, MSS
  Parker, Arthur C., MSS
  Seward, William H., MSS
  Skivington, George J., Collection
Vassar College, Poughkeepsie, N.Y.
  Parrish, Jasper, MSS

GOVERNMENT PUBLICATIONS

American State Papers: Documents, Legislative and Executive of the Congress of the United States. 38 vols. Class 2: *Indian Affairs.* 2 vols. 1832–34. Washington, D.C.: Gales and Seaton, 1832–61.

The Balloting Book and Other Documents Relating to Military Bounty Lands in the State of New York. Albany, N.Y.: Packard and Van Benthuysen, 1825.

Brannan, John, comp. *Official Letters of the Military and Naval Officers of the United States During the War with Great Britain in the Years 1812, 13, 14, 15.* Washington, D.C.: Way and Gideon, 1823.

Birdseye, Ruth A. *Indian Education in New York State, 1846–1953/1954.* Albany, N.Y.: New York State Department of Education, 1954.

Carter, Clarence E., and John Porter Bloom, eds. *The Territorial Papers of the United States.* 28 vols. Washington, D.C.: U.S. Government Printing Office, 1934–56; National Archives, 1858–1962, 1969–75.

Colden, Cadwallader D., comp. *Memoir, Prepared at the Request of a Committee of the Common Council of the City of New York and Presented to the Mayor of the City, at the Celebration of the Completion of the New York Canals.* New York: W. A. Davis, 1825. Reprint. Ann Arbor: Univ. Microfilms International, 1967.

Donaldson, Thomas, comp. *The Six Nations of New York.* Extra Census Bulletin of the Eleventh Census [1890] of the United States. Washington, D.C.: U.S. Census Printing Office, 1892.

Ford, Worthington C., et al., eds. *Journals of the Continental Congress.* 34 vols. Washington, D.C.: U.S. Government Printing Office, 1904–37.

Gallatin, Albert. *Report of the Secretary of the Treasury on the Subject of Public Roads and Canals, 1808*. Washington, D.C.: Weightman, 1808. Reprint. New York: Augustus M. Kelley, 1968.

Hastings, Hugh, ed. *Public Papers of Daniel D. Tompkins, Governor of New York, 1807–1817*. 3 vols. New York: J.B. Lyon and Wynkoop, Hallenback and Crawford, 1898–1902.

———. *The Public Papers of George Clinton*. 10 vols. Albany, N.Y.: Wynkoop, Hallenback and Crawford, 1899–1914.

Kappler, Charles J., comp. *Indian Affairs: Laws and Treaties*. 5 vols. Washington, D.C.: U.S. Government Printing Office, 1903–41.

Laws of New York. 1st sess. (1777)–74th sess. (1851).

Lincoln, Charles Z., comp. *The Constitutional History of New York*. Vols. 1 and 2. Rochester, N.Y.: Lawyers Cooperative Publishing, 1906.

———, ed. *Messages from the Governors* [NYS]. Vols. 1–3. Albany, N.Y.: J. B. Lyon, 1909.

Morse, Jedidiah. *A Report to the Secretary of War of the United States on Indian Affairs, Comprising a Narrative of a Tour Performed in the Summer of 1820 for the Purpose of Ascertaining, for the Use of the Government, the Actual State of the Indian Tribes in Our Country*. New Haven, Conn.: S. Converse, 1822.

New York State Adjutant General's Office, comp. *Index of Awards: Soldiers of the War of 1812*. Baltimore, Md.: Genealogical Publishing, 1969.

New York State Board of Canal Appraisers. *Digest of Claims from 1818 to 1858*. Rochester, N.Y.: A. Strong, 1858.

———. *Digest of Claims from 1866 to 1870, Inclusive*. Albany, N.Y.: Argus, 1870.

New York State Board of Canal Commissioners. *Annual Report* [1811–78].

———. *Official Report of the Canal Commissioners of the State of New-York, and the Acts of the Legislature Respecting Navigable Communications Between the Great Western and Northern Lakes and the Atlantic Ocean*. New York: T. and W. Mercein, 1817.

New York State Board of Land Commissioners. *Proceedings of the Commissioners of the Land Office for the Year 1924*. Albany, N.Y.: J. B. Lyon, 1924.

New York State. *Census of the State of New York for 1855*. Compiled by Franklin B. Hough. Albany, N.Y.: Charles Van Benthuysen and Sons, 1857.

New York State Constitutional Convention. *Documents of the Convention of the State of New York, 1867–1868*. Albany, N.Y.: Weed, Parsons, 1868.

———. *Reports of the Proceedings and Debates of the New York State Constitutional Convention, 1821*. New York: Da Capo Press, 1970.

New York State Legislature. Assembly. Doc. no. 51, *Report of the Special Committee to Investigate the Indian Problem of the State of New York*. Appointed by the Assembly of 1888. 2 vols. Albany, N.Y.: Troy Press, 1889. (Cited herein as the *Whipple Report*.)

———. *Assembly Journal*.

———. *Laws (Statutes) of the State of New York, 1777–1851*.

———. *Report of the Joint Committee of the Legislature of New-York, on the Subject of the Canals*. Albany, N.Y.: Websters and Skinners, 1817.

———. *Senate Journal*.

New York State Secretary of State. *Calendar of New York Colonial Manuscripts, Indorsed Land Papers, 1643–1803.* Edited by Edmund B. O'Callaghan. Reprint. Harrison, N.Y.: Harbor Hill Books, 1987.

———. *Census of the State of New York for 1825.* Albany, N.Y., 1826.

———. *Census of the State of New York for 1835.* Albany, N.Y.: Croswell, Van Benthuysen and Burt, 1836.

———. *Census of the State of New York for 1845.* Albany, N.Y.: Carrol and Cook, 1846.

Richardson, James D., comp. *A Compilation of the Messages and Papers of the Presidents, 1789–1897.* 10 vols. Washington, D.C.: U.S. Government Printing Office, 1896–99.

Royce, Charles C., comp. *Indian Land Cessions in the United States.* 18th Annual Report of the Bureau of American Ethnology, 1896–97. Pt. 2. Washington, D.C.: U.S. Government Printing Office, 1899.

U.S. Bureau of the Census. 1st (1790)–9th (1860) censuses.

U.S. Congress. *Annals of Congress,* 1789–1824.

———. *Congressional Globe,* 1833–51.

———. House of Representatives. Committee on Foreign Affairs. Hearings on H.R. 2498, 11756, 16542, 16547, and 16587: Diversion of Water from the Niagara River. 63d Cong., 2d sess. July 15, 1914. Washington, D.C.: U.S. Government Printing Office, 1914.

———. House of Representatives. Committee on Indian Affairs. Report no. 209: *To Hold a Treaty with the Seneca Indians.* 19th Cong., 1st sess. May 13, 1826. Serial set 142.

———. House of Representatives. *Journal of the House of Representatives* [1789–1815]. Washington, D.C.: Gales and Seaton, 1826.

———. *Register of Debates in Congress,* 1825–37.

———. Senate. *Journal of the Executive Proceedings of the Senate* [1789–1828]. 3 vols. Washington, D.C.: Duff Green, 1828.

———. Senate. *Journal of the Senate* [1789–1815]. 5 vols. Washington, D.C.: Gales and Seaton, 1820–21.

U.S. Indian Claims Commission. *Decisions of the Indian Claims Commission.* Microfiche ed. New York: Clearwater Publishing, 1973–78.

U.S. Interior Department. Commissioner of Indian Affairs. *Annual Report* [1849–60].

———. Secretary of the Interior. *Annual Report* [1849–60].

U.S. War Department. Commissioner of Indian Affairs. *Annual Report* [1824–48].

———. Secretary of War. *Annual Report* [1789–1848].

Washington, George. *The Writings of George Washington from the Original Manuscript Sources, 1745–1799.* Edited by John C. Fitzpatrick. 39 vols. Washington, D.C.: U.S. Government Printing Office, 1931–44.

Whitford, Noble E. *History of the Canal System of the State of New York.* 2 vols. Albany, N.Y.: Brandon Printing (supplement to the annual report of the state engineer and surveyor of the State of New York), 1906.

BOOKS, BOOKLETS, AND PAMPHLETS

Abler, Thomas S., ed. *Chainbreaker: The Revolutionary War Memoirs of Governor Blacksnake as Told to Benjamin Williams.* Lincoln: Univ. of Nebraska Press, 1989.

Abrams, George H. J. *The Seneca People.* Phoenix, Ariz.: Indian Tribal Series, 1976.

Adams, Charles Francis, ed., *Memoirs of John Quincy Adams.* Vol. 7. Philadelphia, Pa.: J. B. Lippincott, 1875.

Adams, William, ed. *Historical Gazetteer and Biographical Memorial of Cattaraugus County, N.Y.* Syracuse, N.Y.: Lyman, Horton, 1893.

Albion, Robert G. *The Rise of New York Port.* New York: Charles Scribner's Sons, 1939.

Alden, Timothy. *An Account of Sundry Missions Performed among the Senecas and Munsees.* New York: J. Seymour, 1827.

Anson, Bert. *The Miami Indians.* Norman: Univ. of Oklahoma Press, 1970.

Armstrong, William H. *Warrior in Two Camps: Ely S. Parker: Union General and Seneca Chief.* Syracuse, N.Y.: Syracuse Univ. Press, 1978.

Austin, Alberta, comp. *Ne Ho Ni Yo De: No—That's What It Was Like.* 2 vols. New York: Rebco Enterprises, 1986–89.

Axtell, James. *The Invasion Within: The Contest of Cultures in Colonial North America.* New York: Oxford Univ. Press, 1985.

Barbour, Hugh, et al., eds. *Quaker Crosscurrents: Three Hundred Years of Friends in the New York Yearly Meetings.* Syracuse, N.Y.: Syracuse Univ. Press, 1995.

Barton, Lois. *A Quaker Promise Kept: Philadelphia Friends' Work with the Allegany Seneca, 1795–1960.* Eugene, Ore.: Spencer Butte Press, 1990.

Beauchamp, William M. *A History of the New York Iroquois. New York State Museum Bulletin* 78. Albany, N.Y., 1905.

Belknap, Jeremy, *Journal of a Tour from Boston to Oneida, June 1796.* Edited by George Dexter. Cambridge, Mass.: John Wilson, 1882.

Benn, Carl. *The Iroquois in the War of 1812.* Toronto, Ont.: Univ. of Toronto Press, 1998.

Berkhofer, Robert F., Jr. *Salvation and the Savage: An Analysis of Protestant Missions and American Indian Response, 1787–1862.* Lexington: Univ. of Kentucky Press, 1965. Reprint. New York: Atheneum, 1976.

Bieder, Robert E. *Native American Communities in Wisconsin, 1600–1960: A Study of Tradition and Change.* Madison: Univ. of Wisconsin Press, 1995.

Bloomfield, Julia. *The Oneidas.* 2d ed. New York: Alden Bros., 1907.

Bouchette, Joseph. *The British Dominions in North America or a Topographical and Statistical Description of the Provinces of Lower and Upper Canada.* 2 vols. London: Longman, Rees, Orme, Brown, and Green and Longman, 1832.

Bourne, Russell. *Floating West: The Erie and Other American Canals.* New York: W. W. Norton, 1992.

Brown, Robert H. *The Republic in Peril: 1812.* New York: Columbia Univ. Press, 1964.

Brown, Thomas. *Politics and Statesmanship: Essays on the American Whig Party.* New

York: Columbia Univ. Press, 1985.

Calloway, Colin G. *The American Revolution in Indian Country: Crisis and Diversity in Native American Communities.* New York: Cambridge Univ. Press, 1995.

————. *Crowns and Calumet: British-Indian Relations, 1783–1815.* Norman: Univ. of Oklahoma Press, 1987.

Campbell, William W. *Annals of Tryon County.* Cherry Valley, N.Y.: Cherry Valley Gazette Printers, 1880.

————, ed. *The Life and Writings of De Witt Clinton.* New York: Baker and Scribner, 1949.

Campisi, Jack, Michael Foster, and Marianne Mithun, eds. *Extending the Rafters: Interdisciplinary Approaches to Iroquoian Studies.* Albany, N.Y.: State Univ. of New York Press, 1984.

Campisi, Jack, and Laurence M. Hauptman, eds. *The Oneida Indian Experience: Two Perspectives.* Syracuse, N.Y.: Syracuse Univ. Press, 1988.

Catlin, George. *Letters and Notes on the North American Indians.* Edited by Michael M. Mooney. 1825. Reprint. New York: Clarkson N. Potter, 1975.

Chazanof, William. *Joseph Ellicott and the Holland Land Company: The Opening of Western New York.* Syracuse, N.Y.: Syracuse Univ. Press, 1970.

Clark, John G. *The Grain Trade in the Old Northwest.* Urbana: Univ. of Illinois Press, 1966.

Clark, Joshua V. H. *Onondaga; or, Reminiscences of Early and Later Times.* 2 vols. Syracuse, N.Y.: Stoddard and Babcock, 1849.

Clarke, Joseph. *Travels among the Indians, 1797.* Doylestown, Pa.: Charles Ingerman, Quixott Press, 1968.

Clarke, T. Wood. *Utica: For a Century and a Half.* Utica, N.Y.: Widtman Press, 1952.

Cohen, Felix S. *Handbook of Federal Indian Law, 1942.* Reprint. Albuquerque: Univ. of New Mexico Press, 1972.

Colden, Cadwallader. *The History of the Five Nations Depending on the Province of New-York in America.* 1727. Reprint. Ithaca, N.Y.: Cornell Univ. Press, 1964.

————. *Memoir, Prepared at the Request of a Committee of the Common Council of the City of New York and Presented to the Mayor of the City at the Celebration of the Completion of the New York Canals.* New York: W. A. Davis, 1825. Reprint. Ann Arbor: Univ. Microfilms International, 1967.

Cole, Donald B. *Martin Van Buren and the American Political System.* Princeton, N.J.: Princeton Univ. Press, 1984.

Colles, Christopher. *Proposals for the Speedy Settlement of the Waste and Unappropriated Lands on the Western Frontiers of the State of New York, and for the Improvement of the Inland Navigation Between Albany and Oswego.* New York: Samuel London, 1785.

————. *Proposal of a Design for the Promotion of the Interests of the United States of America, Extending Its Advantages to All Ranks and Conditions of Men by Means of Inland Navigable Communication of a New Construction and Mode.* New York: Samuel Wood, 1808.

————. *A Survey of the Roads of the United States of America, 1789.* Edited by Walter W. Ristow. Cambridge, Mass.: Belknap Press, Harvard Univ. Press, 1961.

Colton, Calvin. *Tour of the American Lakes and among the Indians of the Northwest Territory in 1830.* 2 vols. (1833). Reprint. New York, 1972.

Congdon, Charles E. *Allegany Oxbow: A History of Allegany State Park and the Allegany Reserve of the Seneca Nation.* Little Valley, N.Y.: Straight Publishing, 1967.

Cornplanter, Jesse. *Legends of the Longhouse.* New York: Lippincott, 1938.

Covington, James W. *The Seminoles of Florida.* Gainesville: Univ. Press of Florida, 1993.

Croffut, W. A. *Fifty Years in Camp and Field: Diary of Major-General Ethan Allen Hitchcock.* New York: G. P. Putnam's Sons, 1909.

Cruikshank, E. A., ed. *The Documentary History of the Campaign Upon the Niagara Frontier, 1812–1814.* 9 vols. Welland, Ont.: Lundy's Lane Historical Society, 1896–1908.

Current, Richard N. *The History of Wisconsin: The Civil War Era, 1848–1873.* Madison: State Historical Society of Wisconsin, 1976.

Curtis, James C. *The Fox at Bay: Martin Van Buren and the Presidency.* Lexington: Univ. of Kentucky Press, 1970.

Cusick, David. *Sketches of Ancient History of the Six Nations 1827.* 2d ed. Lockport, N.Y.: Cooley and Lothrop, 1828.

Dearborn, Henry A. S. *Journals of Henry A. S. Dearborn.* Edited by Frank H. Severance. Buffalo Historical Society *Publications* 7. Buffalo, N.Y.: Buffalo Historical Society, 1904, 35–235.

Delafield, Joseph. *The Unfortified Boundary.* Edited by Robert MacElroy and Thomas Riggs. New York: Privately published, 1943.

Dilts, James D. *The Great Road: The Building of the Baltimore & Ohio, the Nation's First Railroad, 1828–1853.* Stanford, Calif.: Stanford Univ. Press, 1993.

Disturnell, John, comp. *A Gazetteer of the State of New-York.* Albany, N.Y., 1842.

Doty, Lockwood L. *History of Livingston County, New York.* Geneseo, N.Y.: Edward E. Doty, 1876; 2d ed., 2 vols. Jackson, Mich.: W. J. Van Deusen, 1905.

Doty, Lockwood R. *History of the Genesee Country.* 4 vols. Chicago.: S. J. Clarke Publishing, 1925.

Downes, Randolph C. *Council Fires on the Upper Ohio: A Narrative of Indian Affairs in the Uppper Ohio Valley Until 1795.* Pittsburgh, Pa.: Univ. of Pittsburgh, 1940.

Driver, Harold E. *Indians of North America.* Chicago: Univ. of Chicago Press, 1961.

Duncan, John M. *A Sabbath Among the Tuscarora Indians, a True Narrative.* 2d ed. Glasgow, U.K.: A. and J. M. Duncan, 1821.

Durrenberger, Joseph A. *Turnpikes: A Study of the Toll Road Movement in the Middle Atlantic States and Maryland.* Valdosta, Ga.: Southern Stationary Printing, 1931.

Ellicott, Joseph. *Holland Land Company Papers: Reports of Joseph Ellicott.* Publication 37. Edited by Robert W. Bingham. 2 vols. Buffalo, N.Y.: Buffalo Historical Society, 1941.

Ellis, Franklin. *History of Cattaraugus County, New York.* Philadelphia, Pa.: L. H. Everts, 1879.

Ellis, Richard E. *The Union at Risk: Jacksonian Democracy, States' Rights and the Nullification Crisis.* New York: Oxford Univ. Press, 1987.

Evans, Paul D. *The Holland Land Company.* Buffalo, N.Y.: Buffalo Historical Society, 1924.

Evarts, Jeremiah. *Cherokee Removal: The "William Penn" Essays and Other Writings.* Edited by Francis Paul Prucha. Knoxville: Univ. of Tennessee Press, 1981.

Fenton, William N. *American Indian and White Relations to 1830: Needs and Opportunities for Study.* Chapel Hill: Univ. of North Carolina Press, 1957.

———. *The Great Law and the Longhouse: A Political History of the Iroquois Confederacy.* Norman: Univ. of Oklahoma Press, 1998.

———. *The Iroquois Eagle Dance: An Offshoot of the Calumet Dance.* Washington, D.C.: Bureau of American Ethnology, 1953. Reprint. Syracuse, N.Y.: Syracuse Univ. Press, 1991.

———, ed. *Symposium on Local Diversity.* Bureau of American Ethnology Bulletin 149. Washington, D.C., 1951.

Fenton, William N., and John Gullick, eds. *Symposium on Cherokee and Iroquois Culture.* Bureau of American Ethnology Bulletin 180 (1961).

Ferguson, E. James, ed. *The Papers of Robert Morris.* 7 vols. Pittsburgh, Pa.: Univ. of Pittsburgh Press, 1973–88.

Finger, John R. *The Eastern Band of Cherokees, 1819–1900.* Knoxville: Univ. of Tennessee, 1984.

Fitzpatrick, John C., ed. *The Autobiography of Martin Van Buren.* 1920. Reprint. New York: Da Capo Press, 1973.

Flexner, James Thomas. *Mohawk Baronet: A Biography of Sir William Johnson.* 1959. Reprint. Syracuse, N.Y.: Syracuse Univ. Press, 1989.

Foreman, Grant. *The Last Trek of the Indians.* 1946. Reprint. New York: Russell and Russell, 1972.

Fowler, John. *Journal of a Tour in the State of New York, in the Year 1830.* London: Whittaker, Treacher and Arnot, 1831.

Fox, Dixon Ryan. *The Decline of Aristocracy in the Politics of New York, 1801–1840.* 1919. Reprint. Edited by Robert V. Remini. New York: Harper Torchbook, 1965.

Frazier, Patrick. *The Mohicans of Stockbridge.* Lincoln: Univ. of Nebraska Press, 1992.

French, J. H., comp. *Gazetteer of the State of New York.* Syracuse, N.Y.: R. Pearsall Smith, 1860.

Gabriel, Ralph. *Elias Boudinot, Cherokee, and His America.* Norman: Univ. of Oklahoma Press, 1941.

Garraty, John. *Silas Wright.* New York: Columbia Univ. Press, 1949.

Gerber, David A. *The Making of an American Pluralism: Buffalo, New York, 1825–1860.* Urbana: Univ. of Illinois Press, 1989.

Gerlach, Don R. *Proud Patriot: Philip Schuyler and the War of Independence, 1775–1783.* Syracuse, N.Y.: Syracuse Univ. Press, 1987.

Gibson, Arrell, ed. *America's Exiles: Indian Colonization in Oklahoma.* Oklahoma City: Oklahoma Historical Society, 1976.

Goldman, Mark. *High Hopes: The Rise and Decline of Buffalo.* Albany, N.Y.: State Univ. New York Press, 1983.

Goodrich, Carter, ed. *Canals and American Economic Development.* New York: Columbia Univ. Press, 1961.

————. *Government Promotion of American Canals and Railroads, 1800–1890.* New York: Columbia Univ. Press, 1960.

Gottschalk, Louis R. *Lafayette Between the American and the French Revolutions (1783–1789).* Chicago: Univ. of Chicago Press, 1950.

Graymont, Barbara. *The Iroquois in the American Revolution.* Syracuse, N.Y.: Syracuse Univ. Press, 1972.

Grumet, Robert S. *Historic Contact: Indian People and Colonists in Today's Northeastern United States in the Sixteenth Through Eighteenth Centuries.* Norman: Univ. of Oklahoma Press, 1995.

Gundersen, Robert G. *The Log-Cabin Campaign.* Lexington: Univ. of Kentucky Press, 1957.

Gunn, L. Ray. *The Decline of Authority: Public Economic Policy and Political Development in New York, 1800–1860.* Ithaca, N.Y.: Cornell Univ. Press, 1988.

Hagan, William T. *American Indians.* 3d ed. Chicago: Univ. of Chicago Press, 1993.

Hale, Horatio E. *The Iroquois Book of Rites.* 2 vols. Philadelphia, Pa.: D. G. Brinton, 1883.

Hammond, Jabez D. *The History of Political Parties in the State of New York.* 2 vols. Albany, N.Y.: Charles Van Benthuysen, 1842.

Hanson, Lee, and Dick Ping Hsu. *Casemates and Cannonballs: Archeological Investigations of Fort Stanwix, Rome, New York.* Washington, D.C.: National Park Service, 1975.

Hanyan, Craig. *De Witt Clinton and the Rise of the People's Men.* Montreal, Que.: McGill-Queen's Univ. Press, 1996.

Hauptman, Laurence M. *Between Two Fires: American Indians in the Civil War.* New York: Free Press, 1995.

————. *Formulating American Indian Policy in New York State, 1970–1986.* Albany, N.Y.: State Univ. of New York Press, 1988.

————. *The Iroquois and the New Deal.* Syracuse, N.Y.: Syracuse Univ. Press, 1981.

————. *The Iroquois in the Civil War: From Battlefield to Reservation.* Syracuse, N.Y.: Syracuse Univ. Press, 1993.

————. *The Iroquois Struggle for Survival: World War II to Red Power.* Syracuse, N.Y.: Syracuse Univ. Press, 1986.

————. *Tribes and Tribulations: Misconceptions About American Indians and Their Histories.* Albuquerque: Univ. of New Mexico Press, 1995.

Haydon, Roger, ed. *Upstate Travels: British Views of Nineteenth-Century New York.* Syracuse, N.Y.: Syracuse Univ. Press, 1982.

Hemphill, W. Edwin, Robert Lee Meriwether, and Clyde N. Wilson, eds. *The Papers of John C. Calhoun.* 16 vols. Columbia: Univ. of South Carolina Press, 1959–84.

Herrick, John P. *Empire Oil: The Story of Oil in the Empire State.* New York: Dodd, Mead, 1949.

Hewitt, J. N. B. *Iroquois Cosmology.* Pt. 1, Bureau of American Ethnology, *21st Annual Report.* Washington, D.C.: U.S. Government Printing Office, 1899–1900, 127–339.

————. *Iroquoian Cosmology.* Pt. 2, Bureau of American Ethnology, *Annual Report.* Washington, D.C.: Bureau of American Ethnology, 1928.

Hickey, Donald R. *The War of 1812: A Forgotten Conflict.* Urbana: Univ. of Illinois Press, 1989.

Hill, Forrest G. *Roads, Rails and Waterways: The Army Engineers and Early Transportation.* Norman: Univ. of Oklahoma Press, 1977.

Hitchcock, Ethan Allen. *A Traveler in Indian Territory: The Journal of Ethan Allen Hitchcock.* Edited by Grant Foreman. Cedar Rapids, Iowa: Torch Press, 1930.

Hitsman, J. Mackay. *The Incredible War of 1812.* Toronto, Ont.: Univ. of Toronto Press, 1965.

Hodge, Frederick Webb, ed. *Handbook of American Indians North of Mexico.* 2 vols. Washington, D.C.: U.S. Government Printing Office, 1907–10.

Horsman, Reginald. *Expansion and American Indian Policy, 1783–1812.* East Lansing: Michigan State Univ. Press, 1967.

———. *The Frontier in the Formative Years, 1783–1815.* New York: Holt, Rinehart and Winston, 1970.

Hosack, David, comp. *Memoir of De Witt Clinton.* New York: J. Seymour, 1829.

Hough, Franklin B. *Notices of Peter Penet and His Operations among the Oneida Indians.* Lowville, N.Y.: Albany Institute, 1866.

———, comp. *Proceedings of the Commissioners of Indian Affairs Appointed by Law for the Extinguishment of Indian Titles in the State of New York.* 2 vols. Albany, N.Y.: Munsell, 1861.

Houghton, Frederick. *The History of the Buffalo Creek Reservation.* Buffalo Historical Society *Publications* 24. Buffalo, N.Y.: Buffalo Historical Society, 1920.

Howe, Daniel Walker. *The Political Culture of the American Whigs.* Chicago: Univ. of Chicago Press, 1979.

Hulbert, Archer B. *Historic Highways of America.* Vol. 12, *Pioneer Roads and Experiences of Travelers.* Cleveland, Ohio: Arthur H. Clark, 1904.

Hungerford, Edward. *Men of Erie: A Story of Human Effort.* New York: Random House, 1946.

Hurt, R. Douglas. *Indian Agriculture: Prehistory to the Present.* Lawrence: Univ. Press of Kansas, 1987.

Idzerda, Stanley J., ed. *Lafayette in the Age of the American Revolution: Selected Letters and Papers, 1776–1790.* 2 vols. Ithaca, N.Y.: Cornell Univ. Press, 1977.

Israel, Fred L., ed. *The State of the Union Messages of the Presidents.* Vol. 1. New York: Chelsea House, 1967.

Jackson, Halliday. *Civilization of Indian Natives.* Philadelphia, Pa.: Marcus Gold, 1830.

Jackson, Harry F. *Scholar in the Wilderness: Francis Adrian Van der Kemp.* Syracuse, N.Y.: Syracuse Univ. Press, 1963.

Jennings, Francis. *Empire of Fortune: Crowns, Colonies and Tribes in the Seven Years War in America.* New York: W. W. Norton, 1988.

Jennings, Francis, William N. Fenton, et al., eds. *The History and Culture of Iroquois Diplomacy: An Interdisciplinary Guide to the Treaties of the Six Nations and Their League.* Syracuse, N.Y.: Syracuse Univ. Press, 1985.

Johnson, E. Roy. *The Tuscaroras: History—Traditions—Culture.* 2 vols. Murfreesboro, N.C.: Johnson Publishing, 1968.

Johnson, Elias. *Legends, Traditions and Laws of the Iroquois, or, Six Nations, and History of the Tuscarora Indians.* Lockport, N.Y.: Union Printing and Publishing, 1881.

Johnson, Marlene, comp. *Iroquois Cookbook.* 2d ed. Tonawanda Indian Reservation: Peter Doctor Memorial Fellowship Foundation, 1989.

Johnson, Sir William. *The Papers of Sir William Johnson.* 14 vols. Edited by James Sullivan et al. Albany, N.Y.: Univ. of the State of New York, 1921–65.

Johnston, Charles M., ed. *The Valley of the Six Nations.* Toronto, Ont.: Univ. of Toronto, 1964.

Jones, Howard. *To the Webster-Ashburton Treaty.* Chapel Hill: Univ. of North Carolina, 1977.

Kelsey, Isabel Thompson. *Joseph Brant, 1743–1807: Man of Two Worlds.* Syracuse, N.Y.: Syracuse Univ. Press, 1984.

Kelsey, Rayner W. *Friends and the Indians, 1655–1917.* Philadelphia, Pa.: Associated Committee of Friends on Indian Affairs, 1917.

Kent, James. *Commentaries on American Law.* 3 vols. New York: O. Halsted, 1826. Reprint. New York: Da Capo Press, 1971.

Ketchum, William. *An Authentic Comprehensive History of Buffalo.* 2 vols. Buffalo, N.Y.: Rockwell, Baker and Hill, 1864–65.

Klinch, Carl F., and James J. Talman, eds. *The Journal of Major John Norton, 1816.* Toronto, Ont.: Champlain Society, 1970.

Kvasnicka, Robert, and Herman Viola, eds. *The Commissioners of Indian Affairs, 1824–1977.* Lincoln: Univ. of Nebraska Press, 1979.

Lafitau, Joseph François. *Customs of the American Indians* (1724). 2 vols. Edited by William N. Fenton and translated by Elizabeth Moore. Toronto, Ont.: Champlain Society, 1974.

Larned, Josephus N. *A History of Buffalo, Delineating the Evolution of the City.* 2 vols. New York: Progress of the Empire State, 1911.

Lennox, H. J. *Samuel Kirkland's Mission to the Iroquois.* Chicago: Univ. of Chicago Libraries, 1935.

Liberty, Margot, ed. *American Indian Intellectuals.* St. Paul, Minn.: American Ethnological Society, 1978.

Lincklaen, Jan [John]. *Travels in the Years 1791 and 1792 in Pennsylvania, New York and Vermont: Journals of John Lincklaen, Agent of the Holland Land Company.* New York: G. P. Putnam's Sons, 1897.

Livermore, Shaw. *Early American Land Companies: Their Influence on Corporate Development.* Cambridge, Mass.: Harvard Univ. Press, 1939. Reprint. New York: Octagon Books, 1968.

Lord, Philip, Jr. *Heading West.* Albany, N.Y.: New York State Museum, 1991.

Lurie, Nancy O. *Wisconsin Indians.* Madison: State Historical Society of Wisconsin, 1987.

Luzader, John F., Louis Torres, and Orville W. Carroll. *Fort Stanwix.* Washington, D.C.: National Park Service, 1976.

Mahon, John K. *History of the Second Seminole War, 1835–1842.* Gainesville: Univ. Press of Florida, 1967.

Mancall, Peter C. *Deadly Medicine: Indians and Alcohol in Early America*. Ithaca, N.Y.: Cornell Univ. Press, 1995.

Manley, Henry S. *The Treaty of Fort Stanwix, 1784*. Rome, N.Y.: Sentinel, 1932.

Martin, Albro. *Railroads Triumphant: The Growth, Rejection, and Rebirth of a Vital American Force*. New York: Oxford Univ. Press, 1992.

Martin, Deborah B. *History of Brown County, Wisconsin: Past and Present*. Chicago: S. J. Clarke, 1913.

Martineau, Harriet. *Retrospect of Western Travel*. 3 vols. London: Saunders and Otley, 1838.

Mau, Clayton, ed. *The Development of Central and Western New York*. New York: DuBois Press, 1944.

Maximilian, Prince of Wied. *Travels in the Interior of North America*. Translated by H. Evans Lloyd. London: Ackerman, 1843.

McCallum, James Dow, ed. *The Letters of Eleazar Wheelock's Indians*. Hanover, N.H.: Dartmouth College, 1932.

McKelvey, Blake. *Rochester on the Genesee: The Growth of a City*. Syracuse, N.Y.: Syracuse Univ. Press, 1973.

————. *Rochester: The Water-Power City, 1812–1854*. Cambridge, Mass.: Harvard Univ. Press, 1945.

McNall, Neil Adams. *An Agricultural History of the Genesee Valley, 1790–1860*. Philadelphia: Univ. of Pennsylvania Press, 1952.

Meinig, D. W. *The Shaping of America: A Geographical Perspective on 500 Years of History*. 2 vols. New Haven, Conn.: Yale Univ. Press, 1986 and 1993.

Miller, Nathan. *The Enterprise of a Free People: Aspects of Economic Development in New York State During the Canal Era, 1792–1838*. Ithaca, N.Y.: Cornell Univ. Press, 1962.

Minard, John S. *History of Allegany County*. New York: W. A. Ferguson, 1876.

————. *The Indian Oil Spring*. Gowanda, N.Y.: Privately published, 1901.

Mitchell, Stewart. *Horatio Seymour of New York*. Cambridge, Mass.: Harvard Univ. Press, 1938.

Mogavero, I. Frank. "The Joint Mixed Boundary Commission under the Treaty of Ghent." Paper delivered at the sixth College Conference on New York History, D'Youville College, Buffalo, N.Y. Pamphlet found in New York State Library.

Morgan, Lewis Henry. *League of the Ho-de-no-sau-nee, or Iroquois*. Rochester, N.Y.: Sage and Bros., 1851. Reprint. Edited by William N. Fenton. New York: Corinth Books, 1962.

Morris, Richard, ed. *John Jay: The Making of a Revolutionary: Unpublished Papers, 1745–1780*. 2 vols. New York: Harper and Row, 1975.

Moss, Richard J. *The Life of Jedidiah Morse: A Station of Peculiar Exposure*. Knoxville: Univ. of Tennessee Press, 1995.

Moulton, Gary E. *John Ross: Cherokee Chief*. Athens: Univ. of Georgia Press, 1978.

————, ed. *The Papers of Chief John Ross*. 2 vols. Norman: Univ. of Oklahoma Press, 1985.

Namias, June. *White Captives: Gender and Ethnicity on the American Frontier*. Chapel Hill: Univ. of North Carolina Press, 1993.

Niven, John. *John C. Calhoun and the Price of Union: A Biography.* Baton Rouge:
    Louisiana State Univ. Press, 1988.

————. *Martin Van Buren: The Romantic Age of American Politics.* New York:
    Oxford Univ. Press, 1983.

O'Callaghan, Edmund B., ed. *Documentary History of the State of New York.* 4 vols.
    Albany, N.Y.: Weed, Parsons, 1849–51.

O'Callaghan, Edmund B., and Berthold Fernow, eds. *Documents Relative to the
    Colonial History of the State of New York.* 15 vols. Albany, N.Y.: Weed, Parsons,
    1853–87.

O'Reilly, Henry. *Sketches of Rochester.* Rochester, N.Y.: William Alling, 1838.

Ourada, Patricia K. *The Menominee Indians: A History.* Norman: Univ. of Oklahoma
    Press, 1979.

Parker, Arthur C. *The Life of General Ely S. Parker, Last Grand Sachem of the Iroquois
    and General Grant's Military Secretary.* Buffalo Historical Society *Publications* 23.
    Buffalo, N.Y.: Buffalo Historical Society, 1919.

————. *Parker on the Iroquois.* Edited by William N. Fenton. Syracuse, N.Y.:
    Syracuse Univ. Press, 1968.

————. *Seneca Myths and Folk Tales.* 1923. Reprint. With an introduction by
    William N. Fenton. Lincoln: Univ. of Nebraska Press, 1989.

Peterson, Merrill D. *The Great Triumvirate: Webster, Clay, and Calhoun.* New York:
    Oxford Univ. Press, 1987.

Phillips, Joseph W. *Jedidiah Morse and New England Congregationalism.* New
    Brunswick, N.J.: Rutgers Univ. Press, 1983.

Pierce, Harry H. *Railroads of New York: A Study of Government Aid, 1826–1875.*
    Cambridge, Mass.: Harvard Univ. Press, 1953.

Pierce, Maris B. *Address on the Present Condition and Prospects of the Aboriginal
    Inhabitants of North America with Particular Reference to the Seneca Nation.*
    Speech at the Baptist Church in Buffalo, N.Y., Aug. 28, 1838. Buffalo, N.Y.:
    Steele's Press, 1838. Pamphlet.

Pierson, George Wilson. *Tocqueville and Beaumont in America.* New York: Oxford
    Univ. Press, 1938.

Pilkington, Walter, ed. *The Journals of Samuel Kirkland.* Clinton, N.Y.: Hamilton
    College, 1980.

Poor, Henry Varnum. *History of the Railroads and Canals of the United States of
    America.* New York: A. M. Kelley, 1970.

Prucha, Francis Paul. *American Indian Policy in the Formative Years: The Indian Trade
    and Intercourse Acts, 1790–1834.* Cambridge, Mass.: Harvard Univ. Press, 1962.

————. *American Indian Treaties: The History of a Political Anomaly.* Berkeley and
    Los Angeles: Univ. of California Press, 1994.

————. *The Great Father: The United States Government and the American Indians.*
    2 vols. Lincoln: Univ. of Nebraska Press, 1984.

Quimby, Robert S. *The U.S. Army in the War of 1812: An Operational and Command
    Study.* 2 vols. East Lansing: Michigan State Univ. Press, 1997.

Rayback, Robert, ed. *Richards Atlas of New York State.* Rev. ed. Phoenix, N.Y.: Frank
    E. Richards, 1965.

Remini, Robert V. *Andrew Jackson and the Course of American Empire.* 3 vols. New York: Harper and Row, 1977–84.

———. *Henry Clay: Statesman for the Union.* New York: W. W. Norton, 1991.

———. *Martin Van Buren and the Making of the Democratic Party.* New York: Columbia Univ. Press, 1959.

Richards, Cara E. *The Oneida People.* Phoenix, Ariz.: Indian Tribal Series, 1974.

Richter, Daniel K. *The Ordeal of the Longhouse: The Peoples of the Iroquois League in the Era of European Colonization.* Chapel Hill: Univ. of North Carolina Press, 1992.

Richter, Daniel K., and James H. Merrell, eds. *Beyond the Covenant Chain: The Iroquois and Their Neighbors in Indian North America, 1600–1800.* Syracuse, N.Y.: Syracuse Univ. Press, 1987.

Ristow, Walter W. *American Maps and Mapmakers.* Detroit, Mich.: Wayne State Univ. Press, 1985.

Ritzenthaler, Robert E. *The Oneida Indians of Wisconsin.* Public Museum of the City of Milwaukee *Bulletin* 19 (Nov. 1950): 1–50.

Royce, C. C., comp. *Indian Land Cessions in the United States.* Bureau of American Ethnology. *18th Annual Report, 1896–1897.* Part 2. Washington, D.C.: U.S. Government Printing Office, 1899.

Russo, David J. *The Major Political Issues of the Jacksonian Period and the Development of Party Loyalty in Congress, 1830–1840.* Transactions of the American Philosophical Society, 62, pt. 5. Philadelphia, Pa.: American Philosophical Society, 1972.

Ryan, Mary P. *Cradle of the Middle Class: The Family in Oneida County, New York, 1790–1865.* Cambridge, U.K.: Cambridge Univ. Press, 1981.

Sakolski, A. M. *The Great American Land Bubble.* New York: Harper and Bros., 1932.

Satz, Ronald. *American Indian Policy in the Jacksonian Era.* Lincoln: Univ. of Nebraska Press, 1975.

Savery, William. *A Journal of the Life, Travels, and Religious Labours of William Savery, Late of Philadelphia, A Minister of the Gospel of Christ, in the Society of Friends.* London: Charles Gilpin, 1844.

Schoolcraft, Henry R. *Narrative Journal of Travels Through the Northwestern Regions of the United States Extending from Detroit Through the Great Chain of American Lakes to the Sources of the Mississippi in the Year 1820.* Edited by Mentor L. Williams. East Lansing: Michigan State Univ. Press, 1953.

———. *Notes on the Iroquois, or Contributions to American History, Antiquities and General Ethnology.* Albany, N.Y.: Erastus H. Pense, 1847.

Seaver, James E., comp. *A Narrative of the Life of Mrs. Mary Jemison.* 1824. Reprint. With a foreword by George H. J. Abrams. Syracuse, N.Y.: Syracuse Univ. Press, 1990.

———. *A Narrative of the Life of Mrs. Mary Jemison.* 1824. Reprint. With an introduction by June Namias. Norman: Univ. of Oklahoma Press, 1992.

Severance, Frank H., ed. *Correspondence on the Holland Land Company and Canal Construction in Western New York: Buffalo–Black Rock Harbor Papers. Journals and Documents.* Buffalo Historical Society *Publications* 14. Buffalo, N.Y.: Buffalo Historical Society, 1910.

Seward, William H. *The Works of William H. Seward.* 4 vols. Edited by George E. Baker. Boston, Mass.: Houghton, Mifflin, 1884.

Shattuck, George C. *The Oneida Indians Land Claims: A Legal History.* Syracuse, N.Y.: Syracuse Univ. Press, 1991.

Shaw, Ronald E. *Canals for a Nation: The Canal Era in the United States, 1790–1860.* Lexington: Univ. Press of Kentucky, 1990.

———. *Erie Water West: A History of the Erie Canal, 1792–1854.* Lexington: Univ. Press of Kentucky, 1966.

Sheriff, Carol. *The Artificial River: The Erie Canal and the Paradox of Progress, 1817–1862.* New York: Hill and Wang, 1996.

Sherman, Daniel. "The Six Nations." Speech delivered before the Chautauqua Society of History and Natural Science, Jamestown, N.Y., Jan. 29, 1885. Cleveland, Ohio: W. W. Williams, 1885. Pamphlet found in New York State Library.

Shirreff, Patrick. *A Tour Through North America.* Edinburgh, U.K.: Oliver and Boyd, 1835.

Smith, Alice. *The History of Wisconsin.* Vol. 1, *From Exploration to Statehood.* Madison: State Historical Society of Wisconsin, 1973.

Smith, H. Perry. *History of the City of Buffalo and Erie County.* 2 vols. Syracuse, N.Y.: D. Mason, 1884.

Smith, Richard. *A Tour of the Hudson, the Mohawk, the Susquehanna and the Delaware in 1769.* Edited by Francis W. Halsey. 1906. Reprint. Fleischmanns, N.Y.: Purple Mountain Press, 1989.

Snow, Dean, Charles Gehring, and William A. Starna, eds. *In Mohawk Country: Early Narratives About a Native People.* Syracuse, N.Y.: Syracuse Univ. Press, 1996.

Snyder, Charles M., ed. *Red and White on the New York Frontier. A Struggle for Survival. Insights from the Papers of Erastus Granger, 1807–1819.* Harrison, N.Y.: Harbor Hill Books, 1978.

Society of Friends (Hicksite). Executive Committee. *Report of the Proceedings of an Indian Council at Cattaraugus in the State of New York, 1843.* Baltimore, Md.: William Wooddy, 1843.

———. Executive Committee of the Yearly Meetings. *Report of the Proceedings of an Indian Council Held at the Buffalo Creek Reservation, State of New York, Fourth Month, 1842.* (Includes Proceedings of the Second Indian Council Held at the Buffalo Creek Reservation, State of New York, fifth month, 1842.) Baltimore, Md.: William Wooddy for the Executive Committee of the Yearly Meetings, 1842.

———. Joint Committee on Indian Affairs. *The Case of the Seneca Indians in the State of New York.* Philadelphia, Pa.: Merrihew and Thompson, 1840. Reprint with Quaker pamphlets dated 1841 and 1872. Stanfordville, N.Y.: Earl M. Coleman, 1979.

Spafford, Horatio Gates. *A Gazetteer of the State of New-York.* Albany, N.Y.: B. D. Packard, 1824.

Stagg, J. C. A. *Mr. Madison's War.* Princeton, N.J.: Princeton Univ. Press, 1983.

Stevens, Kenneth R. *Border Diplomacy.* Tuscaloosa: Univ. of Alabama Press, 1989.

Stone, William L. *The Life and Times of Red Jacket or Sa-go-ye-wat-ha; Being the Sequel to the History of the Six Nations.* New York: Wiley and Putnam, 1841. Reprint. Albany, N.Y.: Joel Munsell, 1866.

———. *Life of Joseph Brant-Thayendanegea, Including the Border Wars of the American Revolution.* 2 vols. New York: George Dearborn, 1838.

———. *Narrative of the Festivities Observed in Honor of the Completion of the Grand Erie Canal.* In *Memoir, Prepared at the Request of a Committee of the Common Council of the City of New York and Presented to the Mayor of the City at the Celebration of the Completion of the New York Canals,* compiled by Cadwallader D. Colden. New York: W. A. Davis, 1825. Reprint. Ann Arbor: Univ. Microfilms International, 1967, 289–408.

Syrett, Harold C., et al., ed. *The Papers of Alexander Hamilton.* 27 vols. New York: Columbia Univ. Press, 1961–87.

Tanner, Helen Hornbeck, et al., eds. *Atlas of Great Lakes Indian History.* Norman: Univ. of Oklahoma Press, 1987.

Taylor, Francis R. *Life of William Savery of Philadelphia (1750–1804).* New York: Macmillan, 1925.

Taylor, George Rogers. *The Transportation Revolution, 1815–1860.* New York: Rinehart, 1951.

Tocqueville, Alexis de. *Democracy in America.* 2d ed. Translated by Henry Reeve, preface and notes by John C. Spencer. New York: Adlard, 1838.

———. *Journey to America.* Translated by George Lawrence and edited by J. P. Mayer and A. P. Kerr. Reprint. Garden City, N.Y.: Doubleday, Anchor Paperbacks, 1971.

Tooker, Elisabeth. *The Iroquois Ceremonial of Midwinter.* Syracuse, N.Y.: Syracuse Univ. Press, 1970.

———, ed. *Proceedings* of the 1965 Conference on Iroquois Research. Albany, N.Y.: New York State Museum and Science Service, 1967.

Trennert, Robert A., Jr. *Indian Traders on the Middle Border: The House of Ewing, 1827–1854.* Lincoln: Univ. of Nebraska Press, 1981.

Trigger, Bruce G., ed. *Handbook of North American Indians.* Vol. 15, *The Northeast.* Washington, D.C.: Smithsonian Institution, 1978.

Trigger, Bruce G., and Wilcomb E. Washburn. *The Cambridge History of the Native Peoples of the Americas: North America.* 2 vols. Cambridge, U.K.: Cambridge Univ. Press, 1996.

Trollope, Francis Milton. *Domestic Manners of the Americans* (1832). Edited by Donald Smalley. Reprint. Gloucester, Mass.: Peter Smith, 1974.

Truettner, William H. *The Natural Man Observed: A Study of Catlin's Indian Gallery.* Washington, D.C.: Smithsonian Institution Press, 1979.

Turner, Orasmus. *History of Phelps and Gorham's Purchase.* Rochester, N.Y.: William Alling, 1851.

———. *Pioneer History of the Holland Purchase of Western New York.* Buffalo, N.Y.: George H. Derby, 1850.

Tuttle, Sarah. *Letters and Conversations on the Indian Missions at Seneca, Tuscarora, Cattaraugus, in the State of New York, and Maumee in Ohio.* Boston: Massachusetts Sabbath School Union, 1831.

Tyler, Lyon G. *The Letters and Times of the Tylers.* 2 vols. Richmond, Va.: Whittet and Shepperson, 1885.

Upton, Helen M. *The Everett Report in Historical Perspective: The Indians of New York.* Albany, N.Y.: New York State American Revolution Bicentennial Commission, 1980.

Vance, James E., Jr. *Capturing the Horizon: The Historical Geography of Transportation since the Transportation Revolution of the Sixteenth Century.* New York: Harper and Row, 1986.

Vandewater, Robert J. *The Tourist Pocket Manual for Travelers on the Hudson River, the Western Canal and Stage Road to Niagara Falls.* New York: Harper and Bros., 1834.

Van Every, Dale. *Disinherited: The Lost Birthright of the American Indians.* New York: Avon Books, 1966.

Vecsey, Christopher, and William A. Starna, eds. *Iroquois Land Claims.* Syracuse, N.Y.: Syracuse Univ. Press, 1988.

Viola, Herman, J. *Diplomats in Buckskin: A History of Indian Delegations in Washington City.* Washington, D.C.: Smithsonian Institution Press, 1981.

————. *Thomas L. McKenney: Architect of America's Early Indian Policy, 1816–1830.* Chicago: Swallow Press, 1974.

Wallace, Anthony F. C. *The Death and Rebirth of the Seneca.* New York: Alfred A. Knopf, 1969.

Washburn, Wilcomb E., ed. *The American Indian and the United States: A Documentary History.* 4 vols. Westport, Conn.: Greenwood, 1973.

Watson, Elkanah. *History of the Rise and Progress and Existing Condition of the Western Canals in the State of New York.* New York: D. Steele, 1820.

Watson, Winslow C. *Men and Times of the Revolution; or, Memoirs of Elkanah Watson.* New York: Dana, 1956.

Waugh, Frederick W. *Iroquois Foods and Food Preparation.* Anthropological Series 12, Memoirs of the Canadian Geological Survey 86. Ottawa, Ont., 1916.

White, Richard. *The Middle Ground: Indians, Empires, and Republics in the Great Lakes Region, 1650–1815.* New York: Cambridge Univ. Press, 1991.

Wilson, Major L. *The Presidency of Martin Van Buren.* Lawrence: Univ. Press of Kansas, 1984.

Wyckoff, William. *The Developers Frontier: The Making of the Western New York Landscape.* New Haven, Conn.: Yale Univ. Press, 1988.

ARTICLES

Abler, Thomas S. "Friends, Factions and the Seneca Nation Revolution of 1848." *Niagara Frontier* 21 (Winter 1974): 74–79.

————. "Protestant Missionaries and Native Cultures: Parallel Careers of Asher

Wright and Silas T. Rand." *American Indian Quarterly* 26 (Winter 1992): 25–37.

Abler, Thomas S., and Elisabeth Tooker. "Seneca." In *Handbook of the North American Indians.* Vol. 15, *The Northeast,* edited by Bruce G. Trigger. Washington, D.C.: Smithsonian Institution, 1978, 505–17.

Allen, Lewis F. "The Founding of the City of Ararat on Grand Island by Mordecai M. Noah." In Buffalo Historical Society *Publications* 1. Buffalo, N.Y.: Bigelow Bros. for the Buffalo Historical Society, 1879, 305–7.

Allen, Orlando. "Personal Recollections of Captain Jones and Parrish, and the Payment of Indian Annuities in Buffalo." In Buffalo Historical Society *Publications* 6, edited by Frank H. Severance. Buffalo, N.Y.: Buffalo Historical Society, 1903, 539–46.

Avery, Joseph. "Visit of Rev. Joseph Avery." In Buffalo Historical Society *Publications* 6, edited by Frank H. Severance. Buffalo, N.Y.: Buffalo Historical Society, 1903, 223–30.

Bacon, David. "Rev. David Bacon's Visits to Buffalo in 1800." In Buffalo Historical Society *Publications* 6, edited by Frank H. Severance. Buffalo, N.Y.: Buffalo Historical Society, 1903, 183–86.

Barsness, John C. "John C. Calhoun and the Military Establishment, 1817–1825." *Wisconsin Magazine of History* 50 (Autumn 1966): 43–53.

Bauman, Richard. "An Analysis of Quaker-Seneca Councils: 1798–1800." *Man in the Northeast* (1972): 49–54.

Berkhofer, Robert F., Jr. "Faith and Factionalism among the Senecas: Theory and Ethnohistory." *Ethnohistory* 12 (1965): 99–112.

Billington, Ray Allen. "The Fort Stanwix Treaty of 1768." *New York History* 25 (1944): 182–94.

Bingham, Robert W. "The History of Grand Island." In *Niagara Frontier Miscellany,* edited by Robert W. Bingham. Buffalo Historical Society *Publications* 34. Buffalo, N.Y.: Buffalo Historical Society, 1947, 59–78.

Bird, William A. "Reminiscences of the Boundary Survey Between the United States and the British Provinces." In Buffalo Historical Society *Publications* 4. Buffalo, N.Y.: Buffalo Historical Society, 1896, 1–14.

Blau, Harold. "The Iroquois White Dog Sacrifice: Its Evolution and Symbolism." *Ethnohistory* 11 (1964): 97–119.

Blau, Harold, Jack Campisi, and Elisabeth Tooker. "Onondaga." In *Handbook of North American Indians.* Vol. 15, *The Northeast,* edited by Bruce G. Trigger. Washington, D.C.: Smithsonian Institution, 1978, 491–99.

Borchert, John R. "American Metropolitan Evolution." *Geographic Review* 57 (1967): 301–33.

Burke, Joseph C. "The Cherokee Cases: A Study in Law, Politics, and Morality." *Stanford Law Review* 21 (Feb. 1969): 500–531.

Burrows, Roswell. "Visit of Rev. Roswell Burrows, 1806." In Buffalo Historical Society *Publications* 6, edited by Frank H. Severance. Buffalo, N.Y.: Buffalo Historical Society, 1903, 231–38.

Campisi, Jack. "Consequences of the Kansas Claims to Oneida Tribal Identity." In *Proceedings* of the First Congress, Canadian Ethnology Society, edited by Jerome

H. Barkow. Ottawa, Ont.: Canada National Museum of Man, Ethnology Division. Mercury ser. 17 (1974), 35–47.

————. "New York–Oneida Treaty of 1795: A Finding of Fact." *American Indian Law Review* 4 (Summer 1976): 71–82.

————. "Oneida." In *Handbook of North American Indians*. Vol. 15, *The Northeast*, edited by Bruce G. Trigger. Washington, D.C.: Smithsonian Institution, 1978, 481–90.

————. "The Oneida Treaty Period, 1783–1838." In *The Oneida Indian Experience: Two Perspectives,* edited by Jack Campisi and Laurence Hauptman. Syracuse, N.Y.: Syracuse Univ. Press, 1988.

Chernow, Barbara A. "Robert Morris: Genesee Land Speculator." *New York History* 58 (Apr. 1977): 195–220.

Coates, Isaac. "Journal of Journeys to the Indian Country." *The Friends' Intelligencer and Journal* 44 (1887), sec. 2: 468–70; sec. 3: 482–84; sec. 8: 562–64; sec. 9: 557–80; sec. 10: 593–95; sec. 11: 610–12.

Colman, Henry. "Recollections of Oneida Indians, 1840–1845." In *Proceedings* of the State Historical Society at its Fifty-ninth Annual Meeting. Madison, Wis.: State Historical Society, 1912, 152–59.

Cope, Alfred. "Mission to the Menominee: A Quaker's Green Bay Diary." *Wisconsin Magazine of History* 49 (1966): 302–23; 50 (1966): 18–42, 120–44, 211–41.

Covell, Lemuel. "Visit of Rev. Lemuel Covell to Western New York and Canada, 1803." In Buffalo Historical Society *Publications* 6, edited by Frank H. Severance. Buffalo, N.Y.: Buffalo Historical Society, 1903, 207–17.

Cumming, John, ed. "A Missionary among the Senecas: The Journal Bingham, 1822–1828." *New York History* 60 (Apr. 1979): 157–93.

Davidson, John Nelson. "The Coming of the New York Indians to Wisconsin." In *Proceedings* of the State Historical Society of Wisconsin 47. Madison, Wis.: Democrat Printing, 1899, 153–85.

Deardorff, Merle, and George Snyderman. "A Nineteenth-Century Journal of a Visit to the Indians of New York." *Proceedings* of the American Philosophical Society 100 (Dec. 1956): 582–612.

Densmore, Christopher. "More on Red Jacket's Reply." *New York Folklore* 13 (1986): 121–22.

Draper, Lyman C. "Additional Notes on Eleazer Williams." *Wisconsin Historical Collections* 8 (1879): 353–69. Reprint. Madison: State Historical Society of Wisconsin, 1908.

Elkinton, Joseph. "The Quaker Mission among the Indians of New York State." In Buffalo Historical Society *Publications* 18. Buffalo, N.Y.: Buffalo Historical Society, 1914, 169–89.

Ellis, Albert G. "Fifty-four Years' Recollections of Men and Events in Wisconsin." *Wisconsin Historical Collections* 7 (1876): 207–68. Reprint. Madison: State Historical Society of Wisconsin, 1908.

————. "Recollections of Rev. Eleazer Williams." *Wisconsin Historical Collections* 8 (1879): 322–52. Reprint. Madison: State Historical Society of Wisconsin, 1908.

————. "Some Accounts of the Advent of the New York Indians into Wisconsin." *Wisconsin Historical Collections* 2 (1856): 415–49.

Evans, Griffith. "Journal of Griffith Evans, 1784–1785." Edited by Hallock F. Raup. *Pennsylvania Magazine of History and Biography* 65 (1941): 202–33.

Evans, Paul D. "The Frontier Pushed Westward." In *History of the State of New York.* Vol. 5, *Conquering the Wilderness,* edited by Alexander C. Flick. New York: Columbia Univ. Press, 1934.

Fenton, William N., ed. "Answers to Governor Cass's Questions by Jacob Jameson, a Seneca (ca. 1821–1825)." *Ethnohistory* 16 (Spring 1969): 113–39.

————, ed. "A Further Note on Jacob Jameson's Answers to the Lewis Cass Questionnaire." *Ethnohistory* 17 (1970): 91–92.

————. "The Iroquois in History." In *North American Indians in Historical Perspective,* edited by Nancy O. Lurie and Eleanor Leacock. New York: Random House, 1971, 129–68.

————, ed. "The Journal of James Emlen Kept on a Trip to Canandaigua, N.Y., September 15 to October 30, 1794, to Attend the Treaty Between the United States and the Six Nations." *Ethnohistory* 12 (1965): 279–342.

————. "Locality as a Basic Factor in the Development of Iroquois Social Structure." Bureau of American Ethnology *Bulletin* 149 (1951): 302–21.

————. "Northern Iroquoian Culture Patterns." In *Handbook of North American Indians.* Vol. 15, *The Northeast,* edited by Bruce Trigger. Washington, D.C.: Smithsonian Institution, 1978, 296–321.

————, ed. "Seneca Indians by Asher Wright (1859)." *Ethnohistory* 4 (1957): 302–21.

————. "Toward the Gradual Civilization of the Indian Natives: The Missionary and Linguistic Work of Asher Wright (1803–1875) among the Senecas of Western New York." *Proceedings* of the American Philosophical Society 100 (1956): 567–81.

Galpin, W. Freeman. "The Genesis of Syracuse." *New York History* 30 (Jan. 1949): 19–32.

Graymont, Barbara. "New York State Indian Policy after the Revolution." *New York History* 58 (Oct. 1976): 438–74.

————. "The Oneidas and the American Revolution." In *The Oneida Indian Experience: Two Perspectives,* edited by Jack Campisi and Laurence M. Hauptman. Syracuse, N.Y.: Syracuse Univ. Press, 1998, 31–42.

Gunther, Gerald. "Governmental Power and New York Indian Lands—A Reassessment of a Persistent Problem of Federal-State Relations." *Buffalo Law Review* 7 (Fall 1958): 1–14.

Hall, Niki, and Thomas Blosoom. "The Postal Service of the United States in Connection with the Local History of Buffalo." In Buffalo Historical Society *Publications* 4. Buffalo, N.Y.: Peter Paul Book, 1896, 299–315.

Harris, Frank H. "Neosho Agency, 1838–1871." *The Chronicles of Oklahoma* 43 (1965): 35–58.

Harris, George H. "The Life of Horatio Jones." In Buffalo Historical Society *Publications* 6, edited by Frank H. Severance. Buffalo, N.Y.: Buffalo Historical Society, 1903, 381–514.

Harris, Thompson S. "Journals of Rev. Thompson S. Harris, Missionary to the Senecas, 1821–1828." In Buffalo Historical Society *Publications* 6, edited by Frank H. Severance. Buffalo, N.Y.: Buffalo Historical Society, 1903, 281–380.

Hauptman, Laurence M. "Compensatory Justice: The Seneca Nation Settlement Act." *National Forum* 71 (Spring 1991): 31–33.

———. "Four Eastern New Yorkers and Seneca Lands: A Study in Treaty-Making." *Hudson Valley Regional Review* 13 (Mar. 1996): 1–19.

———. "The Historical Background to the Present-Day Seneca Nation–Salamanca Lease Controversy: The First Hundred Years, 1851–1951." Working paper no. 20, Nelson A. Rockefeller Institute of Government, 1985: 1–23.

———. "Refugee Havens: The Iroquois Villages of the Eighteenth Century." In *American Indian Environments,* edited by Christopher Vecsey and Robert W. Venables. Syracuse, N.Y.: Syracuse Univ. Press, 1980, 128–39.

———. "Samuel George (1795–1873): A Study of Onondaga Indian Conservatism." *New York History* 70 (Jan. 1989): 4–22.

———. "State's Men, Salvation Seekers and the Senecas: The Supplemental Treaty of Buffalo Creek, 1842." *New York History* 78 (Jan. 1997): 51–82.

Hogan, Thomas E. "City in a Quandary: Salamanca and the Allegany Leases." *New York History* 55 (Jan. 1974): 79–117.

Holmes, Elkanah. "Letters of Rev. Elkanah Holmes from Fort Niagara." In Buffalo Historical Society *Publications* 6, edited by Frank H. Severance. Buffalo, N.Y.: Buffalo Historical Society, 1903, 187–206.

Holmes, Oliver W. "The Turnpike Era." In *History of the State of New York,* edited by Alexander C. Flick. New York: Columbia Univ. Press, 1934, 257–93.

Hopkins, Gerard. "Visiting of Gerard T. Hopkins: A Quaker Ambassador to the Indians Who Visited Buffalo in 1804." In Buffalo Historical Society *Publications* 6, edited by Frank H. Severance. Buffalo, N.Y.: Buffalo Historical Society, 1903, 217–22.

Hopkins, Vivian C. "De Witt Clinton and the Iroquois." *Ethnohistory* 8 (Spring 1961): 113–43; (Summer 1961): 213–41.

Horsman, Reginald. "The Origins of Oneida Removal to Wisconsin, 1815–1822." In *An Anthology of Western Great Lakes Indian History,* edited by Donald Fixico. Milwaukee: American Indian Studies Program of the University of Wisconsin, Milwaukee, 1987, 203–32.

Houghton, Frederick. "Report on Neuter [*sic*] Cemetery, Grand Island, N.Y." Buffalo Society of Natural Sciences *Bulletin* 9, no. 3 (1909): 376–85.

Howland, Henry R. "The Old Caneadea Council House and Its Last Council." In Buffalo Historical Society *Publications* 6, edited by Frank H. Severance. Buffalo, N.Y.: Buffalo Historical Society, 1903, 34–40. Reprint. Perry, N.Y.: Comfort Craftsmen, 1932. (The reprint contains a supplement about Letchworth State Park.)

———. "The Seneca Mission at Buffalo Creek." In Buffalo Historical Society *Publications* 6, edited by Frank H. Severance. Buffalo, N.Y.: Buffalo Historical Society, 1903, 125–61.

Hyde, Jabez Backus. "A Teacher among the Senecas: A Narrative of Rev. Jabez Backus Hyde, 1811–1820." In Buffalo Historical Society *Publications* 6, edited by Frank H. Severance. Buffalo, N.Y.: Buffalo Historical Society, 1903, 239–74.

Jackson, Halliday. "Halliday Jackson's Journal to the Seneca Indians, 1798–1800."

Edited by Anthony F. C. Wallace. *Pennsylvania History* 19 (Apr. 1952): 117–47; (July 1952): 325–449.

Kemper, Jackson. "Journal of an Episcopalian Missionary's Tour to Green Bay, 1834." *Wisconsin Historical Collections* 14 (1898): 394–449.

Kent, Donald H. "Historical Report on the Niagara River and the Niagara River Strip to 1759." In *Iroquois Indians II. Commission Findings: Indian Claims Commission.* New York: Garland Publishing, 1974, 1–177.

Kent, Donald H., and Merle H. Deardorff, eds. "John Adlun on the Allegheny: Memoirs for the Year 1794." *Pennsylvania Magazine of History and Biography* 84 (1960): 265–324, 435–80.

Lehman, J. David. "The End of the Iroquois Mystique: The Oneida Land Cession Treaties of the 1780s." *William and Mary Quarterly* 47 (Oct. 1990): 523–47.

Lindley, Jacob. "Jacob Lindley's Journal, 1797." In Buffalo Historical Society *Publications* 6, edited by Frank H. Severance. Buffalo, N.Y.: Buffalo Historical Society, 1903, 165–68.

Low, Esther Rutgers. "Narrative of Esther Rutgers Low, 1819–1820." In Buffalo Historical Society *Publications* 6, edited by Frank H. Severance. Buffalo, N.Y.: Buffalo Historical Society, 1903, 275–80.

Mahon, John K. "Two Seminole Treaties: Payne's Landing, 1832, and Fort Gibson, 1833." *Florida Historical Quarterly* 41 (July 1962): 1–21.

Manley, Henry S. "Buying Buffalo from the Indians." *New York History* 28 (July 1947): 313–29.

———. "Indian Reservation Ownership in New York." *New York State Bar Bulletin* 32 (Apr. 1960): 134–38.

———. "Red Jacket's Last Campaign." *New York History* 31 (Apr. 1950): 149–68.

Marryat, Frederick. "An English Officer's Description of Wisconsin in 1837." *Wisconsin Historical Collections* 14 (1898): 137–54.

McKelvey, Blake. "The Erie Canal: Mother of Cities." *New York Historical Society Quarterly* 30 (Jan. 1951): 54–71.

Meinig, D. W. "Geography of Expansion, 1785–1855." In *Geography of New York State, Supplement,* edited by John H. Thompson. Rev. ed. Paperback. Syracuse, N.Y.: Syracuse Univ. Press, 1977, 140–71.

Miller, Nathan. "Private Enterprise in Inland Navigation: The Mohawk Route Prior to the Erie Canal." *New York History* 31 (Oct. 1950): 398–413.

Murphy, Joseph Hawley. "The Salt Industry of Syracuse: A Brief Review." *New York History* 30 (July 1949): 304–15.

Niemcewicz, Julian Ursyn. "Journey to Niagara, 1805." Edited by Metchie J. E. Budka. *New-York Historical Society Quarterly* 74 (Jan. 1960): 72–113.

Parker, Arthur C. "The Senecas in the War of 1812." *Proceedings* of the New York State Historical Association 15 (1916): 78–90.

Parrish, Stephen, comp. "The Story of Jasper Parrish, Captive, Interpreter and United States Sub-Agent to the Six Nations Indians." In Buffalo Historical Society *Publications* 6, edited by Frank H. Severance. Buffalo, N.Y.: Buffalo Historical Society, 1903, 527–38.

Pound, Cuthbert W. "Nationals Without a Nation: The New York State Tribal

Indians." *Columbia Law Review* 22 (Feb. 1922): 97–102.

Prucha, Francis Paul. "Thomas L. McKenney and the New York Indian Board." *Mississippi Valley Historical Review* 48 (Mar. 1962): 635–55.

"Register of the Seneca Mission Church, 1823–1848." In Buffalo Historical Society *Publications* 6, edited by Frank H. Severance. Buffalo, N.Y.: Buffalo Historical Society, 1903, 379–80.

Remini, Robert V. "The Albany Regency." *New York History* 39 (Oct. 1958): 341–55.

Richter, Daniel K. "War and Culture: The Iroquois Experience." *William and Mary Quarterly* (1983): 528–59.

Robie, Harry. "Red Jacket's Reply: Problems in the Verification of Native American Speech Text." *New York Folklore* 12 (1986): 99–117.

Ronda, James P. "Reverend Samuel Kirkland and the Oneida Indians." In *The Oneida Indian Experience: Two Perspectives,* edited by Jack Campisi and Laurence M. Hauptman. Syracuse, N.Y.: Syracuse Univ. Press, 1988, 23–30.

Rothenberg, Diane. "The Mothers of the Nation: Seneca Resistance to Quaker Intervention." In *Women and Colonization: Anthropological Perspectives,* edited by Mona Etienne and Eleanor Leacock. New York: Praeger, 1980.

Rubin, Julius. "An Innovating Public Improvement: The Erie Canal." In *Canals and Economic Development,* edited by Carter Goodrich. New York: Columbia Univ. Press, 1961, 15–66.

Severance, Frank H. "The Quakers among the Senecas." In Buffalo Historical Society *Publications* 6, edited by Frank H. Severance. Buffalo, N.Y.: Buffalo Historical Society, 1903, 165–68.

Shoemaker, Nancy. "The Rise and Fall of Iroquois Women." *Journal of Women's History* 2 (Winter 1991): 39–57.

Snyderman, George S. "Behind the Tree of Peace: A Sociological Analysis of Iroquois Warfare." *Pennsylvania Archaeologist* 38 (Fall 1948): 3–93.

———, ed. "Halliday Jackson's Journal of a Visit Paid to the Indians of New York (1806)." *Proceedings* of the American Philosophical Society 101 (Dec. 1957): 565–88.

Stambaugh, Samuel. "Report on the Quality and Condition of Wisconsin Territory, 1831." *Wisconsin Historical Collections* 15 (1900): 399–438.

Starna, William A. "The Oneida Homeland in the Seventeenth Century." In *The Oneida Indian Experience: Two Perspectives,* edited by Jack Campisi and Laurence M. Hauptman. Syracuse, N.Y.: Syracuse Univ. Press, 1988, 9–22.

Starna, William A., and Jack Campisi. "On the Road to Canandaigua: The Treaty of 1794." *American Indian Quarterly* 19 (Fall 1995): 467–90.

Sturtevant, William C. "Seneca-Cayuga." In *Handbook of the North American Indians.* Vol. 15, *The Northeast,* edited by Bruce G. Trigger. Washington, D.C.: Smithsonian Institution, 1978, 537–43.

Sublett, Audrey J. "Osteological Analysis of the Van Son Site." Buffalo Society of Natural Sciences, Anthropology Contributions, *Bulletin* 24 (1968): 49–66.

Taylor, Alan. "The Art of 'Hook and Snivey': Political Culture in Upstate New York During the 1790s." *Journal of American History* 80 (Mar. 1993): 1371–96.

Tooker, Elisabeth. "Iroquois Since 1820." In *Handbook of North American Indians.*

Vol. 15, *The Northeast,* edited by Bruce G. Trigger. Washington, D.C.: Smithsonian Institution, 1978, 449–65.

———. "The Iroquois White Dog Sacrifice in the Latter Part of the Eighteenth Century." *Ethnohistory* 12 (1965): 129–40.

———. "The League of the Iroquois: Its History, Politics and Ritual." In *Handbook of the North American Indians.* Vol. 15, *The Northeast,* edited by Bruce G. Trigger. Washington, D.C.: Smithsonian Institution, 1978.

———. "On the Development of the Handsome Lake Religion," *Proceedings of the America Philosophical Society* 133 (1989): 35–50.

———. "On the New Religion of Handsome Lake." *Anthropological Quarterly* 41 (1968): 187–200.

Tustin, E. B., Jr. "The Development of the Salt Industry in New York." *New-York Historical Society Quarterly* 33 (1949): 40–46.

Vernon, Howard. "The Cayuga Claims: A Background Study." *American Indian Research and Culture Journal* 4 (Fall 1980): 21–35.

———. "Maris Bryant Pierce." In *Indian Lives: Essays on Nineteenth and Twentieth Century Native American Leaders,* edited by Raymond Wilson and L. George Moses. Albuquerque: Univ. of New Mexico Press, 1985, 19–42.

Wallace, Anthony F. C., ed. "Halliday Jackson's Journal to the Seneca Indians, 1798–1800." *Pennsylvania History* 19 (1952): 117–46, 325–49.

Wallace, Michael. "Changing Concepts of Party in the United States: New York, 1815–1828." *American Historical Review* 74 (Dec. 1968): 453–71.

White, Marian E. "A Reexamination of the Historic Van Son Cemetery on Grand Island." Buffalo Society of Natural Sciences, Anthropology Contributions, *Bulletin* 24 (1968): 1–48.

Wilkinson, Norman B. "Robert Morris and the Treaty of Big Tree." *Mississippi Valley Historical Review* 40 (Sept. 1953): 257–78.

Wilner, Merton M. "Grand Island: Independent State." *York State Tradition* 17 (Spring 1963): 27–28.

PERIODICALS

Albany Argus
Buffalo Emporium
Charleston Gazette (South Carolina)
Commercial Advertiser (Buffalo)
The Friend
Geneva Gazette
Green Bay Intelligencer
The Mental Elevator
Monroe Republican (Rochester)
New York Herald
New York Times

New York Tribune
Niles Register
Onondaga Standard (Syracuse)
People's Friend (Little Falls)
Republican Advocate (Batavia)
Republican Monitor (Cazenovia)
Rochester Daily Advertiser
Rochester Daily Democrat
Utica Intelligencer
Utica Patriot & Patrol
Western Argus (Lyons)

DISSERTATIONS AND THESES

Abler, Thomas S. "Factional Dispute and Party Conflict in the Political System of the Seneca Nation (1845–1895): An Ethnohistorical Analysis." Ph.D. diss., Univ. of Toronto, 1969.

Basehart, Harry S. "Historical Changes in the Kinship System of the Oneida Indians." Ph.D. diss., Harvard Univ., 1952.

Boyce, Douglas W. "Tuscarora Political Organization, Ethnic Identity and Socio-historical Demography, 1711–1825." Ph.D. diss., Univ. of North Carolina, 1973.

Campisi, Jack. "Ethnic Identity and Boundary Maintenance in Three Oneida Communities." Ph.D. diss., State University of New York, Albany, 1974.

Conable, Mary. "A Steady Enemy: The Ogden Land Company and the Seneca Indians." Ph.D. diss., Univ. of Rochester, 1995.

Geier, Philip Otto. "A Peculiar Status: A History of the Oneida Indian Treaties and Claims: Jurisdictional Conflict Within the American Government, 1775–1920." Ph.D. diss., Syracuse Univ., 1980.

Goldstein, Kalman. "The Albany Regency: The Failure of Practical Politics." Ph.D. diss., Columbia Univ., 1969.

Grande, Joseph A. "The Political Career of Peter Buell Porter, 1797–1829." Ph.D. diss., Notre Dame Univ., 1971.

Haigh, Elizabeth B. "New York Antimasons, 1826–1833." Ph.D. diss., Univ. of Rochester, 1980.

Hogan, Thomas E. "A History of the Allegany Reservation, 1850–1900." Master's thesis, State University of New York, Fredonia, 1974.

Karas, Faith E. "Material Culture on the Buffalo Creek Reservation, 1780–1842." Master's thesis, State University of New York, Buffalo, 1963.

Kay, Jeanne. "The Land of La Baye: The Ecological Impact of the Green Bay Fur Trade, 1634–1836." Ph.D. diss., Univ. of Wisconsin, 1977.

Mogavero, I. Frank. "Peter Buell Porter: Citizen and Statesman." Ph.D. diss., Univ. of Ottawa, 1950.

Patrick, Christine. "Samuel Kirkland: Missionary to the Oneida Indians." Ph.D. diss., State University of New York, Buffalo, 1992.

Rapp, Marvin A. "The Port of Buffalo, 1825–1880." Ph.D. diss., Duke Univ., 1947.

Rothenberg, Diane B. "Friends Like These: An Ethnohistorical Analysis of the Interaction Between Allegany Senecas and Quakers, 1798–1823." Ph.D. diss., City University of New York, 1976.

Schein, Richard H. "A Historical Geography of Central New York: Patterns and Processes of Colonization on the New Military Tract, 1782–1820." Ph.D. diss., Syracuse Univ., 1989.

Spiller, Roger J. "John C. Calhoun as Secretary of War." Ph.D. diss., Louisiana State Univ., 1977.

Tripp, Wendell E., Jr. "Robert Troup: A Quest for Security in a Turbulent Nation." Ph.D. diss., Columbia Univ., 1973.

Van Hoeven, James W. "Salvation and Indian Removal: The Career Biography of Rev. John Freeman Schermerhorn, Indian Commissioner." Ph.D. diss., Vanderbilt Univ., 1972.

INDEX

Page numbers in italics denote illustrations.

Conspiracy of Interests: Iroquois Dispossession and the Rise of New York State was composed in 10.5/14 Adobe Garamond in QuarkXpress 4.04 on a Macintosh by Kachergis Book Design; printed by sheet-fed offset on 60-pound Glatfelter Natural, and Smyth-sewn and bound over binder's boards in Arrestox B-grade cloth with dust jackets printed by four-color process and laminated by Cushing-Malloy of Ann Arbor, Michigan; designed by Kachergis Book Design of Pittsboro, North Carolina; published by Syracuse University Press, Syracuse, New York 13244-5160.